ADIRONDACK BIBLIOGRAPHY

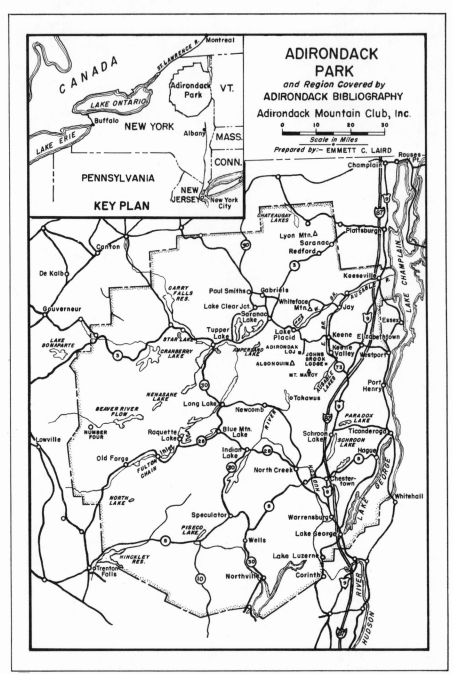

Region Covered by the *Adirondack Bibliography Supplement*:
Adirondack Park Boundary as of 1965.

ADIRONDACK BIBLIOGRAPHY SUPPLEMENT 1956 — 1965

*A List of Books, Pamphlets
and Periodical Articles*

*Compiled by
the Bibliography Committee*
ADIRONDACK MOUNTAIN CLUB

DOROTHY A. PLUM, *Chairman*

THE ADIRONDACK MUSEUM
Blue Mountain Lake, N.Y.
1973

Library of Congress Catalogue Card No. 58-6822

ISBN 0-910020-29-9.

Distributed by Syracuse University Press,
P.O. Box 8, University Station,
Syracuse, N.Y. 13310

Manufactured in the United States of America

PREFACE

Since the publication of the basic volume of the *Adirondack Bibliography* in 1958, a committee of the Adirondack Mountain Club has been compiling annual supplements to the Bibliography. These supplements included not only newly published material but older items discovered since the completion of the basic volume. The present list is a cumulation of the annual lists and the material gathered for the three-year period when no annual supplements were issued. We should emphasize that the dates on the title page "1956-1965" are not to be interpreted literally; the supplement is not limited to titles published in this ten-year span, but includes a number of earlier books, pamphlets and periodical articles, as well as a list of corrections and additions to items in the basic bibliography. The numbering of entries in this new volume continues that of the original; to make consultation of only one index possible, the index of the ten-year supplement has been expanded to include that in the original volume. The introductory note to the index should be read before using the index itself.

In general the scope of the supplement follows that of the original list, as outlined on page v of the *Adirondack Bibliography* (1958); several new subject headings have been added, reflecting new trends and new material. A slight change in typographical style should be noted. Four dashes, ----, at the beginning of an entry, indicate that the name of the author is the same as in the previous entry, a practice which was followed in the annual supplements.

Initials following annotations indicate that information was supplied by one of the following:

Warder Cadbury	WC	P. Schuyler Miller	PSM
G. Glyndon Cole	GC	Arthur Newkirk	AN
C. Eleanor Hall	CEH	Leslie Rist	LR
	William Verner	WV	

No bibligrapical work as extensive as the *Adirondack Bibliography* could be undertaken without the active cooperation of historians, librarians and Adirondack buffs, as well as the hard-working members of the Bibliography Committee. We are particularly indebted to G. Glyndon Cole, Associate Librarian of the State University College at Plattsburgh and director of the New York History Research Center there. His enthusiastic help and interest have been unfailing. Another major contributor is Warder Cadbury, Research Associate of the Adirondack Museum. He has supplied the listing of dime novels, as well as leads to much scarce and valuable material. To the late Leslie Rist of Newcomb, an amateur who requested anonimity, we are indebted for little-known material on Newcomb and the Methodist Church in the Adirondacks. Our blanket thank-you must include Koert D. Burnham, Dirk De Waard, Philip Ham, Dwight Webster, Louise Hargreaves and Marjorie L. Porter.

Most of all we are indebted to H. J. Swinney, former director of the Adirondack Museum, and to his staff, including Marcia Smith and William Verner. Especial gratitude goes to Harold K. Hochschild, President of the Adirondack Historical Association which has made possible the printing and publication of this supplement.

June 1, 1972   Dorothy A. Plum, *Editor*

MEMBERS OF THE COMMITTEE ON THE *Adirondack Bibliography*

Warder H. Cadbury	Member at Large
Laura A. Greene	Albany Chapter
John Hammond	Albany Chapter
Marion Hemstreet	Albany Chapter
Robert W. Livingston	New York Chapter
George Marshall	Member at Large
Arthur E. Newkirk	Schenectady Chapter
Erica Schinn Parmi	Albany Chapter
Dorothy A. Plum	Hurricane Mountain Chapter
Marcia Smith	Cold River Chapter
William K. Verner	Cold River Chapter

CONTENTS

INTRODUCTION

> When we were out the Towne, diverse of the men and women followed us, and broughte us to the toppe of the forsayde mountaine, which we named *Mount Roiall*, it is aboute a league from the Town. When as we were on the top of it, we myght discerne, and plainely see thirtie leagues off. On the North side of it there are manye hilles to be seene, running Weaste and Easte, and as manye more on the South, amongst and betweene the whiche the Countrey is as fayre and as pleasaunte as possiblye can bee seene, being leavell, smoothe, and verye playne, fitte to be husbanded and tilled....

These words of the French explorer Jacques Cartier concerning his visit to the site of Montreal in the fall of 1535 contain the earliest reference in English to what were later to be known as the Adirondack Mountains. The passage quoted is from a little book published at London in 1580 and called *A Short and Brief Narration of the Two Navigations and Discoveries to the Northweast Partes Called Newe France*. The English text was the work of John Florio, contemporary of Shakespeare and translator of Montaigne, who had probably been encouraged to undertake it by Richard Hakluyt. Florio's work, with some minor changes, subsequently appeared again in the third volume of Hakluyt's *The Principall Navigations, Voiages and Discoveries* published in 1600, also at London; but in order to get a better grasp of Florio's place in the bibliographical order of Cartier material we should go back to the beginning.

Jacques Cartier made three voyages to the New World in the service of Francis I, King of France. The first took place in 1534. The second began the following year, lasted through the winter, and ended back at St. Malo in the spring of 1536. Cartier's last trip took place in 1541, and like the rest had the St. Lawrence River as its geographical focus. It was the second trip which began in 1535 that interests us here. Cartier and his party penetrated the St. Lawrence as far as the site of Montreal by October 2nd and found there an Indian settlement named Hochelaga. The next day, October 3rd (October 13th in terms of the modern, or Gregorian, calendar), Cartier and his companions were escorted to the top of what he called Mount Royal, and from there beheld the view as described in the quoted passage.

In *Adirondack Country* (Adirondack Bibliography entry 58, hereafter given as "AB 58"), William Chapman White suggested that "It may have been one of those high autumn days, so common in the northland, with infinite blue sky above, with clear air that brings distant horizons near."[1] Indeed, it must have been, for Cartier himself speaks of visibility extending some "thirtie leagues," a

---

1. William Chapman White, *Adirondack Country* (New York, 1954), p. 3. White incorrectly dates Cartier's visit to Mount Royal as October 2, 1536, rather than as October 3, 1535.

distance, depending upon how you reckon it, of somewhere between 72 and 138 miles. To the north were the Laurentians, the "manye hilles to be seene" running west and east. To the south were "as manye more," undoubtedly the Adirondacks and Green Mountains. Possibly Cartier was able to see the ninety miles south from Montreal to Mt. Marcy and others of the major Adirondack high peaks. He also saw the great beauty of the St. Lawrence Valley, and in this beauty he saw potential—the promise of civilization in the guise of agriculture eventually investing that valley. Between the wild mountains, on the one hand, and the valleys inviting civilization, on the other, the images perceived by Cartier and conveyed in his account coincidentally established the poles within which the general shape of Adirondack history would ultimately play itself out. Indeed, it is probably not too much to say that it is between such poles that Adironack history continues to play itself out, the only significant difference being, perhaps, that in the twentieth century the primary identity of civilization with agriculture no longer holds.

There remains a further level of suggestion in the Cartier account which is worth noting before picking up the bibliographical thread again. As a member of the vanguard of Eruopean explorers in North America, Cartier must inevitably remind us of the profound identification of American culture with the exploratory spirit, a theme which runs throughout American history from the earliest days, through westward expansion, to modern space exploration. Another manifestation of essentially the same thing can be found in the record of attempts to legally preserve wild open space in park and wilderness systems in this country, a story in which the Adirondacks plays an important role. It is a pleasant happenstance, then, that it was a major early figure such as Cartier who was the first to write, even if only tangentially in the phrase "and as manye more on the South," of Adirondack mountains where it is still possible today for individuals to recreate for themselves the unique experience of primitive exploration.

The raw bibliographical record offers similarly intriguing associations. The first published account of Cartier's second voyage actually appeared in 1545, almost a decade after his return to France, in a little book entitled *Brief Recit, & Succincte Narration, de la Navigation Faicte es Ysles de Canada, Hochelage & Saguenay & Autres....* It was published at Paris and is believed to have been drawn from Cartier's personal log of the trip and to have been edited by a member of the exploratory party, one Jean Poullet of Dol. The book has a further bibliographical distinction, aside from being "a first." A copy in the Grenville Collection of the British Museum is the only copy known to exist anywhere in the world today, and the copy in question has been the only one for over a century. Another copy is said to have been on its way to America by ship back in 1852 but, unlike its author who three centuries before had successfully made three trips across the Atlantic and back under then very difficult circumstances, it went to the bottom of the ocean with the ship that was carrying it.[2]

But back to the sixteenth century. Following publication of the *Brief Recit* in French, the Italian chronicler Giovanni Battista Ramusio included Cartier's

---

2. For further bibliographical details on this and related books see the following: H. Harisse, *Notes pour Servir a L'Histoire, a la Bibliographie et la Cartographie de la Nouvelle-France* (1872), pp. 1-6; Justin Winsor, ed., *Narrative and Critical History of America* (New York, 1967), Vol. IV, pp. 64-8; and Samuel Eliot Morison, *The European Discovery of America: The Northern Voyages, A.D. 500-1600* (New York, 1971), pp. 424-5. See also, H.P. Biggar, *The Early Trading Companies of New France* (New York: Argonaut Press, Ltd., 1965), pp. 11-14, 210-220.

account, in Italian, in volume III of his *Delle Navigationi et Viaggi* published at Venice in 1556. It was Ramusio's version upon which John Florio based his translation. Thus the passage quoted earlier, for all its antiquity, is but a third generation account, if one which can boast truly international ancestry. As a final note, thanks to facsimile printing the Florio version became currently available, beginning in 1966, as Number 10 in the *March of America Facsimile Series* published at Ann Arbor, Michigan by University Microfilms.

In beginning this introduction with Cartier, his trip to Montreal, and a consideration of the bibliographical details relative thereto, we are signalling, if a bit obliquely, the course the rest of this introduction is to take. Our intent is to select books and articles of prime Adirondack importance and to discuss these in terms of Adirondack history. A by-product of such an approach is the attainment of an overview of publishing history as it relates to the Adirondacks. The precedent for an introductory essay of this general sort was set in 1958 upon publication of the original *Adirondack Bibliography*. In the introduction to that volume the late Russell M. L. Carson listed and discussed a number of important Adirondack titles, and his essay remains required reading for all serious students of the Adirondacks. It is partly for this very reason that the present introduction differs from Carson in two basic respects. Where the approach here will be historical and chronological, Carson's was topical. And where the very approach we have chosen requires being a bit long-winded, Carson's lent itself to brevity. All of which is to say that it would have been far easier on both writer and reader if we could simply have updated and improved Carson somewhat and left it at that, except for the fact that Carson's work was so well done he left minimal room for improvement. As a result the only option open was to attempt a reexamination of Adirondack literature from a totally different angle, such as the historical.

Before launching beyond Cartier, a few additional preliminary comments are in order, however. To begin with, we have divided the history of the Adirondacks and of Adirondack writings into seven major periods. The first of these will be the colonial era, spanning the three and a half centuries between Cartier and the establishment of the United States. This epoch is characterized by the relative lack of Adirondack history in any direct sense and with positive emphasis on exploration, discovery, military conflicts, and the beginnings of settlement in the outer periphery of the Adirondack region. Following the American Revolution there is a half century of consolidation in which the Adirondack region itself, particularly the central area, played little if any significant role. It is with the mid-1830's that the Adirondacks begins coming into its own finally, both as an entity receiving some public recognition and as the subject of literature in a positive sense. This thirty year period, lasting through the Civil War, which we shall call the Age of the Adirondack Wilderness, was succeeded by another three decades in which the central Adirondack region was opened up in a variety of ways and became subjected to the uses and styles of the Gilded Age. By the end of this period too, a number of laws had been passed, including the establishment of the Forest Preserve and the Adirondack Park, both of which continue to play a major role in the region down to the present. The twenty years preceeding the First World War are of a transitional and somewhat conservative character, but the thirty years of the inter-World War period are rife with ferment. Here begin active programs in public outdoor recreation, the germination of the wilderness movement, and court tests questioning the public functions and management of the region. As the present supplement to the *Adirondack Bibliography* deals with titles published through the year 1965, the final period covers the two decades since the end of the Second World War, a period of continued controversy in many fields and one notable for the volume and quality of published material about the region.

The selection of specific titles included within each of the seven historical periods also requires comment. Our primary concern is to point out what strikes us as the most important and characteristic of books, articles and periodicals which apply to the region in whole or in part. Generally, most of the items discussed are listed in either the *Adirondack Bibliography* or in this supplement, but there are some instances where this is not the case. For instance, the Cartier accounts which we have already discussed are not listed in either volume, and the reason, most probably, is that, despite the distinctive position Cartier may occupy in any chronological consideration of Adirondack history, his actual writings are, at best, only slightly connected to the region. In other cases, however, the lack of a listing at this time may confirm that as in the "making of many books there is no end" so in the making of bibliographies there is also no end. Titles such as Thomas Pownall's geographical works may well merit inclusion in a further supplement to this series at a later time. On the other hand, items principally of an illustrative character, such as some of the plates which appeared in *Every Saturday* and *The Aldine* in the early 1870's, may better be dealt with in some yet-to-be-complied *Iconography of the Adirondacks*.

The criteria for inclusion of titles here will remain open to dispute for other reasons as well. Having unleashed subjectivity by invoking the criterion of quality in the first place, it is not surprising that in some cases it may go too far. Undoubtedly important titles will have been overlooked, and dubious ones may have been included for reasons of simple personal bias. Rather than attempt to hide behind of cloak of false objectivity, however, we can point out that there remains the *Adirondack Bibliography* and supplement listings to which the reader can always turn for his own purposes and from which he can make his own interpretations. Indeed, the essential purpose of this introduction will have been fulfilled if it encourages the reader to go beyond regarding the *Bibliography* as merely "for reference only" and to peruse its listings for all they have to suggest in terms of solid history. With all due respect to Adirondack historians and others whose job it is to synthesize the raw materials of history, the dividends to the student who would sift the leads to raw material as represented in the *Bibliography* may prove more valuable than dependency upon anyone else's interpretation.

I. THE COLONIAL PERIOD: 1535 - 1785

Prime material relating to the early discovery and exploration in and about the Adirondacks is scarce. In fact, until well after the Revolutionary War, material pertinent to the Adirondack region proper is practically non-existent. Early material concerning the Adirondack periphery is rare at first also but gradually increases in volume as the various European-based powers — France, Holland, and England — make deeper inroads upon the American continent.

As we have seen, the original edition of Cartier's account of his visit to Montreal exists in but one known copy. Following Cartier, the bibliographical record remains a practical blank until the publication in 1613 of *Les Voyages du Sieur de Champlain Xaintongeois* by Jean Berjon of Paris. This volume included Samuel de Champlain's account of his trip south from the St. Lawrence the summer of 1609 into what came to be called Lake Champlain. Accompanied by Algonquin Indians, Champlain encountered and did battle with a group of Mohawk Indians at a site believed to have been near the present Ticonderoga. Champlain thus became the first Caucasian known to have set foot upon soil that was to become the State of New York, and, coincidentally, territory now included within the Adirondack Park. Translations of the account of the 1609 voyage can be found in a variety of places, including O'Callaghan's *Documentary History of New York* (AB 312) which was published in the 1850's, in Grant's edition of Champlain's voyages (AB 313), and, more recently, in an issue of *North Country Life* (AB 7710). Here and elsewhere in the early periods of Adirondack history we must often rely upon secondary sources and thus at the outset must sidestep our intent of generally dealing only with works which are contemporary with the events they treat.

After Champlain, the record again becomes sparse. An exception, and a notable one, is provided in the *Jesuit Relations*, particularly in the letters of Isaac Jogues written in the 1640's (AB 24; see also the 73 volumes of the complete *Jesuit Relations* edited by Reuben Gold Thwaites and published as a collected edition around the turn of the present century). Otherwise, we must, again, generally depend upon secondary sources including O'Callaghan's *Documentary History* (AB 15) published in two editions between 1849 and 1851 and Brodhead's fifteen volume *Documents Relating to the Colonial History of New York* (AB 16). Here we are dealing with monuments of mid-nineteenth century scholorship, and here too we encounter a case where Adirondack history is defined rather by the very absence of positive history than by its presence. Another way of saying this is that the history of what took place outside the Adirondacks proper must stand, for lack of anything else, as the negative image of Adirondack history. All of this would amount to little more than playing with words were it not for the fact that in later centuries, when there came to be an Adirondack history in a directly positive sense, the flavor of that history — its aroma of wildness and relatively unencumbered naturalness — was due in no small measure to man's not having managed to subordinate the region to his conventionally civilized purposes.

A perennial Adirondack question is, what of Indians? What of the Iroquois, of Mohawks, Oneidas and the rest; what of the Algonquins, and especially the "Adirondack" Indians; what of the Abenaki, and particularly of the St. Francis Indians, several of whom (Sabattis and Sabael, for example) were notable adornments of the nineteenth century Adirondack scene? Again, the primary record is slim. Indians were not given to record-keeping, and the records of whites, both primary and secondary, are often confusing. The *Adirondack Bibliography* devotes sections to Archaeology and to Aborigines (AB 2ll - 278 and 7676 - 7698), but we recommend no single title which unequivocally unravels the story of Indians and the Adirondacks. The *Jesuit Relations* and other similar accounts provide a feel of what was happening around the Adirondacks in aboriginal terms in the seventeenth century. J. Franklin Jameson's edition, *Narratives of New Netherland, 1609 - 1664* (New York: Barnes & Noble, Inc., 1909) contains some intriguing items, and so do O'Callaghan and Brodhead. A number of French accounts, particularly from the early eighteenth century, e.g., Lafitau, remain to be studied and possibly added to the *Adirondack Bibliography* at a later time. One book, Cadwallader Colden's *History of the Five Nations*, originally published in 1727, supplemented in 1747 (see AB 7583 for a 1902 reissue), is fundamental. Colden is essential not so much because he is accurate in all details (he most probably is not) but because he is the source to which many subsequent historians and others have gone for information. For example, it is possible, even probable, that it was from Colden, or from a source based on Colden, that Ebenezer Emmons derived the term *Adirondack* which he used to designate Northern New York's "Adirondack group" of mountains in 1838. Colden frequently used the term *Adirondack* to signify the Algonquin Indian enemies of the Iroquois in his books.

Another subject where the *Bibliography* provides general guidance is the matter of French settlement on the edges of the Adirondacks (AB 60 - 81 and 7576 - 7577). Here again, most references to early settlement are to secondary sources, and a considerable portion of such listings deal, in fact, with later French settlements, both American and French post-revolutionary. Still, the beginnings of first-hand accounts of the Adirondack periphery are now coming to hand. Especially notable is Pehr (Peter) Kalm's *En Resa til Norra America* published at Stockholm in three volumes between 1753 and 1761. A German translation appeared in Leipzig between 1754 and 1764, and it was upon this German version that an English version published in 1770-71 was based (AB 3385). Kalm's observations remain basic to the history of natural science, particularly botany, in America. For the Adirondacks, Kalm represents one of the first of a long series of European travellers who were to write up the impressions of their American travels including what they encountered in the valleys — Hudson-Champlain, St. Lawrence, and Mohawk — which encircle the Adirondacks proper.

The French and Indian Wars, during which so much important action transpired on the edges of the Adirondacks, have bred a considerable amount of published material (AB 82 - 133 and 7578 - 7601). Only a few select items shall we mention here, one of which — Samuel Blodgett's *A Prospective Plan of the Battle near Lake George, on the 8th Day of September, 1755* (AB 87) and published that same year — has been called by the distinguished historian of American art, E. P. Richardson, the "first historical print engraved in America."[3] There is, of course, the *Journals* of Robert Rogers, originally published in 1763, more recently available in a 1961 reprint (AB 10313).

The Revolution itself (AB 134 - 179 and 7602-7604) was again an affair largely peripheral to the Adirondack interior — with the possible exception of Sir John Johnson's escape to Canada in 1776. A particularly interesting contribution to the historical geography of the Adirondacks lies in the work of Lewis Evans and Thomas Pownall. Proceeding chronologically, in 1755 Lewis Evans published his *General Map of the Middle British Colonies* at Philadelphia. At the same time, Evans's *Geographical, Historical, Political, Philosophical and Mechanical Essays: Containing an Analysis of a General Map of the Middle British Colonies in America* was published by Benjamin Franklin and David Hall, also at Philadelphia. Thomas Pownall, who in 1757 became royal Governor of Massachusetts, had worked with Evans on his *Map* and *Analysis,* and in 1776 published his own *Topographical Description of North America* (London: J. Almon), a work intended to update Evans. Pownall anticipated yet a further edition of his work and completed revisions of text and map in 1784. This material did not get into print, however, until 1949, with the appearance of Lois Mulkearn's edition of Pownall, *A Topographical*

---

3. E. P. Richardson, *Painting in America: From 1502 to the Present* (New York, 1965), p. 82.

Description of the Dominions of the United States of America (Pittsburgh: University of Pittsburgh Press). Some of Pownall's comments about the sources of the Hudson River provide as accurate a report for the time of man's knowledge of the Adirondack region as we are likely to find. Speaking of the Hudson's sources, Pownall writes that "those which come from the North rise in a Tract of Country called Couxsachrage [our Couchsachrage], the Principal of which is that called Canada Creek...."[4] Further along, he notes that the "main Branch of this River Hudson rises from Lakes in the Mountains of Couxsachrage to the West of Lake Champlain, and is called Sacondaga [Sacandaga] River...." Finally, not fully content with his comments thus far, Pownall closes this section of his book with the following:

> ...I must just passing (rather to mark my Ignorance than presuming to give Information) observe, that the Country, lying to the West of these Lakes [George and Champlain], bounded on the North West by Canada River [the St. Lawrence], and on the South by the Mohawks [Mohawk] River, called by the Indians Couxsachrage, which signifies the Dismal Wilderness or Habitation of Winter, is a triangular, high mountainous Tract, very little known to the Europeans; and although a hunting Ground of the Indians, yet either not much known to them, or, if known, very wisely by them kept from the Knowledge of the Europeans. It is said to be a broken unpracticable Tract; I own I could never learn any Thing about it....[5]

Besides providing a sound description as to the state of man's knowledge of the Adirondack region just after the Revolution, Pownall also provides an apt and amusing example of humility's place in scholarship.

II. AFTER THE REVOLUTION: 1786 - 1835

In the post-revolutionary years, as the valleys surrounding the Adirondacks began accomodating permanent settlement, personal travel accounts — particularly those of European visitors — provided the first hand documentation on the outer Adirondacks. Isaac Weld's *Travels through the States of North America* (AB 395), Timothy Dwight's *Travels* (AB 1825), and Jacques Milbert's *Itineraire Pittoresque* (AB 409) are examples. Milbert's account, based on his travels in the 1810's, and accompanied by an impressive collection of lithographed views, was published in 1828-29. The *Travels in North America* (AB 8093) of Capt. Basil Hall covered the years 1827 and 1828 and provide a Briton's view. The War of 1812 only touched the Adirondacks peripherally (AB 180 - 210 and 7641 - 7668).

The native American's concern — or, more particularly, the native New Yorker's concern — for his national geography is reflected in the emergence of such practical works as H. G. Spafford's *A Gazetteer of New York State,* first issued in 1813 (AB 1255) and again, revised, in 1824 (AB 1256). Spafford combines basic information about places in New York along with often pithy comments on particular subjects which happened to move him at the time. This latter quality continues to make his books eminently readable and entertaining long after their practical purposes have been superseded by works of the same

---

4. Thomas Pownall, *A Topographical Description of the United States of America,* edited by Lois Mulkearn (Pittsburgh, 1949), p. 37.

5. *Ibid.,* pp. 50-1.

type. In 1829, the first D. H. Burr *Atlas of the State of New York* (AB 1277), a work containing individual county maps and pertinent statistics, was issued. It was updated and reissued in 1839 and 1840. Geological and mining interest in the North Country manifested itself early, and the *Bibliography* provides chronological listings of material on these subjects (AB 2983 - 3148 and 8605 - 8709, and AB 4126 - 4330 and 8936 - 8964, respectively), with coverage running from the 1820's through 1965.

Finally, fiction should not be overlooked. James Fenimore Cooper's romance of the year 1757, *The Last of the Mohicans* (AB 10451), it may be noted, was first published in 1826. There is relatively little pure local history in these early years of a young nation, with the exception of W. W. Campbell's *Annals of Tryon County* (AB 140), originally published in 1831 and reissued in 1849 and 1924.

III. THE ADIRONDACK WILDERNESS: THE GOLDEN YEARS, 1836 - 1865

From the middle 1830's until the end of the Civil War in 1865, the Adirondack region — especially the central third, approximately, of what we now know as the Adirondack Park — constituted a very special, almost a unique, part of the northeastern American cultural scene. An island of wildness in a part of the country becoming rapidly civilized, it inspired an extraordinarily interesting body of writing and art. Now the bibliography of the Adirondacks acquires a notable bulge as the region truly begins to come into its own historically. Both primary and secondary sources become abundant, the primary materials reflecting the discovery of yet another new found land to Americans, many of the secondary works exhibiting the growth of strong retrospective interest in the colonial and immediate post-colonial history of the young country.

Where the Adirondacks had formerly played a role as a sort of collective back-country for the relatively civilized valleys which surrounded it, the region now emerges as a focal point of general public interest in its own right. The central event signalling this shift was the discovery, ascent, and naming of Mount Marcy in 1837 and the designation of the major northern New York mountains as the "Adirondack group" in 1838. On August 15, 1837, a letter — written ten days earlier on the summit of Marcy by James Hall — appeared in an Albany paper informing the outside world of the Marcy ascent (reprinted in AB 7817). The ascent had officially been under the auspices of the State Geological Survey, but the climbing party included several non-official participants. One of these was William Redfield who issued accounts of the trip both in the New York City press (*Journal of Commerce*) and in at least two periodicals (AB 40). Charles Fenno Hoffman, a New York journalist, found the news emanating from the Adirondack high peak area irresistible, and he made a trip north to get into the act. His accounts appeared serially, at first in the *New York Mirror* (AB 8094 and 405) and later in book form in English editions (AB 1005) at both London and New York and in German (AB 1006) at Dresden.

The formal reports of Geological Survey group leader Ebenezer Emmons came out annually over a five year period, the work of the 1836 - 1840 seasons appearing in State legislative documents in 1837 - 1841 (AB 2985). As such they constituted an important part of what has since been called "the classic model of the state survey."[6] In addition to the Marcy report of 1837 (published early in 1838), Emmons's account of his trip through the central Adirondack lakes region in 1840 (published 1841) is especially interesting. The summation of his geological findings in northern New York appeared in 1842 (AB 2990) as a volume in the monumental *Natural History of New York,* and other contributions to that same series which involve the Adirondacks in greater or lesser degree include the following: DeKay's multi-volume *Zoology* (AB 3520), John Torrey's *Flora* (AB 3497), Emmons's *Agriculture* (AB 4336), and James Hall's *Paleontology* (AB 2994). All of these volumes appeared in the 1840's with the exception of some of Hall's work, publication of which was not completed until 1894.

Charles Fenno Hoffman's *New York Mirror* pieces introduced a somewhat new kind of pure literary and descriptive genre into Adirondack letters, and his *Vigil of Faith and Other Poems* (AB 7428 and 6892) continued the style. John Todd's little *Long Lake,* published in book form in 1845 (AB 900) and again that same year in his *Simple Sketches* (AB 901), added a pastoral touch in two ways. On the one hand he foresaw, incorrectly, a viable agricultural future for the central Adirondack valleys, and on the other he was determined to bring Christ to the then rather heathen Long Lakers. The Minister was not above larding his homilies with an occassional hunting or fishing story now and then, however.

Other writers dwelt more on the pleasures of Nimrod to be had in the Adirondacks at mid-century. Another preacher, George Washington Bethune, who wrote anonymously, appended the journal of the Piseco Lake Trout Club to his 1847 edition of Walton's *Compleat Angler* (AB 6105), and two other authors contributed significantly to making the Adirondacks better known to the outside world. Charles Lanman included a number of Adirondack chapters in his *A Tour to the River Saguenay in Lower Canada* (AB 5989), issued at New York in 1848 and at London the same year but under the title *Adventures of an Angler in Canada, Nova Scotia and the United States* (AB 5988). Lanman's Adirondack stories appeared again in 1854 (AB 1027) and in 1856 (AB 1028) in books with yet different titles. Possibly the most influential and widely distributed book of its period, however, was Joel Tyler Headley's *The Adirondac; or, Life in the Woods* (AB 1003). It remained the standard traveller's book to the Adirondacks for two decades and underwent several editions, revisions, additions, and plagiarizations over the years.

The 1840's also saw a number of practical publications which were either devoted to the Adirondacks or which included the region among other subjects. Disturnell's *New-York State Guide* of 1842 (AB 1178) contained some of the new information about the region developed by the Geological Survey, and his *Northern Traveller* of 1844 (AB 1180) provided information on how to get *to* the Adirondacks, if not *into* the region. Developmental schemes of various sorts were also very much in evidence during this period as indicated by the reports of the New York Canal Board (AB 1154 - 1155). The *Memorial of George A. Simmons and Others* addressed to the New York State Senate in 1846 (AB 4413) includes material developed by Prof. Farrand N. Benedict relative to possible railroad and steamboat routes through the Adirondacks.

It is worth bearing in mind that by suggesting that the mid-nineteenth century was the golden age for wilderness in the Adirondacks we are not

---

6. William H. Goetzmann, *Exploration and Empire: The Explorer and the Scientist in the Winning of the American West* (New York, 1966), p. 355.

suggesting that the entire region we now know as the Adirondack Park was still a wilderness. Rather it is necessary to observe certain basic geographical and functional distinctions when considering the region. It was the central Adirondacks, and by central Adirondacks we mean a territory considerably larger than the high peaks area alone, which constituted what people then called "the wilderness." It was a region of several million acres and included, in addition to most of the major Adirondack mountains, the central and western lake chains as well. It was a territory penetrated by relatively few, and mostly quite primitive, roads. Its resident population numbered a few hundred at most. This central Adirondack wilderness was the focus at mid-century of Adirondack travel accounts — the tales of hunting, fishing and camping — through which some persons learned for the first time of the adventure to be had in the region and through which the experienced recalled the odor of oil and pine tar and the feel of sore muscles.

At the same time, however, new elements in the Adirondack bibliographical record after 1850 indicate a distinctly different kind of cultural orientation, and the geographical locus of such inspiration was the large outer portion of the present Adirondack Park region which surrounded the wild heartland. The population density of this outer region, for example, was already very nearly as great as it is today. For over half a century farming, mining, lumbering and the creation of communities had been markedly changing the face of the landscape. Places such as the Lake George valley which to Peter Kalm in 1750 had been "wilderness" could no longer be so characterized in 1850, and the cultural changes implicit in these geographical changes had their reflection in the greater numbers of serious local histories which rapidly began to be published about this time. Northern New Yorkers, like their cousins elsewhere in the United States, were beginning to look back and take stock of the roots from which they had come.

An example of the new type of book was Jeptha R. Simms's *Trappers of New York* (AB 6712), published in 1850. Another, and perhaps more serious work going even further back in time for its subject matter, was Lewis Morgan's *League of the Ho-de-no-sau-nee* (AB 241) which dealt with the Iroquois confederation and which was first published in 1851. It was during this period that the indefatigable Dr. Franklin B. Hough of Lowville began turning out such county histories as his work on St. Lawrence and Franklin counties published in 1853 (AB 565), and his book on Lewis County (AB 663) published in 1860 and revised in 1883 (AB 664). Peter S. Palmer's *History of Lake Champlain* (AB 365), first published in 1853, Elkanah Watson's *Men and Times of the Revolution* (AB 1104), edited by his son W. C. Watson, and the latter's *Pioneer History of the Champlain Valley* (AB 394) are all examples of this new genre.

This period is not without its serious, practical publications as well — books, articles and pamphlets which either explicitly or implicitly belie an essentially economic, developmental, or utilitarian attitude towards the Adirondacks. W. C. Watson, again, prepared a survey of agricultural practice and potentiality for Essex County (AB 4344 and 4345), work also valuable as history. Farrand N. Benedict, the presumed author of an article called "The Wilds of Northern New York" (AB 956) which appeared in the September *Putnam's* for 1854 takes a larger geographical canvas and teeters a bit uncertainly between extolling the virtues of pure wildness, on the one hand, and of developmental potential on the other. W. C. H. Waddell's material on the proposed Sackett's Harbor and Saratoga Railroad (AB 1102) and H. J. Raymond's "A Week in the Wilderness" (AB 1058) which appeared in the *New York Times* in 1855 were both directed at attracting outside interest and capital into the region. For the Adirondacks and for New York State as a whole (and still indispensable as a reference work) J. H. French's 1860 *Gazetteer* (AB 1260) pinned down the geographical facts of New York life with considerable thoroughness.

Still, the dominant flavor of the age remains recreational and romantic. The "picturesque" was a major element of mid-nineteenth century sensibility in America, and the Adirondacks provided excellent material in this respect both figuratively and literally. Examples can be found in *The Home Book of the Picturesque* (AB 7220, reissued as AB 7224), in T. A. Richard's *American Scenery Illustrated* (AB 7231), and in the same author's *Appleton's Illustrated Handbook of American Travel* (AB 1187), which was first issued in 1857. Richards had also done a two-part series, "A Forest Story" (AB 1060), for *Harper's Monthly* a few years earlier, an account which placed a certain emphasis on the then promising mining activities at the village of Adirondac. By 1859, however, when Benson J. Lossing visited Adirondac, the mine had failed, and the "deserted village" and other central Adirondack themes constituted fit subject matter for both pen sketches and narrative by Lossing. Some of his material appeared originally in *The Art Journal* (London) in 1861 but received far broader circulation in 1866 with the publication of his important and handsome *The Hudson: From the Wilderness to the Sea* (AB 407).

Other travellers of the fifties and sixties placed a good deal of emphasis on sport. Charles Wilkins Webber's Adirondack stories appeared in a number of guises (AB 5689, and 5690 - 5692) as did some of the work of Samuel H. Hammond, an Albany newspaper editor. Hammond's *Hills, Lakes and Forest Streams* (AB 5615) of 1854, for example, appeared subsequently between 1856 and 1865 under the title *A Hunter's Adventures in the Northern Wilds* (AB 5617), and again in 1890 as *In the Adirondacks* (AB 5618). Hammond also collaborated with L. W. Mansfield on another book, published in 1855, which deals with the Adirondacks in part (AB 5769), and alone Hammond produced yet another Adirondack title, *Wild Northern Scenes* (AB 5619) which appeared in 1857.

The illustrated article was a popular medium beginning at mid-century as many periodicals adopted the wood-engraving which had finally come into its own. We have already cited Thomas Addision Richards's work for *Harper's Monthly*. Another example is provided in an anonymous piece (AB 463) which appeared in the *Great Northern Monthly* in 1859, an article with illustrations we have since learned was the work of the painter Jervis McEntee. In 1851, McEntee and another artist, Joseph Tubby, spent several summer months in the Adirondacks. They entered the wilderness from the west via Lowville, camped at Raquette Lake, hiked from Long Lake to Newcomb, ascended Mount Marcy, and left the region via Schroon River. McEntee's original journal has found its way into the Adirondack Museum's collection although the original sketches and paintings made on the trip have disappeared. Only the published article continues to provide us a link, through its wood-engravings, with those original art works.

One of the most delightful of all early Adirondack travel accounts was written by a lady in waiting to Queen Victoria, The Honorable Amelia Matilda Murray. Her *Letters from the United States...*(AB 1043), published in 1856, contains an account of a trip by boat through the Adirondacks with a party that included Governor Horatio Seymour. Lady Murray tells us that like McEntee she too made sketches on this trip; as with the McEntee sketches hers too are lost. Unfortunately, unlike the McEntee sketches, none of Lady Murray's were reproduced in her book. Such was not the case with another travel account published in *Leslie's Illustrated* in 1858 where wood-engravings after drawings by Charles Whitehead embellished Frederick S. Stallknecht's text on their "Sporting Tour" of 1858 (AB 9774). In itself, their trip was typical for the period — a boat tour through the Adirondack lakes under the wing of experienced guides. Along the way Stallknecht and Whitehead encountered another party in the woods which was also characteristic of the time, the so-called "Philosophers" — Ralph Waldo Emerson, Louis Agassiz, and others — encamped at Follensby Pond. Emerson's own tribute to "The Adirondacs" (AB 7416) came out in a book of his collected verse in the 1860's. Still other accounts of like-minded individuals in search of fish, game, and relaxation can be found in such items as the listings for the North Woods Walton Club (AB 6662 - 3).

In the 1860's a notable author of books on the Adirondacks, State Librarian Alfred Billings Street, was quite active. His *Woods and Waters* (AB 1083 and 1084) came out in 1860, his *Forest Pictures in the Adirondacks* (AB 7481) with illustrations by John Hows in 1864 and again in 1865, and his *The Indian Pass* (AB 627) in 1869. Other books of interest were Coffin's *Forest Arcadia of Northern New York* (AB 974) and C. H. Burt's *The Opening of the Adirondacks* (AB 35).

We should not forget that the would-be hunter and fisherman had some help in the form of general guidebooks on hunting, fishing, and trapping, many of which had things to say about the Adirondacks specifically. *Frank Forester's Fish and Fishing of the United States* (AB 5969) by H.W. Herbert, published in 1855, includes comments on the region as does Thaddeus Norton's *The American Angler's Book* (AB 6126) of a decade later. Mention should be made too of Sewell Newhouse's *The Trapper's Guide* (AB 6235).

A chronological review of Adirondack bibliography reminds us that an era was coming to an end, both locally and nationally. An item in a *Williams Quarterly* for 1864 (AB 6850) tells us of the passing of Ebenezer Emmons — who had helped open the era by leading the first recorded ascent of Mt. Marcy and who gave the name Adirondacks to the mountains. Emmons had died in the South in 1863, the same year in which Charles C. Ingham, the artist who had accompanied the Emmons party up Marcy, passed away. James Redpath's *Public Life of Brown* (AB 6779), published in 1860, recalls to us the death of John Brown at Harper's Ferry, his burial at North Elba, and the beginnings of the Civil War. By the end of the war a new era dawned for the nation and for the Adirondacks, an era fittingly enshrined in the title of a novel published in the early 1870's by Mark Twain and Charles Dudley Warner, *The Gilded Age*.

IV. THE WILDERNESS BREACHED: THE GILDED AGE, 1866 - 1895

In 1868 a railroad line reached south from Plattsburgh into the northeastern Adirondacks at Point of Rocks. By 1874 it was extended to Ausable Forks. On the southeast, the Adirondack Railroad reached North Creek in 1871. By 1875 a railroad had been completed along the entire western side of Lake Champlain. In 1882 a spur line connected Glens Falls on the southeast with Caldwell (Lake George); by 1887 another line reached around from Plattsburgh to Saranac Lake (extended to Lake Placid by 1893); and by 1889 railroad lines had reached Tupper Lake from the north and Benson Mines on the west. By 1892, the line between Utica and Malone traversed the western Adirondacks, and spurs reached Raquette Lake in 1900 and Cranberry Lake from Childwold in 1913. From 1900 until 1930, thirteen hundred feet of track carried the Marion River Carry train back and forth in the heart of the Adirondacks. Change, in the guise of technology, had come to the Adirondacks, first poking into the outer reaches, where stage lines then took visitors into the central Adirondacks, and finally extending well into and through the region.

The post Civil War period brought not only the mixed blessings of new technology to the region. The war itself had wrought sociological changes which made it possible for a wider spectrum of humanity to seek out what the Adirondacks had to offer. Finally, books, and maps, and periodical articles contributed mightily to the breaching of the old Adirondack Wilderness.

It has been said that W. H. H. ("Adirondack") Murray's *Adventures in the Wilderness; or, Camp-Life in the Adirondacks* (AB 7327), published in 1869, caused the opening up of the Adirondacks. Perhaps it did and perhaps it didn't; the argument is probably as fruitless as trying to decide definitively whether Murray's book represented the end of an era or the beginning of a new one. In truth, Murray's book both ended and began eras, and its success was both caused by and the cause of a host of other factors. More simply put, Murray's book was pivotal. It provided a summary of a style of life that had characterized the golden age of the Adirondack Wilderness, and it was a precursor of those forces that brought the gilded age to the Adirondacks and, in the process, helped undo the integrity of that wilderness. Another thing is fairly certain: the young Murray's first Adirondack book was to remain his best Adirondack writing and was never outdone by his later Adirondack tales (AB 7322-7326 and 7328 - 7342).

Adventures in the Wilderness also served to breed a considerable literary progeny. Later books and articles either satirized or capitalized upon Murray, and among these were Charles Hallock's "The Raquette Club" (AB 6642) which appeared in *Harper's Monthly* in 1870 and was subsequently reissued in the same author's *Fishing Tourist* (AB 5967). Hallock lampooned Murray, whereas another writer, H. P. Smith, appears rather to have admired Murray, which Smith's *Modern Babes in the Wood* (AB 1068) of 1872 demonstrates. While Murray's reminiscences hit pay dirt, those of other authors tried in various ways — though never as successfully — to do the same; examples include W. C. Prime's *I Go A-Fishing* (AB 6018), S. I. Prime's *Under the Trees* (AB 1054), Charles Dudley Warner's *In the Wilderness* (AB 7244; see also AB 5183), Samuel Gold Appleton's *Windfalls* (AB 951), George Dawson's *Angling Talks* (AB 5947), and, completing a circle of sorts which had begun with Street's *The Indian Pass* published the same summer as Murray's book, Henry Van Hoevenberg's *Indian Pass* (AB 7495), a pamphlet published in 1888.

For a time the small boat and the canoe still remained the principal means of central Adirondack travel. The Adirondack guide-boat was the ultimate flowering of this style of life, while literary manifestations of interest in small boats and canoes can be found in such books as W. H. Bishop's *Voyage of the Paper Canoe* (AB 959), published in 1878, and the series of letters addressed to *Forest and Stream* in the 1880's by "Nessmuk" (George Washington Sears), including "Rough Notes from the Woods" (AB 5161), "Cruise of the *Nipper*" (AB 5302), "In Defense of the Adirondack Guides" (AB 5240), "Cruise of the *Sairy Gamp*" (AB 5241), and "The *Sairy Gamp*" (AB 5303). Nessmuk's *Woodcraft* (AB 5162), first issued in 1884 and still in print today, helped establish the "go light" style of travel which has had a notable revival in recent years.

Perhaps even more indicative of Murray's impact and of changing times were the maps and guidebooks which now became an established part of the Adirondack scene. W. W. Ely's map of "The New York Wilderness" (AB 988) was probably the first of the pure tourist maps to be devoted exclusively to the Adirondacks. It was in any case the first important map of its type. First issued in 1867, it went through frequent revisions, and ultimately came to be known under its publisher's name, "Colton's Map." It accompanied the Tourist Edition of Murray's book (issued the summer of 1869) and was adopted by various guidebooks, most notably Wallace's. Asher and Adams's *New Topographical Atlas and Gazetteer of New York* (AB 1284), although not solely devoted to the Adirondacks, came out in 1871.

Of guidebooks, Benjamin F. DeCosta's *Lake George* (AB 1195) came out in 1868. Like the *Descriptive and Historical Guide* of 1871 written by W. C. Watson, it appeared only once. The guidebooks of E. R. Wallace and S. R. Stoddard most effectively captured the Adirondack market and continued to appear in frequent, even annual, revisions for many years after their initial publication. Wallace's first *Descriptive Guide* (AB 1202) appeared as a supplement to Smith's *Babes in the Wood,* but later editions, until cessation of publication altogether in 1899, came out on their own. Stoddard, the Glens Falls photographer and artist, issued a wide variety of guidebooks, including *Ticonderoga Past and Present* (AB 807) in 1873, and, in annual revisions from 1871 to 1913, a *Lake George Illustrated* (AB 1200). In 1874 he issued his *Adirondacks Illustrated* (AB 1206) for the first time, and this little book — at first illustrated with line drawings by Stoddard, later with halftone photographs — went through annual revisions until two years before the author's death in 1917. Other guidebooks of the period included Charles Possons' books on Lakes George and Champlain (AB 1217) and, indicative of the growing importance of railroads in the Adirondack tourist economy, Frank Hamilton Taylor's *Birch Bark from the Adirondacks* (AB 1088) prepared for the Adirondack Railroad Co. and issued between 1886 and 1888.

The outdoor life still figured strongly in the Adirondacks as reflected in new generations of national sporting periodicals. Among these were *Forest and Stream* which began publication in 1873 and *The American Angler* which flourished from 1881 until 1900. Yet new life styles and institutions were grafting themselves to the old outdoor ways, and there is perhaps no better nor any stranger an example of this phenomenon than is provided in the Rev. John Patterson Lundy's *The Saranac Exiles* (AB 7317). Published at Philadelphia in 1880 and bearing an author's attribution of "Not by Shakespeare," this is a peculiar, diffuse, and often bitter book. Although dealing with the outdoors in part, it is equally devoted to taking pot-shots at everything from Murray to

Charles Dudley Warner, from forest destruction in the Adirondacks to the natives of Saranac Lake village. The book also has something to say about the rise of institutionalized tuberculosis treatment in the Adirondacks and serves as a reminder that it was only three years later that Dr. Edward Livingston Trudeau opened "Little Red," the first of many small separate buildings which characterized The Adirondack Cottage Sanitarium (later Trudeau Sanatorium). The rise and fall of this important Adirondack institution, its very fall a measure of its success in contributing to modern cures for tuberculosis, can be traced in the annual reports issued between 1886 and 1951 (AB 4858).

Another kind of Adirondack institution — the private club — arose in this period as well. *Forest and Stream* editorialized on this subject in 1889 (AB 6462), and the various publications of the Adirondack League Club (AB 6493-6), further illustrate this phenomenon.

The *Adirondack Bibliography* is by no means devoted solely to new phenomena in this period, however. Older literary traditions, including the writing of history and biography, continued to flourish. B. C. Butler's *Lake George and Lake Champlain* (AB 279), published in 1868, carried the history of those areas up to the year 1759, and in 1869 Watson's *Military and Civil History of the County of Essex* (AB 685) was issued in Albany by Joel Munsell, publisher of a distinguished list of well-designed books of local history. The ever-busy Dr. Hough, prior to immersing himself in a series of national forestry studies for the Department of Agriculture, revised and updated French's *Gazetteer* in 1872 (AB 1269). The list of books on local history grew considerably. A. W. Holden's *A History of the Town of Queensbury* (AB 286) came out under Munsell's imprint in 1874 and Peter S. Palmer's *History of Plattsburgh* (AB 719) — based on an 1871 newspaper series — in 1877. N. B. Sylvester's *Sketches of Northern New York* (AB 53) came out that same year, his *History of Saratoga County* (AB 680) the year following. Other county histories, increasingly the products of national publishers of local history, followed, including Hurd's *Clinton and Franklin Counties* (AB 666) in 1880; two works by H. P. Smith, a *History of Warren County* (AB 678) and one on *Essex County* (AB 677) in the 1880's; and Francis Parkman's *Historic Handbook of the Northern Tour* (AB 294) in 1885. Other historical items included Jeptha R. Simms's *Frontiersmen of New York* (AB 46) and Henry Dornburgh's primitive but curious pamphlet "Why the Wilderness Is Called Adirondack" (AB 18) — a question it really doesn't answer correctly. In 1893, there appeared the first in a series of monographs on the Indians of New York by William M. Beauchamp, his *Indian Names in New York* (AB 228).

In biography, the publication in the 1870's of O. B. Frothingham's *Gerrit Smith* (AB 7108) and J. E. Todd's *John Todd: The Story of His Life* (AB 7150) reminds us of individuals associated with earlier phases of Adirondack history. In much the same way, F. E. Pond's *Life and Adventures of "Ned Buntline"* (AB 6944-5) published in 1888, shortly after the death of the dime-novel writer, evokes an earlier, colorful period in the Adirondacks. Buntline, whose real name was Edward Zane Carroll Judson, had lived for several years at Eagle Lake, near Blue Mountain, but he wrote practically no Adirondack fiction. Other writers did turn out dime-novels with Adirondack settings, however, particularly following the Civil War. From the 1870's until the First World War fictional characters such as Jack, Jerry and Joe, Diamond Dick, Frank and Dick Merriwell, and Fred Fearnot all had their share of fantastic Adirondack adventures. An eager public apparently took very much to such alliterative or otherwise colorful series titles as *Pluck and Luck, Brave and Bold, Diamond*

Dick, Jr., Happy Days, Do and Dare, and *Tip Top Weekly* (AB 10574 - 10601), and publishers such as Frank Tousey, now forgotten, and Street and Smith, still familiar to generations raised on comic books, were happy to oblige. Not all Adirondack fiction was of the dime-novel variety, however. Robert Louis Stevenson's *The Master of Ballantrae* (AB 10477), written at Saranac Lake and published in 1889, had episodes set in the Adirondacks.

No consideration of the Adirondacks and of writings about the Adirondacks can afford to gloss over the work of Verplanck Colvin or the emergence of the conservation movement in the region. In a sense, both Colvin and Adirondack conservation owe a great deal to George Perkins Marsh's seminal *Man and Nature* (AB 8422). Although there was only bare mention of the Adirondacks in the first edition of 1864, the revised editions of 1874 and 1885 — published under the title *The Earth As Modified by Human Action* — expanded upon northern New York at greater length. Marsh's book has been called "the fountainhead of the conservation movement"[7] in America, and to a certain extent the theories it expounded undoubtedly played a similar role for the Adirondacks. It is likely, too, that the book had a decisively formative influence on the views of Verplanck Colvin who was in his 'teens when it was originally published. It was Marsh who brought the attention of America — indeed the world — to the need for exercising caution in dealing with those mountainous regions from which emanated the water supplies that nurtured civilization, whether agricultural or industrial. In the case of the Adirondacks, it was, above all, the concern for watershed protection that precipitated the creation by law in 1885 of the New York Forest Preserve and which contributed significantly to placing the preserve under constitutional protection in 1894.

Verplanck Colvin's own writings on the Adirondacks began innocently enough with the pamphlet *Narrative of a Bear Hunt* (AB 5878), published in 1870. His most influential work — perhaps, in retrospect, rather more for its narrative color and its conservation message than for its purely scientific virtues — lay in his survey writings, beginning with "The Ascent and Barometrical Measurement of Mt. Seward" (AB 1117), made public in 1872, and the various topographical and state land survey reports produced in an official capacity between 1873 and the end of the century (AB 1118 - 1145). These reports, especially the first through seventh reports covering the key transitional years of the 1870's (AB 1118 - 1120), constitute what is possibly the greatest single body of writing ever produced in or about the Adirondacks. In addition to the romantic color Colvin imparted to his narratives, his arguments favored sound conservation in the Adirondacks. In his recommendations regarding the desirability of creating an Adirondack Park, he also noted the rapid changes which were being wrought in the wilderness. In 1880, for instance, he wrote the following — a passage that has often been quoted but which bears repeating:

> Viewed from the standpoint of my own explorations, the rapidity with which certain changes take place in the opening up to travel of the wild corners of the wilderness has about it something almost startling.... I find following in the footsteps of my explorations the blazed-line and the trail; then the ubiquitous tourist, determined to see all that has been recorded as worth seeing. Where first comes one — the next year there are ten — the year after full a hundred. The woods are thronged; bark and log huts prove insufficient; hotels spring up as though by magic, and the air resounds with laughter, song and jollity.... The

7. Lewis Mumford, *The Brown Decades: A Study of the Arts in America, 1865-1895* (New York, 1931), p. 78.

genius of change has possession of the land; we cannot control it. When we
study the necessities of our people, we would not control it if we could.[8]

The beginnings of control in the Adirondacks were taking shape,
nonetheless. In this respect, the *Adirondack Bibliography* provides convenient
chronological breakdowns of a number of vital subjects, including the Forest
Preserve, for the years 1872 through 1894 (AB 1350 - 1464 and 8196 - 8198), on
fish and game from 1864 through 1965 (AB 2317 - 2755 and 8443 - 8533), and
on soil and water conservation from 1874 through 1965 (AB 2756 - 2878 and
8534 - 8574). Certain purely scientific and technological works bear mentioning
here too, as the work of people such as Marsh and Colvin and the efforts of the
early conservation movement were very much imbued with the scientific spirit.
One such example — and this one is technological in its implications — is
Farrand N. Benedict's swan song to the Adirondacks, his 1875 *Report on a
Survey of the Waters of the Upper Hudson and Raquette Rivers* (AB 4388).
More purely scientific are such studies as J. A. Lintner's *Entomological
Contributions* (AB 2965), Colvin's *Winter Fauna of Mt. Marcy* (AB 3677), C.
H. Peck's *Plants of the Summit of Mt. Marcy* (AB 3490), Lintner's
Lepidoptera (AB 2969), and Fred Mather's *Memoranda Relating to
Adirondack Fishes* (AB 3544). Most of these studies, by the way, were first
published as appendices in various of Colvin's survey reports. Another basic
work is Clinton Hart Merriam's *The Mammals of the Adirondack Region*
which was published in several formats during the 1880's (AB 3705, 3701, and
3700).

If the scientific spirit played an important role in the rise of the conservation
movement in America and in the Adirondacks, the practical application of
conservation measures required a kind of human activity far removed from the
ivory tower. Given a certain amount of raw scientific data to begin with,
choices of action were still very much dependent upon judgments based upon
human wishes and public need. At this point conservation veered off into the
realms of politics and law, propaganda and persuasion. Early documentation of
an important effort to come to grips with the conservation of the Adirondacks
on the governmental level is provided in the *First Annual Report of the
Commissioners of State Parks* (AB 1350), submitted to the State legislature in
May of 1873 and published as a pamphlet in an edition of 4,000 copies early in
1874. The Commission was headed by former Governor Horatio Seymour,
Lady Amelia Murray's host in the 1850's, and included Franklin B. Hough in
its membership. Verplanck Colvin was secretary to the Commission, signed the
letter of transmittal to the legislature, and may have had an important role in
the drafting of the report. Little, if any, significant action followed upon this
report, however. Indeed, it was a decade before decisive legal moves were made
relative to the State's interest in the Adirondacks. Meanwhile, conservation
action continued to be carried on largely outside of government in such media
as the columns of the press and the miscellaneous writings of people like Colvin
(AB 1146 - 1153).

It was not until 1883 that the roughly 700,000 acres of Adirondack land then
in State ownership were withdrawn from further sale to the public. It was in this
year too that Charles Sprague Sargent, first director of the Arnold Arboretum
at Harvard, wrote in the *Nation* on "The Adirondack Forests" (AB 2092), thus

---

8. Verplanck Colvin, *Seventh Annual Report on the Progress of the Topographical Survey of the Adirondack
Region of New York* (Albany, 1880), pp. 7-8.

commencing his deep, if relatively brief, involvement in establishing the Forest
Preserve. Another Commission, this one headed by Sargent, came up with the
forest preserve recommendations in 1885 (AB 1400). With the passage of the
law establishing protection for the Preserve in May of that year a permanent
Forest Commission was finally established in New York State and the regular
publication of information on the Adirondacks commenced in the form of
annual reports (AB 1400). Once established in law, the Forest Preserve would
become the object of litigation, and here the *Adirondack Bibliography* again
offers chronological listings beginning with the year 1886 (AB 1875 - 2039 and
8391b - 8391d).

The Adirondack Park, whose history paralleled that of the forest preserve,
came into being only after establishment of the preserve. "Shall a Park Be
Established in the Adirondack Wilderness?" the Forest Commission asked in
1891 (AB 1438). A year later an affirmative answer to that question was given
by the legislature, the rationale being to provide geographical focus for the
accretion of further forest preserve lands and to designate a place for public
health and recreation in addition but still subordinate to the essentially
utilitarian purposes for which the Forest Preserve had originally been
established.

All was not well with the preserve, nonetheless. At the constitutional
convention of 1894 it was placed under even more stringent protection. The
convention itself, including the speeches of David McClure in support of
constitutional protection, is covered in the revised record published in 1900 (AB
1936-7) while the subsequent constitutional history of the Forest Preserve can
be traced chronologically in the *Bibliography* (AB 1935-74).

Finally, a word should be said about the importance of the printed
illustration during this critical transitional period in Adirondack history. In
1867 *Harper's Weekly,* for example, based a page of wood-engravings upon the
work of the Malone photographers, Fay and Farmer (AB 934). Following the
attention brought to the Adirondacks by W. H. H. Murray, several magazines
ran Adirondack illustrations, most notably in the Boston-based *Every
Saturday,* a weekly published by the same firm that published Murray. Though
not covered in the *Adirondack Bibliography,* a number of full-page wood-
engravings based on drawings by Homer Martin and by Winslow Homer can
be found in some of the issues for late 1870 and early 1871. Similarly, the 1872
and 1873 volumes of *The Aldine* contain engravings of a considerable number
of Adirondack subjects originally drawn or painted by such artists as George
H. Smillie, John Hows, Fred T. Vance (AB 8078), and Alexander Lawrie. In
the two large and sumptuous volumes of William Cullen Bryant's *Picturesque
America* (AB 968-9), issued in 1872 and 1874, can be found sections devoted to
both the Adirondacks and Lakes George and Champlain with numerous wood-
engravings by Harry Fenn.

In the 1880's there were a number of striking instances where pictorial art
worked hand in hand with conservation. One is inevitably reminded of the
Sierra Club Exhibit Format books of the 1960's, only in the 1880's the
engraving, not the photograph, and black and white, not color, were
characteristic of the medium employed. Examples include the front cover of the
December 6, 1884, issue of *Harper's Weekly* where Julian Rix's two panel
"Destruction of Forests in the Adirondacks" appears, while inside the same
issue there are related illustrations by the same artist and a short article calling
attention to "wantoness" on the part of the lumbering industry (AB 1384). In
January of the next year, accompanying an article on "Forest Destruction"

(AB 1388) by Sargent, were two further Rix illustrations, these showing a feeder of the Hudson River before and after logging and fire. The wildlife of the Adirondacks — notably the extirpated or near-extirpated mammals of the region — received visual attention in February, 1885, in a full-page engraving after Daniel Beard (AB 3681). The "Evicted Tenants" included the moose, elk, wolverine, beaver, panther, and wolf, species which in recent years have again come to public attention through the work of the Temporary Study Commission on the Future of the Adirondacks.

V. CONSERVATION AND PRESERVATION: 1896 - 1915

During the two decades between the achievement of constitutional protection for the Forest Preserve and the beginning of the First World War, the Adirondacks and the literature of the Adirondacks found themselves in a curious state of suspension. The rapid changes which had taken place in the previous thirty year period needed digesting, or so it would appear from the bibliographical record. Retrospection was in the air. At the same time, the vital relationship which had once existed between individuals and the Adirondack environment and which had found expression in Adirondack art and literature of an earlier day appears to have diminished somewhat. At least the reflection of this love affair achieved less frequent or original expression. Instead, there is a notable gain in material reflecting the increased roles of industrialization and institutionalization in the period immediately preceding the First War.

The place of industry, for example, can be noted in the continuing and even greater influence of the railroad corporations. The Delaware and Hudson's *A Summer Paradise* (AB 1221) invited the city dweller to the North Country with regularity from 1895 until 1942, and again, for a time, following the Second World War. In 1914, the D.&H. sponsored Warwick S. Carpenter's *The Summer Paradise in History* (AB 280), an excellent little historical handbook of its type. Carpenter's work represented a further development of Henry P. Phelps's *Literary and Historic Note Book* (AB 1233) which had been published in 1907, also by the D. & H.

Although the taste for woodcraft and sport was by no means totally eradicated in this period, as illustrated by W. H. Boardman's *Lovers of the Woods* (AB 5071) and A. N. Cheney's "Angling Notes" (AB 5932), published between 1893 and 1901 in *Forest and Stream,* the rise of the institutional view of matters Adirondack was increasingly apparent. Such items as the *Lake Placid Club Handbook* (AB 6580), the organization pamphlet of the Adirondack Trail Improvement Society (AB 6606), the *St. Regis Yacht Club Book* (AB 6673), and a *Forest and Stream* article on Litchfield Park (AB 6652) — all of these published in the waning years of the nineteenth century — help reinforce the point. The role of the organized institution in early twentieth century Adirondack life likewise continued to be reflected in such titles as the Lake Placid *Club Notes* (AB 5579) issued from 1905 to 1935 and in the Ausable Club's *Yearbook* for 1908 (AB 6612).

Several new periodicals, some devoted exclusively or almost exclusively to the Adirondacks, are further illustrative of the collective or institutionalized approach to the region. Among these was Harry V. Radford's *Woods and Waters* (AB 4771), which was issued between 1898 and 1906 and which helped keep alive the spirit and attitudes expressed in an earlier day by "Adirondack" Murray. *Forest Leaves* (AB 4745), published at Gabriels, and *Journal of Outdoor Life* (AB 4746), both issued between the early 1900's and about 1935, emanated from the health industry. *Stoddard's Northern Monthly* (AB 4765) represented an attempt by the author of Adirondack guidebooks and photographer of the Adirondack scene to enter the periodical field; but the magazine was short-lived.

Attempts to resolve conflicting views as to the meaning and purpose of forestry and conservation in the Adirondacks continued to be dominant issues of the period. The bibliography on the Forest Preserve for these years can be followed chronologically (AB 1465 - 1649). Meanwhile, from 1895 through 1899, the agency responsible for the preserve — the State Fish, Game and Forest Commission — commenced the publication of annual reports in an impressive large page format, liberally illustrated (AB 2041). This series was continued by successor organizations until 1911. The role of the commission itself, however, remained a subject of scrutiny, and the publication of State Senator Martin V. B. Ives's *Through the Adirondacks in Eighteen Days* (AB 1488) in 1899 was a by-product of legislative committee work, as was the change in name to the Forest, Fish and Game Commission. A reordering of priorities is implied by the new name, although the Commission's reports (AB 2043) continued the tradition and format established earlier. In 1911 another name change took place, when the Forest Preserve and other natural resource responsibilities came under the Conservation Commission. In 1927, the name was changed again, this time to Conservation Department, and, more recently still, it has become the Department of Environmental Conservation. Annual reports of the Conservation Commission and Department adopted a more modest format and continued to be issued through the year 1965 (AB 2055).

The dominance of the forestry question was reflected in a great number of titles published in the pre-war period. The emergence of a fledgling forestry profession in America, based in large measure upon European scholarly and institutional models, played a considerable, if often frustrated, role upon the Adirondack scene. The problem was to demonstrate whether it was possible economically, technically, and politically for sustained-yield forestry to thrive on State lands in coexistence with the requirements of watershed, aesthetic conservation and private interests. The attempt was not particularly successful, principally for political and aesthetic reasons, and professional forestry of the applied sort was eventually driven to take refuge on private lands in the State and on State lands outside the Adirondacks and other than those of the Forest Preserve. Despite the ultimate outcome, the effort was valiant, and many leaders in Adirondack forestry were to become prominent in national applied conservation. W. F. Fox's *The Adirondack Black Spruce* (AB 3508) came out in 1894 and Gifford Pinchot's *The Adirondack Spruce* (AB 4023) four years later, shortly before Pinchot became first Director of the U. S. Forest Service under Theodore Roosevelt. In 1900 R. S. Hosmer and E. S. Bruce prepared *A Forest Working Plan for Township 40* (AB 2116), dealing with the Raquette Lake area. About the same time the Prussian trained B. E. Fernow was undertaking to prove the practicability of applied forestry on State lands at Axton, a program of the ill-fated New York College of Forestry at Cornell. Fernow's *Beginnings of Professional Forestry in the Adirondacks* (AB 4949), his *Progress of Forest Management in the Adirondacks* (AB 2115), and the annual reports of the forestry school issued between 1899 and 1904 (AB 4955) describe an arc of anticipation, conflict, and defeat for forest management on State lands. The emergence of such organizations as the Association for the Protection of the Adirondacks in 1902 (see AB 6568-9) is indicative of the kind of antagonism which Fernow and others faced.

Still, the practical forester continued to have plenty to keep him busy in the Adirondacks, even on State lands. The disastrous forest fires of 1903, about which Fox wrote the following year (AB 2138), and the equally devastating fires of 1908 indicated the need to bring destructive natural and manmade forces under control in northern New York. The establishment of fire towers and other control measures under the Conservation Commission was a result. Another was a hesitancy on the part of the Constitutional Convention of 1915 to consider any loosening of the Forest Preserve provision, particularly as the impact of the earlier fires could be attributed, at least in part, to poor logging practices of the past. Louis Marshall, who had been a delegate to the previous convention of 1894, was the chief spokesman for maintaining strict control on the Forest Preserve at the 1915 convention, the record of which (AB 1942) suggests that the essentially utilitarian issues of forestry and watershed were still dominant and caution the wise course.

The literature of science in this period continues to be impressive, and, like other subjects of the time, it too has a decidedly retrospective, monumental, and synthetic character. From the engaging romanticism of the early Colvin surveys, for instance, we find ourselves confronted with the results of spirit levelling in New York as prepared by the U. S. Geological Survey and published between 1895 and 1917 (AB 926-7). It was upon this work that the early Geological Survey quadrangle maps were based, a series superceded by the post Second World War maps based on aerial photogrammetry. In natural history, Tarleton H. Bean's *Catalogue of the Fishes of New York* (AB 3525) and E. H. Eaton's *Birds of New York* (AB 3592) date from 1903 and 1910 - 1914, respectively. A more specialized study, though not without touches of the romantic and promotional, was Radford's "History of the Adirondack Beaver" (AB 3763) which was included in the volume of Forest, Fish and Game Commission reports covering the years 1904 - '06. Radford's arguments led to the restocking of beaver in the Adirondacks, an attempt that proved highly successful. Similar attempts by Radford and others to restock other species (see entries between AB 2364 and 2374 and AB 8452-3) were not successful, however.

Even Adirondack fiction is not without a retrospective air in some cases. Examples include Irving Batcheller's *Eben Holden* (AB 7240) and S. Paige Johnson's *Zebadiah Sartwell* (AB 7310), although the action of Gertrude Atherton's *The Aristocrats* (AB 7248) is contemporary with the immediate post turn-of-century period when all three titles were published.

The period's retrospective and monumental tendencies were perhaps most thoroughly expressed in its books of history and biography. Francis Parkman's great studies of the French and British in North America, begun in 1852, were completed shortly before the end of the century and soon brought together in a uniform edition. Titles particularly bearing on the Adirondacks, especially its periphery, included *Pioneers of New France* (AB 7567), *Montcalm and Wolfe* (AB 38), *The Jesuits in North America* (AB 37), and *A Half Century of Conflict* (AB 366). W. M. Beauchamp's continuing researches into the Indians of New York were published as State Museum bulletins early in the century and included *Aborginal Occupation of New York* (AB 226), a *History of the New York Iroquois* (AB 227), and *Aborginal Place Names of New York* (AB 1300). More recent events were subjected to the retrospective treatment of history as well. Logging, for instance, was treated in W. F. Fox's "History of the Lumber Industry in the State of New York" (AB 3942-3) which first appeared in 1900, while the first volume of J. E. Defebaugh's *History of the*

Lumber Industry in America (AB 3927) appeared that same year, the second volume in 1907.

Although the craze for local history that was characteristic of the middle and late nineteenth century seemed to have died down a bit, examples continued to come forth. There was W. K. Stone's *Washington Co., N. Y.* (AB 679), for example, and Hanson and Frey's edition of the *Tryon County Committee of Safety Minute Book* (AB 7639). Charles Z. Lincoln turned out two sizable works in the early years of the century, his five volume *Constitutional History of New York* (AB 1338), which includes material on the Forest Preserve as might be expected, and the eleven volumes of the *Messages of the Governors* (AB 1341), some of which pertain to the Adirondacks. The year 1909 marked the tercentennial of Champlain's first visit to the territory of New York State and the attendant celebrations included a good deal of printed material (AB 354 - 7).

The titles of a number of biographies and biographical notices published in the years shortly before the First World War remind us of what had gone before. J. Howard Redfield's *Recollections* (AB 7060) takes us back as far as the 1830's and his father's involvement with Emmons and others in the exploration of the High Peaks region. Other titles are reminders of the remarkable changes that had come over the Adirondacks since the end of Civil War. In 1912, for instance, F. J. Mather's small book, *Homer Martin: Poet of Landscape* (AB 7228), provided a fitting, sometimes impassioned, tribute to an artist whose work spanned the entire period. Martin's work had its beginnings in the traditional style inherited from the old Hudson River school. Some of his drawings had been published as wood-engravings in periodicals celebrating the "Adirondack" Murray phenomenon in 1870. And yet, in 1895, one of his last canvases — called variously "Adirondack Scenery" or simply "Adirondacks" — was in the vivid style called American impressionism. This last Adirondack painting of Martin's could well be the single most exciting pure work of art inspired by the region.

And, speaking of Murray, his old guide, John Plumley of Long Lake had died just after the turn of the century, and Murray penned an eloquent tribute to him, an "In Memoriam" (AB 7049), which appeared in Radford's *Woods and Waters* in 1901. Murray himself died in 1904. The following year, Harry Radford's little book on Murray appeared (AB 7009). Six years later, Radford — then only thirty-one — was murdered in Canada by an Eskimo guide.

VI. THE RISE OF PUBLIC RECREATION: 1916 - 1945

In August 1914, Europe became embroiled in the First World War. The United States managed to stay out of it until April, 1917, but by then significant new steps had been taken both nationally and in the Adirondacks relating to public use of outdoor resources. The National Park Service was established in 1916, thus providing professional custodianship for certain national land resources dedicated to purposes of public recreation. The initial emphasis was upon what has been called aesthetic conservation. In New York State, and in the Adirondacks particularly, programs of a similar sort were beginning. In a sense, such undertakings represented the concrete fulfillment of obligations which had been implied nearly a quarter of a century earlier when the Adirondack Park had been established by law.

A major force behind these new activities was George DuPont Pratt, since 1915 State Commissioner of Conservation. His "The Use of New York State

Forests for Public Recreation" (AB 5142), published in the *Proceedings of the Society of American Foresters,* was indicative of the new trend. So too was the publication, beginning in 1917, of a quarterly State magazine called *The Conservationist* (AB 4742) which lasted for four years until budgetary difficulties halted it. The issuance by the Commission of a new series of Recreation Circulars, including C. R. Pettis's *Public Use of the Forest Preserve* (AB 1934) and Arthur S. Hopkins's *The Trails to Marcy* (AB 5321), provided further evidence of the same phenomenon, and many of these same circulars, revised and updated, are still published today, now by the Department of Environmental Conservation.

The new policies had their physical manifestations as well. The erection of fire towers had begun some years earlier, but now there was an increased effort to build and mark trails purely for recreational purposes. Open camps, or leantos, were provided by the State in various locations, and, with the advent of the automobile, it was not long before the first of the drive-in campsites in the Adirondacks were under development. Because of budgetary limitations in the early 1920's, however, many of these State programs had to be curtailed for a time, with the result that some of them were taken up by private organizations. One of the most important of these was the Adirondack Mountain Club, the creation, in part, of George Pratt after he had stepped down as Commissioner. The Club adopted a constitution and bylaws in 1922 (AB 6512), and, in addition to addressing itself to its own internal purposes, undertook projects of a quasi-public character, including the sponsorship in 1922 of construction of the Northville-Lake Placid trail through the heart of the region. W. G. Howard wrote of this project (AB 5322), while the Club, in the meantime, had initiated its own program of publishing a periodical and monographs dealing with the Adirondacks and outdoor recreation. Its periodical *High Spots* (AB 6546) was supplemented and ultimately succeeded by such titles as the *Bulletin* (AB 6510), the *High Spots Bulletin* (AB 6513), and the *High Spots Yearbook* (AB 6547) through the year 1944. The first of Club-sponsored monographs or books was Robert Marshall's *The High Peaks of the Adirondacks* (AB 5393) issued in 1922. Russell M. L. Carson's *Peaks and People of the Adirondacks* was published by Doubleday Page and Company with Club backing in 1927. In 1935, the first edition of the Club's *Guide to Adirondack Trails* (AB 5317) was issued, while an eighth edition has just recently appeared.

Meanwhile, publications under other auspices, such as Walter Collins O'Kane's *Trails and Summits of the Adirondacks* (AB 5326), brought the Adirondacks to the attention of an ever expanding public. So too did the automobile, which carried a new clientele to the region and provided the means for diffusing use over a greater extent of territory than had been possible in the days of rail. In 1927, the newly designated Conservation Department issued a new Recreation Circular, *Adirondack Highways* (AB 5542), which confirmed in print the new technological phenomenon. This Circular was superceded after 1931 by W. D. Mulholland's *Adirondack Campsites* (AB 5536).

In conservation philosophy new ideas and new conflicts emerged during the inter-war period. Where much of the earlier conservation had been concerned primarily with such purely utilitarian issues as timber production versus watershed maintenance, the requirements of outdoor recreation, of aesthetic conservation, and, finally, of an emerging concern for wilderness preservation *per se* assumed an increasingly dominant position after the First World War. A. B. Recknagel's *The Forests of New York* (AB 1705), published in 1923, provided a synthesis of the manipulative forester's views on the Adirondacks, but the literature of the Forest Preserve after 1915 (AB 1650 - 1788 and 8199 - 8208) is indicative of a spectrum of public concern relative to the Adirondacks far broader than could be encompassed even within the professional competence of the conventional forester. It is perhaps no wonder, then, that the major court test of the constitutional provision governing the Forest Preserve, the so-called bobsled case of 1930 (AB 2011), went beyond the old issues. Although the outcome of the case hinged in part on a negative technicality as to what constituted the cutting of a "substantial number of trees," the courts seemed at least equally concerned about the positive virtues implicit in maintaining the "wild forest character" of the Forest Preserve.

Yet the bobsled case did not provide, even temporarily, definitive answers to such questions as what the new functions of the Forest Preserve might be or how the preserve should be managed specifically. Issues raised following the case were widely discussed, and many are still unresolved even today. Some were to prove of national significance. During 1933, in the pages of *High Spots* (AB 1766), Russell M. L. Carson considered such matters under the title "Sabbath is for Man, Not Man for the Sabbath" (AB 1766) and took a position favoring modest degrees of physical development of the Forest Preserve for recreational purposes, but development nonetheless. Simultaneously, a new recreational heresy was beginning to be codifed, something called wilderness recreation. It was taken up by the nationally oriented Wilderness Society, formed in 1935, which assumed a more strictly preservationist stance than did other recreationists or foresters who advocated the techniques of total environmental manipulation. The foundation of the Wilderness Society owed a great deal to Robert and George Marshall, both of whom had learned their early wilderness lessons in the Adirondacks, having been the first persons, along with their guide Herb Clark, to climb all of the major Adirondack peaks. The Society's periodical was *The Living Wilderness* (AB 4748), and its first issue contained Raymond H. Torrey's "Truck Trails in the Adirondacks" (AB 1773), covering an issue of basic importance and indicative of the intellectual ferment characteristic of the Depression which extended even into the field of conservation. Despite the controversies of the time, however, the Constitutional Convention of 1938, though holding firmly to the constitutional provision covering the preserve, assumed a middle of the road course in its interpretation of just what that provision meant relative to the preserve.

The inter-war period was particularly notable for historical writing pertaining directly and exclusively to the Adirondacks. Of a somewhat general nature were Arthur C. Parker's *Archaeological History of New York* (AB 218), and Landon's *The North Country: A History* (AB 26), and, in the field of recreational history, Charles Eliot Goodspeed's *Angling in America* (AB 5941). In natural history there were W. J. Miller's *Geological History of New York State* (AB 3059) and his *The Adirondack Mountains* (AB 3071), as well as works of a more general nature such as T. M. Longstreth's *The Adirondacks* (AB 27), published in 1917, F. J. Seaver's *History of Franklin County* (AB 673), and the multi-volume *William Johnson Papers* (AB 25), commenced in 1921 and only completed in 1965 with volume fourteen. It was Alfred L. Donaldson's *A History of the Adirondacks* (AB 17) published in 1921 which really established a firm basis for books devoted solely to the Adirondacks, however. Published in two volumes, Donaldson's work contained a number of factual errors and suffered somewhat from an overdependence upon the vagaries of verbal tradition, but it was rich in excellently drawn character studies and demonstrated to subsequent authors that there was a place for books dealing solely with the rather specialized topic of Adirondack history. At the same time, Donaldson's own pioneering bibliographical list (AB 2), which appeared as an appendix in his *History,* established an even more specialized tradition, of which the present *Adirondack Bibliography* represents the fulfillment. Thoughout the 1920's and 1930's other books, often dealing with very particular Adirondack locales or subject matter, followed. Arthur M. Masten's *The Story of Adirondac* (AB 864) was privately printed in 1923; Russell M. L. Carson's *Peaks and People of the Adirondacks* (AB 8), already mentioned, came out in 1927. In 1933, Joseph F. Grady's *The Adirondacks: Fulton Chain - Big Moose Region* (AB 20) was published, and in 1935 a half century of the forest preserve was honored in Gurth Whipple's *Fifty Years of Conservation in New York State* (AB 2069), a state publication.

Another anniversary, the centennial of the first recorded ascent of Mt. Marcy, was celebrated the summer of 1937. An entire issue of *High Spots* was devoted to the subject and included Carson's "The First Ascent of Mt. Marcy" (AB 582), a story which, it should be noted, is now subject to some modification in light of the recent discovery of fresh primary sources. Finally, T. Wood Clarke's *Emigres in the Wilderness* (AB 65), which dealt with the French settlements on the northwestern fringes of the Adirondacks, came out in 1941 as America entered the Second World War.

The Adirondack region figured in other types of books and periodicals as well. Harold W. Thompson's *Body, Boots, and Britches* (AB 4731) dealt with the folklore of New York State, including the Adirondacks, while Edith Cutting's *Lore of An Adirondack County* (AB 4688) was more particularly concerned with Essex County. There were also historical periodicals such as the *Fort Ticonderoga Museum Bulletin* (AB 4767), which began publication in 1927, and the shortlived but intriguing *Moorsfield Antiquarian* (AB 4750) which was issued between 1937 and 1939.

The 1930's were preoccupied with anniversaries of all sorts, besides the ones already mentioned. Dedicated to institutional observations in particular were such titles as M. A. Osborn's *Camp Dudley: First 50 Years* (AB 6664), Elizabeth Cole's *Fifty Years at Trudeau Sanatorium* (AB 4841), Arthur Masten's *Tahawus Club: 1898 - 1933* (AB 6656), and Henry S. Coffin's *Adirondack Mountain Reserve: 1887 - 1937* (AB 6627). Elizabeth D. McIver's *Early Days at Putnam Camp* (AB 6653) appeared about 1941.

Biography and autobiography had their place as well. E. L. Trudeau's *Autobiography* (AB 7188) and Stephen Chalmer's short biography of Trudeau, *The Beloved Physician* (AB 7157), both appeared in the mid-teens not long after the death of that pioneer in the treatment of respiratory disease. Another doctor's autobiography, Arpad Gezya Gerster's *Recollections of a New York Surgeon* (AB 5611) also came out in the 1910's, and both text and illustrations pertained in part to that talented man's associations with the central Adirondack lakes region. James M. Clarke's *James Hall of Albany* (AB 6875) dealt with a man who was a member of the party which made the first ascent of Mt. Marcy and who subsequently became a major force in American paleontology and in the training of younger men who were to make their mark in the scientific exploration of the American West. The passing of Adirondack historian Alfred Donaldson was noted in a pamphlet prepared in 1923 by T. M. Longstreth (AB 6842), and Herb Clark, companion of the Marshall brothers in the ascents of the forty-six major Adirondack peaks, was memorialized by Robert Marshall in a moving *High Spots* article of 1933 (AB 6903). Another remarkable figure — Lowville physician, statistician, author of local histories and State gazetteers, student of forestry and early figure in national forest conservation — Franklin B. Hough, was the subject of a study (AB 6903) by Edna L. Jacobson which appeared in *New York History* in 1934.

Books on the fine arts dwindled somewhat, just as the attention of artists themselves had shifted away from subjects such as the Adirondacks and their preferred styles moved away from the representational. Nevertheless, Eliot Clark's *Alexander H. Wyant: Sixty Paintings* (AB 7235) came out in 1920, and in 1929 and 1931 the two volumes of Harry T. Peter's monumental study of *Currier & Ives: Printmakers to the American People* (AB 722) were issued. In fiction and poetry there continued to be some market. Longstreth's *Mac of Placid* (AB 7313) was a study of an Adirondack guide and old-timer. Ernest Thompson Seton's *Rolf in the Woods* (AB 7537), published in 1926, has been called the best example of Adirondack juvenilia. Louis Untermyer's *Adirondack Cycle* (AB 7494) provided the poetic touch. Probably the major work of American fiction based upon Adirondack events was, and remains, Theodore Dreiser's *An American Tragedy* (AB 7285), published in 1929, which was based on the murder of Grace Brown by Chester Gillette at Big Moose Lake in 1906.

As had been the case in the previous period, first hand accounts of adventure deep in the Adirondacks remained few and far between. Perhaps there were few "new discoveries" to be made in an Adirondacks which had been thoroughly mapped, whose more dangerous species of animals had, for the most part, been exterminated, and whose once romantic offerings had become the public property of thousands. Still, there were some exceptions, including Henry Abbott's nineteen birchbark books (AB 7326) published annually by the author from 1914 to 1932 and given away by him to friends at Christmas time. These little accounts dealt in a quiet way with Abbott's own experiences and those of his guide "Bige" Smith in the central Adirondack woods. They remain gentle reminders of one man's love of the woods and perpetuate such woodland standbys as bear stories and deer hunting tales, of being lost in the woods, and of secret places seen, even today, by few. Paulina Brandreth's *Trails of Enchantment* (AB 5072), issued under the pseudonym Paul Brandreth, is not dissimilar in effect. In 1940 appeared Rockwell Kent's eminently readable *This Is My Own* (AB 6953), an autobiographical work covering the Kents' falling in love with an old Essex County farmstead, conservation battles engaged in, and the quagmires a non-native can get himself into when he tries to penetrate the mysteries of local Adirondack politics.

As in an earlier period, however, institutions appear to have had the upper hand between the wars. Published reports of the Olympic Committee (AB 6341) remind us of the winter games held at Lake Placid in 1932. Beginning in 1939, there appeared *Lumber Camp News* (AB 4749) which reached fourteen volumes until, in 1952, it became the *Northeastern Logger* (AB 4761) and later the *Northern Logger,* which it remains. The Adirondacks also figured in another, and very important, cooperative publishing enterprise, the New York Writers Program's *New York: A Guide to the Empire State* (AB 1247), which appeared in 1940. Then came the war.

VII. AFTER ANOTHER WAR: 1946 - 1965

The twenty years following the end of the Second World War saw a veritable explosion of books, periodicals, and articles about the Adirondacks. Four of the books from this period are among the most useful, comprehensive, and enjoyable of all Adirondack literature. Three of them we shall mention here at the outset, the fourth at the close of this section.   First in order of publication is Harold K. Hochschild's *Township 34* (AB 285) which was privately printed in 1952. Based on over two decades of both primary and secondary research into the history of the central Adirondacks, with Blue Mountain Lake as its focus, the book is gargantuan in bulk, is loaded with illustrations based on old maps, photographs and drawings, and in its thoroughness establishes a standard of local history writing that will probably remain unsurpassed, in the Adirondacks or anywhere else, for a long time to come. The book has another distinction. It is not unusual for a museum, once established, to produce books, but it is definitely uncommon for a book to constitute the cornerstone of a museum. Yet *Township 34* did become the figurative cornerstone of the Adirondack Museum at Blue Mountain Lake, an institution Walter Muir Whitehill has called an "extra-illustration of *Township 34* in three dimensional terms."[9] The collector who covets a copy of *Township 34* for his personal library, however, is forwarned that it is practically impossible to obtain. Printed only in a limited edition, it can be found in many libraries, but it has never been for sale and its appearance on second-hand lists is extremely rare. Parts of it at least, updated and revised in some respects, were issued by the Adirondack Museum as separate pamphlets in the early 1960's.

Next is William Chapman White's *Adirondack Country* (AB 58). Originally published in 1954 by Duell, Sloan and Pearce as a volume in its American Folkways series, *Adirondack Country* remains the best single volume dealing with the Adirondack region in general. The original edition was reprinted several times. In 1967 the book was updated and reissued by Alfred A. Knopf and remains readily available.

The third book is Paul Jamieson's superb collection of Adirondack writings published in 1964, *The Adirondack Reader* (AB 10415). Here can be found excerpts from the best writings on the region as well as a number of plates which reproduce photographs and historical prints. Unfortunately, copies of the book itself are practically impossible to find. Already out of print, it richly deserves reprinting.

Aside from their intrinsic excellence, books such as those by Hochschild, White, and Jamieson are also symptomatic of a general burgeoning of publications about the Adirondacks which began after the lull of the early 1940's. First there were the periodicals. The Adirondack Mountain Club continued its *Bulletin* under a new title, *Adirondac* (AB 6507), in 1945. The following year the State Conservation Department began publication of another bi-monthly, the *New York State Conservationist* (AB 4759), its first attempt along these lines since the demise in 1921 of the old Commission's quarterly *Conservationist*. The same year there began to appear *North Country Life* (AB 4760), later *York State Tradition,* under the editorship of G. Glyndon Cole. The National Lead Company launched its *Tahawus Cloudsplitter* (AB 4766) in 1949 as the house organ for its Adirondack titanium mining operations. In 1954, the

9. Walter Muir Whitehill, *Independent Historical Societies* (Boston, 1962), p. 531.

State began publication of the *New York Fish and Game Journal,* a scientific periodical which contained a considerable amount of material pertinent to the Adirondacks or based upon research undertaken in the region. Other periodicals of the period ran the gamut from the mimeographed *Backwoods Journal* (AB 9294) published at Paradox Lake beginning in 1957 to the old *Adirondack Life* (AB 9289), which appeared beginning in 1960 at irregular intervals as a tabloid supplement to such newspapers as the *Warrensburg-Lake George News.* Twice a year, beginning in 1963, the Adirondack 46-ers began issuing its mimeographed *Adirondack Peeks* (AB 9291) to members, suggesting the growing viability of that organization. There were also periodicals devoted to local history, including the St. Lawrence Historical Association's *Quarterly* which began publication in 1956 and the *Franklin County Historical Review* (AB 9304) which commenced in 1964.

An embellishment of some periodicals was the special column, and there were a number of new Adirondack columns. Bill Roden's "Adirondack Sportsman" (AB 9336) began to appear in several Adirondack newspapers in 1955. Edgar B. Nixon's "Armchair Mountaineer" (AB 10436) was a staple of the *Adirondac* for several years beginning in 1956, and Marjorie Lansing Porter's "Upstate Things and Stuff" (AB 9335) became a feature of the *Plattsburgh Press-Republican* beginning in 1963. Mrs. Porter's remarkable collection of Adirondack folklore had been the subject of a piece in the *New York Folklore Quarterly* (AB 4721) a decade earlier.

Of individual books and articles there seems to have been no end. W. H. Cook's *Letters of a Ticonderoga Farmer: 1851 - 1885* (AB 6998) came out in 1946 under the editorship of Frederick G. Bascom. In 1948 there were such books as Morris Bishop's *Champlain: The Life of Fortitude* (AB 6806) and David Beetle's *Up Old Forge Way* (AB 957). In the 1950's there were the following, among many others: Andrew Denny Rodgers' *Bernhard Eduard Fernow* (AB 4065), Barbara Kephart Bird's *Calked Shoes* (AB 3887), Harvey L. Dunham's very popular *French Louie* (AB 7093), George Marshall's *New York History* article on "Dr. Ely and His Adirondack Map" (AB 6849), and a number of offset publications compiled by Howard Becker, including Livonia Stanton Emerson's "Early Life at Long Lake" (AB 8005) and "Some Early Long Lake Documents" (AB 7994). Samuel Reznikoff's two volume *Louis Marshall: Champion of Liberty* (AB 8190) contained a good deal of material on Marshall's prominent role in Adirondack and New York State forest conservation.

The first half of the 1960's also produced its fair share of material on the Adirondacks. This included Charles Sleicher's *The Adirondacks* (AB 7570), Jesse David Roberts' *Bears, Bibles and a Boy* (AB 10470), *Tales of an Adirondack County* (AB 9256) by Ted Aber and Stella King, and their *History of Hamilton County* (AB 7839). In 1963 a new history of Warren County (AB 7840) was published under the editorship of William H. Brown. Edward Hamilton's *French and Indian Wars* (AB 7589) had been published the year before, and the same author's edition of the Bougainville journals, *Adventure in the Wilderness* (AB 7581), came out in 1964. Harrison Bird was also busy turning out books dealing with the wars that had touched the eastern fringes of the Adirondacks, including *Navies in the Mountains* (AB 755), *March to Saratoga* (AB 7607), and *Battle for a Continent* (AB 7580). Diversion and, in many cases, raised eyebrows were provided by Stephen Birmingham's *Holiday* magazine article of August, 1964 on the "Beautiful, Bedevilled Adirondacks"

(AB 8080). The piece pointed out, among other things, some of the less attractive aspects of the Adirondack scene, social conflicts in particular. But the following year a reader could, if he wished, lose himself in the past by studying William Ritchie's *Archaeology of New York State* (AB 7681). Perhaps it did not matter that Ritchie concluded there was relatively little to be said, on archaeological grounds at least, of Indians in the Adirondacks.

The past was by no means the sole focus of Adirondack writings in the period, however. New recreational forms were taking hold in the region as was evident, for instance, in Jim Goodwin's articles on rock climbing (AB 5501 - 4) and in the Adirondack Mountain Club's *Adirondack Winter Mountaineering Manual* (AB 9830) of 1957. The vitality of an older form of recreation was demonstrated by the publication in 1957 and 1962, respectively, of sixth and seventh editions of the popular *Guide to Adirondack Trails* (AB 9621 -2). Both editions were under the editorship of L. Morgan Porter. The 46-ers also entered the book field with a collection about their organization and its interests (AB 10023), a volume published in 1958 and since followed by another.

Scientists were busy as well. The State's *The Ruffed Grouse* (AB 3577), edited by Gardiner Bump, came out in 1947 and was hailed with critical acclaim as a model study. Work by Jamnback and Collins on Adirondack entomology mixed pure and applied science and resulted in such titles as their *Control of Blackflies* (AB 8603). Much the same can be said of William Severinghaus's studies on the white-tailed deer such as his "Deer Weights as an Index of Range Conditions" (AB 3802), which was published in the *Fish and Game Journal.* Concern for another prime Adirondack natural resource was reflected in the publications of the Atmospheric Sciences Research Center (AB 9447 - 8).

If the Adirondack forest and park environment continued to be the source of such wealth and well-being as the region could provide, the relationship of man's economic requirements to the resource itself demanded new approaches both organizationally and informationally. An article on "The Adirondack Park Association" (AB 6692) by Margaret (Wilson) Lamy was indicative of new attempts to bring people together for effective action in the region. The forest as utilitarian resource resulted in a series of informational studies issued by the State University College of Forestry at Syracuse in the 1950's. Among these were C. C. Larson's *Timber Resources and the Economy of the Saranac Lake - Lake Placid Areas* (AB 3983), *Forest Acreage and Timber Volume in the Adirondack and Catskill Regions* (AB 4013) by Miles Ferree and James Davis, the same authors' studies for Clinton, Essex, and Franklin counties (AB 8860), Larson's *Forest Economy of the Adirondack Region* (AB 8885), and the *Atlas of Forestry of New York State* (AB 8892) edited by Neil Stout. Another primary resource, water, was the subject of Roscoe C. Martin's *Water for New York* (AB 8563). Meanwhile, local economics, forestry, and water supply all had to contend with the question of the Forest Preserve.

Again, Forest Preserve material in general can be reviewed chronologically in the *Bibliography* for the periods 1938 to 1955 (AB 1789 - 1934 and 8209 - 8220) and 1956 - 1965 (AB 8221 - 8372); selected titles are indicative of special problems which characterized the period up to 1965. For instance, the serial *The Forest Preserve* (AB 1833), edited by Paul Schaefer and which began publication in 1947, is a reminder of the Panther and Higley Mountains dam controversies of the late 1940's and early 1950's. Put out by the Friends of the Forest Preserve, the purposes addressed by this periodical were served also by a number of *Supplement Bulletins* (AB 1850) begun in 1949. Another major crisis was precipitated on November 25, 1950, when a hurricane, the great "Blowdown," ripped through the Adirondacks and felled acres and acres of timber on both public and private lands throughout the region (see AB 2280). The effects of the storm were not solely physical, however. A year later, an editorial in the October - November, 1951 *Conservationist* posed four questions about the Forest Preserve and its functions which resulted in a reader reaction which has been aptly named the great "Blowup" of 1951. The four questions related to forest preservation, game management, economics, and public recreation. The then Conservation Commissioner commented upon them in the next issue of the magazine (AB 1329), as did specialists in the Department (AB 1865). By the following issue public reaction had been formulated and was also printed (AB 1871, 1873, 1874). Editor of the *Conservationist* at the time of this controversy was Pieter Fosburgh, and a resume of the debate as seen from one viewpoint was contained in his 1959 book, *The Natural Thing* (AB 8406).

The "Blowup" was withdrawn from the *Conservationist* before long and the whole matter shifted to a Joint Legislative Committee on Natural Resources whose annual reports and those of its successor Committees (AB 1167 - 8, 1171, 1173, and 8399) continued through 1965 to try and untangle the knotty problem of the preserve. Yet if open controversy over the preserve was put aside for a time, ferment continued nonetheless. In the late 1950's the proposal to build the Adirondack Northway called forth more hot debate, including an article in *Harper's* magazine by Robert Rienow called "Why Spoil the Adirondacks" (AB 8262). This was followed by a rebuttal written by Roger Tubby (AB 8265). Meanwhile, there was also concern about Adirondack conservation problems and history in the halls of academe. Darwin Benedict chose "The New York Forest Preserve: Formative Years, 1872 - 1895" (AB 1324) as the topic for a Maxwell Graduate School of Syracuse University master's thesis in 1953. Marvin Kranz's "Pioneering in Conservation: A History of the Conservation Movement in New York State, 1865 - 1903" (AB 8410) was a doctoral dissertation in history done at Syracuse in 1961. A year later Roger C. Thompson wrote a particularly fascinating doctoral dissertation at the College of Forestry which he called "The Doctrine of Wilderness: The Policy and Politics of New York's Adirondack Forest Preserve - Park" (AB 8195). Some of the ideas developed in this thesis were used in Thompson's "Politics in the Wilderness: New York's Adirondack Forest Preserve" (also AB 8195) which appeared in the Winter, 1963 issue of *Forest History*.

For all the problems it seems to have created, the Forest Preserve as both principle and reality had had, and was continuing to have, decisive impact upon national conservation thinking. This had been so in the late nineteenth century as national forestry emerged; it had been so in the 1930's as national wilderness policies were established, particularly in the Forest Service; and in the 1950's it remained the case. A measure of this impact since the Second World War can be found in a number of books and articles. For instance, in a statement made before New York's Joint Legislative Committee on Natural Resources in 1953 (AB 8217), the executive director of the Wilderness Society, Howard Zahniser, pointed out the debt owed to the Forest Preserve by federal wilderness legislation which was then being considered by Congress. In 1964 a federal Wilderness Act was ultimately passed. Hans Huth's *Nature and the American* (AB 10413) was published in 1957 and included the Adirondacks in its consideration of the history of aesthetic conservation in America. In *Wilderness and Recreation* (AB 9584), a study report prepared in 1962 for the Outdoor Recreation Resources Review Commission, the Mount Marcy area of the Adirondacks was recognized as the only wilderness area in the Northeast meeting the study's criteria.

Energies expended in attempting either to protect or undo the Forest Preserve in these years were not the sole expressions of interest in the Adirondacks. There remained a considerable number of books content to concentrate on less controversial but no less valid aspects of the Adirondack scene, whether expounding upon a personal relationship to the area, its history, or its folklore. Among books of this type are several groups of titles by individual authors, including Martha Reben's *The Healing Woods* (AB 4808), *The Way of the Wilderness* (AB 4809), and *A Sharing of Joy* (AB 10468) which were all quite popular. Hugh Fosburgh wrote several novels set in the Adirondacks, including *Sound of White Water* (AB 7289) and *The Drowning Stone* (AB 10457), and his *One Man's Pleasure,* based on a year's journal of personal experience in the Adirondacks, was a vivid and sensitive expression of involvement with place. Among historical books, the works of two authors dealt particularly with the southwestern Adirondacks and periphery. Thomas C. O'Donnell's *Birth of a River* (AB 479) and *River Rolls On* (AB 7782) were concerned with the Black River. Howard Thomas published his own books, including *Trenton Falls: Yesterday and Today* (AB 897), *Folklore from the Adirondack Foothills* (AB 9282), *Tales from the Adirondack Foothills* (AB 9283), *Boys in Blue* (AB 7675), and *Black River in the North Country* (AB 7791). Other examples of author-published books were William Wessels' *Adirondack Profiles* (AB 10074) and *Moses Cohen* (AB 10150).

At the same time, Adirondack history was being subjected to other forms of expression and interpretation as two articles in the July 1958 issue of *New York History* demonstrated. One piece by Richard W. Lawrence, Jr. dealt with the founding of the Adirondack Center Museum at Elizabethtown (AB 9524), the other, by R. B. Inverarity, with the Adirondack Museum at Blue Mountain Lake (AB 9522).

It was in 1959 that the Adirondack Museum itself turned to the publication of books as one of its activities. Its first title was *Cranberry Lake: An Adirondack Miscellany* (AB 7762). Edited by Albert Vann Fowler, this title soon went out of print, but subsequent titles remain available at this writing. *Winslow Homer in the Adirondacks* (AB 10406), also published in 1959, was both a catalogue of an exhibit at the Adirondack Museum and a checklist of Homer's Adirondack work. In 1960 a posthumous collection of William Chapman White's miscellaneous Adirondack writings was published under the title *Just About Everything in the Adirondacks* (AB 10441). A facsimile and transcript of a *Journal of a Hunting Excursion to Louis Lake, 1851* (AB 9755) came out in 1961 with an introduction by Warder Cadbury. The same year the first (AB 9169) of seven pamphlets representing revised extracts of H. K. Hochschild's *Township 34* was published, to be followed early in 1962 by the others (AB 9163, 9227, 9032, 9211, 8955, and 8875). In 1962 there also appeared Dan Brenan's edition of *The Adirondack Letters of George Washington Sears, Whose Pen Name Was "Nessmuk"* (AB 9574). In 1963 came Kenneth Durant's *Guide-Boat Days and Ways* (AB 9589) and in 1964 two small books — Charles W. Bryan's *The Raquette: River of the Forest* (AB 7757) and Mildred Phelps Stokes Hooker's *Camp Chronicles* (AB 9551). The latter was based on a booklet which had originally appeared in a private printing twelve years before (AB 5102).

We have saved for last the remaining title of what we consider to have been the four most important books issued since the end of the Second World War.

The item in question is the *Adirondack Bibliography* itself (AB 7540), which also happens to be the first item listed in the present supplement. The genesis of the *Bibliography* has been explained in the preface to that volume. Suffice to say that it was the work over many years of the Adirondack Mountain Club's Bibliography Committee; the original volume was published at Gabriels, N. Y. by the Club. We have already mentioned the important introduction in the book done by Russell Carson. The editor of that volume, as with this one, was the indefatigable Dot Plum. The *Bibliography* remains the first, and most important, book any serious collector or student of Adirondackana should have at his fingertips.

SINCE 1965

This supplement to the *Adirondack Bibliography* covers material published through 1965, but since that time publishing activity within and about the Adirondacks has continued unabated. Books from institutional and commercial publishers and in private printings continue to roll off the presses. There is even a new magazine, and an important one, *Adirondack Life*. There has been another constitutional convention, a proposal to turn the central Adirondack region into an Adirondack Mountains National Park, a State report recommending against the National Park, a Temporary Study Commission on the Future of the Adirondacks, and, finally, an Adirondack Park Agency. All of these have added considerable grist to an Adirondack bibliographer's mill. Yet these publications and others that are inevitably to come will have to wait their turn until such time as there is a further supplement to the *Adirondack Bibliography*, just as the present supplement itself will have to wait until it is provided its own bibliographical listing and assigned a serial number (judging from where the present volume leaves off, we suspect that number will be AB 10642). All of which only reinforces what was noted earlier that, as with the making of many books themselves, with the making of bibliographies there is no end.

William K. Verner
Blue Mountain Lake, N. Y.   Curator
September 1, 1972   The Adirondack Museum

ADIRONDACK BIBLIOGRAPHY

HISTORY OF THE ADIRONDACK REGION

BIBLIOGRAPHY

Adirondack mountain club, inc. Bibliography committee. Adirondack bibliography: a list of books, pamphlets and periodical articles published through the year 1955... Gabriels, N.Y. 1958. 354p. map, pictorial end-papers. Described briefly in the *New York State Conservationist*, Feb.-Mar. 1959, 13:no.4:40. Reviewed by A.E. Newkirk in *Adirondac*, Nov.-Dec. 1958, 22:122; by Harold K. Hochschild in *New York History*, Jan. 1959, 40:81-83. Other reviews in *North Country Life*, Fall 1958, 12:no.4:53-54 and in *Appalachia*, June 1958, mag.no.126:143. Summary of reviews in *Adirondac*, July-Aug. 1959. 23:74-75.   7540

----. Same, supplements, 1956 and 1957. Gabriels, N.Y. 1960. 20p. Reprinted from *Adirondac*, Jan.-Feb. - Mar.-April 1958; Jan.-Feb. - Mar.-April 1959. 22:20-23,43-48; 23:19-24, 42-47.   7541

----. Same, supplement 1958... Gabriels, N.Y. 1960. 15p. Reprinted from *Adirondac*, Jan.-Feb. - Mar.-April 1960. 24:20-24, 37-44.   7542

----. Same, supplement 1959... Gabriels, N.Y. 1961. 16p. Reprinted from *Adirondac*, Jan.-Feb. - Mar.-April 1959. 23:19-24, 42-47.   7542a

----. Same, supplements, 1960, 1961-1962, 1963. Gabriels, N.Y. 1962-1965. v.p. Review of 1961-1962 supplement by C. Eleanor Hall in *Adirondac*, Jan.-Feb. 1965. 29:14.   7543

Casgrain, Henri Raymond. The French-war papers of the Marechal de Lévis, described by the Abbe Casgrain with comments by F. Parkman and J. Winsor. Cambridge, Mass. J. Wilson & son, 1888. 11p. 50 copies privately printed, reproduced from the Proceedings of the Massachusetts Historical Society, April 12, 1888.   7544

Cole, G. Glyndon. New York's year of history: a reading list for junior and senior high schools. Part I. New York state; Part II. Hudson-Champlain valley. Unpaged (16p.) illus. Supplement to the Spring 1959 issue of *North Country Life*.   7545

Cone, Gertrude E. A selective bibliography of publications on the Champlain valley. Plattsburgh, N.Y. 1959. 144p. Reviewed by G.C. in *North Country Life*, Spring 1959, 13:no.2:48-49; by D.A. Plum in *New York History*, Jan. 1960, 41:109-111; unsigned review in *New York Historical Society Quarterly*, Jan. 1961, 45:105-106.   7546

New York (state) University. Bureau of secondary curriculum development. Hudson-Champlain reading list. Albany, 1959? 21p.   7547

GENERAL HISTORY

GENERAL

Allen, Ethan. A brief narrative of the proceedings of the government of New-York, relative to their obtaining the jurisdiction of that large district of land, to the northwest from the Connecticut river... Hartford, Eben Watson, 1774. 211p. Appendix: A state of the rights of the colony of New-York, so far as concerns the grant formerly made by the French government of Canada, of lands on Lake Champlain, and at and to the southward of Crown Point, p.189-211.   7548

Baudry, P.-J.-U. Un vieux fort français. *In* Royal society of Canada. Proceedings and transactions. Memoires section 1, v.5, p.93-114.

Montreal, 1887. History of the French settlement of Fort St. Frederic at Crown Point, 1609-1760.   7549

Bird, Harrison. Navies in the mountains: the battles on the waters of Lake Champlain and Lake George, 1609-1814. N.Y. Oxford university press, 1962. 361p. illus. maps. Reviewed by Frances Herman in *Adirondack Life*, Jan. 1962 and by E.M. Miller in *Vermont History*, July 1962, 30:241-45. Other reviews in the *Journal of Modern History*, Sept. 1962, 34: 324-25 and in the *William and Mary Quarterly*, Jan. 1963.   7550

Clarke, Rosemary A. Hudson and Champlain. *NYS Con*, June-July 1959. 13:no.6:2-3. illus.   7551

Crockett, Walter Hill. Vermont; the Green mountain state. N.Y. Century history co. 1921. 4v. plates, maps. Vol.1, ch.2, Champlain's discovery; ch.13, The capture of Ticonderoga; Vol.2, ch.16, The naval battle of Lake Champlain.   7552

Fiske, John. New France and New England. Boston, Houghton, 1902. 378p. front. maps (double) Chapter IX, Crown Point, Fort William Henry and Fort Ticonderoga, p.294-325.   7553

Folsom, William R. Vermonters in battle and other papers. Montpelier, Vt. Vermont historical society, 1953. 236p. maps. Ch.3, The battle of Valcour Island; ch.5, The battle of Plattsburg; ch.8, Benedict Arnold.   7554

Forts of the Champlain-Lake George valley area. In New York (state) Legislature. Joint legislative committee on preservation and restoration of historic sites. Report, 1959. Albany, 1959. p.39-44. illus. (Legislative Document 1959, no.82)   7555

Gifford, Stanley M. Fort William Henry, a history. Glens Falls, N.Y.? 1955. 16p. illus. (part col.)   7556

Hamilton, Edward Pierce. Fort Ticonderoga, key to a continent. Boston, Little Brown, © 1964. 241p. illus. ports. maps, incl. map on end papers.   7557

Hall, Radcliffe. "History was made where you live". Troy, N.Y. Troy savings bank, 1938. v.p. port. Thirteen radio broadcasts over WGY, Feb.-May 1938. Includes Lake George, Port Henry and Ticonderoga.   7558

Hammersley, Sydney Ernest. The Lake Champlain naval battles of 1776-1814. Hudson-Champlain, 1959, 350th anniversary edition. Waterford, N.Y. privately printed, 1959. 28p. illus.   7559

Hill, Ralph Nading. Gateway struggle. Ver Life, Summer 1959. 13:no.4:35-47. illus. map.   7560

Historic sites committee plans catalog of sites in four counties of valley. Reveille, Sept. 1960. 5:no.19:1. Clinton, Essex, Warren and Washington counties.   7561

Hulbert, Archer Butler. Portage paths: the keys of the continent. Cleveland, A.H. Clark co. 1903. 194p. (Historic Highways of America) New York portages, p.122-150.   7562

New England folks "saw-conquered" Adirondack lands. Reveille, Sept. 1960. 5:no.19: 2,3,4.   7563

Palmer, George W. An American's role in the Papineau revolt. No Country Life, Summer 1962. 16:no.3:12-15,18.   7564

Parkman, Francis. The battle for North America; edited by John Tebbel. Garden City, N.Y. Doubleday, 1948. 746p. map on end pap-

ers. An abridgment of "France and England in North America". Part 2, The Jesuits in North America includes "Isaac Jogues", p.127-46, Part 6, Montcalm and Wolfe includes "Fort William Henry", p.591-608; "Winter of Discontent", p.609-14; "The Battle for Ticonderoga", p.627-38; "Amherst's Campaign", p.684-92.   7565

----. The Parkman reader...selected and edited ...by Samuel Eliot Morison. Boston, Little, Brown, 1955. 533p. port. maps (one folded) References to Champlain, Jogues and Ticonderoga.   7566

----. Pioneers of France in the new world. Boston, Little, Brown, 1897. 473p. Ch.10, Lake Champlain.   7567

Robinson, Rowland Evans. Vermont: a study of independence. Boston, Houghton, 1892. 370p. front. (folded map) (American Commonwealth). Ch.7, Ticonderoga; Ch.9, Lake Champlain; Ch.11, Ticonderoga, Hubbardton.   7568

Ross, John. This happened here; the story of the Lake Champlain territory reprinted from the North Countryman. Rouse's Point, N.Y. Northern pub.co. 1955. unpaged.   7569

Sleicher, Charles Albert. The Adirondacks: American playground...N.Y. Exposition press, 1960. 287p. illus. ports. map. Reviewed in North Country Life, Winter 1960, 14:no.4:47.   7570

Struik, D.J. Mathematicians at Ticonderoga. Sci Mo, May 1956. 82:236-40. Part played by Des Barres, Holland, Lotbinière and Bougainville at Fort Carillon.   7571

Stuart, E. Rae. Jessup's rangers as a factor in loyalist settlement. In Ontario. Department of public records and archives. Three history theses. Toronto, Ont. 1961. p.V-158. Reproduced from typewritten copy.   7572

Tyrrell, William G. Champlain and the French in New York. Albany, University of the State of New York, 1959. 56p. illus. maps.   7573

The underground railroad. No Country Notes, May 1965. no.23:4. Reprinted from April 1965 News Letter of Ausable River Lodge 149, F. & A.M., Keeseville, N.Y.   7574

Wool, John E. Fortifying the Canadian-United States border... No Country Notes, Mar. 1962. no.8:2-3. Letter to John H. Eaton, Secretary of War, 19 Nov. 1830.   7575

FRENCH SETTLEMENTS, ETC.

Muhl, Gerard. The Castorland story. York State Trad, Fall 1964 18:no.4:41-48. map.7576

Webster, Clarence J. French emigres in the wilderness. York State Trad, Spring 1963. 17:no. 2:43-47. Text of a radio address.   7577

FRENCH AND INDIAN WARS

Amherst, Jeffrey Amherst, 1st baron. Letter from Maj. Gen. Amherst to Mr. secretary Pitt, dated Crown-Point, August 5. *Gent Mag,* Sept. 1759. 29:435-36.   7578

Berkofer, Robert F. The French and Indians at Carillon. *Ft Ti Mus Bul,* 1956. 9:no.6:134-72. illus.   7579

Bird, Harrison. Battle for a continent. N.Y. Oxford university press, 1965. 376p. illus. ports. Reviewed in *York State Tradition,* Fall 1965, 19:no.4:59-60.   7580

Bougainville, Louis Antoine de. Adventure in the wilderness: the American journals...1756-1760. Translated and edited by Edward P. Hamilton. Norman, Okla. University of Oklahoma press, 1964. 344p. illus. ports. maps. (American Exploration and Travel Series, 42)   7581

Charland, Thomas M. The Lake Champlain army and the fall of Montreal. *Ver Hist,* Oct. 1960. n.s.28:293-301.   7582

Colden, Cadwallader. The history of the five nations... N.Y. New Amsterdam publishing co. 1902. 2v. Originally published in 1727-1747.   7583

Cruelties of the Indians at Ticonderago (sic) *Gent Mag,* Oct. 1757. 27:476.   7584

Dwight, Melatiah Everett. The journal of Capt. Nathaniel Dwight of Belchertown, Mass. during the Crown Point expedition, 1755. *NY Gen & Biog Rec,* Jan.-July 1902. 33:3-10, 65-70, 164-66.   7585

Farther account of the defeat of the French by General Johnson. *Gent Mag,* Nov. 1755. 25:519-20.   7586

Furnis, James. An eyewitness account...of the surrender of Fort William Henry, August 1757; edited by William S. Ewing. *NY Hist,* July 1961. 42:307-16. facsim.   7587

General orders of 1757 issued by the Earl of Loudoun and Phineas Lyman in the campaign against the French. N.Y. Dodd, Mead, 1899. 144p. front. (facsim.) 250 copies printed by the Gilliss Press.   7588

Hamilton, Edward Pierce. The French and Indian wars: the story of battles and forts in the wilderness. Garden City, N.Y. Doubleday & co. 1962. 318p. maps. (Mainstream of America Series) Reviewed in the *New-York Historical Society Quarterly,* April 1964, 48:178-79.   7589

Hamilton, Milton W. Battle report: General William Johnson's letter to the governors, Lake George, September 9-10, 1755. *Am Ant Soc Proc,* 1964. 74:19-36.   7590

----. Hero of Lake George: Johnson or Lyman? *NE Quar,* Sept. 1963. 26:371-82.   7591

A letter to a friend in the country, upon the news of the town. London, Printed for J. Raymond, 1755. 47p. Extensive reference to the building of Crown Point.   7592

Lévis, François Gaston, duc de. Collection des manuscrits du Marichal de Lévis. Quebec, L.J. Demers et Frère, 1889-1895. 12v.   7593

Niles, Grace Greylock. The Hoosic valley; its legends and its history. N.Y. Putnam, 1912. 584p. plates, maps. Ch. 7, Ephraim Willaims and the battle of Lake George, 1747-1755; Ch.15, The heroes of Fort Ticonderoga.   7594

O'Conor, Norreys Jephson. A servant of the crown in England and in North America, 1756-1761, based upon the papers of John Appy, secretary and judge advocate of His Majesty's forces. N.Y. Appleton-Century, 1938. 256p. front. illus. plates, ports. facsims. (Society of Colonial Wars in the State of New York. Publication no.47) Includes original account of the failure of the British at Fort Ticonderoga, 1758.   7595

Particulars of Major Robert Rogers' last expedition against the enemy. *Gent Mag,* May 1759. 29:203-205. map.   7596

A scheme proposed for driving the French out of the continent of America in one year's time. *Gent Mag,* Sept. 1755. 25:389-91.

7596a

Siege and surrender of Fort William Henry. *Gent Mag,* Oct. 1757. 27:475.   7597

Smith, Bradford. Rogers' rangers and the French and Indian war...N.Y. Random house, 1956. 184p. illus. (Landmark Series, no. 63)

7597a

Stiles, Fred T. Dieskau's march thru South Bay. *No Country Life,* Summer 1959. 13:no. 3:29-33. map.   7598

----. 1755-59 in the Champlain valley. *No Country Life,* Summer 1961 - Winter 1962. 15:no. 3:51; 15:no.4:26-29; 16:no.1:35-37. illus. The Winter 1962 issue includes the story of Duncan Campbell; Fall 1961, Massacre at Fort William Henry.   7599

Tomlinson, Abraham. The military journals of two private soldiers, 1758-1775, with numerous illustrative notes. Poughkeepsie, N.Y. 1855. 128p.front. Includes Lemuel Lyon's military journal for 1758, at Ticonderoga.   7600

Walworth, Ellen (Hardin) Battle of Lake George and Baron Dieskau, 1755. *NY State Hist Assn Proc,* 1901. 1:54-57.   7601

THE REVOLUTION

Account of American affairs. *Gent Mag,* Sept. 1777. 47:454-56. Includes letters from Schuyler, St. Clair and Burgoyne.   7602

Arnold, Benedict. Benedict Arnold's regimental memorandum book, written while at Ticonderoga and Crown Point, 1775. *Pa Mag,* Dec. 1884. 8:363-76.   7603

Barton, John A. The battle of Valcour island. *Hist Today,* Dec. 1959. 9:791-99. illus. ports. map.   7604

Beach, Janice. The capture of Ticonderoga by the Green Mountain boys. *Ver Hist,* Oct. 1958. 26:229-35.   7605

Bennett, C.E. Advance and retreat to Saratoga: Burgoyne campaign... n.p. Union-Star press, n.d. 57p. illus. Another edition ©1927, 80p. folded map.   7606

Bird, Harrison. March to Saratoga: General Burgoyne and the American campaign, 1777. N.Y. Oxford university press, 1963. 300p. illus. maps. Reviews in *York State Tradition,* Summer 1963, 17:no.3:55, in *New York History,* Jan. 1964, 15:82-83, and in the *New-York Historical Society Quarterly,* April 1964, 48:181-82.   7607

The British occupation of Point au Fer. *No Country Notes,* Sept. 1963. no.14:2-3.   7608

A British view of the Battle of Valcour. *No Country Notes.* April 1963. no.13:2-3. Report found in the Canadian Archives differing from American versions of the battle.   7609

Burgoyne, John. Letter from Lieut.-Gen. Burgoyne to Lord Geo. Germain. *Gent Mag,* Aug. 1777. 47:398-402.   7610

----. Orderly book of Lieut. Gen. John Burgoyne, from his entry into the State of New York until his surrender at Saratoga, 16th Oct., 1777...ed. by E.B. O'Callaghan, M.D. Albany, J. Munsell, 1860. 221p. plates, port. folded map.   7611

----. A state of the expedition from Canada, as laid before the House of Commons...with a collection of authentic documents... London, printed for J. Almon, 1780. 140p. front. (folded map) folded plans. His own account of the ill-fated expedition through the Adirondacks.
                                                  7612

DePeyster, John Watts. The Burgoyne campaign of July-October,1777... Philadelphia, L.R. Hamersly & co. 1883. 17p. Reprinted from *United Service,* Oct. 1883.   7613

Du Roi, August Wilhelm. Journal of Du Roi, the elder, lieutenant and adjutant in the service of the Duke of Brunswick, 1776-1778. Trans. from the original German manuscript in the Library of Congress...by Charlotte S.J. Epping. Philadelphia, University of Pennsylvania, 1911. 189p. facsims. tables. (Americana Germanica, n.s. Monograph no. 15) Ticonderoga in 1776.
                                                  7614

Frazer, Persifer. Letters from Ticonderoga, 1776. *Ft Ti Mus Bul,* Feb. 1961. 10:386-96. To his wife.   7615

From Cambridge to Champlain, March 18 to May 5, 1776. A manuscript diary, with a foreword by Bruce Lancaster. Middleboro, Mass. Privately printed and published by Lawrence B. Romaine, 1957. 30p. front. (facsim.) Diary of unknown soldier, includes Lake George, Ticonderoga and Crown Point. 250 copies printed.   7616

Gen. Carleton's letter to Ld. G. Germaine, on passing the lakes and destroying the enemy's fleet... *Gent Mag.* Nov. 1776. 46:525-26. The letter was first published in the *London Gazette* November 23, 1776.   7617

General Fraser's account of Burgoyne's campaign on Lake Champlain...*In* Vermont historical society. Proceedings, Oct. 18 and Nov. 2, 1898. p. 139-51.   7618

Hamilton, Edward Pierce. Was Washington to blame for the loss of Ticonderoga in 1777? *Ft Ti Mus Bul,* Sept. 1963. 11:65-74.   7619

Hatch, Eugene. The ordeal of John Johnson. *Quar,* April 1963 8:no.2:6-8. illus.port.map. Escape route through the Adirondacks.   7620

Hough, Franklin Benjamin, ed. The northern invasion of October 1780...against the frontier of New York... N.Y. Bradford club, 1886. 227p. front. folded map. 80 copies printed.
                                                  7621

Journal of the party sent to secure Ticonderoga. *Gent Mag,* July 1775. 45:343-44.   7622

The last chapter in the *Philadelphia* story. *No Country Life,* Spring 1962. 16:no.2:44-45. Gundelo, formerly on display near Willsboro, transferred to Smithsonian Institution. 7623

Letter written in 1776 by A. Moore returns to Fort Mount Hope. *Reveille,* Dec. 1956. 1:no.8:1,3,4.   7624

Lossing, Benson John. The pictorial fieldbook of the revolution... N.Y. Harper, 1851-52. 2v. col. front. illus. Vol.1, Ch.5 and 6 contain references to Lake George, Lake Champlain, etc.   7625

Mahan, Alfred Thayer. The major operations of the navies in the war of American independence. Boston, Little, Brown, 1913. 280p. plates, maps. Ch.1, The naval campaign on Lake Champlain.   7626

Neilson, Charles. An original...corrected account of Burgoyne's campaign and the memorable battles of Bemis's Heights, Sept. 19 and Oct. 7, 1777...and a map of the battleground. Albany, J. Munsell, 1844. v.p. map.   7627

Nickerson, Hoffman. The turning point of the revolution; or, Burgoyne in America. Boston, Houghton, Mifflin, 1928. 500p. Ch.5, The fall of Ticonderoga.   7628

Ostrander, William S. Old Saratoga and the Burgoyne campaign... Schuylerville, N.Y. 1897. 42p. front. illus. map.   7629

Palmer, Peter Sailly. Battle of Valcour on Lake Champlain October 11, 1776. Plattsburgh. N.Y. 1876. 24p.   7630

Peixotto, Ernest Clifford. A revolutionary pilgrimage... N.Y. Scribner, 1917. 369p. illus. plates, front. Ticonderoga and Lake Champlain.   7631

Proceedings of the army under Gen. Burgoyne from the beginning of September till its surrender on the 17th of Oct. *Gent Mag,* Dec. 1777. 47:576-87.   7632

Scammell, Alexander. Letter from Colonel Alexander Scammell. *Reveille,* June 1958. 2:no.12:2. Dated Aug. 24, 1777 and addressed to Sullivan's headquarters. Describes retreat from Ticonderoga.   7633

Sewall, Henry. The diary of Henry Sewall. *Ft Ti Mus Bul,* Sept. 1963. 11:75-92. June 15, 1776 to July 7, 1777, describing experience at Ticonderoga.   7634

Skerrett, Robert G. Wreck of the Royal Savage recovered. *USN Inst Proc,* Nov. 1935. 61:1646.
                                                   7635

Smith, William Henry. The St. Clair papers. The life and public services of Arthur St. Clair ...with his correspondence and other papers... Cincinnati, O. Robert Clarke & co. 1882. 2v. fronts. folded map.   7636

Some of the circumstances which inevitably retard the progress of a northern army through the uninhabited countries of America. *Gent Mag,* Oct. 1777. 47:472-74. Poor roads, etc.
                                                   7637

Stone, William Leete, 1835-1908. Memoir of the centennial celebration of Burgoyne's surrender, held at Schuylerville, N.Y...on the 17th of October, 1877... Albany, J. Munsell, 1878. 189p. front.   7638

Tryon county, N.Y. Committee of safety. Minute book of the Committee of safety of Tryon county, the old New York frontier. Now printed verbatim for the first time; with an introduction by J. Howard Hanson and notes by Samuel Ludlow Frey. N.Y. Dodd, Mead, 1905. 151p. front. plates, facsim. map.   7639

Van de Water, Frederic Franklyn. Day of battle. N.Y. Ives Washburn, inc. 1958. 365p. Includes retreat from Ticonderoga, 1777.   7640

WAR OF 1812

Barnes, James. Naval actions of the War of 1812. N.Y. Harper, 1896. 263p. front. plates. Includes Battle of Lake Champlain.   7641

Beirne, Francis F. The war of 1812; maps by Dorothy De Fontaine. N.Y. Dutton, 1949. 410p. maps. Plattsburgh, p.289-303.   7642

Cobbett, William, 1763-1835. Letters on the late war between the United States and Great Britain... N.Y. J. Belden and co. 1815. 407p. Includes Lake Champlain and the Battle of Plattsburgh.   7643

Cooper, James Fenimore. The history of the navy of the United States of America. Philadelphia, Lee and Blanchard, 1839. 2v.   7644

Dispatch from Lieut.-gen. Sir George Prevost, bart. *Gent Mag,* Dec. 1814. 84:pt.2:589-90. Battle of Plattsburgh.   7645

Everest, Allan S. Alexander Macomb at Plattsburgh, 1814. *NY Hist,* Oct. 1963. 44:307-35.
                                                   7646

----. British objectives at the Battle of Plattsburgh. Champlain, N.Y.Moorsfield press, 1960. 21p. Foreword by Wayne S. Byrne.   7647

Everest, Allan S., ed. Recollections of Clinton county and the Battle of Plattsburgh, 1800-1840. Memories of early residents from the notebooks of Dr. D.S. Kellogg. Plattsburgh, N.Y. Clinton county historical association, 1964. 75p. maps. Corrections in *North Country Notes,* Jan. 1965, no.21:4.   7648

Feinberg, Robert J. Extemporaneous address ...on...the 149th anniversary of the Battle of Plattsburgh...September 11, 1963. n.p. n.d. unpaged (4p.)   7649

Fitch, Asa, jr. Incident of the battle on Lake Champlain. *Ver Hist Soc News,* Sept. 1959. 11:no.1:6.   7650

Folsom, William R. The battle of Plattsburg. *Ver Quar,* Oct. 1952. n.s.20:235-59.   7651

Forester, C.S. Victory on Lake Champlain. *Am Heritage,* Dec. 1963. 15:no.1:4-11,88-90. illus. (part col.) map.   7652

Hamilton, Edward Pierce. The battle of Plattsburgh. *Ver Hist,* April 1963. 31:84-105. illus.
                                                   7653

Hunt, Gilbert J. The battle of Plattsburgh... *York State Trad,* Summer 1964. 18:no.3:30-37. illus.   7654

Hunter, Charles W. A British deserter. *No Country Notes,* Sept. 1964. no.19:2. Part of a letter written from Plattsburgh.   7655

Letter from Commodore Sir J.L. Yeo, commander in chief on the lakes of Canada. *Gent Mag,* supplement to 84, pt.2:663-65. Defeat of the British by Macdonough.   7656

Lossing, Benson John. The pictorial field-book of the war of 1812...N.Y. Harper, 1869. 1084p. figures, maps. Ch. 37, Events on Lake Champlain.   7657

The near armistice of 1814. *No Country Notes,* May 1964. no.18:3   7658

New York (state) Legislature. Senate. Mr. Hubbard's report. In Senate, October 10, 1814. N.Y. 1814. 2p. Concerning that part of the Governor's message recommending expression of gratitude to the heroes of the Niagara army and the army and navy of Plattsburgh.   7659

Nichols, Caleb. Crab island. *No Country Notes,* Nov. 1964. no.20:2. Bill to United States for damages. Reprinted from the Plattsburgh Republican.   7660

Roosevelt, Theodore. The naval war of 1812... N.Y. Putnam, 1882. 498p. diagrs.   7661

Ross, John. The significance of the battle of Plattsburgh. An address...September 11, 1957. Plattsburgh, Battle of Plattsburgh day commission, 1958. unpaged (8p.)   7662

U.S. Congress. Senate. Committee on the library. Commemoration of the battle of Plattsburgh. Hearing before a subcommittee of the Committee on the library...March 12, 1914 ... Washington, 1914. 26p.   7663

U.S. Navy, Secretary of. Letter...to the chairman of the Naval committee, transmitting sundry documents from Captain MacDonough, relating to the capture of the British fleet in Lake Champlain... Albany, National commercial bank and trust company, 1957. 18p. illus. Facsimile of pamphlet published in 1814.   7664

Vermont. Adjutant and inspector general's office. ...Roster of soldiers in the war of 1812-14... St. Albans, Vt. 1933. 474p. Over half of Vermont's soldiers were stationed at or near Plattsburgh.   7665

Wood, James W. A citizen complains. *No Country Notes,* Sept. 1964. no.19:3-4. Wilkinson invasion.   7666

Wool, John E. The battle of Beekmantown in 1814. *No Country Notes,* Sept 1965. no.24:2. Letter written Jan. 6, 1859.   7667

----. Major Wool's account of the battle of Plattsburgh. *No Country Notes,* Sept. 1961. no.5:2-3. Extracts from a letter to Benson J. Lossing, May 10, 1860.   7668

CIVIL WAR

Beaudrye, Louis N. Historic records of the Fifth New York cavalry...2d ed. Albany, S.R. Gray, 1865. 358p. front. plates, ports. tables. Company H from Crown Point.   7669

Morhous, Henry C. Reminiscences of the 123d regiment N.Y.S.V... Greenwich, N.Y. People's journal, 1879. 220p. Washington county.   7670

Mould, Henry Munroe. Army life with Co. K 118th New York volunteers, 1862-3. *Reveille,* Mar.-June 1961. 6:no.21:2-4, 6:no. 22:2-4.   7671

Ninety-sixth infantry. *In* New York (state) Adjutant general. Annual report, 1902. Albany, 1903. p.503-736.   7672

One hundred and eighteenth infantry. *In* New York (state) Adjutant general. Annual report, 1903. Albany, 1904. p.695-991.   7673

Simmons, Julia (Gardelphe) GI, 1863. *York State Trad,* Winter 1964. 18:no.1:14-16. Based on letters of Forrest Fisher, a soldier from Clinton County.   7674

Thomas, Howard. The boys in blue from the Adirondack foothills. Maps by John D. Mahaffy. Prospect, N.Y. Prospect books, 1960. 297p. illus. Reviewed in *New York State and the Civil War,* June 1962, 2:no.1:25-27, port.   7675

ARCHAEOLOGY

Fadden, Ray. A pottery find, Adirondack rock shelters. *Yester,* Mar. 1960. 3:no.11:21-24. illus. map.   7676

----. Rare pottery discovery on Silver lake mountain. *No Country Life,* Winter 1960. 14: no.1:21-23,49. illus.   7677

Huden, John Charles. Archaeology in Vermont: some reviews supplemented by materials from New England and New York. Burlington, Vt. University of Vermont, 1960. 107p. plates. Rock shelter at Ticonderoga, p.78-79.   7678

Huey, Paul R. New discoveries at Crown Point, N.Y. A report of the historic-site archaeology carried on by Education Adventure, a teenage work group. Troy, N.Y. Rensselaer county junior museum, ©1959. 33p. illus. maps. Reproduced from typewritten copy.   7679

Plea to skin divers. *Trailmarker,* Summer 1963.

2:no.1:32. illus. Caution in recovery of archeological material urged by Bruce Inverarity.   7680

Ritchie, William Augustus. The archaeology of New York state. Garden City, N.Y. Garden City press, 1965. 357p. plates, maps (including end papers) figures. Prehistory of Indian occupation, c.7000 B.C. to A.D. 1600. Printed for the American Museum of Natural History.   7681

----. The pre-Iroquoian occupation of New York state. Rochester, N.Y. Rochester museum of arts and sciences, 1944. 416p. illus. tables, diagrs. (part folded) (Rochester Museum Memoir, no.1)   7682

----. Traces of early man in the northeast. Albany, New York state museum and science service, 1957. 91p. illus. charts, folded map in pocket. (Bulletin 358)   7683

ABORIGINES

Carse, Mrs. Mary Rowell. The Mohawk Iroquois. *In* Archaeological Society of Connecticut. Bulletin no. 23, June 1949. p.3-53. Revision of her Master's thesis, Yale University, 1943 entitled "Contributions to Mohawk Ethnology". 7684

Drumm, Judith. Iroquois culture. Albany, New York state museum and science service, 1962. 14p. Mimeographed. (Educational Leaflet no. 5) 7685

Fadden, Ray.Conservation as the Indian saw it, by Aren Akweks; illustrations by the author. Hogansburg, N.Y. Akwesasne counselor organization, St. Regis Mohawk reservation, ©1948. 7p. illus. Includes poem by June Fadden, "Contrast". 7686

----. The formation of the Ho-de-no-sau-ne or League of the five nations, by Aren Akweks ... Hogansburg, N.Y. Akwesasne counselor organization, St. Regis Mohawk reservation, n.d. 26p. illus. 7687

----. Migration of the Iroquois, by Aren Akweks. Onchiota, N.Y. Akwesasne Mohawk counselor organization, 1961. 36p. illus. History of the group which settled in New York State, told in pictographs with accompanying text. 7688

Headley, Joel Tyler. The St. Regis Indians. *In* his Miscellaneous works... N.Y. John S. Taylor, 1849. v.1,p.262-69. 7689

Huden, John Charles. Indian legacy. *Ver Life,* Summer 1959. 13:no.4:21-26. illus. 7690

Lighthall, William Douw, and Armstrong, Louis Oliver. The book of the play of Hiawatha the Mohawk depicting the seige of Hochelaga and the battle of Lake Champlain... n.p. n.pub. 1909. 24p. Libretto of the Indian pageant presented at the Lake Champlain Tercentenary. 7691

Perkins, George Henry. The Calumet in the Champlain valley. *Pop Sci,* Dec. 1893. 14:238-47. illus. 7692

Radisson, Pierre Esprit. Voyages...being an account of his travels and experiences among North American Indians... Boston, Prince society, 1885. 385p. (Publications of the Prince Society, v.16) 7693

Ritchie, William Augustus. Indian history of New York state: Pt.3. The Algonkian tribes. Albany, New York state museum and science service, 1956. 24p. illus. 7694

Shonwatchawicket. *No Country Life,* Spring 1962. 16:no.2:19-21. port. illus. Indian dancers, part of the Order of the Arrow program of the Adirondack Council, Boy Scouts of America. 7695

Society for the preservation of Indian lore, inc. The Ticonderoga Indian festival. n.p. n.d. unpaged (12p. incl. covers) illus. Cover title: Annual Indian Pageant. 7696

----. 24th annual Indian pageant...August 15, 1958. Ticonderoga, N.Y. 1958. 4 leaves. mimeographed. 7697

Wallace, Paul Anthony Wilson. The white roots of peace.Philadelphia,University of Pennsylvania, 1946. 57p. front. Includes Iroquois legends and references to the Adirondacks. 7698

LOCAL HISTORY

Becker, Howard I. comp. A history of South Pond and the origin of Long Lake township. Rexford, N.Y. 1963. 274 leaves. illus. maps. Reproduced from typewritten copy. 7699

Hamilton, Edward Pierce. Lake Champlain and the upper Hudson valley. Ticonderoga, N.Y. Fort Ticonderoga association, ©1959. 47p. illus. maps (part col.) 7700

Hibbard, Wallace G. Scenes on Lake George and Lake Champlain famous for their historic and scenic attractions. Glens Falls, N.Y. author, ©1904. unpaged (52p.) illus. Copy at the Adirondack Museum. 7701

Sawyer, Willoughby Lord. Some facts concerning our local history. Hudson Falls, N.Y., Swigert press, ©1930. 62p. maps. 7702

THE CHAMPLAIN VALLEY

American historians re-live the pageant of Champlain history, on the last of the great white fleet of side-wheelers - the Ticonderoga. *Ver Life,* Winter 1949-50. 4:no.2:12-13. illus. Brief text. 7703

Andrews, Buel C. Who discovered Lake Champlain. *Vermonter,* Nov. 1915. 20:245-46. 7704

Beach, Allen Penfield. Lake Champlain as the centuries pass. Burlington, Vt. Lane press, 1959. 82p. 7705

Bredenberg, Oscar E. Military activities in the Champlain valley after 1777. Champlain, N.Y. Moorsfield press, 1962. 37p.   7706

Brown, Levant Frederick. Lake Champlain: an appreciation. *Four Tr News*, Aug. 1906. 11:156-57. illus.   7707

Canfield, Thomas H. Discovery - navigation and navigators of Lake Champlain. Burlington, Vt. Burlington savings bank, 1959. 30p.   7708

Carmer, Carl Lamson. The Champlain valley. *Holiday*, June 1959. 25:no.6:66-69,130-31, 133, 135-38. illus. (part col.)   7709

Champlain, Samuel de. Champlain's account of his voyage up Lake Champlain as translated and recorded in E.B. O'Callaghan's Documentary history of the State of New York. *No Country Life*, Summer 1959. 13:no.3:34-39. illus.   7710

Childs, Laura Clark. The peace rock. *Vermonter*, Sept. 1930. 35:202. Rock Dunder or Mohawk Rock in Lake Champlain, the legendary dividing point of the Six Nations and the Algonquins.   7711

Copeland, Fred O. Anyhow, I sailed Lake Champlain. *Vermonter*, July 1940. 45:149-51.   7712

----. Bomb shelters and sunshine along Champlain. *Vermonter*, Jan. 1942. 47:6-11.   7713

----. The Burlington ferry ride. *Vermonter*, April 1941. 46:75-78.   7714

----. Lake Champlain: a guide and story handbook. Rutland, Vt. Tuttle, 1958. 88p. col. front. illus. folded map.   7715

Couchy, Sid. Lake Champlain. Essex, N.Y. ©1957. unpaged (16p.) illus. map. Prepared for the 350th Champlain anniversary. Many cartoons.   7716

----. Our Champlain story; historical cartoons and text... n.p. 1964. 59p. illus. Issued for the Battle of Plattsburgh Commission.   7717

Dean, Leon W. Champlain ace in the hole. *Ver Life*, Summer 1959. 13:no.4:19. illus. Lake serpent.   7718

----. Champlain's famous rock. *Vermonter*, Feb.-Mar. 1914. 19:29. Rock Dunder or Mohawk Rock.   7719

De Voto, Bernard. The Champlain corridor. *Ford Times*, Feb. 1959. 51:no.2:10-13. col. illus.   7720

Essex county republican. Art annual: supplement. Plattsburgh, 1898. unpaged. illus. (part col.) Contains "Chronological History of the Champlain Valley".   7721

The first conference of Lake Champlain historians, July 1, 1939. *Ver Hist Soc Proc*, Sept. 1939. n.s.7:185-206.   7722

Gagné,Leonne. Lake Champlain and its importance during the wars. *Ver Hist*, April 1961. 29:87-91.   7723

Hard, Walter. Land and water. *Ver Life*, Summer 1959. 13:no.4:2-7. illus. map. Signed:W.H.   7724

Hoyt, Murray. Why I love Lake Champlain *Sat Eve Post*, Feb. 28, 1959. 231:no.35:32-33, 82-84. col. illus. map.   7725

Interstate commission on the Lake Champlain basin. The face of the basin, by Sargent-Webster-Crenshaw & Folley, Syracuse, N.Y., Northeast planning associates, Burlington, Vt., Project planning associates, ltd. Toronto, Ontario. Burlington, Vt.? 1961. Large broadside, printed on both sides and folded into thirty sections. Map on one side, text on other. 7726

----. The Lake Champlain basin: "the highway of the nations". n.p. 1958. unpaged (16p. incl. cover) illus. tables, map. The Commission also issued a 4p. folder entitled "The Champlain Valley 350th Anniversary Festival, 1609-1959" and a folded broadside, printed on both sides, with map and illustrations, called "The Champlain Valley".   7727

----. Profile of the Champlain anniversary festival. n.p. n.d. 8p. For another account of the festival see Thomas B. Lesure's "Into the Land of Legend" in the *Redbook*, September 1959.   7728

----. Report. Albany, 1958. 131p. illus. (New York State Legislative Document 1958 no.12) Cover title: The Champlain Valley 350th Anniversary Festival. Annual reports also issued for 1959-1962.   7729

Lake Champlain committee. Why a Lake Champlain committee? n.p. 1963. unpaged (8p.)   7730

Mace, Mrs. H.S. October on Champlain. *Vermonter*, Oct. 1933. 38:265-66.   7731

MacLeod, Audrey. Champlain guide. *Ver Life*, Summer 1959. 13:no.4:27-34. illus. map. Handbook of the main attractions and little-know by-ways of the Champlain Valley. 7732

Morse, Stella R. Lovely Lake Champlain. *Vermonter*, Dec. 1915. 20:274-75.   7733

New York (state) Lake Champlain bridge commission. Annual report, 1959. Albany, 1960. 8p. plus appendix. Mimeographed. Also issued for 1960 and 1961.   7734

New York's Champlain celebration July 4 to 9, 1909. n.p. n.pub. 1909? 8p.   7735

The One hundred and fiftieth anniversary of the American revolution in the Crown Point area... Albany, Fort Orange press, 1927. 40p. illus. port. "The Champlain Valley", by Frank E. Brimmer, p.5-17.   7736

Pell, John H.G. The Champlain celebration. *Ft Ti Mus Bul,* Feb. 1960. 10:305-14. illus. 7737

Pierce, Mark G. Putt-putt ahoy! Samuel! *Vermonter,* Mar. 1934. 39:69-75 illus. Motorboat trip with visit to Fort Ticonderoga. 7738

Schuyler, Montgomery. Notes on the patroonships, manors and seigneuries in colonial times. N.Y. Watkins, 1950. 43p. (Order of Colonial Lords of Manors in America. Publication, no. 31) 7739

U.S. Congress. House. Tercentenary celebration of discovery of Lake Champlain, by Mr. Foster. Washington, 1909. 9p. (60th Congress, 2d Session, Report no. 2169) 7740

U.S. General accounting office. Audit of the Hudson-Champlain celebration commission, May 1960: report to Congress...by the Comptroller general... Washington, 1960. 8 leaves. 7741

U.S. Hudson-Champlain celebration commission. The 350th anniversary of the exploration of Henry Hudson and Samuel de Champlain. Final report... N.Y. 1960. 81p. illus. ports. facsim. 7742

Vermont. Lake Champlain tercentenary commission. ...Celebration of the three hundredth anniversary of the discovery of Lake Champlain. Message from the President...transmitting a report of the secretary of state... Washington, G.P.O. 1908. 14p. (U.S. 60th Congress, 1st Session, Senate Document 456) The commission also issued an unpaged report August 20, 1908, printed in Burlington. 7743

Vermont Life, Lake Champlain: 350 years. The entire Summer 1959 issue, volume 13, number 4, with sixty illustrations, part colored, including facsimiles and maps. 7744

THE HUDSON

Bruce, Wallace. The Hudson; illustrated by Alfred Fredericks with photoengravings of scenery. N.Y. Bryant literary union, ©1894. 310p. illus. 7745

Carmer, Carl Lamson. The Hudson river. N.Y. Holt, Rinehart and Winston, 1962. 114p. Reviewed in *North Country Life* (quoting New York Times *Book Review)* Fall 1962, 16:no.4:50. 7746

Hoffman, Charles Fenno. The last man. *NY Mirror,* Sept. 15, 1837. 15:74. Includes poem "To the Hudson". Notes that he accompanied the party surveying the source of the Hudson "over many a romantick tract". 7747

The Hudson, river of history. *No Country Life,* Spring 1959. 13:no.2:10-16. illus. 7748

Lewis, Jack. The Hudson river. n.p. n.pub. ©1964. 67p. Reproductions of water colors accompanied by brief text. Includes the Adirondacks. Noah John Rondeau, p. 24-25. 7749

Price, Willard. Henry Hudson's river. *Nat Geog Mag,* Mar. 1962. 121:364-403. col. illus. col.maps. Adirondacks, p.396-402. 7750

LAKES AND STREAMS
General

Au Sable valley chamber of commerce, inc. The Au Sable valley. Lake George, N.Y. Adirondack resorts press, 1958? unpaged folder. illus. maps. 7751

----. Au Sable valley, heart of the Adirondacks. Lake George, N.Y. Adirondack resorts press, n.d. Broadside printed on both sides and folded into 24p. illus. (part col.) col. map. 7752

----. Your pleasure guide to the Au Sable valley. n.p. 1963? 64p. illus. maps. Cover title: "A Valley to Remember". Marjorie L. Porter prepared p.17-51. 7753

Blackmar, Abel Edward. Diary of Fourth lake, 1870. *Adirondac,* July-Aug. - Nov.-Dec. 1959. 23:85-88, 92-97, 118-22. 7754

Bowes, Anne La Bastille. The Beaver river flow country... *Con,* June-July 1965. 19:no.6:18-20. illus. (part col.) 7755

Bruce, Dwight Hall. In the wilderness - Beaver river country. *Rod & Gun,* June 17, 1876. 8:179. 7756

Bryan, Charles W. The Raquette river of the forest. Blue Mountain Lake, N.Y. Adirondack museum, 1964. 122p. illus. ports. map. Reviewed in *York State Tradition,* Winter 1965. 19:no.1:56-57. 7757

Buchner, Marion Yates. Legacy of the lakes in play and pageant. n.p. 1959. 20p. Caroga, Canada and Stoner lake region. 7758

Cadbury, Warder H. Eagle lake. *NYS Con,* Feb.-Mar. 1960. 14:no.4:46. Quotes a letter by David Read from the second edition of Headley's "Adirondacks". 7759

De Sormo, Maitland C. Meacham-then and now. *No Country Life,* Fall 1960-Winter 1961. 14:no.4:33-38; 15:no.1:43-47. illus. See correction in Spring 1961 issue, 15:no.2:54. 7760

Exploring New York state: New York's lakes. Text and photos by New York state department of commerce. *No Country Life,* Fall 1957. 11:no.4:47-52. illus. Includes a number of Adirondack lakes. 7761

Fowler, Albert Vann, ed. Cranberry lake, 1845-1959. An Adirondack miscellany... Blue Mountain Lake, N.Y. Adirondack museum, ©1959. 150p. map. Reviewed by A.S. Merrill in *New York History,* Jan.1960, 41:108-109; other reviews in *North Country Life,* Fall 1959, 13: no. 4:57-58 and in *Adirondac,* Sept.-Oct. 1959, 23:102,107. 7762

Fulton chain club. The Fulton chain region. N.Y. Giles co. 1891? 23p. illus. maps. Title supplied. Copy in the Adirondack Museum lacks cover.   7763

Fynmore, Jim. Along the Fulton chain. *No Country Life,* Summer 1956. 10:no.3:28-33. Pictures with brief text.   7764

Gerling, V.B. Historical notes on the Sacandaga reservoir area. Rexford, N.Y. Howard I. Becker, 1958. 24p. maps. mimeographed. 7765

Gordon, Wellington E. Scattering memories of a Sacondaga home, 1850-1870. Rexford, N.Y. Howard I. Becker, 1960. 97 leaves. mimeographed.   7766

Hiscock, L. Harris. Changing times. *Adirondac,* Sept.-Oct. 1957. 21:92-94,98. Meacham Lake. See also his "In Bygone Years" in issue for May-June 1956, 20:44-46, also on Meacham Lake.   7767

Hornaday, William Temple. In the heart of an autumn forest. *Four Tr News,* Sept. 1905. 9:163-65. illus. Big Moose Lake.   7768

Hugh R. Jones co. inc. The Beaver lake country. Utica, N.Y. ©1923. 17p. illus. maps. Advertising brochure of the Fisher Forestry and Realty Company.   7769

Indian lake country. *No Country Life,* Summer 1958. 12:no.3:48-49,57. illus. Reprinted from *Town Topics.*   7770

James Bayne co. Souvenir of the Fulton chain section of the great Adirondack wilderness... Grand Rapids, Mich. n.d. unpaged. illus. lp. text.   7771

Jamieson, Paul F. The Oswegatchie highlands... *Adirondac,* May-June 1963. 27:36-41,47. illus.   7772

Katz, E.C. A star in the wilderness. *Four Tr News,* June 1906. 10:443-45. illus. Star Lake.   7773

Lake Placid chamber of commerce. Don't miss the boat tour of Lake Placid... Lake Placid, N.Y. 1935? broadside, printed on both sides, folded into 8p. illus map.   7774

McCoy, Mrs. June. Chateaugay chasm. *Franklin Hist R,* Aug. 1965. 2:no.1:12-14. illus. 7775

MacGregor, T.D. A king on American soil. *Four Tr News,* Feb. 1905. 8:93-95. illus. Lake Bonaparte.   7776

McKenney, Clara (Bush). The Cranberry lake dam. *Quar,* Oct. 1965. 10:no.4:6-7,19. illus.   7777

Marshall, Robert. One hundred largest lakes in the Adirondacks. *Cloud Splitter,* July-Aug. 1962. 25:no.4:2-3. Excerpts from the Adirondack Mountain Club archives.   7778

Merrill, David Shepard. The education of a young pioneer in the northern Adirondacks...

NY Hist, July 1958. 39:238-55. Chateaugay lakes.   7779

Mystery at Morehouse lake. *NYS Con,* April-May 1957. 11:no.5:47. Questions identity of photograph of custodian's cottage, printed in August-September issue.   7780

Northrup, Ansel Judd. A summer vacation on Cranberry lake (North woods) New York, July 1878. Syracuse, N.Y. Truair, Smith & Bruce, 1879. 40p. Reprinted from the Syracuse *Daily Journal.* Copy in the collection of Albert Vann Fowler.   7781

O'Donnell, Thomas Clay. The river rolls on: a history of the Black river from Port Leyden to Carthage... Prospect, N.Y. Prospect books, 1959. 142p. illus. The second of the author's series on the Black River. Includes some Adirondack material. Reviewed in *North Country Life,* Winter 1960, 14:no.1:63.   7782

Priest, Irvin M. Continued history of Lake Bonaparte, N.Y. Book no.2... n.p. 1946. 26p. illus. 2d printing. Followed by ...Book no.3, 1940,21p. illus. port. Joseph Bonaparte and family.   7783

----. Lake Bonaparte: map and camps. n.p. n.pub. n.d. unpaged leaflet (8p.) port. maps. Map copyrighted 1934 by I.M. Priest. 7784

----. The why of Lake Bonaparte and Natural Bridge, New York. n.p. n.d. 16p. illus. port. maps. One picture is ©1938.   7785

Pringle, Larry. A place called Sargent's pond. *Am For,* Dec. 1962. 68:no.12:27,56. illus. Includes comments on the future if Forest Preserve is opened.   7786

Roden, William M. An Adirondack adventure in conservation. *NYS Con,* Aug.-Sept. 1958. 13:no.1:32-33. illus. Harrisburg Lake.   7787

Stewart, Gustav L. III. Hewitt reflections: a short history. Princeton, N.J. Princeton printing co. 1955. unpaged (64p.) illus. map. Three generations at Hewitt Lake. Privately printed in a limited edition.   7788

Stiles, Fred T. More about South bay. *York State Trad,* Fall 1963-Winter 1964. 17:no.4:47-51,53; 18:no.1:42-46. illus.   7789

----. South bay settlement. *No Country Life,* Fall 1958. 12:no.4:8-13. maps.   7790

Thomas, Howard. The Black river in the north country. Prospect, N.Y. Prospect books, 1963. 220p. illus.   7791

Ward, Mrs. Mary L. Foothills and footnotes. *Adirondac,* Mar.-April 1958. 22:41-43. illus. Summers spent at Star Lake.   7792

Woodbridge, John R. Camp Lookout on Clear pond, 1881-1909. *Adirondac,* Sept.-Oct. 1957. 21:84-89,97-98. illus. See letter by George W. Whitson in Mar.-April 1958 issue, 22:35. 7793

Zilliox, Robert G. Brant lake. *NYS Con,* Aug.

-Sept. 1956. 11:no.1:31. Map with brief text. Similar maps were issued as follows: Brown tract ponds, April-May 1962,16:no.5:5; Forked lake, June-July 1960, 14:no.6:30; Franklin county: Fish creek ponds, Rollins pond, Aug.-Sept. 1960, 15:no.1:28-29; Lake Eaton (Clear pond) Long lake, South pond, Aug.-Sept. 1959, 14:no.1:14-15; Lake Luzerne (Warren county), Dec. 1958-Jan. 1959, 13:no.3:33; Loon lake, Dec. 1957-Jan. 1956, 12:no.3:15; Sacandaga lake, Lake Pleasant, Aug.-Sept. 1957, 12:no.1: 9. A letter referring to Lake Luzerne appears in the April-May 1959 issue, p.45.   7794

Ausable Chasm

Ausable chasm; one of the natural wonders of the world. n.p. n.d. Broadside printed on both sides and folded into 8p. illus.   7795

----. Same. n.p. n.d. Broadside printed on both sides and folded into 12p. illus. map. Map is ©1914.   7796

Ausable chasm company. Ausable chasm... N.Y. F.W. Robinson co. 1900? unpaged. illus. (part col.).   7797

----. Same. Troy, N.Y. Troy times art press, n.d. unpaged (12 leaves) One page of text. 7798

----. Explore Ausable chasm... Watertown, N.Y. Kamargo press, n.d. Broadside printed on both sides and folded into 12p. col. illus. col. map. Also another edition with title "Ausable chasm One of the World's Wonders", undated, printed in Albany by the J.B. Lyon Company.   7799

Guide to Ausable chasm... Troy, N.Y. Troy times art press, n.d. 12p. illus. folded map.7800

Possons, Charles H. publisher. Souvenir of Ausable chasm. Glens Falls, N.Y. 1890? 12 leaves. illus.   7801

Souvenir of Ausable chasm. n.p. New York photogravure co. n.d. unpaged. illus. Photographs with brief text; copyright by W.H. Tracy, proprietor.   7802

Lake George

Crook, Mel. Lake George patrol. *Yachting,* Jan. 1964. 115:no.1:96-97,360-61. illus. map.   7803

Davis, Albert T. Shoreline survey of Lake George. *NYS Con,* Aug.-Sept. 1959. 14:no. 1:16-18. illus.   7804

Historic Lake George in picture. Saratoga Springs, N.Y. Robson & Adee, n.d. unpaged. Plates with one page of text.   7805

Historical association recovers bateau from Lake George, N.Y. *Hist News,* Dec. 1960. 16:no.2:15. Colonial bateau.   7806

New York (state) Conservation department. Division of lands and forests. Lake George. Albany, 1960. 8p. Accompanied by folded map. Also issued in 1961 and 1963.   7807

Stiles, Fred T. On the road to Shelving rock. *No Country Life,* Summer 1960. 14:no.3:37-41. illus. Knapp Estate, Lake George.   7808

----. Recollections of the Knapp estate. *No Country Life,* Fall 1960 - Spring 1961. 14:no. 4:25-32; 15:no.1:40-42; 15:no.2:30-33. illus.   7809

----. Tales of Lake George. *York State Trad,* Summer 1963. 17:no.3:45-52. illus.   7810

Stoddard, Seneca Ray. Lake George: a book of pictures. Glens Falls, N.Y. ©1899. unpaged. illus. One page of text.   7811

----. Lake George: artotype illustrations by Edward Bierstadt. Glens Falls, N.Y. 1883. 45p. illus.   7812

Street, Alfred Billings. The wilds of Lake George, *New Yorker,* April 25, 1840. 9:81. See also anonymous "Lake George" on same page.   7813

Tuttle, Charles Henry and Tuttle, Helene (Wheeler) One hundred years on Lake George, New York...1856-1956. Lake George, N.Y. Adirondack resorts press, 1956. 36p. illus. A family chronicle.   7814

Tuttle, Helene (Wheeler) On our way rejoicing; including Houses in the sun... Lake George, N.Y. Halcyon press, ©1964. 279p. illus. port. Fifty-seven summers at Lake George.   7815

Views of historic Lake George, from photographs taken by Mr. L. E. Heath. Saratoga Springs, N.Y. Robson & Adee, n.d. unpaged. plates. One page of text.   7816

MOUNTAINS AND PASSES
Mount Marcy

Hall, James. The naming of Mt. Marcy. *Tahawus Cloudsplitter,* Feb. 1965. 17 i.e. 16:no. 2:3. Reprint of article from Albany *Daily Advertiser,* Aug. 15, 1837.   7817

Ketchledge, Edwin H. Mount Marcy, New York's highest mountain, a scenic and scientific wonder. *NYS Con,* Dec. 1961-Jan. 1962. 16:no.3:30-32. illus.   7818

Lindstrom, John D. Mount Marcy. *Summit,* July-Aug. 1963. 9:no.7:31-33.   7819

Lowrie, Walter. Marcy reminiscences. *Adirondac,* Mar.-April 1956. 20:30-33. Preceded by a letter from Sarah D. Lowrie to William B. Glover. See also letter from Dr. Ernest Sachs in the July-Aug. issue, 20:73.   7820

Shorey, Archibald Thompson. Buds, bees and skimmers. *Adirondac,* Nov.-Dec. 1956. 20: 119. A farewell climb.   7821

Victory mountain park committee. Following is a list of Victory mountain park committee which held its first meeting...June 26, 1919. n.p. n.d. 8p. Title reported by Warder H. Cadbury.   7822

Other Mountains and Passes

Cadbury, Warder H. An introduction to Robert Clarke's account of the first ascent of Mt. Colden in 1850. *Adirondac,* Jan.-Feb. 1957. 21:4-5.   7823

Clarke, Robert. The first ascent of Mt. Colden. *Adirondac,* Jan.-Feb. 1957. 21:5-7, 20-21. illus. Letter to his mother dated Adirondac, August 17, 1850. Original at Headquarters House, Ticonderoga.   7824

Gore mountain, N.Y. *Rocks & Min,* Nov.-Dec. 1958. 33:486. Brief review of article in the rotogravure section of the Syracuse *Post-Standard,* July 6, 1958.   7825

Hubinski, Paul. Hoffman peak. *Cloud Splitter,* Mar.-April 1957. 20:no.2:2.   7826

Jamieson, Paul F. Catamount mountain. *Adirondac,* Sept.-Oct. 1959. 23:99-102. In southwest corner of Clinton County. See also "More about Catamount" and "Source of Quote", on p.107.   7827

Jones, Garfield. Helicopter crash on Basin. *Adirondac,* Sept.-Oct. 1964. 28:76. illus. 7828

Jones, Walter Rysam. The Indian pass. *Home Office,* Oct.-Nov. 1936. p.18-20. illus. 7829

Muiry, James M. Resurrection of Whiteface lodge. *NYS Con,* Dec. 1951-Jan. 1952. 6:no. 3:22-23. illus. Brief text.   7830

Power at the summit. *No Country Life,* Spring 1961. 15:no.2:24-26. illus. Gore Mountain. Reprinted from Niagara Mohawk *News.* 7831

Rist, Leslie. How did Mount Adams get its name. *Tahawus Cloudsplitter,* Feb. 1965. 17 i.e.16:no.2:10. Another letter on the same subject in the April 1965 issue, p.11. Also letter from A.T. Shorey in the Sept. 1965 issue, p.10.   7832

Slade, Bertha, and Slade, Orville. Colvin's peaks. *NYS Con,* Feb.-Mar. 1960. 14:no.4:42. illus. Hurricane Mountain.   7833

Street, Alfred Billings. Saved in mid-air. *Beadles M,* April 1866. 1:345-48. Adventure on Whiteface.   7834

Van Dyke, Paul A. Tragedy on Wright... *Adirondac,* Mar.-April 1962. 26:27, 29. Crash of B-47 bomber on Wright Peak.   7835

Weld, Paul W. Nye mountain in May. *Adirondac,* Nov.-Dec. 1965. 29:90-92,93. port. Includes brief biography of William Watson Ely.   7836

Witte, Frederick P. Algonquin peak. *Summit,* June, 1964. 10:no.5:22-23. illus.   7837

Yandom, Thomas. Sleeping giant. *York State Trad,* Winter 1963. 17:no.1:19-21. On Hoffman; winner of the 1963 Hudowalski Folklore Essay contest.   7838

COUNTIES

Aber, Ted and King, Stella (Brooks) The history of Hamilton county. Lake Pleasant, N.Y. Great wilderness books, 1965. 1209p. illus. ports. maps. Copyright by Frederick C. Aber, jr. and Stella King.   7839

Brown, William H. ed. History of Warren county, New York. Glens Falls, N.Y. Board of supervisors of Warren county, 1963. 302p. illus. maps. Includes chapter on Adirondack Forest Preserve and State Park. Reviewed in *York State Tradition,* Fall 1953, 17:no.4:56.   7840

Christie, Mrs. Elizabeth and Christie, Robert jr. Hamilton county. Albany, New York state conservation department, 1959. 4p. col. maps. (Information Leaflet) Reprinted from the *New York State Conservationist.*   7841

Clinton county. Board of elections. List of registered voters in Clinton county in 1911... n.p. n.d. 75p.   7842

Clinton county and the California gold rush. *No Country Notes,* May 1962. no.9:2-3. 7843

Clinton county goes to war. *No Country Notes,* Nov. 1961. no.6:1-4. Extracts from Civil War letters.   7844

Concerning slavery in Clinton county. *No Country Notes,* Jan. 1961. no.2:2. Extracts from Town of Plattsburgh records. See also p.3.   7845

Cornell university. Agricultural experiment station. Department of rural sociology. The people of Clinton county, New York. Trends in human resources and their characteristics, 1900-1960. Ithaca, N.Y. 1963. 50p. tables, map. (Bulletin no.62-9, August 1963) Similar reports have been issued for Essex, Franklin, Fulton, Hamilton, Herkimer, Lewis, Oneida, Saratoga, St. Lawrence, Warren and Washington counties.   7846

Dean, Willamay T. Memories of my youth. *York State Trad,* Summer 1963. 17:no.3:33-36. Franklin county.   7847

Durkee, Cornelius E. comp. Index of names in Sylvester's History of Saratoga county, 1878. Rexford, N.Y. Howard I. Becker, 1965. 151p. Reproduced from typewritten copy. Completed by Henry C. Ritchie, Historian, Town of Charlton.   7848

Essex county. Board of supervisors. Journal of the proceedings... Keeseville, N.Y. Boynton, 1862-. v.p. Place and publisher vary. Incomplete files at Adirondack Museum and Keene Valley Public Library. Consult Supervisors Office in each county for complete record of publication.   7849

Essex county development corporation. Initial overall economic development program for Essex county, New York. n.p. n.d. 54p. tables, map. Cover title. Report submitted Feb. 1962.   7850

Essex county men who knew Lincoln. *Reveille*, Mar.-April 1962. 6:no.24:1-4; 7:no.25:4.
7851

Hall, Robert. Old-timer recalls murder cases of 75 years ago. *Reveille*, Sept. 1957. 2:no.10: 1,4. Harry Allen's reminiscences.   7852

Hamilton county. Board of supervisors. Proceedings. n.p. v.d. v.p. 1927 and 1929 at the Adirondack Museum.   7853

Hanna, Mark B. Essex county in the Civil war. *Reveille*, Dec. 1959. no.17:3.   7854

Hayes, Margaret F. Historical facts of Clinton county. n.p. 1958. 4p. Reproduced from typewritten copy. By the Clinton County Historian.
7855

King, Stella (Brooks) Hamilton county. *Sup News*, Jan. 1962. 12:no.1:18-19,36,39-40, illus. Offprints, with map were published without source or date. W.C.   7856

MacMorris, Mary W. Washington county. *Sup News*, June 1961. 11:no.2:17,30,41. port.
7857

New York (state) Legislature. Assembly. ...Report of the committee on internal affairs of town and counties on petition of supervisors and others, of Hamilton county. Albany, 1860. 17p. (Document no. 94) Dated Feb. 24, 1860.
7858

Noxon, Horace E. Some pertinent facts concerning real property taxes in Essex county. *Sup News*, Jan. 1964. 14:no.1:12,36. port. 7859

Official program of the home coming celebration by the people of Essex county to those in national service in the World war 1917-19 held in Port Henry, N.Y. September 1, 1919. n.p. n.d. unpaged (16p.) Includes lists of soldiers.   7860

Olds, Carlton and Olds, Ethel. St. Lawrence county. *County Gov*, May 1961. 11:no.3:26-31. illus. See also later article with same title in *Supervisors News* June 1962, 12:no.2:14, 17-21. illus.   7861

One hundredth anniversary of the formation of Warren county, New York. n.p. n.pub. 1913? 74p. illus. Includes historical sketch of the county and each town, also biographical sketches.   7862

Palmer, Robert Morris. Fulton county. *Sup News*, June 1961. 11:no.2:32-37. illus.   7863

----. Historical Fulton county, New York. Johnstown, N.Y. Fulton county publicity, n.d. unpaged. illus. map.   7864

Saratoga county. Board of supervisors. Rules ...in relation to auditing accounts of justices of the peace... Saratoga Springs, N.Y. 1867. 16p.
7865

Sheldon, Oscar F. Early settlers. *Reveille*, Dec. 1963; Mar. 1964. 8:no.32:4; 9:no.33:1-3. Essex county.   7866

U.S. Census office. Washington county state of New York 1800 and 1810; also the town of Fair Haven, Vt. 1800 and 1810. St. Johnsville, N.Y. Enterprise and news, n.d. 15p.   7867

Warren county, N.Y. furnishes 1964 national Christmas tree. *N Logger*, Dec. 1964, 13:no. 6:18,68.   7868

Warren county committee for the observance of 1959 as a year of history. Presenting a bit of Warren county history... n.p.1959. 23p. col. illus. maps (one in col.)   7869

Warrensburg chamber of commerce. Warrensburgh, N.Y. Queen city of the Adirondacks. Warrensburg, n.d. Broadside printed on both sides and folded into 12p. illus.   7870

Young, Lois. Odd quotes from old deeds in Essex county. *Cloud Splitter*, May-June 1960. 23:no.3:3-4. Extract from article submitted for the Hudowalski Essay Contest.   7871

CITIES AND VILLAGES
Crown Point

Barker, Elmer Eugene, comp. Crown Point, New York in the Civil war. Albany, New York state Civil war centennial commission, 1961. 133 leaves. illus. Reproduced from typewritten copy.   7872

Barker, Elmer Eugene. Crown Point's part in New York State's year of history. *Cloud Splitter*, Mar.-April 1959. 32:no.2:2-3.   7873

Barnett, Ethel. Recalling the old country store. *No Country Life*, Spring 1962. 16:no.2:40-41. Store at Crown Point used as school and post-office.   7874

Clark, William Colton. The hand clasp of the states. *Vermonter*, Oct. 1929. 34:145. Good relations between New York and Vermont; the Crown Point bridge.   7875

Crown Point foundation. Colonial trouble spot: Crown Point on Lake Champlain, 1609-1783. A major historical site in New York state. N.Y. 1964? Broadside, printed on both sides and folded into 12p. illus. map.   7876

Crown Point trading post. Crown Point reservation: Fort Amherst; Fort St. Frederic, the Lake Champlain bridge. Crown Point, N.Y. n.d. unpaged. Published after completion of the bridge, dedicated in 1929. 7877

Fort St. Frederic. *NYS Con*, Dec. 1961-Jan. 1962. 16:no.3:40. Crown Point tract now an historic site.   7878

Glenn, John E. The Crown Point story. *NYS Ed*, Dec. 1964. 52:no.3:12-13. port. Attempt to force resignation of school principal. 7879

Hopkins, Arthur S. Old Fort St. Frederic - French relic at Crown Point. *NYS Con*, Aug.-Sept. 1962. 17:no.1:13-15. illus. plan.   7880

Lonergan, Carroll Vincent. Fort St. Frederic. *No Country Life,* Summer 1958. 12:no.3:43-44   7881

The one hundredth and fiftieth anniversary of the American revolution in the Crown Point area... July 4, 1927... n.p. n.pub. n.d. 40p. port. illus. Contains Historical pageant by Elizabeth B. Carey and Carrie Wood Porter; the Champlain valley, by Frank E. Brimmer, p. 5-17.   7882

Penfield foundation. Report to members and friends. Crown Point, N.Y. 1965. unpaged (16p.) illus. ports. Includes brief history of Crown Point and report of E. Gilbert Barker, president of the Board of Trustees, Penfield Foundation.   7883

The Penfield foundation, Ironville, Crown Point, New York. n.p. 1962. Folded broadside, printed on both sides, illus. The Foundation was formed to maintain the Penfield Homestead as an historic site and as a museum of local history for Crown Point.   7884

Plan of Fort Frederick at Crown Point. *Gent Mag,* Nov. 1755. 25:525. plan, map.   7885

Redford, Kenneth. Crown Point supporters. *Con,* Dec. 1962-Jan. 1963. 17:no.3:44. Fort St. Frederic.   7886

Spalding, Cora. Crown Point's white church and the angel Gabriel. *No Country Life,* Spring 1956. 10:no.2:39-40,46. illus.   7887

Standish, Jared B. Region about new Champlain bridge has vast historic association. *Vermonter,* Oct. 1929. 34:152-54. illus.   7888

Elizabethtown

Barnes, Mary Clark. A woodland epic: a story of the poetry and tragedy of the trees. *Four Tr News,* Oct. 1903. 5:199-203. illus. Describes the region around Elizabethtown.   7889

Bishop, M.E. Story of Elizabethtown told by Dr. Bishop, 1904. *Reveille,* Sept. 1960. 5:no. 19:3. Extracts from the Elizabethtown *Post and Gazette,* Mar. 10, 1904.   7890

1852 county jailhouse construction agreement. *Reveille,* Nov. 1958. 2:no.14:2. Essex County Jail.   7891

Elizabethtown chamber of commerce. Meet you in Elizabethtown... n.p. n.d. Broadside printed on both sides and folded into 8p. illus. map.   7892

----. Welcome! Adirondack festival, Elizabethtown, New York. Elizabethtown, N.Y. 1964. unpaged (8p.) illus. map.   7893

Elizabethtown social center, Elizabethtown, New York. n.p. n.d. unpaged (8p.) illus.   7894

Great fire at Elizabethtown, 1895. *Reveille,* July 1959. no.16:1-2. illus. Reprint from the *Essex County Republican,* Jan. 31, 1895.   7895

Hand, Augustus N. Local incidents of the Pap-

ineau rebellion. *NY Hist,* Oct. 1934. 15:376-87. Includes raid on the Elizabethtown armory, Feb. 16, 1838.   7896

Lawrence, Richard W. jr. Elizabethtown: its Adirondack center museum and colonial garden. Elizabethtown, N.Y. Chamber of commerce, ©1960. Folded broadside, printed on both sides. illus. maps. Tour guide with brief historical notes.   7897

Old mill art school, June 19th-Sept. 5th...Elizabethtown, N.Y. n.p. n.d. Broadside, printed on both sides and folded into 24p. illus. map.   7898

Pleasant valley almanac, v.1, no.1. Elizabethtown, N.Y. 1958. 4p. illus. map. Folio directory of Elizabethtown published by Robert Hall, Warrensburg.   7899

Rainey, John J. The players come to town. *No Country Life,* Summer 1960. 14:no.3:12-15. Ben Greet Players.   7900

Upstate New Yorkers have big time on sugaring off day. *Friends,* Mar. 1960. p.25.   7901

Keene and Keene Valley

Adirondack communities council, inc. Adirondack communities council, inc.1953-1957. A report to members and a plea for your support. Keene Valley, N.Y. 1957. unpaged (4p.) Town of Keene.   7902

----. The villages of Keene and Keene Valley... n.p. 1958. unpaged folder, illus. map.   7903

Easton, Mrs. Emily. Keene club hears speech on town planning, Nov. 15. Broadside reprinted from the Ausable Forks *Record-Post,* Dec. 5, 1963.   7904

Holt, Charles N. comp. Mallory grant... Keene Valley, N.Y. 1959? 34 leaves. mimeographed. A collection of extracts with comments documenting the history of Keene Valley. Title supplied from first page of text.   7905

Isham, Edward. Reminiscences of Ed Isham of Keene Valley; foreword by William B. Glover. *Adirondac,* Jan.-Feb. 1957. 21:9-11. port.   7906

Keene Valley, N.Y. Board of trade. Keene and Keene Valley, N.Y. surrounded by the most famous Adirondack peaks. Watertown, N.Y. Kamargo press, n.d. Broadside printed on both sides and folded into 8p. illus. map.   7907

Keene Valley country club. Constitution, 1906. n.p. n.d. 8p. Copy at the Adirondack Museum.   7908

Keene Valley garden club. Keene Valley wild flower, plant and bird sanctuary and the Nature museum, Keene Valley, N.Y. n.d. unpaged folder (6p.)   7909

Keene Valley memorial corporation. Keene

Valley memorial corporation. n.p. n.d. unpaged leaflet (8p.)   7910

LaDuke, John T. ...The Keene Valley. *Trailmarker*, Oct.-Nov. 1962. 1:no.3:11-12. illus.   7911

Lippitt, Marion Almy. A vignette of the valley. *Adirondac*, May-June 1958. 22:64,67.   7912

MacIntosh, J. Oswald. Johns Brook memories. *Adirondac*, Sept.-Oct. 1956. 20:89-91. illus.   7913

Porter, Lewis Morgan. Mrs. MacCormack's stone jug. *Adirondac*, Sept.-Oct. 1951. 15:96, 99. A bit of local history.   7914

Porter, Marjory (Lansing) East Hill: two experiments in social living. *No Country Life*, Fall 1957. 11:no.4:27-32. illus. Thomas Davidson and Glenmore; Prestonia Mann Martin and Summerbrook.   7915

Winding up the crank. *Tel Rev*, Mar. 1951. p.13. illus. On closing the telephone building at Keene Valley.   7916

Lake Placid

The family goes to Lake Placid. *Today's Liv*, Dec. 13, 1959. p.4-5, 20. illus. (part col.)   7917

Freemasons. Lake Placid lodge no.834, F & A M. Souvenir of Lake Placid in the Adirondacks. n.p. n.d. unpaged (12p.) illus. One page of text, folder of pictures.   7918

Lake Placid chamber of commerce. Lake Placid-in-the-Adirondacks. N.Y. Whitney Paddenburg, inc. n.d. Broadside printed on both sides and folded into 4p. illus.   7919

Lake Placid in New York's Adirondacks invites you for your next vacation. n.p. n.pub. n.d. unpaged (8p. incl. cover) col. illus. map. Advertising leaflet published around 1962.   7920

Russell D. Bailey and associates. Community characteristics. Population trends. Land use. Village of Lake Placid, Essex county and Town of North Elba, New York. Utica, N.Y. 1964? 41 leaves, illus. tables, charts, maps (one folded)   7921

----. Lake Placid; North Elba. The master plan. Utica, N.Y. 1964. 30 leaves. maps. Summary of 8 volumes of reports. Cover title.   7922

----. Land development program & capital improvement program. Village of Lake Placid. Town of North Elba... Utica, N.Y. 1964. unpaged charts.   7923

----. The quality of housing, Village of Lake Placid, Essex county and Town of North Elba, New York. n.p. 1964? 11 leaves. maps. No.2 of a series of studies made through the New York State Department of Commerce Urban Planning Assistance Program.   7924

Tanner, Hudson H. and Cunningham, Mary E. Trails, timber and tourists. Lake Placid, convention capital. *Yorker*, Mar.-April 1957. 15:no.4:52-56. illus.   7925

Thomas, Lowell. The legacy of Lake Placid. *Ski Life*, Feb. 1960. 2:no.5:42-45. Influence of 1932 Olympics on American skiing.   7926

Plattsburgh

Barnes, John Bryson. Letters of a Plattsburg patriot, by O.N.E. Washington, D.C. United states infantry association, 1917. 80p. illus. Training camp.   7927

Beckwith, George M. The great freshet of 1830 in Plattsburgh. *No Country Notes*, April 1963. no.13:4. Reprinted from the Plattsburgh *Republican*, Mar. 31, 1883.   7928

Behan, Frank. A picture record helps city expand water system. *Am City*, Nov. 1955. 70: no.11:124-25. illus.   7929

A bit of history of Old Plattsburgh. *Reveille*, June 1958. 2:no.12:1.   7930

Carnright, Jason J. Detroit in the North country. *No Country Notes*, Mar. 1965. no.22:3. Lozier Motor Company.   7931

Clinton county agricultural society. Plattsburgh, N.Y. Big Clinton county fair...1925. Plattsburgh, N.Y.Imperial press, 1925. 110p. illus.   7932

Cole, G. Glyndon. A way of life long since vanished. The Kent-Delord house. *No Country Life*, Summer 1957. 11:no.3:23-28. illus.   7933

Gauvreau, Charles F. Soldier's homecoming, 1898. *No Country Life*, Fall 1962. 16:no. 4:26-30. 21st Infantry.   7934

Hildreth, Dick. Plattsburgh air force base. Syracuse Post-Standard *Pictorial*, June 1, 1958, p. 4-5 illus. (incl. front cover)   7935

Historic Plattsburgh. *Lines*, Winter 1954. p.4-6. illus. (part col.)   7935a

Hundreds of rare old documents... *No Country Life*, Summer 1958. 12:no.3:51. Note from Lake Placid *News*, May 11, 1956, on files found in the Kent-Delord house.   7936

Kent Delord house. n.p. ©1924. unpaged (36p.) illus.   7937

The Kent-Delord house... *Motorgram*, Nov. 1960. 31:no.11:12-13. illus. (incl. front cover)   7938

Langworthy Bess (Hagar) History of Cumberland head. Plattsburgh, N.Y. Clinton county historical association, 1961. 25p. Reproduced from typewritten copy.   7939

Lovejoy, George Newell. A delightful summer city. *Four Tr News*, Mar. 1906. 10:244-46. illus.   7940

Monroe, James. A narrative of a tour of observation, made during the summer of 1817...

Philadelphia, S.A. Mitchell and H. Ames, 1818. 228p. Plattsburgh, p.180-87.   7941

Mooney, Charles. North country bootlegging days. *No Country Life,* Spring 1959. 13: no.2:39-40.   7942

A new era in the Plattsburgh story. *No Country Life,* Spring 1957. 11:no.2:7-12. illus.   7943

New York (state) Plattsburgh centenary commission. Pageant of the Champlain valley... n.p. 1914. 15p. illus. ports. maps. Program.   7944

Plattsburgh, N.Y. Ordinances of the city of Plattsburgh, New York. n.p. n.d. 74p.   7945

Plattsburgh, N.Y. Charter. The charter of the city of Plattsburg (Laws of 1902, ch.269, as amended) *In* New York (state) Department of audit and control. Municipal affairs division. Charters of the cities of New York state. Albany, 1949. v.8.   7946

----. Charter of the city of Plattsburgh, New York as amended. n.p. 1912. 161p. With this is bound Ordinances (see above) and Municipal civil service rules for the classified service...1908, 30p. Copy in the Plattsburgh Public Library.   7947

Plattsburgh, N.Y. Common council. A message to the citizens of Plattsburg from the mayor & council. n.p. 1936. unpaged.   7948

Plattsburgh chamber of commerce. Plattsburgh: the international city for your plant. Plattsburgh, N.Y. n.d. unpaged (12p. incl. cover) illus. map.   7949

----. Plattsburgh panorama, heart of the Champlain valley; 1950 ed. n.p. n.d. 30p. illus. map (col.)   7950

Plattsburgh, frontier of freedom. *Diamond Dig,* Feb. 1958. p.10-15. illus. (part col.) Continued in the Spring 1958 issue, p.8-11, illus.   7951

Plattsburgh. *Tel Rev,* Nov. 1941. p.10-11,40-41,46. illus.   7952

Plattsburgh's new museum. *No Country Notes,* Jan. 1964. no.16:1.   7953

Porter, Marjorie (Lansing) Plattsburgh: 1785 - 1815 - 1902. Plattsburgh barracks, 1814. n.p. George Little press, ©1964. 122p. illus. map.   7954

----. Plattsburgh souvenir tour guide... Plattsburgh, N.Y. Clinton press, n.d. 32p. maps.   7955

Russell, Francis. When gentlemen prepared for war. *Am Heritage,* April 1964. 15:no.3: 24-27,89-93. port. illus. Military training camp.   7956

Saranac Lake

Baldwin, Edward Robinson. The development of Saranac Lake as a health resort. *J Outd Life,* May 1931. 28:292-94. illus.   7957

Disabled veterans of the world war. New York State department. Official program...sixteenth annual state convention...Saranac Lake, N.Y. June 10,11,12,1937. n.p. n.d. unpaged (38p.) illus. map laid in. Cover title: Saranac Lake in the Adirondacks.   7958

Gardner, Leroy Upson. Saranac Lake as a research center. *J Outd Life,* May 1931. 28:298-302. illus. port.   7959

Goldthwaite, Kenneth W. Picturesque Saranac Lake. Saranac Lake, N.Y. ©1914. unpaged (32p.) illus. One page of text followed by pictures.   7960

In the Saranac Country: world famous resorts lure the traveler to delights of lake and mountain. *Motordom,* June 1930. 24:no. 1:26. illus.   7961

Let a cop drive you home New Year's eve. *Sat Eve Post,* Dec. 18, 1954. 227:no.25:12. Editorial describing Saranac Lake plan.   7962

McDonald, John and Ricciardi, Franc. The business decision game. *Fortune,* Mar. 1958. 57:no.3:140-42,208,213-14. col. charts. American Management Association, Trudeau.   7963

Park, Nancy. "The little city of hope". *J Outd Life,* June 1935. 32:224.   7964

Saranac Lake, N.Y. Board of trustees. Saranac Lake: the little city in the Adirondacks. Saranac Lake, N.Y. n.d. Broadside, printed on both sides and folded into 16p. illus. map.   7965

----. Same. Saranac Lake, N.Y. 1920. Broadside printed on both sides and folded into 12p. illus. map. Drawings by Mills Thompson; text by Roy Dayton.   7966

Saranac Lake chamber of commerce. What a new hotel will mean to Saranac Lake. Saranac Lake, N.Y. Enterprise press, 1922. Broadside printed on both sides and folded into 8p. illus. On the location of Hotel Ampersand.   7967

Saranac Lake. *No Country Life,* Summer 1956. 10:no.3:45-50. illus.   7968

Saranac Lake, N.Y. hub of the Adirondacks. Saranac Lake, N.Y. Currier press, n.d. Broadside printed on both sides and folded into 12p. illus. map. Map, copyright 1935 by T.W. Sheridan.   7969

Saranac Lake society for the control of tuberculosis, inc. Saranac Lake, New York. In the Adirondacks. Pioneer health resort. n.p. n.d. unpaged (4p.) illus.   7970

Saranac Lake study and craft guild. Report of activities July 1, 1946-June 30, 1947... Saranac Lake, N.Y. n.d. 32p. illus.   7971

Saranac Lake taxpayers association, inc. How your taxes were spent...a survey of public expenditures in the village of Saranac

Lake, N.Y. 1937-1938. Saranac Lake, N.Y. 1939. 15p. Also an undated broadside entitled "Taxpayers - Attention"; "Taxpayer's Voice", a 4p. leaflet dated September 4, 1934. 7972

Smith, Robert E. 82 years in Saranac Lake. Dedicated to my wife Lillian who has shared with me the last fifty. n.p. n.pub. 1947. unpaged (8p.) mimeographed. 7973

Whiting, Edward Clark. Plans for the improvement of Saranac Lake, reprinted from the *Adirondack Enterprise,* April 1, 1909. Saranac Lake, N.Y. Village improvement society, 1910. 27p. illus. map. Original typescript in the Saranac Lake Free Library. 7974

Ticonderoga

Allen, Henry M. Letters to the editor of the Citizen-Advertiser. Auburn? N.Y. 1934-1936. n.p. n.d. 7 leaves. mimeographed. 7975

Fort Ticonderoga. Museum. Fort Ticonderoga. A visitor's guide and some important dates. n.p. n.d. unpaged (4p.) 7976

Hamilton, Edward Pierce. Guide book to Fort Ticonderoga. Ticonderoga, N.Y. Fort Ticonderoga museum, n.d. 16p. 7977

----. An historic mortar. *Ft Ti Mus Bul,* Feb. 1960. 10:299-303. illus. On parade ground at the fort. 7978

Lonergan, Carroll Vincent. Ticonderoga, historic portage. Ticonderoga, N.Y. Fort Mt. Hope society, ©1959. 248p. illus. ports. facsims. maps. Prepublication note in *North Country Life,* Summer 1958, 12:no.3:60; reviews in *North Country Life,* Winter 1960, 14:no.1:60-61 and in *New York History* Jan. 1960,41:98-99. 7979

Lonergan, James M. The narrative from Mt. Defiance... n.p. c1953. 16p. illus. 7980

Lord, Clifford L. and Lape, Jane (McCaughlin) New York state historical association. The headquarters house... Ticonderoga, N.Y. 1943. 23p. illus. 7981

Mills, Edgar MacKay. Honor to four nations. Fort Ticonderoga... *Chr Sci Mon,* April 24, 1935. p.8-9 illus. 7982

...Mt. Defiance. *No Country Life,* Spring 1958. 12:no.2:34-38. illus. Site of revolutionary fort at Ticonderoga made accessible by road. 7983

Northern gateway. *Ver Life,* Spring 1948. 2:no.3:22-31. col. plates, figs. maps. Brief text accompanied by photographs by T. H. and E. Kleffel. Fort Ticonderoga. 7984

Shallies, Maude Eleanor. In the shadow of the past: a Ticonderoga reverie. *Four Tr News,* May 1906. 10:394-97. illus. 7985

Ticonderoga chamber of commerce. Historical Ticonderoga. Troy, N.Y. Regal art press, n.d. unpaged (16p.) illus. map. 7986

----. Ticonderoga, New York. Place where history was made... n.p. n.d. 42p. illus. map. 7987

Ticonderoga, N.Y. Its advantages and resources...also a directory of its inhabitants... Whitehall, N.Y. Press of Times, 1893. 80p. illus. map. Cover title: Directory of Ticonderga. Copy at the Penfield Foundation, Crown Point. 7988

Ticonderoga, Town of. Historic Ticonderoga. Ticonderoga, N.Y. 1933. 28p. illus. map. Edited by Julian Boyd. C.E. Hall. 7989

A valley of forts. A tribute to its history. *In* New York (state) Legislature. Joint legislative committee on preservation and restoration of historic sites. Report, 1959. Albany, 1959. p.45-65. 7990

Wickes, Sheldon F. Ticonderoga: where history was made. *No Country Life,* Fall 1959. 13:no.4:20-22. 7991

Wickser, Josephine Wilhelm. Ticonderoga. n.p. Privately printed, 1934. 5p. 7992

Other Cities and Villages

Barber's Point - Feb. 20, 1846. *Reveille,* July-Dec. 1959. no.16:4; no.17:2,3. Reprint from a contemporary newspaper. 7993

Becker, Howard I. comp. Some early Long Lake documents. Rexford, N.Y. 1957. v.p. ports. plates, maps. multilithed. Section I: The Shaws, by Howard I. Becker; Autobiography of Robert Shaw; Early views of Long Lake Village. Section II: Stories of the Adirondack, by Livonia Stanton Emerson. Section III: Rev. Frederick B. Allen's Sketches; Comments on Allen, by Warder H. Cadbury. Section IV: Visits to Long Lake, by Rev. John Todd. Section V: Footnotes to John Todd's Visits, by Warder H. Cadbury; New York State Assembly Report no.94 (1860) on Agricultural Possibilities in Hamilton County and Some New Road Costs. Section VI: Amos Dean's Pamphlet (1846) on Land for Sale in Township 21 (Long Lake); Dean's Map of the Lots; Comments on Amos Dean; Comments on Senate Document no.61 - 1840-vol.2, O.L. Holley, Hoffman; Comments on Senate Document no.73 - 1846-vol.3, George A. Simmons and Committee; Comments on Assembly Document no.68 - 1850-vol.4, H.J. Raymond. 7994

Biskin, Mrs. Miriam. The house on the pink Staffordshire plate. *NY Folk Q,* Autumn 1961. 17:183-85. Home of Jeremy Rockwell at Hadley Falls, Lake Luzerne. 7995

Blankman, Lloyd G. Secret places of the Adirondacks. *Trailmarker,* Oct.-Nov. 1962. 1:no.3:14. illus. Withers homestead, North Wilmurt. 7996

Bonn, John Louis. Gates of Dannemora. Garden City, N.Y. Doubleday, 1951. 276p.   7997

The bridge at Keeseville. *Ballou,* July 17, 1858. 15:34.   7998

Burger, William. Coll Bay. *Reveille,* April-July, 1956. 1:no.5:1,4; 1:no.6:2. Early history of Westport.   7999

Burton, Harold B. Inside Dannemora. *Sat Eve Post,* Dec. 29, 1956. 229:no.26:11-13, 66-67. illus.   8000

Champlain community exhibit. Historical program. Champlain, N.Y. n.d. v.p. Annual; 1933-1936 located.   8001

Chateaugay, N.Y. Fire department. Chateaugay fire department 1860-1960...Program for inspection and 100th anniversary field day... n.p. n.d. unpaged (24p.) illus. Includes fire department history.   8002

Craigie, Donald. The epoch of booze and bedlam. *Cloud Splitter,* Mar.-April 1962. 25:no.2:2-4. Rum-running at Schroon Lake during prohibition. Submitted for the Hudowalski Essay contest.   8003

Donovan, Gilbert .C. 'Round Saratoga and Lake George. *Woods & Wat,* Autumn, 1899. 2:no.3:11.   8004

Emerson, Livonia (Stanton) Early life at Long Lake, N.Y. Rexford, Howard I. Becker, 1956. 63p. multilithed. Text is entitled: True stories of the Adirondacks for Children and Young People.   8005

Farmer, Edward and others. Birthplace of the United States navy.   Whitehall, N.Y. Whitehall chamber of commerce, 1965. unpaged (8p.) illus.   8006

First celebration of July 4, 1802. *Reveille,* Dec. 1963. 8:no.32:2-3. From newspaper clipping given by Koert D. Burnham, being reminiscences of Mary A. Sheldon of Willsborough Falls.   8007

Fowler, Barnett. Fort William Henry. *No Country Life,* Summer 1957. 11:no.3:29-33, 60. illus. Restoration of the fort.   8008

Granger, Marcus E. Guide to Schroon lake and vicinity... Warrensburg, N.Y. Newsprint, n.d. 23p. Copy in the Warrensburg Public Library has pencilled note: This book was written about 1876 or 1877. A.M. Jenks. The Guide is in doggerel.   8009

Haberly, Lewis. Here lies Schroon lake. *NY Folk Quar,* Winter 1962. 18:265-73. Cemetery inscriptions.   8010

Hall, Arthur. Our town - Willsboro. *No Country Life,* Summer 1960. 14:no.3:49-50. Reprinted from the *Essex County Republican.*   8011

A history of the old Durant homestead... Blue Mountain Lake... written as a newspaper story under date of July 17, 1915. n.p. n.pub. n.d. unpaged leaflet (4p.)   8012

Indian legend, Schroon Lake, N.Y., Adirondack mountains; illustrated with choice photographs of the region by Maude E. Taylor. Watertown, N.Y. Santway photo craft co. n.d. unpaged (16p.) illus.   8013

Johnson, Ellen (Adkins) Streetroad, its history and its people; facts, folks and fancies. Ithaca, N.Y. Linguistica, 1956. 64 leaves, illus. Reproduced from typewritten copy.   8014

Jones, Mabel (Merryfield) Brief history of Minerva. *Reveille,* July 1956. 1:no.6:2-3. 8015

Lake George. *Ballou,* Oct. 16, 1853. 1:249. See also article with same title in issue for July 8, 1854. 7:9.   8016

Lake George chamber of commerce, inc. Queen of American lakes: Lake George in the Adirondacks, New York. Lake George, N.Y. Adirondack resorts press, 1960. 83p. illus. (part col.) maps (part col.) Another edition, 1958, 86p.   8017

Lake George on the air. *NYS Con,* Aug.-Sept. 1957. 12:no.1:33. illus. Radio program. 8018

Lange, Willem M. III Letters from an old timer. Elizabethtown, Denton publications, inc. 1965. 48p. illus. port. History of the Town of Willsboro prepared for the Willsboro Bicentennial Committee.   8019

Magee, Catherine M. comp. Thurman fifty years ago. n.p. n.pub. 1961. 18 leaves. mimeographed. Copy in the Adirondack Museum.   8020

Magee, James A. Fort William Henry: reasons why it is a national shrine. *Ad Life,* June 17, 1965. p.2-3,8. illus. port.   8021

Manley, Atwood. The Ripley papers and Matildaville. *Quar,* April 1960. 5:no.2:3-9, 12.   8022

Mann, Mina. Stony Creek mt. days in 11th year. *Ad Life,* Aug. 13, 1964. p.4. illus. The entire issue is on the Stony Creek Mountain Days. Mann's "History of Stony Creek" reprinted in *Adirondack Life,* Part I, August 19, 1965, p.8-9.   8023

Miner, W.H. inc. 1894. 50th anniversary year. 1944. Chicago, 1944. unpaged. illus. ports. Includes Heart's Delight Farm, Chazy Central Rural School, Kent-Delord House. 8024

Miner, William Henry. Heart's delight farm, Chazy, New York, U.S.A. Chicago, Lammers Shilling co. n.d. 114p. illus. (part col.) Folded map in color tipped in back.   8025

Morton, Doris (Begor) Skenesborough harbor model. *No Country Life,* Winter 1960. 14:no.1:36-39. illus.   8026

Murphy, Daniel J. Cheever diary. *Reveille,* Mar. 1964. 9:no.33:3-4.   8027

Nation's Christmas tree comes from Chestertown. *Tahawus Cloudsplitter,* Dec. 1964. 5:no.8:4. Photographs with captions. 8028

New York legion's great Adirondack "camp" completes 40 years of service to disabled men & women vets and legion families. *Am Leg Mag,* Oct. 1962. 73:no.4:26-27 illus. Brief text, describing camp at Tupper Lake. 8029

Newcomb, Minerva. In the Adirondacks. n.p. n.pub. n.d. Broadside printed on both sides and folded into 16p. illus. map. 8030

Port Henry, N.Y. Programme of Old home week. Port Henry, New York, 1904... n.p. n.d. unpaged. illus. Also issued in 1903. 8031

----. Rules, ordinances and by-laws of the village of Port Henry, New York, revised, established and adopted by the Board of trustees... 1919... n.p. n.d. 16p. 8032

----. Board of water commissioners. Ordinances relating to the use of village water... n.p. 1921. 11p. 8033

----. Fire department. 75th anniversary Labor day celebration... Port Henry, N.Y. September 6-7. 1964. n.p. n.pub. n.d. unpaged (36p.) Program including unsigned article by C. Eleanor Hall on the history of the Labor Day celebration. 8034

Port Henry on Lake Champlain: gateway to the Adirondacks. n.p. n.d. Broadside folded into 8p. illus. 8035

Port Kent, N.Y. *Weekly Novelette,* Oct. 19, 1861. 10:88. illus. 8036

R. Prescott and son at Keeseville, New York. *Northeast Log,* Oct. 1958. 7:no.4:22-23, 46-48. illus. Cabinet maker. 8037

Rist, Leslie. A short roundup of facts on Pendleton settlement. *Tahawus Cloudsplitter,* Sept. 1965. 17 (i.e. 16):no.5:10. Another letter on the same subject in the Dec. 1965 issue, p. 11. On Newcomb. 8038

Roberts, Marion E. The story of Chateaugay. *Franklin Hist R,* Aug. 1964. 6 leaves. 8039

Rolleston, Mrs. Ruth E. High spots in the town of Thurman. *Cloud Splitter,* May-June 1964. 27:no.3:2-3. 8040

Ross, John. The story of 'Fort Blunder' and Fort Montgomery at Rouses Point, N.Y. n.p. n.d. unpaged (4p.) "Compliments of the *North Countryman".* 8041

Rouses Point. *Ballou,* Jan. 1858. 14:17. 8042

Schroon Lake chamber of commerce. Schroon Lake, N.Y. in the Adirondacks... Watertown, N.Y. Kamargo press, n.d. Broadside printed on both sides and folded into 12p. illus. (part col.) map. 8043

Schroon Lake, N.Y. Publicity committee. The great Adirondack summer and winter resort.

Schroon Lake and vicinity. n.p. n.d. 44p. illus. Copy at the Adirondack Museum. 8044

Seaman, Ruth, comp. Bolton, Warren co. N.Y. *Yester,* Feb. 1959. no.6:1-5. Local history written by school children. 8045

Shorey, Mabel (Pitkin) The early history of Corinth, once known as Jessup's Landing. Corinth, N.Y. 1959. 71p. illus. maps. Also includes Hadley, Conklingville and Mt. McGregor. Reviewed in *North Country Life,* Summer 1960, 14:no.3:53. Extract with title "Jessup's Landing" in same issue, p.24-25. 8046

Smith, Mrs. Hartwell. Newcomb note. *NYS Con,* April-May 1952. 6:no.5:38. Letter to the editor. 8047

Souvenir book of important events in the history of Star Lake, N.Y. From 1878-1953. Wilderness-progress. n.p. n.d. unpaged (44p.) Foreword by Murray R. Hawley, village historian. 8048

Stanyon, Minnie (Patterson) The quiet years: with illustrations by Mildred Stanyon Colvin. n.p. n.pub. ©1965. 112p. illus. Life at Speculator in southern Hamilton County. 8049

Steamboat landing at Lake George. *Ballou,* Oct. 1, 1853. 5:216. 8050

Stegmyer, J.J. Wells in prose, song and pictures. Wells, N.Y.Press of the Hamilton county record, 1905. 25p. illus. 8051

Stony Creek, N.Y. Town board. Publicity committee. 1852-1952. Stony Creek centennial... n.p. n.d. 32p. illus. Stony Creek History, by Mina Mann, town historian, p.1-12. The committee also issued a 4p. folder entitled "Stony Creek, Warren County, N.Y." 8052

Sullivan, Mrs. Nell B. comp. Historical facts, Town of Chazy... Chazy, N.Y. 1960. unpaged (24p.) 8053

Tahawus sportsmen's show, 1951, Apr. 28-29. Tahawus, N.Y. Glens Falls, N.Y. Glens Falls Post co. 1951. 24p. illus. ports. Program with portraits and vignettes of leading participants, including Noah John Rondeau. 8054

Thistlethwaite, W.J.The romance of Old Forge. Old Forge, N.Y. Adirondack development corporation, n.d. 8p. Reprinted from the Utica *Daily Press,* Dec. 8, 1915. 8055

Tippetts, William Henry. Lake George and its picturesque attractions. Lake George, N.Y. 1901. Broadside printed on both sides and folded to 16mo. illus. map. Includes directory of hotels. 8056

Torrance, Elizabeth. A brief history of the Town of Jay. *Reveille,* Dec. 1960. 5:no.20:1-4. illus. 8057

Tupper Lake national bank. 50 years of progress...1906-56. Tupper Lake, N.Y. 1956. 12p. illus. 8058

Village of Lake George in the southern Adirondacks... Lake George, N.Y. Adirondack resorts press, n.d. Broadside printed on both sides and folded into 12p. illus. map. Map is ©1929, by A.S. Knight.   8059

Westport chamber of commerce. Westport; queen village of Lake Champlain, New York. n.p. n.d. Broadside printed on both sides and folded into 8p. illus. map. Also variant edition with title "Westport on Lake Champlain, N.Y.", broadside printed on both sides and folded into 6p. with illustrations and map.   8060

White, Byron E. Trenton Falls yesterday and today; a famous beauty spot and fashionable resort of the nineteenth century retains its charm while contributing to Utica's demand for power. *Synchronizer,* Sept. 1927. 8:no.3. 13p. port. illus. Photocopy in the Saranac Lake Free Library. This periodical was listed as unlocated in the Adirondack Bibliography, p.295.   8061

White, Philip. Early settlers in Beekmantown. *No Country Notes,* Jan. 1965. no.21:2.   8062

Whitehall, N.Y. Charter of the village of Whitehall passed March 16th, 1850 and acts amendatory thereto. Whitehall, N.Y. Washington county chronicle print, 1869. 48p. Copy in the Sherman Library, Port Henry.   8063

----. Chamber of commerce. Birthplace of the United States navy. Whitehall, N.Y. 1955. unpaged (8p.) illus.   8064

Willsboro, Essex county, New York...on Lake Champlain where the mountains meet the lake. n.p. n.d. Broadside, green paper, printed in green on both sides and folded into 8p. illus. map. Map is dated 1955.   8065

Wilmington Falls. *Aldine,* 1879. 9:226-27. Illustration by John S. Davis on p.224.   8066

Wineburgh, Dorris. Newcomb in history. n.p. 1916. unpaged (8p.) Copy in the Adirondack Museum.   8067

Wood, Marjorie S. Story of Sabattis. n.p. Watchung area council, Boy scouts of America, 196-? unpaged (19p.) illus. map. mimeographed. Long Lake West, now Sabattis. Copy at the Adirondack Museum.   8068

Young, Charles H. Reminiscences of St. Regis Falls, N.Y. *Franklin Hist R,* Aug. 1965. 2:no.1:21-22.   8069

GEOGRAPHY

GENERAL

Adirondacks. *Woods & Wat,* Summer 1899. 2:no.2:4-6. 8070

The Adirondacks (editorial) *Northeast Log,* July 1957. 6:no.1:18. Brief summary. 8071

Rafinesque, Constantine Samuel. Physical geography. Elevations of land and water, mountains and hills in the state of New York. *In* his Atlantic journal and friend of knowledge, Autumn 1833. 1:188-91. Includes "Region, northern or of Saranac". 8072

EXPLORATION, DESCRIPTION AND TRAVEL

GENERAL

Adirondack park association. Discover New York state's beautiful Adirondack park. Area map and information guide. Adirondack, N.Y. 1965? Broadside, printed on both sides and folded into 6p. illus. map. 8073

----. The Adirondacks invite you. Saranac Lake, N.Y. 1961. Broadside printed on both sides and folded into six sections. illus. (part col.) map. 8074

Adirondack resorts association. The Adirondacks. Buffalo, Cleveland and New York, Matthews-Northrup works, n.d. unpaged (12p. incl. cover) illus. map. Map is ©1922. 8075

----. The Adirondacks: map and directory. Buffalo, N.Y. Whitney, Gresham co. inc. n.d. Broadside printed on both sides, folded into 16p. illus. (part col.) maps. The maps are copyrighted 1932 by B.T. Fay. 8076

----. In the Adirondacks. N.Y. Richardson press. n.d. unpaged (16p.) illus. maps. 8077

The Adirondacks. *Aldine,* Aug. 1873. 6:154-55. illus. Other illustrations on p.158-59. Engravings by F.T. Vance. 8078

The Adirondacks: larger than Yellowstone, Yosemite, Grand Canyon, Glacier and Olympia national parks combined. *Summit,* April 1961. 7:no.4:18-19. 8079

Birmingham, Stephen. The beautiful, bedeviled Adirondacks. *Holiday,* Aug. 1964. 36:no.2:42-47, 89-94, 102. col. illus. incl. port. 8080

Brice, Evelyn. The Adirondacks. *No Country Life,* Winter 1959. 13:no.1:48. 8081

Bryant, F. Hastings. ...Nooks in the north. N.Y. New York view co. ©1887 154p. illus. Copy at the Adirondack Museum. 8082

Central Adirondack association. Central Adirondacks of New York state. Vacationist's directory. Old Forge, N.Y. n.d. 26p. illus. folded map. 8083

Chateaugay fish and game club, inc. Beauty spots in Franklin and Clinton counties, New York. Chateaugay lakes and vicinity... n.p. 1936? unpaged (64p.) 8084

Cole, Thomas. The course of empire, Voyage of life and other pictures of Thomas Cole, N.A. with selections from his letters and miscellaneous writings... N.Y. Cornish, Lampert & co. 1853. 415p. Journey to the Adirondacks with John Cheney as guide, p.373-75. Brief description of Schroon Lake, p.206. 8085

Essex county republican. The heart of the mountains in the beautiful region of the upper Ausable valley. Keene Valley, Keene, Jay, Upper Jay and Wilmington. Keeseville, N.Y. 1902. unpaged (4p.) illus. Supplement to v.4, no.52, Friday Sept. 5, 1902. 8086

An excursion to the Adirondack mountains in the summer of 1861. *Friends In,* 1861-1862. 18:650-52,665-67, 699-701,715-17, 726-28, 742-43. illus. From Westport to Tupper Lake; includes description of the John Brown farm and an ascent of Whiteface. 8087

Extract from a letter describing a visit to the Adirondacks, dated Hudson, 8th mo.3, 1863. *Friends In,* 1863-64. 29:489. Visit to John Brown's grave and description of Dannemora prison. 8088

The favorite summer route to the Adirondacks, Ausable chasm and Whiteface mountain. n.p. n.pub. n.d. Broadside, printed on both sides, folded into 8p. illus.   8089

Freligh, Michael. 1806. Diary of Dr. Michael Freligh's trip from Schenectady to Plattsburgh, N.Y. Rexford, N.Y. Howard I. Becker, 1960. 10p. mimeographed. An extract entitled "A trip to Plattsburgh in 1806" appears in *North Country Notes*, Jan. 1962, no.7:2.   8090

Grey, Sidney. The Adirondacks. *Aldine*, 1879. 9:18-19. Illustration by John S. Davis on p.22.   8091

Hadfield, Joseph. An Englishman in America, 1785, being the diary of Joseph Hadfield; ed. and annotated by Douglas S. Robertson. Toronto, Hunter-Rose co. ltd. 1933. 232p. port. Lake George and Lake Champlain.   8092

Hall, Basil. Travels in North America in the years 1827 and 1828. 3d ed. Edinburgh and London, Robert Cadell and Simpkin & Marshall, 1830. 3v. Includes Trenton Falls, Lake George and Lake Champlain. Title from W.K. Verner.   8093

Hoffman, Charles Fenno. Editorial correspondence. *NY Mirror,* Sept. 23-30, 1837. 15:103,111. Signed:H. Letters from Whitehall and McIntyre describing his journey to the Adirondacks. Introduction to his "Scenes at the Sources of the Hudson" (AB405)   8094

James Bayne co. Among the Adirondacks. Grand Rapids, Mich. n.d. 2v. illus. Entry from cover title. Title pages differ and some pictures are duplicated.   8095

Jefferson, Thomas. Th: Jefferson on birch bark. *Yorker,* Mar.-April 1961. 19:no.4:12-13. facsim. Two letters about trips to the Adirondacks, May-June 1791. Originals in the Morgan Library.   8096

Johnson, Clifton. What to see in America. N.Y. Macmillan, 1919. 541p. plates, figures. Adirondacks, 89-98.   8097

Knight, Ralph. New York wilderness. *Sat Eve Post,* Aug. 27, 1960. 233:no.9:32,52-53,56. col. illus.   8098

Leland, Oscar H. 1834 journey to Lewis. *Reveille,* Nov. 1958. 2:no.14:1,2,4. A letter written in 1892.   8099

Miller, Flora Smith. Sunday rock. *No Country Life,* Fall 1953. 7:no.4:31-33.   8100

Miller, Seaver Asbury. The Adirondacks. *Shoot & Fish,* Oct. 27, 1898. 25:26.   8101

Myers, J.C. Sketches on a tour through the northern and eastern states, the Canadas and Nova Scotia. Harrisonburg, Va. J.H. Wartmann and bros. 1849. 475p. Lake Champlain and Lake George.   8102

Nutting, Wallace. New York beautiful... N.Y. Dodd, Mead, 1927. 305p. plates, front. (col.)

Poem by Mildred Hobbs, "The Adirondack Trail", p.17. Lake George and Lake Champlain.   8103

Our great summer playground... *Munsey,* June 1898. 15:259-84. illus. Includes Adirondacks.   8104

Pomeroy, Mark M. The great Adirondack forest. *Advance Thought,* Aug. 1890. 4:no.1:12-15. Account of a trip to Jock's Lake by one of the founders of the Adirondack League Club. Copy at the Adirondack Museum.   8105

Rath, Frederick L. jr. The Adirondack country. *Yorker,* Mar.-April 1961. 19:no.4:4-7. illus.   8106

Rosenberg, James Naumberg, and MacDougal, Harry M. Adirondacks: area's splendors are unique in America. *County Gov,* July 1961. 11:no.4:6-10. illus.   8107

Secret places of the Adirondacks. *Trailmarker,* July-Aug. 1962. 1:no.2:7. Jock's Lake road near Nobleboro. The May-June issue, 1:no.1:19, featured the site of a long-lost lead mine.   8108

Sellar, Robert. Morven: the Highland United empire loyalist. Huntington, Quebec, Gleaner Bookroom, 1911. 177p. Describes journey through the Adirondack wilderness during the War of the Revolution. Copy in Rare Book Room, McGill University Library.   8109

Silliman, Benjamin. Remarks, made, on a short tour, between Hartford and Quebec, in the autumn of 1819...2d ed. New Haven, S. Converse, 1824. 443p. front. plates. This edition, reprinted from the London edition, has fewer plates than the first edition, New Haven, S. Converse, 1820. Also published under the title: A Tour to Quebec in the Autumn of 1819... Lake Champlain.   8110

Stewart, Donald. A new Holiday shunpike tour - The Adirondacks... *Holiday,* Aug. 1965. 38:no.2:100a-100c, 100f. map.   8111

Stillman, William James. Sketchings: editorial correspondence. *Crayon,* Sept. 25-Oct. 18, 1855. 2:216-17, 232, 264-65, 280-81, 296, 312-13, 328-29,344-45,360. Letters signed W.J.S. describing vacation trip from Newburgh to Saranac Lake, Raquette Pond, Tupper Lake and Long Lake.   8112

Stoddard, Seneca Ray. The Adirondacks. Glens Falls, N.Y. n.d. 8p. text accompanied by plates, accordion binding. Inscribed: Christmas 1888.   8113

----. Picturesque Adirondack resorts; phototype views of Lake George, the Adirondacks and the Hudson river valley... Glens Falls, N.Y. ©1892. unpaged. front. plates. 50 copies printed, variant editions. Maitland de Sormo.   8114

Valley news, Elizabethtown. Visitor's guide to eastern Essex county, Elizabethtown, Westport, Lewis, Essex, Willsboro. Elizabethtown, N.Y. 1958. 12p. folio. Edited by Robert Hall.   8115

Weeks, Charles L. Adirondacks: health and happiness... Schroon Lake, N.Y. 1923. unpaged (8p.)   8116

Wessels, William L. New York's Adirondack trail. *Travel,* Sept. 1965. 124:no.3:38-39. illus.
8117

What to do - what to see this summer in northern New York. *No Country Life,* Summer 1956. 10:no.3:5-14. illus.   8118

Your Adirondack holidays. Old Forge, N.Y. ©1957. 32p. illus. (part col.) col. maps. Promotion literature. Covers are colored view from East Hill, Keene.   8119

THE ADIRONDACK AND STATE LAND SURVEYS
Arranged by date

Colvin, Verplanck. Extract from his Adirondack survey, Sept. 1873. *Backwoods J,* Sept.-Oct. 1963. 7:no.2. unpaged.   8120

Marshall, George. Early Adirondack photography. *Adirondac,* May-June 1956. 20:59. Photographic work for Colvin's Topographical Survey.   8121

OTHER SURVEYS

New York (state) Surveyor-general. Report...in answer to a resolution from the senate...requesting him to furnish them with a statement of the lands owned by the state lying within fifteen miles of the proposed new route for a railroad and slack water navigation recently surveyed by Professor Benedict. Albany, 1846. 5p. (Senate Document 88)   8122

GUIDEBOOKS

Arranged by date

Disturnell, John. The New-York state guide... Albany, 1843. 96p. folded map.   8123

----. The traveler's guide to the Hudson river, Saratoga Springs, Lake George...the Fashionable northern tour through the United States and Canada... N.Y. American news co. ©1864. 324p. front. illus.   8124

Rutland, Ogdensburg and Montreal railway. Plattsburgh route to the Adirondacks. n.p. 1869. 12p. tables, map. Bound in copy of Murray's Adventures in the Wilderness, 1869 (AB 7327)
8125

Bruce, Wallace. Thursty McQuill's tourist guide. n.p. n.pub. 1872. 78p. illus. folded map.   8126

...An illustrated guide-book to the principal summer resorts of the United States, including descriptions of the Hudson river, Saratoga Springs, Lakes George and Champlain... N.Y. American and foreign publications co. 1875. 171p. illus. plates, folded maps. (The "Red and Gold" Guides, no.4) Adirondacks, p.63-99.
8127

Lippincott's Illustrated guide book to the principal summer resorts of the United States... descriptions of the Hudson river, Saratoga Springs, Lakes George and Champlain... Philadelphia, 1876. 175p. illus. folded map. Second edition.   8128

West shore railroad. Summer homes and excursions embracing lake, river, mountain and seaside resorts... N.Y. 1886. 128p. illus. folded map. Adirondacks, p.57-60.   8129

Northern Adirondack railroad company. The northern Adirondacks. n.p. 1889. 64p. illus. folded map.   8130

Central Vermont railroad company. Summer homes among the green hills of Vermont and along the shores of Lake Champlain. St. Albans, Vt. 1894. 143p. plates, tables, maps. Includes a colored folded map of Lake Champlain by S.R. Stoddard. Also published with slight change of title, for 1895-1908, 1910. Copies for 1895, 1903-1904, 1908 in Bailey Collection, Middlebury College.   8131

New York central railroad company. Resorts in the Adirondacks, a region of unsurpassed beauty, a wilderness and yet a paradise. N.Y. 1897. Broadside printed on both sides and folded into 20p. illus. map. (Four-Track Series no. 21) Copy at the Adirondack Museum.   8132

Rutland railroad company. The islands of Lake Champlain and beyond. Rutland, Vt. 1902. 79p. plates, tables. Another edition, published in 1903, unpaged.   8133

Adirondack motor guide. n.p. 191-? 48p. illus. Issued by the Associated Adirondack Hotels and Garages.   8134

Adirondack good roads association. Adirondack mountains. Route book... Saranac Lake, N.Y. n.d. unpaged (20p.) illus. maps. One map is dated 1910.   8135

International railway publishing co. Montreal. All round route and panoramic guide of the St. Lawrence... Montreal, 1910. 384p. illus. maps. Includes Adirondacks and Saratoga Springs.
                                                        8136

Van Noy interstate co. Souvenir and guide thru Lake George and Lake Champlain. n.p. G.F. Williams & sons, printer, 1910? 29p. illus. 8137

Adirondack motor guide... Saranac Lake, N.Y. Adirondack enterprise print shop, n.d. 48p. illus. folded map (dated 1914)   8138

New York central railroad company. The Adirondacks. A region of beautiful, verdure clad mountains... Chicago, Poole bros. 1914. 38p. illus. map.   8139

Delaware & Hudson railroad corporation. The Adirondacks: our great national playground... Chicago, Poole bros. 1930. Broadside printed on both sides and folded into 32p. illus. col. map.
                                                        8140

----. Same. Chicago, Poole bros. 1931. Broadside printed on both sides and folded into 36p. illus. maps.   8141

New York state world's fair commission. Adirondack division. Adirondack region. Souvenir New York world's fair, 1939. N.Y. n.d. unpaged (48p.) illus. map.   8142

Chestertown-Pottersville chamber of commerce. Guide to your holiday in the tri-lakes area of the Adirondacks. Friends lake, Loon lake, Schroon lake... Glens Falls, N.Y. Bullard press, 1956? 36p. incl. covers. illus. (part col.) map.   8143

New York Thruway user's guide, 1957-1958 edition... Albany, New York good roads association, inc. ©1957. 222p. illus. Issued annually. Includes Adirondacks.   8144

Undated

Adirondack motor bus co. inc. By motor bus through the Adirondacks. Saranac Lake, N.Y. Currier press, n.d. Broadside printed on both sides and folded into 8p. illus. map.   8145

Adirondack park association. The Adirondacks invite you. Saranac Lake, N.Y. Currier press, n.d. Broadside printed on both sides and folded into 12p. illus. map.   8146

----. Come to the Adirondacks. Saranac Lake, N.Y. Currier press, n.d. Broadside printed on both sides and folded into 12p. illus. map. 8147

----. Off-the-beaten-path (scenic roads) in the Adirondack park area of New York state... Peter A. Ward, ed. Adirondack, N.Y. n.d. 9 leaves. mimeographed.   8148

Adirondack resorts association. The Adirondacks. Buffalo and N.Y. Whitney-Graham co. n.d. Broadside printed on both sides and folded into 16p. illus. (part col.) maps (one col.) The maps are ©1929.   8149

----. The Adirondacks: map and directory. Albany, n.d. Broadside printed on both sides and folded into 16p. illus. map. Map is ©1947. 8150

Central Adirondack association. The central Adirondacks. Old Forge, N.Y. n.d. Broadside printed on both sides and folded into 16p. illus. maps (part col.) Also another edition, with different illustrations and a map which is ©1930.
                                                        8151

Delaware & Hudson railroad corporation. The Adirondacks, Lake George and Lake Champlain: the summer paradise. n.p. n.d. unpaged (20p.) illus. Cover title: The Summer Paradise in Pictures.   8152

----. The Adirondacks: our great national playground. Albany, n.d. Broadside printed on both sides and folded into 36p. illus. (part col.) col. map.   8153

----. Helpful information for tourists and vacationists in "A summer paradise". The Adirondacks, Lake George, Lake Champlain. Albany, N.Y. n.d. 16p. folded map. Location of hotels and summer camps.   8154

----. The Laurentian. Albany, n.d. 23p. col. maps.   8155

----. Pictorial map of the summer paradise... Albany, n.d. Broadside printed on both sides and folded into 24p. illus. (part col.) map.   8156

----. The summer paradise in pictures. n.p. n.d. unpaged (8p.) illus.   8157

----. Your vacation: what it will cost and where to go...Season of 1893... Albany, Walter & Dickerman, n.d. 33p. illus. tables.   8158

Knight, Arthur S. Picture map of the Adirondacks, Lake George and Lake Champlain... Lake George, N.Y. Adirondack resorts press, n.d. Broadside printed on both sides and folded into 24p. illus. col. map. Map is ©1948.   8159

New York central railroad company. Adirondack mountains and how to reach them... n.p. Rand McNally & co. n.d. Broadside printed on both sides, folded into 48p. illus. map. (Travel Series no. 20)   8160

----. The Adirondack mountains: where lakes, forests, rivers and the eternal hills abound. n.p. n.d. 64p. illus.   8161

GAZETTEERS AND DIRECTORIES

Arranged by date

Child, Hamilton. Gazetteer and directory of Franklin and Clinton counties with an almanac for 1862-3... Ogdensburgh, N.Y. Advance office, 1862? 92p. illus. 8162

Kimball's directory of Plattsburgh, with a business directory of Clinton county. Compiled and published by J.C. Kimball... Watertown, N.Y. Hanford & Wood, v.d. v.p. 1869 issue in the Plattsburgh Public Library. 8163

Webb's Plattsburgh directory... N.Y. W.S. Webb & co. v.d. v.p. Issues for 1875/76/77 in the Plattsburgh Public Library. 8164

Plattsburgh directory for the year 1882-83. Embracing also the residents of West Plattsburgh, South Plattsburgh and Cadyville. Albany, R.S. Dillon & co. n.d. 163p. 8165

The Ned Trick Plattsburg, New York, city directory; master edition... Plattsburg, N.Y. Ned Trick directory service, ©1951- v.p. Supplement edition also issued. Set in the New York State Library. 8166

Manning's Plattsburgh (New York) directory... Schenectady, H.A. Manning co. v.d. v.p. Files at the Plattsburgh Public Library and the State University College Library at Plattsburgh. 8167

Directory of Plattsburgh... Newburgh, N.Y. L.P. Waite & co.v.d. v.p. Files at Plattsburgh Public Library and at the State University College Library, Plattsburgh. 8168

ATLASES

Arranged by date

Cram, George F. co. A descriptive review of the commercial, industrial, agricultural, historical development of the state of NewYork with special charts, detail maps... N.Y. ©1914. 300p. incl. illus. maps, plans. 8169

Lamb, Wallace. Northern New York state: includes Essex, Clinton, Franklin, Jefferson, St. Lawrence and Lewis counties; or, Section XI from Lamb's Sectional historical atlas of New York state... n.p. n.pub. 1956. 26p. illus. maps (one folded) School text. 8170

Huden, John Charles, ed. An English captive's map. Ver Hist, Oct. 1958. 26:301-305. Lake Champlain, about 1755-1759. 8171

Becker, Howard I. comp. Town maps of Saratoga county. Rexford, N.Y. 1959. 75p. maps. Taken from Beers, 1866 (AB 1279) 8172

Huden, John Charles. Historical Champlain maps. Ver Hist, Jan. 1959. 27:34-38. 8173

----. Some early maps depicting the Lake Champlain area, 1542-1792. Burlington, Vt. 1959. 20p. maps. (Monograph no.2) Reviewed by Herman R. Friis in Vermont History April 1960, 28: 166-67. 8174

Resources map of Clinton, Essex, Warren and Washington counties available. Emp State Geo, Fall 1964. 3:no.1:17. Brief note of map issued by New York State Museum and Science Service. 8175

PLACE NAMES

Allen, Herbert C. jr. Mountain names and labels. Adirondac, May - June 1959. 13:54-55. illus. Climbing unnamed peaks. 8176

Barker, Elmer Eugene. Origin of name, Bouquet river. Reveille, April 1967. 1:no.9:1,4. 8177

Clinton county place names. No Country Notes, Nov. 1964; May 1965. no.20:4; no.23:1. 8178

Day, Gordon M. Indian place names. NYS Con, April-May 1960. 14:no.5:42. Letter with answer by W.N. Fenton. 8179

Dorothy, Beulah. How Childwold got its name. Quar, Oct. 1961. 6:no.4:11. 8180

Hagerty, Gilbert. How Eagle lake got its name.

No Country Life, 1958. 12:no.1:8-10. Lake near the Fulton Chain. 8181

Lounsbury, Floyd G. Iroquois place names in the Champlain valley. In Interstate commission on the Lake Champlain basin. Champlain basin, past, present and future... Albany, 1960. (Legislative Document 1960 no.9) Reviewed by C.G. Holland in International Journal of American Linguistics, April 1963, 29:178-80. 8182

Wanakena. Quar, Oct. 1962. 7:no.4:13. Includes letter from L.P. Plumley on origin of name and poem "Wanakena", by Lynette McLaughlin and A.W. Bryce. 8183

Why do they call it...? Trailmarker, May-June, July-Aug. 1962. 1:no.1:30; 1:no.2:6. 8184

ADIRONDACK PRESERVE
THE ADIRONDACK PARK, CONSERVATION

GENERAL AND HISTORICAL

Adirondack Forest preserve honored as "historic landmark". *NYS Ranger Sch,* 1964. p.24-25. Certification by National Park Service.   8185

Adirondack mountain club, inc. Schenectady chapter. Conservation committee. The Forest preserve of New York state: a description of the origins, values and need for protection of our great public forest. Schenectady, N.Y. 1964. 36p. illus. charts, maps. Announced by David L. Newhouse in *Adirondac,* Nov.-Dec. 1964, 28: 85. Reviewed by C. Francis Belcher in *Appalachia,* June 15, 1965, no.35:576.   8186

Apperson, John S. New York state Forest preserve 50th anniversary celebration...Dr. Franklin B. Hough presentation... n.p. n.pub. 1953. unpaged (4p.)   8187

Douglas, William O. A wilderness bill of rights. Boston, Little, Brown, ©1965. 192p. illus. Includes Robert Moses against "Forever wild" and other references to the Forest Preserve.   8188

Fosburgh, Pieter W. New York state's Forest preserve. Albany, N.Y. State conservation department, Division of conservation education, 1965. 16p. illus. (part col.) maps. (Information Leaflet) Reprint of articles in the *Conservationist,* Oct.-Nov. 1963; Dec. 1963-Jan. 1964, April-May 1964. 18:no.2:16-19,28; 18:no.3:18-22,35; 18:no.5:17-21.   8189

Marshall, Louis. Louis Marshall: champion of liberty; selected papers and addresses. Edited by Charles Reznikoff...Philadelphia, Jewish publication society of America, 1957. 2v. illus. (Jacob R. Schiff Library of Jewish Contributions to American Democracy) Ch.X, Conservation, contains addresses and letters on the Forest Preserve, constitutional amendments affecting the Preserve, and the New York State College of Forestry at Syracuse. Reviewed by Edgar B. Nixon in *Adirondac,* July-Aug. 1957, 21:75.   8190

Newkirk, Arthur Edward. The birth and growth of the Forest preserve. *Adirondac,* Nov.-Dec. 1960. 24:108-110, 123. maps.   8191

Pomeroy, Robert Watson. ...150 years of the Forest preserve. *In* New York (state) Legislature. Joint legislative committee on natural resources. Report, 1961. p.199-205. Speech at New York State Conservation Council banquet, Oct. 14, 1960. Extract from this speech issued as an undated 4p. pamphlet, accompanied by reprints of editorials from the Saranac Lake *Adirondack Enterprise,* Feb. 6 and Aug. 17, 1960.   8192

----. Wilderness in the Forest preserve - heritage to be guarded. *NYS Con,* Oct.-Nov. 1960. 15:no.2:5-8. illus. maps. Brief history with report on study by the Conservation Department and the Joint Legislative Committee on Natural Resources.   8193

The 75th anniversary. *NYS Con,* Oct.-Nov. 1960. 15:no.2:1. Establishment of the Forest Preserve. See also article entitled "75th Anniversary Forest Preserve..." in *Reveille,* Sept. 1960. 5:no.19:1,4.   8194

Thompson, Roger C. The doctrine of wilderness: a study of the Adirondack preserve-park. Ph.D. thesis, State University College of Forestry, Syracuse, June 1962. 526 leaves, illus. charts, tables, maps. Typewritten. An article based on this thesis was published with title "Politics in the Wilderness: New York's Adirondack Forest Preserve" in *Forest History,* Winter 1963, 6:no.4:14-23, illus. maps. 8195

1872-1955

This section and the three that follow are arranged by date.

Saving the Adirondacks. *Harpers W,* Jan. 26, 1884. 28:55. Recommends state control rather than state ownership.   8196

Preservation of the Adirondack forests. N.Y. 1884. 4p. Letter from special committee on Preservation of the Adirondack forests of the Chamber of Commerce, New York. Dated Jan. 29, 1884.   8197

Wheatley, Richard. The New York board of

trade and transportation. *Harper W,* April 16, 1892. 36:369-72. illus. port.   8198

Torrey, Raymond Hezekiah. State parks and recreational uses of state forests in the United States... Washington, National conference on state parks, 1926. 259p. illus. tables. Forest Preserve, p.182-87.   8199

The organization that will fight the power and pulp grab. Broadside reprint of an editorial from the Saranac Lake *Adirondack Enterprise,* June 2, 1927.   8200

Association for the protection of the Adirondacks. ...State regulation of private forests... n.p. 1927. Broadside, printed on one side. News release on its "Rescue the Forests" (AB 1719)   8201

New York (city) Board of trade and transportation. Docket...April 13, 1927. N.Y. 1927. 8p. Urges revision of the Hewitt amendment. 8202

----. Docket...March 9, 1927. N.Y. 1927. 8p. Includes "Reforestation of Waste Lands", recommending that the Hewitt amendment be laid over.   8203

Apperson, John S. and others. Comments on the questions and answers appearing in pamphlet distributed by the direction of the New York state reforestation commission on Amendment no.3... Schenectady, N.Y. 1931. unpaged (4p.) Against the amendment.   8204

New York state fish, game and forest league. Before the Senate of the State of New York. In the matter of Senate int.33 pr. no.33 and Senate int.814 pr.no.855. N.Y. 1931. 30p. Opposing Hewitt amendment and supporting Baxter amendment. Signed: W.O. Dapping, President.   8205

Schenectady county conservation council and Mohawk valley towns association. Conservation committee. Tree cutting with your money. n.p. 1931. unpaged (4p.) Against Amendment no.3.   8206

Forest preserve association of New York state, inc. "Resolution no. 82". Schenectady, N.Y. 1934. unpaged (6p.) Proposing federal aid for reforestation.   8207

Apperson, John S. Given before a joint meeting of the Burroughs-Audubon nature club and the

Genesee fish and game association... February 28, 1936. n.p. 1936. 3 leaves.   8208

Whiteface area ski council. Memorandum in support of the Whiteface mountain amendment number 4... n.p. 1941. unpaged (12p.)   8209

Hudowalski, Grace (Leach) The lands of the state. *Fed Gard Clubs NY,* Mar.-April 1946. 18:no.3-4:1,3.   8210

Apperson, John S. Preservation of nature's garden urged by Apperson. Schenectady, N.Y. 1946. Broadside reprint from Schenectady *Gazette,* June 11, 1946.   8211

----. Twenty-fifth anniversary Federated garden clubs of New York state, inc. Talk...March 21, 1949. n.p. 1949. 4p. mimeographed.   8212

Forster, Herman. Commercialization of the Forest preserve. *NYS Con Council,* Feb. 23, 1949. no.89:1-3. map.   8213

Conservationists examine state park cutting policies. *Lumber Camp News,* Feb. 1952. 13: no.10:17,19,21.   8214

Apperson, John S. Confusion in conservation. n.p. 1952. Broadside printed on both sides. Talk before the Federated Garden Clubs of New York State, May 15, 1952.   8215

----. New York's forest areas. Schenectady, N.Y. 1952. Broadside reprint of letter to the *New York Times,* Feb. 29, 1952.   8216

Zahniser, Howard. New York's Forest preserve and our American program for wilderness preservation. Washington, Wilderness society, 1953. 14p. Mimeograph press release, presented to the Joint Legislative Committee on Natural Resources, Jan. 27, 1953.   8217

Oneida county forest preserve council, inc. and others. Comments on Joint legislative committee report, Document 72, 1954. "New York state's natural resources". n.p. 1954. 7p. 8218

Forster, Herman. Power dams in the Forest preserve again? n.p. 1954. Broadside printed on both sides. Panther Mountain reservoir. 8219

Forest preserve association of New York state, inc. Comments...at public hearing February 19, 1955... Schenectady, N.Y. 1955. Broadside.   8220

1956-1959

Goldthwaite, George Edgar. Transmission lines over Adirondacks! *Adirondac,* Jan.-Feb. 1956. 20:10-12. illus.   8221

Milmoe, Wheeler. For the Forest preserve. *NYS Con,* Feb.-Mar. 1956. 10:no.4:3.   8222

Wehle, Louis A. For more public lands. *NYS Con,* Feb.-Mar. 1956. 10:no.4:2.   8223

Mills, Borden H. sr. Panther mountain dam: a post mortem. *Adirondac,* Mar.-April 1956. 20: 28,37. See also letter from C.R. Roseberry and reply by Mills in May-June issue, p.54.   8224

Quiz on the Forest preserve. *NYS Con,* April-May 1956. 10:no.5:8-9,36.   8225

Shorey, Anna (Snow) 1956 legislative report. *Cloud Splitter,* May-June 1956. 19:no.3:2-3.   8226

Adirondack mountain club, inc. Conservation committee. A land purchase program for the New York state Forest preserve. *Adirondac,* Nov.-Dec. 1956. 20:104,109. Also in the *Cloud Splitter,* May-June 1956, 19:no.3:5-6.　　8227

Foss, William M. Recreational needs in state Forest preserve for next ten years. *In* New York (state) Legislature. Joint legislative committee on natural resources. Report, 1956. p.48-54. tables.　　8228

Illick, Joseph S. Study areas in state Forest preserve. *In* New York (state) Legislature. Joint legislative committee on natural resources. Report. 1956. p.68-77.　　8229

Forest preserve association of New York state, inc. Another attack on the Forest preserve. Schenectady, N.Y. 1956. Broadside printed on both sides. Four editions issued. Also in *Adirondac,* July-Aug. 1956. 20:72-73.　　8230

Baar, Charles F. Operation blowdown. A review and final summary. *NYS Con,* Dec. 1956-Jan. 1957. 11:no.3:8-9. illus.　　8231

Adirondack mountain club, inc. New York chapter. Mining and the New York state Forest preserve. *Adirondac,* Jan.-Feb. 1957. 21:12-14,20. Condensed. Includes lists of minerals within and outside of the "blue line"　　8232

----. Campsites in the Forest preserve: a report of the New York chapter's conservation committee. *Adirondac,* Mar.-April 1957. 21:36-38. Includes report on roadside picnic areas in New York state.　　8233

Adirondack aircraft. *NYS Con,* April-May 1957. 11:no.5:42. E.W. Littlefield replies to a query from Robert Snyder. See also letter from R.W. Rehbaum in the October-November issue, p.44.　　8234

Johnson, John W. The northway. *NYS Con,* April-May 1957. 11:no.5:4-5. map. The Superintendent of Public Works gives reasons for choice of route.　　8235

The Milmoe committee and the Forest preserve. *NYS Con,* April-May 1957. 11:no.5:40-41. Milmoe reply to a letter from Mrs. Hobart L. Morris of the Oneida County Forest Preserve Council on the detached parcels issue and the purchase of land for the Forest Preserve. See also letter from Robert G. Drevs in the August-September issue, p.42, with comment by D.G. Rankin. Correction in the October-November issue, p.43.　　8236

Welch, Fay. The Forest preserve in the present decade. *Fed Gard Clubs NY,* April-May-June 1957. 29:no.2:5-8. Covers the period to January 1, 1957.　　8237

Westervelt, Earl A. New legislation-1957. *NYS Con,* June-July 1957. 11:no.6:30-31. Includes Forest Preserve, fish and game.　　8238

Wilm, Harold G. Forests and water...in New York state. *Northeast Log,* July 1957. 6:no.1: 30-31,50. illus.　　8239

Adirondack mountain club, inc. Conservation committee. Club opposes change in constitutional safeguards for the Forest preserve. *Adirondac,* Sept.-Oct. 1957. 21:90-91,99. By John T. Jamison, chairman.　　8240

Ham, Philip W. ...Would lose both money and land. Schenectady, N.Y. 1957. Broadside reprint of letter in Schenectady *Union-Star,* Feb. 9 1957. Issued by the Forest Preserve Association of New York State. Against Milmoe Committee recommendation for Forest Preserve lands outside the blue line.　　8241

Milmoe, Wheeler. Conserving our forest resources. *In* New York (state) Legislature. Joint legislative committee on natural resources. Report, 1957. p.33-38. Abstract of talk given June 30, 1956.　　8242

Welch, Fay. Our New York heritage. 2p. reprint from the *News* of the Federated Garden Clubs of New York State, Inc. Jan.-Feb.-Mar. 1957.　　8243

Hudowalski, Edward C. Letter to the editor. *Adirondac,* Jan.-Feb. 1958. 22:4. On the club's stand against the Adirondack route for the Northway. See comment in letters from Arthur Newkirk, Darwin Benedict and Richard Keller in March-April issue, 22:31-32; also letter from Borden H. Mills, sr. in issue for May-June, 22:66.　　8244

Marshall, George. The need to enlarge the Forest preserve. *Adirondac,* Jan.-Feb. 1958. 22:11-12,14.　　8245

Ward, Peter A. Report of APA meeting. *Adirondac,* Mar.-April 1958. 22:28. Adirondack Park Association opposes purchase of land for the Forest Preserve.　　8246

Price, Fraser P. State and private holdings in roadless Adirondack areas. *Adirondac,* July-Aug. 1958. 22:86-87. tables, map.　　8247

Adirondack mountain club, inc. Conservation committee. Must the northway divide the Adirondacks? Gabriels, N.Y. 1958. unpaged (4p.) illus. diagrs. map.　　8248

New York (state) Conservation department. The Forest preserve; water and wilderness, by Sharon J. Mauhs... Albany, 1958. 10p. Mimeographed press release, Dec. 17, 1958.　　8249

----. "The Forest preserve should not be lumbered". Speech delivered by Sharon J. Mauhs...at the annual meeting of the Oneida lake association on April 23, 1958. Mimeographed release. Reprinted in *Adirondac,* July-Aug. 1958, 22:77-81 and in the *New York State Conservationist,* Aug.-Sept. 1958, with title "Our Forest Preserve". Extracts in *Adirondac*, May-June 1958, 22:62. Abstract in *Living Wilderness*, Autumn 1958, no.64:36-37.   8250

----. Project Forest preserve: address of Conservation commissioner Sharon J. Mauhs. Niskayuna forest, fish and game association... October 23, 1958. Albany, 1958. 5p. Mimeographed press release.   8251

New York (state) Legislature. Joint committee to study assessment and taxation of state lands. Report, 1958. Albany, 1958. 36p. (Legislative Document 1958 no.34)   8252

New York (state) Public works, Department of. Interstate route study F A I 502. Adirondack northway & Lake Champlain route from Glens Falls to Keeseville. Albany, 1958. 41p. chart, maps. mimeographed. Lake Champlain route rejected.   8253

----. Same. Schroon lake area. Albany, 1958. 10p. maps. mimeographed. Advocates route to the east of Schroon Lake.   8254

Oneida county forest preserve council, inc. Champlain northway. The water level route vs. Adirondack mountain northway. n.p. 1958. unpaged (4p.) "The context of this bulletin was prepared by Mr. V.L. Ostrander..." 2d printing issued May 1958 with the Forest Preserve Association of New York State. 8255

----. Notes about the Forest preserve. n.p. 1958. 7p. Reproduced from typewritten copy.   8256

Wilderness in New York. Remarks of Leo W. O'Brien...and speeches of Hon. Sharon Mauhs... and Howard Zahniser. Washington, G.P.O. 1958. 12p. Reprint from *Congressional Record*.   8257

Platt, L.B. Largest park. *NYS Con*, Feb.-Mar. 1959. 13:no.4:42. Letter asking about the Adirondack Forest Preserve, with reply by L.L. Huttleston.   8258

Jamison, John T. The northway. *Adirondac*, May-June 1959. 13:57-58. From the ADK Conservation Committee chairman.   8259

Westervelt, Earl A. Conservation legislation - 1959. Summary and review. *NYS Con*, June-July 1959. 13:no.6:32-33.   8260

Adirondack northway opposed. *Liv Wild*, Autumn 1959. no.70:28-29. Quotes article from the July-September *News*, Federated Garden Clubs of New York State.   8261

Rienow, Robert and Rienow, Leona. Why spoil the Adirondacks. *Harper*, Oct. 1959. 219:no. 1313:74-77. Against the Northway. Reviewed in *Living Wilderness*, Autumn 1959, no.70,p.29.   8262

MacMorran, J. Burch. Adirondack northway. *NYS Con*, Oct.-Nov. 1959. 14:no.2:2-4. illus. map (col.) The Superintendent of Public Works urges passage of amendment; with a letter of support from Conservation Commissioner Harold G. Wilm.   8263

The northway. *Fed Gard Clubs NY*, Oct.-Nov. 1959. 31:no.4:4-10. illus. Well presented arguments against the Adirondack route.   8264

Tubby, Roger W. Forest and highways. *Harper*, Nov. 1959. 219:no.1314:8,10. Letter replying to the Rienow article in the October issue.   8265

Northway goes through. *Nat Parks*, Dec. 1959. 33:no.147:12.   8266

Jamison, John T. The Adirondack northway threat. *Liv Wild*, Winter 1959. no.67:12-14. illus. map. See also brief articles "Adirondack Northway Opposed", p.28 of this issue and another on p.28-29 of the Autumn 1959 issue.   8267

Adirondack northway vote. *Liv Wild*, Winter 1959-60. no.71:43.   8268

Citizens northway committee. Your northway. Points to remember... Schenectady, N.Y. 1959. unpaged (4p.) illus. map. Dated April 1959.   8269

----. Vote "No" on Amendment no.2... Schenectady, N.Y. 1959. unpaged (4p.) illus. 8270

----. Which way northway?... Schenectady, N.Y. 1959. unpaged (4p.) illus. Two editions with slight variations, dated June and July 1959; another edition, 2p. mimeographed, Feb. 1959. This Committee also issued "Citizens' Northway Committee News", July 6 and 10, 1959.   8271

----. When you vote NO on Amendment no.2. Schenectady, N.Y. 1959. unpaged (4p.) illus. map. Text reprinted from Federated Garden Clubs of New York State *News*, July-August-September 1959.   8272

Committee for the Adirondack northway. New York needs the Adirondack northway. Glens Falls, N.Y. 1959. unpaged (6p.) map. 8273

----. Would you throw away $28,000,000? Glens Falls, N.Y. 1959. Folded broadside, printed on both sides. illus.   8274

----. Your Adirondack northway. Glens Falls, N.Y. 1959. unpaged (4p.) map.   8275

Maurer, J. Gilbert. The Champlain northway: a brief for business organizations, New York state. n.p. n.pub. n.d. unpaged (12p.) Issued February 1959, sponsored by the Citizens Northway Committee.   8276

New York (state) Conservation department. The northway, your future scenic highway in the beautiful Adirondacks. Albany, 1959. unpaged (6p.) illus. map. Issued jointly by the Conservation Department, the Joint Legislative Committee on Natural Resources and the Department of Public Works.   8277

New York (state) Public Works, Department of. The Adirondack northway: a study in depth with special emphasis on Glens Falls - Keeseville segment. Albany, 1959. 18p. chart, maps.

mimeographed. Advocates route west of Schroon Lake.   8278

New York citizens committee for preservation of state water resources. The Barge canal & state water resources. Should New York give up control? Albany, 1959. 12p. incl. covers, illus. This Committee also issued two 4p. pamphlets, "Protect Your Water Resources" and "Water Is Precious".   8279

Ostrander, V.L. The northway: Champlain route versus mountain route... n.p. n.pub. n.d. unpaged (6p.) Published February 1959. Favors the Champlain route.   8280

Schaefer, Paul. The Siamese ponds wilderness region. *In* New York (state) Legislature. Joint legislative committee on natural resources. Report, 1959. p.103-107.   8281

1960-1965

Adams, Howland K. "The growing problem in wilderness preservation." *Adirondac*, Jan.-Feb. 1960. 24:10-12.   8282

Wakeley mountain gift. *NYS Con*, April-May 1960. 14:no.5:37. illus. 1200 acre tract given to the state by Finch, Pruyn.   8283

Wilm, Harold G. Multiple land use in New York. *Pulp & Pa*, May 1960. 34:93-95. 8284

Lawrence, Robert L. Legislative roundup. *Adirondac*, May-June 1960. 24:58,59. 8285

New York state conservation council, inc. Stop the Hunter mountain land grab... Troy, N.Y. 1960. unpaged (4p.) illus. Catskill Forest Preserve plan would give precedent for Adirondacks.   8286

Pomeroy, Robert Watson. Wilderness in the Forest preserve: a heritage to be guarded. n.p. n.pub. 1960. unpaged (4p.) maps.   8287

Schaefer, Paul. Report on the Siamese ponds wilderness area. *In* New York (state) Legislature. Joint legislative committee on natural resources. Annual report, 1960. p.35-37. 8288

Stout, Neil. Proposed field study program (Adirondack wilderness area project) *In* New York (state) Legislature. Joint legislative committee on natural resources. Annual report, 1960. p.33-34.   8289

Wilm, Harold G. Summary of remarks regarding role of the Conservation department in the Natural resources committee study program. *In* New York (state) Legislature. Joint legislative committee on natural resources. Annual report, 1960. p.27-28. 8290

King, Lawrence H. Do you want an Arietta speedway? *Adirondac*, Jan.-Feb. 1961. 25:7-10. illus. map.   8291

Roosevelt, Eleanor (Roosevelt) I am pleased... *Adirondac*, Jan.-Feb. 1961. 25:18. On the Forest Preserve.   8292

Mauhs, Sharon J. What price protection - is our Forest preserve in danger?... *Adirondac*, Mar.-April 1961. 25:31-32.   8293

Newkirk, Arthur Edward. The Forest preserve, the blue line and a land purchase program.

Adirondac, Mar.-April 1961. 25:35-36. map.   8294

Newhouse, David L. Legislative roundup. *Adirondac*, Mar.-April, May-June, Sept.-Oct. 1961. 25:34,52,91.   8295

Pomeroy, Robert Watson. A long range program for the Forest preserve. *Con Council Com*, April-May 1961. 1:no.1:3.   8296

Burton, Harold B. To the editor. *Adirondac*, May-June 1961. 25:58. On veto of bill authorizing use of state land on the summit of Whiteface for a commercial television tower. 8297

King, Lawrence H. Always opposing? *Adirondac*, May-June 1961. 25:57.   8298

Newhouse, David L. Wilderness areas in the preserve? *Adirondac*, July-Aug. 1961. 25:72-75.   8299

Reed, Mrs. Susan A. Progress comes to the Adirondacks. *Adirondac*, Sept.-Oct. 1961. 25:92-95. Invasion of the Forest Preserve by totegotes and planes.   8300

Welch, Fay. To the editor. *Adirondac*, Sept.-Oct. 1961. 25:101. On the Pomeroy wilderness bill.   8301

LeMaire, Amy. Vignette of the Forest preserve. *Fed Gard Clubs NY*, Oct.-Nov.-Dec. 1961. 33:no.4:16. Followed by brief article "Danger! Axemen at Work", by A. LeMaire. On dangers of the Wilderness Area bill.
                                              8302

Apperson, John S. To the editor. *Adirondac*, Nov.-Dec. 1961. 25:122. For protection of the Forest Preserve.   8303

Newhouse, David L. Wilderness areas in the Forest preserve: some questions and answers. *Adirondac*, Nov.-Dec. 1961. 25:120-21.
                                              8304

Adirondack mountain club, inc. Do you want a speedway...through the Forest preserve land! Gabriels, N.Y. 1961. unpaged (4p.) illus. maps. Issued October 1961.   8305

----. Conservation committee. Do you want an Arietta speedway? Gabriels, N.Y. 1961. un-

paged (4p.) illus. maps. Reprinted with revisions from *Adirondac*. Revised June 1961.
8306

Crosby, John. ...Mr. Moses in the wilderness. n.p. 1961. Broadside reprint of Crosby's Column, New York *Herald Tribune*, Sept. 25, 1961. On the Forest Preserve.   8307

Forest preserve association of New York state, inc. Is the forest law needed? Schenectady, N.Y. 1961. Broadside reprint of letters to *Herald Tribune* and *New York Times*, Mar. 18 and Mar. 4, 1961.   8308

----. Statement to the Joint legislative committee on natural resources...Sept. 12, 1961. Schenectady, N.Y. 1961. Broadside. 8309

New York (state) Board of Hudson river - Black river regulating district. Reserved for the people: the story of the reservoirs in the Adirondack region. Albany, 1961. unpaged. illus. map.   8310

New York (state) Legislature. Joint legislative committee on natural resources. Public hearing, Indian Lake, New York, August 26, 1961. n.p. 1961. 101p. mimeographed.   8311

----. Same, Kingston, New York, September 16, 1961. n.p. 1961. 85p. mimeographed. 8312

----. Same, Saranac Lake, New York, August 29, 1961. n.p. 1961. 102p. mimeographed.
8313

----. Same, Utica, New York. n.p. 1961. 88p. mimeographed.   8314

----. Supplemental wilderness area findings in the Adirondacks. *In* its Annual report, 1961. p.133-65. Addenda to the 1960 report.   8315

Osborne, Lithgow. Speech at a Cornell university seminar, April 26, 1961. N.Y. 1961. *In* Association for the protection of the Adirondacks. Annual report, April 1961. N.Y. 1961. p.12-15. Strong plea for continuing constitutional protection of the Forest Preserve.
8316

Pomeroy, Robert Watson. An open letter to everyone interested in the Forest preserve. n.p. 1961. unpaged (4p.) Wilderness area bill.
8317

----. Remarks... *In* New York (state) Legislature. Joint legislative committee on natural resources. Annual report, 1961. p.206-11. Speech, Jan. 11, 1961 to the Empire State Products Association. On the work of the Committee.   8318

----. Remarks...before the Eastern New York state chapter of Nature conservancy. *In* New York (state) Legislature. Joint legislative committee on natural resources. Annual report, 1961. p.212-17. On the Forest Preserve.   8319

----. Wilderness in the Forest preserve. A heritage to be guarded. n.p. 1961. unpaged (4p.) table, maps.   8320

Robert Moses replies to N.Y. Times on conservation, n.p. n.pub. 1961. Broadside reprint of *Times* editorial "Forest Preserve in Danger" and letter of rebuttal by Robert Moses. 8321

Gaylord, Levi P.M. The story of river regulating reservoirs in the Adirondacks. *Sup News*, Jan. 1962. 12:no.1:15,33,38. port. In favor of Panther Mountain Reservoir.   8322

Johnson, Grant W. The fabulous 60's, our responsibility. *Sup News*, Jan. 1962. 12:no.1:13, 34,37. port. Economic development vs. "forever wild".   8323

Pomeroy comments on Lefkowitz decision. *Con Council Com*, Jan.-Feb. 1962. 1:no.4:4. Attorney-General's decision confirming the authority of the Conservation Department to regulate or prohibit use of motorized equipment in the Forest Preserve.   8324

Reed, Mrs. Susan A. The selfish people: with these modern gadgets where will be wilderness. *Adirondac*, Jan.-Feb. 1962. 26:4,5,19. Motorists, planes, etc.   8325

Buckheister, Carl W. State wilderness needs protection. *Audubon Mag*, Mar.-April 1962. 64:84-85.   8326

Newhouse, David L. Legislative roundup. *Adirondac*, Mar.-April 1962. 26:31,33.   8327

Pomeroy, Robert Watson. What next for the Joint legislative committee?... *Adirondac*, May-June 1962. 26:43,47.   8328

----. Forest preserve is studied by committee. *Con Council Com*, June-July 1962 1:no. 6:12.   8329

Adirondack mountain club, inc. Conservation committee. Motorized transport in the Forest preserve... *Adirondac*, July-Aug. 1962. 26: 58-60,68.   8330

Douglas, William O. An opinion on wilderness values. *Adirondac*, July-Aug. 1962. 26:55. port.
8331

C., J.B. Adirondack preserve - "Forever wild"? Yes, voters say, but pressures continue to mount. *Am For*, Nov. 1962. 68:no.11:4,53-55. Meeting at Lake Placid of the Natural Resources Council of America.   8332

Pomeroy reports on improved use of recreational facilities. *Con Council Com*, Nov. 1962. 1:no.8:3.   8333

Newhouse, David L. Forest preserve under renewed attack... *Adirondac*, Nov.-Dec. 1962. 26:94-95,97. Also in *Appalachia*, Dec. 1962, no.135:365-68.   8334

Tubby, Roger. Natural beauty vs man-made ugliness. *Ad Life*, Dec. 1962. p.5,12. illus. map.

Plea for a planning program for the Adirondacks. 8335

Apperson, John S. "Forever wild." New York state Forest preserve. Schenectady, N.Y. 1962. 1p. Talk given to the Rotary Club of Schenectady. 8336

New York (state) Legislature. Joint committee on appraisal and assessment of state-owned lands. Minutes of the proceedings of a public hearing...at Albany, New York, July 30, 1962. Albany, 1962. 71p. mimeographed. 8337

----. Same, Albany, New York, October 29, 1962. Albany, 1962. 160p. mimeographed. 8338

Stop tampering with the Forest preserve! Syracuse, N.Y. 1962. Unpaged (4p.) Sponsored by the Schenectady County Conservation Council, New York State Isaac Walton League, Onondaga County Federation of Sportsmen's Clubs and the New York State Conservation Council. 8339

Allen, Herbert C. jr. Forest preserve enlargement... *Adirondac*, Jan.-Feb. 1963. 27:12. 8340

New seaway raises its head. *Fin World*, Feb. 20, 1963. 119:no.8:3-4. map. Proposed Champlain waterway. 8341

Ham, Philip W. Legislative roundup. *Adirondac*, Mar.-April 1963. 27:28. Continued in the May-June issue, p.45. 8342

Forest preserve policy adopted by Joint committee. *Adirondac*, May-June 1963. 27:43. "Conforms with spirit and intent of Article 14, Section 1 and expresses positive philosophy". 8343

Newhouse, David L. Saranac Lake dump proposal on ballot... *Adirondac*, May-June 1963. 27:44,45. 8344

Big Forest preserve tract added under bond act. *Con*, June-July 1963. 17:no.6:35. Gould Paper Company land in Hamilton and Herkimer counties. 8345

Reed, Mrs. Susan A. The old way is for the birds... *Adirondac*, July-Aug. 1963. 27:57. The tote-gote in the wilderness. 8346

Bromley, Albert W. The Forest preserve and the gasoline engine. *Con*, Aug.-Sept. 1963. 18:no.1:2-6. illus. Includes list of Forest Preserve roads closed wholly or in part. 8347

King, Lawrence H. What is the enforcement clause? *Adirondac*, Sept.-Oct. 1963. 27:74,78. In relation to the Forest Preserve. 8348

Adirondack mountain club, inc. Conservation committee. Forest preserve newsletter, no.2. n.p. 1963. 4 leaves. Reproduced from typewritten copy. Dated Oct. 22, 1963. 8349

New York (state) Legislature. Joint committee on appraisal and assessment of state-owned wild forest lands. Report, 1963. Albany, 1963.

44p. (Legislative Document 1963 no.20) 8350

Forest preserve snowmobiles. *Con*, Dec. 1963-Jan. 1964. 18:no.3:36. Brief note on amending regulation closing abandoned and unused roads in the Forest Preserve. 8351

Miner lake gift. *Con*, Dec. 1963-Jan. 1964. 18:no.3:36. Brief note on Clinton County tract given by the Miner Foundation. 8352

Road closures in the Forest preserve. *Adirondac*, Jan.-Feb. 1964. 28:9. 8353

'Jewel of the Adirondacks' donated to New York state. *Con Council Com*, April 1964. 3:no.2:10. Elk Lake. 8354

Elk lake area. *Con*, April-May 1964. 18:no.5: 40. illus. map. Bloomingdale gift. 8355

Ham, Philip W. Legislative roundup. *Adirondac*, Mar. - April 1964. 28:31. Continued in May-June issue, 28:44, with title "Legislative Review." 8356

"Here is your Forest preserve". *Adirondac*, Mar.-April 1964. 28:18. Proposed illustrated lecture. 8357

Peterson, Dutton. New York state's Forest preserve. *N Logger*, July 1964. 13:no.1:10-11, 37. Address given to Empire State Forest Products Association, Albany Jan. 15, 1964. In favor of opening the Forest Preserve to lumbering. 8358

Lawrence, Leo A. ...Accomplishments of the Joint legislative committee on conservation law revisions. *Con Council Com*, Dec. 1964. 3:no. 6:15. 8359

Schaefer, Paul and Ripberger, Robert. Forest preserve committee recommendations. *Con Council Com*, Dec. 1964. 3:no.6:10-11. 8360

Newhouse, David L. Piseco airport amendment. *Adirondac*, Jan.-Feb. 1965. 29:14. 8361

Adirondack forest lands change owners. *N Logger*, Feb. 1965. 13:no.8:40. 8362

Adirondacks registered as landmark. *Con Council Com*, Feb. 1965. 4:no.1:12. Forest Preserve. 8363

Snow buggies and the Forest preserve. *Tahawus Cloudsplitter*, April 1965. 17(i.e.16): no.3:3. 8364

Gardner, John Raymond. To the editor. *Adirondac*, May-June 1965. 29:46. Need for a land-acquisition program to protect the Forest Preserve. 8365

Adirondack mountain club, inc. Conservation committee. No more canvas houses. *Adirondac*, July-Aug. 1965. 29:54-55,57. illus. On new regulation concerning tent platforms in the Forest Preserve. David L. Newhouse, chairman. 8366

Proposed Forest preserve policy. *Con Council Com*, July-Aug. 1965. 4:no.4:9.   8367

Newhouse, David L. Legislative review. *Adirondac*, Sept.-Oct. 1965. 29:80.   8368

Ah wilderness! *Newsweek*, Oct. 25, 1965. 66: no.17:58. Brief account of Rockefeller horseback trip in the Forest Preserve.   8369

King, Lawrence H. Northway "progress" report. *Adirondac*, Nov.-Dec. 1965. 29:94-96. illus.   8370

Schaefer, Paul. Council makes historic decisions setting Forest preserve policy. *Con Council Com*, Dec. 1965. 4:no.6:3.   8371

Williams, L.A. The Forest preserve committee reports. *Con Council Com*, Dec. 1965. 4: no.6:3.   8372

UNDATED

Adirondack civic league for the protection and progress of the Adirondacks. ...Adirondack game park. n.p. n.d. unpaged (4p.) illus.   8373

Citizens committee on the protection of the Adirondack forests. Protection of the Adirondack forests. n.p. n.d. 26p. Petition to the legislature. Copy at the New York State Library.   8374

Defeat the "recreational amendment"... n.p. n.pub. n.d. unpaged (4p.)   8375

New York (state) Conservation department. The northway: your toll-free future highway to the beautiful Adirondacks. Albany, n.d. unpaged. illus. map. Issued jointly by the Conservation Department, the Joint Legislative

Committee on Natural Resources and the Department of Public Works.   8376

New York (state) Public works, Department of. A comparison between the Adirondack northway and the Lake Champlain route with particular reference to recently produced pamphlets. n.p. n.d. 15p. map. mimeographed. Refers to publications of the Oneida County Forest Preserve Council and the Adirondack Mountain Club, inc.   8377

----. The northway and the Adirondack forest: a highway location study. Albany, n.d. 33p. illus. charts, maps. Oblong spiral binder. A brochure describing preliminary studies.   8379

CONSTITUTIONAL CONVENTIONS AND AMENDMENTS AFFECTING THE FOREST PRESERVE

Arranged by date

Apperson, John S. Proposed constitutional convention to be voted on November 3rd. Schenectady, N.Y. Forest preserve association of New York state, inc. 1936. Broadside printed in green ink.   8380

Victory in New York. *Sierra Club Bul*, Jan. 1956. 41:no.1:9. Brief note on defeat of Amendment no.7.   8381

Should the highway amendment be passed? A symposium. *Adirondac*, Mar.-April 1957. 21: 28-31. Includes: The Highway Amendment, by Arthur E. Newkirk; Limited Authorization for Improvement of Existing State Highways in the Forest Preserve, by Wheeler Milmoe; Statement against Proposed Highway Amendment, by Robert Rienow.   8382

Adirondack mountain club, inc. Bouquet river lodge chapter. Let's keep the Forest preserve intact. Schenectady, N.Y. 1957. Broadside. Against Amendments 5 and 6, detached parcels and highway amendments.   8383

Illick, Joseph S. State Forest preserve amend-

ments of 1957. *In* New York (state) Legislature. Joint legislative committee on natural resources. Annual report, 1958. p.81-103.   8384

New York (state) Legislature. Joint legislative committee on natural resources. It's your Forest preserve. Facts about proposed constitutional amendments no.5 and no.6. Albany, 1957. 11p. In favor of the amendments.   8385

Hudowalski, Edward C. New York state barge canal. *Cloud Splitter*, Sept.-Oct. 1959. 22:no. 5:2-9. illus. "A brief history...and the implications of Amendment no.6".   8386

Lawrence, Robert L. The northway. Industrial planning. Conservation. Social planning... n.p. n.pub. n.d. unpaged (4p.) Published February 1959. In favor of the Champlain route.   8387

Adirondack mountain club, inc. Statement... in opposition to the so-called Hunter mountain amendment... n.p. 1960. 2 leaves. Presented Dec. 15, 1960 at the public hearing conducted by the Joint Legislative Committees on Natural Resources and on Winter Tourists.   8388

Schaefer, Paul. The barge canal amendment. *In* New York (state) Legislature. Joint legislative committee on natural resources. Annual report, 1960. p.46.   8389

Mills, Borden H. sr. The vote on amendment seven. *Adirondac,* Jan.-Feb. 1962. 26:9,19.   8390

Welch, Fay. The Anderson-Bartlett bill... *Ad-*

irondac, Jan.-Feb. 1963. 27:8-9,15. To repeal Section 1 of Article 14 of the New York State constitution.   8391

Newhouse, David L. Detached parcels and highway straightening. A look at two constitutional amendments. *Adirondac,* Mar.-April 1963. 27:31. Brief note on the application of amendments approved in 1957.   8391a

LITIGATION

Arranged by date

Shepard, Edward Morse. Before the attorney-general. In the matter of the application of Eric P. Swenson, to bring suit (1) to have the title of thirty thousand acres of land conveyed Cornell University vested forthwith in the name of the people of the State of New York, and (2) to abrogate the contract between Cornell university and the Brooklyn cooperage company. Brief in behalf of the Brooklyn cooperage company... n.p. 1903. 34p.   8391b

New York (state) Court of appeals. People of the State of New York, Irving Langmuir, Kathryn Starbuck, C. Everett Bacon, Kenneth G. Reynolds, John S. Apperson, J. Howard Melish and M.F. Witherell, plaintiffs-appellants against System properties, inc. and the Lake George association, defendants - appellants. County of Warren... defendants-respondents... Brief for the Lake George association, defendant-appellant. N.Y. Bar press inc. 1956. 43p. Argued by Charles H. Tuttle.   8391c

New York (state) Court of appeals. The people of the State of New York et al., appellants-respondents v. System properties, inc. et al. defendants; and Trustees of Dartmouth college et al., appellants-respondents. Argued October 17, 1956; decided February 28, 1957. *In* New York reports, 2d series, v.2,p.330-46. Ticonderoga River a navigable stream, title to bed of stream at dam site was owned by Trustees of Dartmouth College. State has complete sovereign power over water levels of lake and river. Modifies previous decision of the Appellate Division of the Supreme Court (281 App. Div. 433) The following documents are reported by Philip W. Ham as being in the library of John Apperson: Supreme court, State of New York, County of Essex. Reply brief for defendant,

System properties, inc. Sept. 1, 1946. Same; Reply brief for plaintiffs, Irving Langmuir et al. n.d. Record on appeal (lists all attorneys as filed 26 March 1948) 7v. Appellate division, 3d judicial department. Reply brief for plaintiffs-intervenors, Jan. 14, 1953. Same; Brief for defendant-respondent, System properties, inc. Jan. 15, 1953. Same; Reply brief for plaintiff-appellant, Jan. 29, 1956. Court of appeals. Brief for plaintiffs-intervenors-appellants, Feb. 1956 to be argued by Richard D. Moot. Same; answering brief of defendant - Trustees of Dartmouth college as respondents to appeal of plaintiffs - intervenors - appellants, Langmuir et al, April 7, 1956, Randall LeBoeuf, Lamb and Leiby, Attys. Same; Brief for the defendant-appellant, Trustees of Dartmouth college, May 11, 1956, to be argued by R.J. LeBoeuf, jr. Same; Record on appeal, exhibits: Plaintiff's exhibit, Book 1, exhibits 1-109; book 2, exhibits 110-238. Defendant's exhibit, Book 1, exhibits 1 to 64; book 2, Exhibits 65 to 427. Panther Mountain Reservoir suit, South Branch of the Moose River: New York (state) Supreme court. Appellate division. In the matter of the application of the Adirondack league club, petitioner, against the Board of the Black river regulating district and William R. Adams, president...respondents. Brief of petitioner in proceeding no.1, argued by Charles H. Tuttle, May 27, 1949. Same; brief for all petitioners in proceeding no.2, to be argued by Curtiss E. Frank and Milo R. Kniffen. n.d. Same; brief for respondents in both proceedings, to be argued by Daniel Scanlon. 1949. Same; brief for Adirondack league club, appellant, argued by Charles H. Tuttle. n.d. Same; brief for Board of the Black river regulating district, et al., respondents, to be argued by Daniel Scanlon. 1950.   8391d

CONSERVATION

Arranged by date

Small, Edwin Williams. The Adirondack region: a study of its development in relation to the conservation and out-of-doors movements during the nineteenth century. Master's thesis, Yale University, 1934. 155 leaves, plate, maps.

Typescript. Microfilm at the Adirondack Museum.   8392

Hosmer, Ralph Sheldon. Fifty years of conservation. *For Leaves,* April 1935. 25:no.5:65-66.   8393

New York (state) Conservation department. 50

years of conservation in New York state. Official program, Lake Placid, September 12-13-14, 1935. Albany, 1935. 14p. See also two illustrated pamphlets entitled "Fifty years of conservation in New York State, 1885-1935", one 4 pages, the other 8 pages. 8394

Mead, James M. Mead outlines his position on conservation. Schenectady, N.Y. 1946. Broadside reprint of article in Schenectady *Union-Star*, 17 September, 1946. 8395

Conservation advisory committee. *NYS Con,* Feb.-Mar. 1956. 10:no.4:39. Brief account of first meeting. 8396

Nature conservancy. Help to save Dome island, Lake George, New York. Washington, D.C. 1956. Illustrated broadside printed on both sides. 8397

New York (state) Legislature. Joint committee on revision of the conservation law. Memorandum relating to an act to amend the conservation law. Albany. 1957. 4 issues. 8398

----. Report, 1956-1957. Albany, 1957. 144p. illus. (Legislative Document 1957 no.11) Issued yearly through 1963-1964. 8399

Roosevelt, Franklin Delano, President U.S. Franklin D. Roosevelt & conservation, 1911-1945. Compiled and edited by Edgar B. Nixon. Hyde Park, N.Y. Franklin D. Roosevelt library, 1957. 2v. port. facsim. Part I contains numerous references to conservation and the Forest Preserve; text of Roosevelt's speech at Lake Placid, Sept. 14, 1935. v.1,p.429-33. Papers selected are limited to those relating to conservation of "natural and renewable resources". 8400

Hardy, Ruth Gillette. Conservation issues in New York. *Appalachia,* June 1958. no.126:127-28. On the Northway. 8401

Rockefeller conservation policies. *Liv Wild,* Autumn 1958. no.64:33. Brief note of campaign promises. 8402

Simkins, Stephen V.R. Co-operative conservation. *NYS Con,* Dec. 1958-Jan. 1959. 13:no.3:10-11. Black and Long Ponds reclaimed, with the aid of the Conservation Department, by Paul Smith's College. 8403

Plum, Dorothy Alice. Clean roadsides drive. *Adirondac,* May-June 1959. 23:53. Mid-Hudson's anti-litter campaign. 8404

Wilm, Harold G. A platform of conservation for New York state. *Northeast Log,* Sept. 1959. 8:no.3:10-11,44-45. illus. 8405

Fosburgh, Pieter W. The natural thing: the land and its citizens N.Y. Macmillan, 1959. 255p. A collection of essays on conservation, some reprinted from the *New York State Conservationist.* Includes the Forest Preserve. Reviewed by A. B. Recknagel in *Northeastern Logger,* April 1960, 8:no.10:26, and by Clay-

ton B. Seagears in the *New York State Conservationist,* Dec. 1959-Jan. 1960, 14:no.3:48. Also a review in *North Country Life,* Winter 1960, 14:no.1:62-63. 8406

Conservation in New York state. *Appalachia,* June 15, 1960. no.130:123-24. Continued in December 15th issue, no.131:272. 8407

Shirley, Hardy L. Conservation issues in New York state. *In* New York (state) Legislature. Joint legislative committee on natural resources. Annual report, 1960. p.137-44. 8408

Newhouse, David L. Conservation committee report: 1961. *Adirondac,* Nov.-Dec. 1961. 25:118-19. 8409

Kranz, Marvin W. Pioneering in conservation: a history of the conservation movement in New York state, 1865-1903. Ph.D. thesis, Graduate School of Syracuse University, 1961. 621 leaves. Typescript. Microfilm at Adirondack Museum. 8410

New York (state) Conservation department. Welcome. Albany, 1961. unpaged (4p.) illus. Rules and regulations, from the conservation law. 8411

----. Division of conservation education. Public campsite locations and activities map. Albany, 1961. Broadside printed in black and red. 8412

Trefethen, James B. Crusade for wild life: highlights in conservation progress. Harrisburg, Pa. Stackpole, 1961. 377p. (Boone and Crockett Club) The Adirondack deer law, p.72-78. 8413

New York (state) Conservation department. Conservation highlights, 1962- Albany, 1962-date. v.p. Summary of annual report. 8414

----. Welcome to public campsites... Albany, 1962? 4p. illus. Rules and regulations. 8415

Seborg, R.M. and Inverarity, Robert Bruce. Conservation of 200-year-old water-logged boats with polyethylene glycol. *In* Studies in conservation, 1962. 7:111-20. Treatment of colonial bateaux, found under water at Lake George in 1960, with polyethylene glycol 1000 reduces checking and shrinking of wood when exposed to the air. 8416

Cross, Charles W. Wildlife use of small forest clearings in the Adirondacks. MS thesis, State University College of Forestry, 1963. 122p. illus. maps, plates. Typescript. 8417

Oliver, Frank J. Conservation in New York. *Appalachia,* June 1964. no.138:195. 8418

New York (state) Conservation department. Division of lands and forests. Rules and regulations...Lands and forests. Albany, 1964. unpaged (20p.) 8419

Newhouse, David L. Elk lake covenant, *Adirondac,* July-Aug. 1965. 29:48. 8420

Quinn, Doris. Register and vote! and help the C.D. men help you. *Adirondac,* July-Aug. 1965. 29:59. Importance of signing the Conservation Department registers.   8421

Marsh, George Perkins. Man and nature; edited by David Lowenthal. Cambridge, Mass. Harvard university press, 1965. 472p.   8422

New York (state) Hudson river valley commission. The Hudson: biological resources... Iona Island, N.Y. 1965. 43p. maps. Prepared by the New York State Museum and Science Service. Includes a few Adirondack sites.   8423

FORESTRY AND FIRE PROTECTION
Arranged by date

Forest protection. *Harper W,* Dec. 15, 1883. 27:799.   8424

The preservation of forests. *Harper W,* April 14, Aug. 11, 1888. 32:263,587.   8425

Barker, S. Omar. The fire lookout on Baldy. *Am For,* Jan. 1927. 33:no.3:97-98.   8426

Forest preserve association of New York state, inc. Man made fire hazard enemy no.1. Schenectady, N.Y. 1936. Broadside printed on both sides in green ink and folded into 6p. Contains letter to Thomas C. Desmond and Lithgow Osborne from J.S. Apperson.   8427

Dean, Leon W. I became a ranger. N.Y. Farrar & Rinehart, 1938. 240p.   8428

Perpetual forests. N.Y. 1949. Broadside reprint of editorial from the *New York Times,* Nov. 13, 1949.   8429

Hopkins, Arthur S. An adventure in cooperation. The northeastern forest fire protection commission. *State Gov,* Sept. 1954. 27:189-92.   8430

Summer fire situation. *Compact News,* Oct. 1, 1955. no.13:4-8. Contains a letter from S. J. Hyde on control of fires on Long Pond Mountain, Hamilton County.   8431

Holmes, Charles H. Saranac Lake chapter adventure. *Adirondac,* May-June 1958. 22:52. Extinguishing a duff fire.   8432

Baar, Charles F. New York's forest practice act - a progress report. *NYS Con,* Oct.-Nov. 1958. 13:no.2:14-15. illus. tables.   8433

Fisk, M.C. Cedar lakes ranger station. *NYS Con,* Feb.-Mar. 1959. 13:no.4:16-17. illus. See also letter from Fred G. Cornish in Aug.-Sept. issue, p.46.   8434

Forest fires in '58. *NYS Con,* June-July 1959. 13:no.6:41. Summary.   8435

Fowler, Albert Vann. The Long Lake West fire. *NYS Con,* June-July 1959. 13:no.6:43. Letter to the editor with reply by Solon J. Hyde. 8436

Forest fires - '59. *NYS Con,* Feb.-Mar. 1960. 14:no.4:32. Brief note.   8437

A "little" fire. *NYS Con,* Oct.-Nov. 1960. 15:no.2:35. On Wolf Jaw.   8438

Terrific fight with forest fires. How John Anderson and his men held back the flames. *Reveille,* Sept. 1962. 7:no.27:1-3. illus.   8439

Miller, Roland B. Fall forest fires mobilize department. *Con,* Feb.-Mar. 1964. 18:no.4:18-21. col. illus.   8440

Greene, Rodney F. Ranger grads on the Preserve. *Con,* April-May 1965. 19:no.5:46-47. Letter to the editor.   8441

Roden, William M. Lumbering the New York Forest preserve. *Con Council Com,* July-Aug. 1965. 4:no.4:12. On amending "forever wild".   8442

FISH AND GAME
General
Arranged by date

B. The game laws. *Wilkes Spirit,* Sept. 24, 1864. 9:57. Letter in answer to a query in the September 10th issue, p.28. The quail law.   8443

Clay, Cecil. Sticks in a deer's body, by C.C. *For & Stream,* June 29, 1876. 6:337.   8444

New York (state) Laws, statutes, etc. The game laws of the State of New York, 1877. New Hartford, N.Y. Sanford F. Sherman, n.d. 21p. excluding index. Copy at the Adirondack Museum.   8445

Fay, Gaston. The disappearance of game. *Harper W,* Oct. 4, 1884. 28:660.   8446

Danaher, Franklin Martin, comp. The game laws of the State of New York, revised to July 1885. Published under the auspices of the Anglers' association of St. Lawrence river... N.Y. American angler, 1885. 63p.   8447

----. Same, revised to July 1886... Albany, W. W. Byington ©1886. 110p.   8448

----. Epitome of the game law of the State of New York...comp...for Robert Lenox Banks. Albany, 1892. 24p.   8449

Whitaker, Edward G. The New York game code... N.Y. and Albany, Banks and bros. 1893. 115p. Koert Burnham reports 1892 edition, 87p.   8450

Radford, Harry V. A "Sun" mistake. *Woods & Wat,* Autumn, 1898. 1:no.3:4-5. The last Adirondack moose.   8451

Restock the Adirondack wilderness with moose. *Woods & Wat,* Autumn 1899. 2:no.3:9. See also comments entitled: "Bring Back the Moose", Winter 1899-1900, 2:no.4:6-7; and "Restore the Moose", Spring 1900, 3:no.1:8.   8452

F., E.N. Bring back the moose. *Woods & Wat,* Autumn 1900. 3:no.3:15.   8453

Murray, William Henry Harrison. Adirondack Murray on the moose question. *Woods & Wat,* Autumn 1900. 3:no.3:9.   8454

New York (state) Conservation commission. Manual of instructions for game protection... Albany, J.B. Lyon, 1916. 115p. 8455

Duncan, John. Antlers: the life story of the Riding mountain elk. *For & Stream*, Aug. 1924. 94:458-59,497-98. illus. 8456

Experiment of Valcour island: a study of predator control. *NYS Con*, Feb.-Mar. 1950. 4:no. 4:33. Control of grouse and hares. 8457

Patric, Earl F. and Webb, William L. A preliminary report on intensive beaver management. *J For*, Jan. 1954. 52:31-32. At Huntington Forest. 8458

Smith, Ralph H. A history and definition of game ranges in New York state. Albany, N. Y.S. Conservation department, Division of fish and game, Bureau of game, 1954. 55,41p. tables, maps (one folded in pocket) Final Report, Pittman-Robertson Project W-23-R. The Adirondacks, one of the game ranges. Synopsis in *New York Fish and Game Journal*, July 1955, p.128-41. 8459

Black bear in New York. *NYS Con*, April-May 1956. 10:no.5:35. Brief note with map and table of distribution. 8460

Bromley, Albert W. New York's 1955 deer kill. *NYS Con*, April-May 1956. 10:no.5:37. tables. 8461

Black, Hugh C. and Drahos, Nicholas. A bear by the tail. *NYS Con*, Oct.-Nov. 1956. 11:no. 2:28-29. illus. New York's big game investigation program. 8462

Benson, Dirck, Foley, Donald D. and Schierbaum, Donald L. The problem of setting duck hunting seasons in New York. *NY Fish & Game J*, July 1957. 4:194-202. figures, map. Based on aerial survey flights in 1948-52. Includes Champlain Valley. 8463

Seagears, Clayton B. The future of fish and wildlife...in the Adirondacks. *Northeast Log*, July 1957. 6:no.1:26-27, 52-53,70. illus. 8464

Hyde, Solon J. The laws of 1885 ... *NYS Con*, Aug.-Sept. 1957. 12:no.1:37. illus. Reproduction of "Rules and Laws of the Forest Commission", January 1887, with comment by the Superintendent of the Bureau of Fire Control. 8465

Bears and the biologists. *NYS Con*, Oct.-Nov. 1957. 12:no.2:26-27. illus. Tagging New York's largest bear. 8466

Burton, Harold B. I'm glad I'm not a game warden. *Sat Eve Post*, Nov. 23, 1957. 230:no. 21:44-45,53,56,59. illus. 8467

Black, Hugh C. Preliminary report on black bear investigation in New York state. n.p. 1957. 15p. mimeographed. (New England Wildlife Conference Transactions) 8468

New York (state) Conservation department. New York's fish and wildlife management act... Albany, 1957. unpaged. 8469

Wildlife gangsters. *NYS Con*, Aug.-Sept. 1958. 13:no.1:43. Franklin County game violation case. 8470

Black, Hugh C. Black bear research in New York. *In* North American wildlife conference. Transactions, 1958. p.433-61. illus. tables. 8471

----. Second progress report on the black bear investigation in New York state. Washington, North American wildlife conference, 1958. 18p. mimeographed. 8472

New York (state) Legislature. Joint committee on revision of the conservation law. Memorandum...act to amend the adoption of fish and wildlife management practices and to furnishing of benefits... Albany, 1958. 6p. mimeographed. 8473

----. Memorandum...act to amend the conservation law in relation to date of expiration of hunting, fishing and trapping licenses. Albany, 1958. 2p. mimeographed. 8474

----. Memorandum...act to amend the conservation law, the penal law and the code of criminal procedure, in relation to punishments for violations of the fish and game law. Albany, 1958. 7p. mimeographed. 8475

Cheatum, Evelyn Leonard. The fish and wildlife management act: where do we stand and what of the future? *NYS Con*, Feb.-Mar. 1959. 13:no.4:2-5. illus. map. 8476

Severinghaus, C.W. New York's big game take - season of 1958. *NYS Con*, April-May 1959. 13:no.5:18-19. tables. Includes Adirondack figures. 8477

Hall, Albert G. The big game season for 1959. *NYS Con*, Oct.-Nov. 1959. 14:no.2:7. Followed by a two page article "1959 Regulations - Special Deer Seasons" with map. 8478

Finch, Pruyn - a co-operator. *NYS Con*, Dec. 1959-Jan. 1960. 14:no.3:36. Signing Fish and Wildlife Management Act agreement. 8479

Severinghaus, C.W. Big game season - 1959. *NYS Con*, April-May 1960. 14:no.5:14-15,33. tables. Includes summary of deer take in Adirondack area. 8480

Hall, Albert G. Game seasons for '60. *NYS Con*, Aug.-Sept. 1960. 15:no.1:6-8. maps. 8481

Webb, William L. and Patric, Earl F. Seeding herbaceous perennials in forest areas for game food and erosion control. *NY Fish & Game J*, Jan. 1961. 8:19-30. table. At Huntington Wildlife Forest. 8482

Chase, Greenleaf T. A holding pen for varying hares. *NY Fish & Game J*, July 1961. 8: 150-51. illus. At DeBar Mountain Game Management Area in Franklin County. 8483

Shot, wounded and killed. *NYS Con*, Oct.-Nov. 1962. 17:no.2:39. From report of H.H.

Covey in the 1895 report of the New York State Fisheries, Game and Forest Commission. 8484

Free, Stuart. Record black bear. *Con,* Feb.-Mar. 1963. 17:no.4:8.   8485

----. The 1962 big game season. *Con,* April-May 1963. 17:no.5:7-10. charts, tables. Includes Adirondacks.   8486

Free, Stuart and Garland, Larry. Early fall bear hunt - 1963. *Con,* Feb.-Mar. 1964. 18:no. 4:5.   8487

Severinghaus, C.W. and Free, Stuart. The 1963-64 big game season. *Con,* June-July 1964. 18:no.6:10-12. tables. Includes Adirondacks.   8488

Hesselton, William T. Winter deer feeding - good or bad? *Con,* Dec. 1964-Jan. 1965. 19: no.3:8-9. illus.   8489

Free, Stuart. Big game harvest good despite woods closing from fires. *Con,* June-July 1965. 19:no.6:6-8. illus. charts.   8490

Trimm, H. Wayne. Old man from Moose river - an obituary. *Con,* Oct.-Nov. 1965. 20:no. 2:15. illus. A trapped deer used for experimental purposes.   8491

Fish

Adirondack league club. Fishery management reports, 1954- n.p. 1954-date. v.p. multilithed. Issued annually. Edited by Dwight A. Webster.   8492

Morrison, Frank H. A new deal for Pitchfork pond. *NYS Con,* Dec. 1955-Jan. 1956. 10:no. 3:16-17. illus. (part col.) Restocking program.   8493

Pasko, Donald G. Carry Falls reservoir investigation. *NY Fish & Game J,* Jan. 1957. 4:1-31. tables, diagrs. map.   8494

Lake George landlocks - again. *NYS Con,* Feb.-Mar. 1958. 12:no.4:36. Another record salmon.   8495

Youngs, William D. Effect of the mandible ring tag on growth and condition of fish. *NY Fish & Game J,* July 1958. 5:184-204. Includes some Adirondack sites.   8496

Lindsey, James J. The fish car - Adirondack - an era passes. *NYS Con,* Dec. 1958-Jan. 1959. 13:no.3:31. illus. Specially equipped car used by the New York Fish Commission.   8497

----. New York's flying trout. *NYS Con,* April-May 1959. 13:no.5:12-13. illus. Stocking remote Adirondack lakes by plane. List of ponds, p.37. See also letter from Walter Hochschild the October-November issue, p.46.   8498

Adirondack league club. Brandon park fish management reports, 1950-1959 summary. n.p. 1959. 70p. multilithed. Issued annually 1960-1964. Edited by Dwight A. Webster and William Flick.   8499

Lindsey, James J. Pelleted dry food as a total diet for trout. *NY Fish & Game J,* Jan. 1960. 7:33-38. tables. Includes Lake George.   8500

Webster, Dwight A. and Flick, William. Results of planting kokanee salmon in two Adirondack mountain lakes, New York. *Prog Fish Culturist,* April 1960. 2:59-63. charts. At Black Pond on Brandon Preserve and Third Bisby Lake, Adirondack League Club.   8501

Falling fingerlings. *NYS Con,* June-July 1960. 14:no.6:37. Brief note on stocking trout by air.   8502

Webster, Dwight A. Toxicity of the spotted newt...to trout. n.p. 1960. Reprinted from *Copeia,* Mar. 25, 1960. p.74-75.   8503

----. A unusual lake of the Adirondack mountains, New York. *Limn & Ocean,* Jan. 1961. 6:no.1:88-90. Survival of trout in Honnedaga Lake. Also issued as a reprint.   8504

----. Artificial spawning facilities for brook trout... *Am Fish Soc Tr,* April 1962. 91:no.2: 168-74. illus. map, table. East Lake, Sylvan Ponds Outlet, Follensby Jr. Pond and Honnedaga Lake. Also issued as a reprint.   8505

Dean, Howard J. Why the lake trout fry died - D.D.T. *Con,* Dec. 1963-Jan. 1964. 18:no.3: 5-7. illus. chart.   8506

Deer

Adirondack, pseud. Natural selection, a modern instance. *Am Nat,* Dec. 1869. 3:552-53. Spike horned deer.   8507

Severinghaus, C.W. Comparison of live weight of Adirondack and southern tier deer. *Pittman RQ,* July 1946. 6:109-10. Abstract of Wildlife Management Research Project on forest game.   8508

----. Relationship of weather to winter mortality and population levels among deer in the Adirondack region of New York. *In* North American wildlife conference. Transactions, 1947. 12:212-23. figures. Studies made on the Moose River plains.   8509

Webb, William L. Environmental analysis of a winter deer range. *In* North American wildlife conference. Transactions, 1948. 13:442-49.   8510

Air-borne fodder for snowbound deer. *Out Life,* Mar. 1949. 103:no.3:34-5. illus.   8511

Chase, Greenleaf T. and Severinghaus, C.W. Winter deer feeding. Albany, N.Y.S. Conservation department, 1949. 16p. illus. tables. (Fish and Wildlife Information Bulletin no.3)   8512

Notes on "wilderness" deer. *NYS Con,* Dec. 1955-Jan. 1956. 10:no.3:38. illus. From "An analysis of the 1954 special 'wilderness' deer season in the Adirondacks", by C.W. Severinghaus.   8513

Severinghaus, C.W. Road block at Lake George. *NYS Con*, Feb.-Mar. 1956. 10:no.4: 37. Inspection of hunters. 8514

Webb, William L., King, Ralph T. and Patric, Earl F. Effect of white-tailed deer on a mature northern hardwood forest. *J For*, June 1956. 54:391-98. tables, diagrs. At Huntington Wildlife Forest. 8515

Cheatum, Evelyn Leonard. Too many deer? *NYS Con*, June-July 1956. 10:no.6:2-4. illus. 8516

Severinghaus, C.W. Winterkill of deer 1955-56. *NYS Con*, Aug.-Sept. 1956. 11:no.1:11. 8517

Hatch, A.B. Twin Falls deer. *NYS Con*, Oct.-Nov. 1957. 12:no.2:12-13. illus. How private clubs view the one-day doe season. 8518

Deer yard. *NYS Con*, Feb.-Mar. 1959. 13:no. 4:38. illus. 8519

Deer starvation, 1958-59. *NYS Con*, Oct.-Nov. 1959. 14:no.2:34. 8520

Severinghaus, C.W. and Gottlieb, Rosalind. Big deer vs. little deer; food is the key factor. *NYS Con*, Oct.-Nov. 1959. 14:no.2:30-31.col. charts. 8521

Adirondack league club. Deer management studies...1959. n.p. 1960. 12p. 8522

----. Same, 1960-61. n.p. 1961. 10p. 8523

Severinghaus, C.W. The future for deer in New York. *NYS Con*, Oct.-Nov. 1962. 17:no.2:2-4. illus. Includes Adirondacks. 8524

Perkins, George F. Wisdom of deer feeding. *Con*, Feb.-Mar. 1963. 17:no.4:42. Letter with comments by C.W. Severinghaus. 8525

Severinghaus, C.W. and Free, Stuart. Management implications of the trend and distribution of the legal deer kill in the Adirondack region. *NY Fish & Game J*, July 1963. 10:201-14. maps. tables. 8526

Four experts discuss deer management in Forest preserve. *Con Council Com*, Nov. 1963. 2: no.5:9-11. Panel discussion by Harold Wilm, Howard A. Hanlon, Richard H. Pough and Fay Welch. 8527

Severinghaus, C.W. and Tanck, John E. Productivity and growth of white-tailed deer from the Adirondack region of New York. *NY Fish & Game J*, Jan. 1964. 11:13-27. charts, tables. 8528

Moose river deer. *Con*, June-July 1964. 18:no. 6:13-15, 40-41. illus. maps. See also letter from Leo Spinning on p.42 of this issue and one from Cecil Brown on p.45 of the August-September issue. 8529

Krull, John N. Deer use of a commerical clearcut area. *NY Fish & Game J*, July 1964. 11: 115-18. table. At Huntington Forest. 8530

Allen, Herbert C. jr. Domesticated white-tails. Why more deer yards in the Preserve? *Adirondac*, Nov.-Dec. 1964. 28:94. Reprinted from *Conservation Council Comments*, September 1964. 8531

Newhouse, David L. Deer and the Forest preserve... n.p. 1964. p.45-48. Offprint from *Adirondac*, May-June 1964. 28:45-48. 8532

Moose river deer hunt. *Con*, Aug.-Sept. 1965. 20:no.1:38. 8533

SOIL AND WATER CONSERVATION
Arranged by date

Floods and forests. *Harper W*, Mar. 1, 1884. 28:143. 8534

Carr, M. Earl and others. Soil survey of Washington county, New York. Washington, 1912. 105-59p. map, tables. (U.S. Bureau of Soils Report 11, 1909) 8535

Maxon, E.T. and Bromley, J.H. Soils survey of Saratoga county, New York. Washington, 1923. 87-124p. maps, tables (U.S. Bureau of Soils Report 19,1917) 8536

Lounsbury, Clarence and others. Soil survey of St. Lawrence county, New York. Washington, 1925? 44p. maps, tables. (U.S. Bureau of Chemistry and Soils, Soil Management Report Series 1925, no.34) 8537

Lewis, Henry Guy. Soil survey, Herkimer county area, New York, by H.G. Lewis...and E.F. Brookins...and F.B. Howe and D.F. Kinsman. Washington, 1929. 1601-1648p. maps (one folded) (U.S. Bureau of Chemistry and Soils, Soil Management Report Series 1923, no.46) 8538

U.S. War department. Chief of engineers. Big Chazy river, N.Y. Letter from the Secretary of war transmitting report...on Big Chazy river, N.Y., covering navigation, flood control, power development, and irrigation. Washington, 1930. 27p. tables. (U.S. Congress. 71st Congress, 2d Session, House Document 490) 8539

James, Emerson W. Stream development. A basic work-plan standardizing some of the fundamentals of stream improvement. n.p. ©1935. unpaged (15p.) Reproduced by photo-offset. Title from Koert Burnham. 8540

Morhouse, Lyman A. Logic and local color. n.p. n.pub. 1942. Broadside reprint of letter in Ticonderoga *Sentinel*, April 23, 1942. Lake George water level. 8541

Causes affecting water levels of Lake George being investigated. *L Geo Mirror*, July 23, 1943. 40:no.4:3,7. 8542

Attorney general says state will appeal Ryan decision on fixing of Lake George levels. n.p. n.pub. 1947. Broadside reprint of news release and letter from J.S. Apperson to Glens Falls *Times*, Oct. 17, 1947. 8543

Decision in water level case hailed by Charles H. Tuttle as assuring lake protection. n.p. n. pub. 1947. Folio broadside. Includes letter from J.S. Apperson, Oct. 14, 1947. 8544

Statement by Attorney general regarding Lake George case is attacked by Assemblyman Reoux. n.p. n.pub. 1947. Broadside reprint of article in Glens Falls *Times* and letter from J.S. Apperson, Oct. 17, 1947. 8545

Wm. G. Huckle assails Reoux resolution on Lake George dispute. n.p. n.pub. 1948. Broadside reprint of letter to Glens Falls *Times,* Mar. 6, 1948. 8546

Lake George protective association, inc. Lake George. n.p. 1950. unpaged (5p.) Includes supplement to 2d edition of "Lake George Water Level History" issued by the Forest Preserve Association of New York State, Inc. August 1948. 8547

Cline, Marlin G. Soils and soil associations of New York. Ithaca, N.Y. 1955. 64p. illus. maps (one folded) (New York State College of Agriculture, Cornell Extension Bulletin 930) Revised 1961. 8548

Lake George association. Wake up, Lake George! Fight the repeal of the Lake George anti-pollution statute... Diamond Point, N.Y. 1955. 7p. 8549

Feuer, Reeshon and Johnsgard, Gordon A. Washington county soils. Ithaca, N.Y. Cornell university, 1956. 6p. text on verso of folded map. (Soil Association Leaflet 6) 8550

World famous scenery being destroyed. *Adirondac,* July-Aug. 1957. 21:67-69,77. illus. Lake George. Also issued as a reprint. 8551

Adirondack mountain club, inc. Bouquet river lodge chapter. New law does not solve problem of Lake George water levels. Schenectady, N.Y. 1957. Broadside. 8552

Lake George protective association, inc. Lake George a mill pond, previously unlawful but now authorized by the Legislature. Bolton Landing, N.Y. 1957. Oblong leaflet, unpaged (12p. incl. cover) illus. Exhibits showing damage caused by high water level. 8553

Miner, Norman H. Watershed hydrology applied to two Adirondack streams. MS thesis, State University College of Forestry, 1957. 71p. illus. 8554

Wilm, Harold G. Forest watershed problems in New York State. *In* Society of American foresters. Proceedings, 1957. Washington, 1958. p.28-29. 8555

Adirondack mountain club, inc. Conservation committee. Lake George and the continuing blunder. n.p. 1958. unpaged. illus. Extract in *Adirondac,* Sept.-Oct. 1958, 22:99. 8556

U.S. Department of agriculture. Soil survey. Franklin county, New York. Washington, 1958.

75p. folded maps (part col.) (Series 1952,no.1). Issued by Soil Conservation in cooperation with the Cornell University Agricultural Experiment Station. 8557

Adirondack mountain club, inc. ADK requests action. Gabriels, N.Y. 1959. unpaged (4p.) Urges club support for bill to provide closer control of water levels in Lake George. 8558

Decision expected on Lake George water level bill. n.p. n.pub. 1959. unpaged (4p.) Reprints of newspaper articles and letters. 8559

Flach, Klaus, Cline, Marlin G., and Feuer, Reeshon. Clinton county soils. Ithaca, N.Y. Cornell university, 1959. 6p. text on verso of folded map. (Soil Association Leaflet 8) 8560

Forest preserve association of New York state, inc. Decision expected on Lake George water bill. n.p. 1959. Broadside, printed on both sides. Reprint of newspaper articles, issued March 16, 1959. Attached is a one-page report from E. MacD. Stanton, made in 1932. 8561

Van Dyke, W.C. Electrical features of the upper Raquette river power project. N.Y. American institute of electrical engineers, 1959. 16p. charts, maps. (Conference Paper) 8562

Martin, Roscoe C. Water for New York: a study in state administration of water resources. Syracuse, N.Y. Syracuse university press, ©1960. 264p. Includes the Adirondacks. 8563

New York (state) Temporary state commission on water resources planning. Progress report. Dynamic planning: first step in water resources planning for New York state. Albany, 1960. 260p. illus. (Legislative Document 1960 no.24) 8564

Pearson, C.S., Cline, Marlin G. and Stone, Earl L. Soil survey of Lewis county, New York. Washington, 1960. 107p. fold.maps. (U.S. Soil Conservation Service, Soil Survey, Series 1954 no.10) 8565

New York (state) State soil conservation committee. Twenty years of soil and water conservation in New York state...1940-1960. Ithaca, N.Y. 1961. 16p. illus. 8566

Newhouse, David L. Huckleberry lake. *Adirondac,* Jan.-Feb. 1964. 28:8. Proposed construction of dam and reservoir on the Salmon River. 8567

Eschner, Arthur R. Forest protection and streamflow from an Adirondack watershed. Ph.D. thesis, State University College of Forestry, 1965. 210p. illus. typescript. 8568

New York (state) Hudson river valley commission. The Hudson river as a resource... Iona Island, Bear Mountain, N.Y. 1965. v.p. maps, charts. Prepared by the New York State Conservation Department, Division of Water Resources. 8569

----. Statements submitted to the commission at public meetings; Warren county center - August 16, 1965 and Rensselaer polytechnic institute, Troy - August 17, 1965. Iona Island, Bear Mountain, N.Y. 1965. 56,40p. illus. map. Reproduced from typewritten copy.   8570

U.S. Department of agriculture and Department of the interior. Wild rivers. Washington, 1965. 44p. illus. (part col.) Printed with private funds. Includes the Hudson in rivers chosen for preliminary study.   8571

Wilm, Harold G. ...Pattern for action: water and recreation resources. Berkeley, Cal. University of California School of forestry, 1965. 33p. port. (Horace M. Albright Conservation Lectureship V) New York program.   8572

Undated

Water level dispute is described by a shore owner on Lake George. n.p. n.pub. n.d. Broadside reprint of letter to *Gazette*.   8573

Lake George association. Helpful hints on sanitation. Diamond Point, N.Y. n.d. unpaged (4p.)
8574

NATURAL HISTORY

GENERAL

Anderson, Richard, ed. Crane mountain cave... *Speleo Dig,* 1958. p.86-92. maps. Contents: Geology by George W. Moore; Hydrology, by John Spence; Mineralogy, by Lawrence O. Chapman.   8575

Barker, Eugene and Barker, Edna. Our field trip with sixth grade pupils. *Cloud Splitter,* Sept.-Oct. 1960. 23:no.5:3-6. Includes student reports on nature walk.   8576

Butcher, O.L. Predators of the Adirondacks. *Con,* Aug.-Sept. 1963. 18:no.1:41-42.   8577

Cox, Donald D. Some postglacial forests in central and eastern New York state as determined by the method of pollen analysis. Albany, University of the State of New York, 1959. 52p. figures, map. (New York State Museum and Science Service Bulletin 377) Includes three Adirondack bogs.   8578

Davis, James F. Field guide to the central portion of the southern Adirondacks. Albany, New York State Museum and Science Service, 1962. 34p. illus. mimeographed. (Educational Leaflet Series no.12)   8579

Dayton, Roy. The Adirondack climate: some notes and comparisons. *J Outd Life,* May 1931. 28:314-16,331-32. illus.   8580

Drahos, Nicholas. Museum in the sky: a weather laboratory is in the making on the roof of New York. *NYS Con,* Aug.-Sept. 1958. 13: no.1:13,36. illus. On Whiteface Mountain. 8581

Fowler, Albert Vann. The great windfall of 1845 in New York state. Reprinted from *Weatherwise.* Aug. 1961, 14:142-46. illus. maps. Reprinted in *The Quarterly,* January 1962, 7:no.1:8-9,12. maps.   8582

Frederick, R. H. and others. Spring and fall freezing temperatures in New York state. Ithaca, N.Y. New York state college of agriculture, 1959. 15p. charts. (Cornell Miscellaneous Bulletin, 33) Includes Adirondack stations.   8582a

Fuller, A.R. Spring at Meacham lake. *For & Stream,* June 17, 1876. 6:301. Record of birds and weather, Mar. 15-May 16, 1876.   8583

Hogan, Ray. Forest forecast. *Trailmarker,* July-Aug. - Oct.-Nov. 1962; Mar. 1963; Summer 1963. 1:no.2:29; 1:no.3:6; 1:no.4:28; 2:no. 1:8. The weather.   8584

Ketchledge, Edwin H. Changes in the forests of New York. A review of the forces that shaped our forests and how some will continue to transform our woodlands. Reprinted from the N.Y. State Conservationist, Feb.-Mar. 1965. Albany, N.Y.S. Conservation department, 1965. 4p. illus. (Information Leaflet)   8585

----. The ecology of a bog. *Con,* June-July 1964. 18:no.6:23,26-27. illus.   8586

Lull, Howard W. and Rushmore, F.M. Snow accumulation and melt under certain forest conditions in the Adirondacks. Upper Darby, Pa. 1960. 16p. illus. (Northeastern Forest Experiment Station, Paper no. 138)   8587

Myers, Frank J. Rotifera from the Adirondack region of New York. *Am Mus Nov,* Jan. 13, 1937. no.963:1-17. Includes Caroga Lake, Peck Lake, Van Denburg Pond, Canada Lake, Pine Lake, Stoner Lakes, Lake Pleasant, Piseco Lake and Sacandaga Reservoir. 8588

Narten, Perry F. and McKeown, Francis A. A reconnaissance of radio-active rock of the Hudson valley and Adirondack mountains, New York. Prepared by the Geological survey for the U.S. Atomic energy commission, technical information service. Oak Ridge, Tenn. 1952. 54p. diagrs. maps (one folded in pocket) (U.S. Atomic Energy Commission TEI 70) Abstract in Selected Annotated Bibliography of the Uranium Geology of Igneous and Metamorphic Rocks in the United States. p.235-36. (U.S. G.S. Bulletin 1059-E)   8589

Neth, Paul C. Changes in bottom fauna production and an evaluation of a bottom sampling problem in Panther lake, New York. n.p. Adirondack league club, 1965. 36p. (Special Report) Title from Dwight A. Webster. 8590

Ogden, Eugene C. and Lewis, Donald M. Airborne pollen and fungus spores of New York state. Albany, 1960. 104p. charts. (New York State Museum and Science Service Bulletin 378) Includes Adirondack stations.   8591

Ogden, Eugene C. Survey of airborne pollen and fungus spores of New York state. A preliminary report. Albany, 1957. 62p. charts. (New York State Museum and Science Service Bulletin 356) Includes Adirondack stations.   8592

Rockwell, Landon G. The great avalanche on Giant... *Adirondac,* Sept.-Oct. 1963. 27:68-70,73. illus. See also notes in the July-August issue, p.62.   8593

Smith, Milford K. Life of the wild. *Ver Life,* Summer 1959. 13:no.4:8-20. illus. Champlain Valley.   8594

Tester, Jefferson. Condensation nuclei counts on the slopes of Little Whiteface mt. in New York state. *Pure & App Geophy,* 1964. 57: 181.   8595

Trembley, Charles C. Tracks in the snow, by C.C.T. *J Outd Life,* Jan. 1907. 3:456-59. illus.
                                                      8596

ENTOMOLOGY

Collins, Donald L. and Yops, Chester J. Paradise at Paradox. *NYS Con,* June-July 1956. 10:no.6:8-10. illus. Blackfly control.   8597

Comstock, G.F. A list of lepidoptera found in the Adirondack mts. Extract from *Entomological News,* June 1903, p.197-200.   8598

DDT. *NYS Con,* June-July 1957. 11:no.6:44-45. Minert E. Hull's criticsm of article on blackfly control in June-July 1956 issue is answered by Donald L. Collins.   8599

Dowden, Philip Berry. Endemic populations of the spruce budworm in the Adirondacks. *J Econ Ent,* Aug. 1961. 54:811-12. table. 8600

Fox, Herbert S. Black-flies. *Con,* June-July

1963. 17:no.6:41. Letter with comment by Donald L. Collins.   8601

Hammer, O.H. Champlain valley has own insect problems. *Farm Res,* Oct. 1935. 2:no. 1:12.   8602

Jamnback, Hugo A. and Collins, Donald L. The control of blackflies (Diptera:Simuliidae) in New York. Albany, 1955. 113p. illus. tables, maps. (New York State Museum Bulletin 350) Control measures in the central Adirondacks.
                                                      8603

Miller, Alfred F. Insect pests and the Forest preserve: a New York chapter conservation committee report. *Adirondac,* Sept.-Oct. 1960. 24:92-94.   8604

GEOLOGY

GENERAL

Arranged by date

Raymond, Percy E. Crown Point section. April 1, 1902. Ithaca, N.Y. Cornell university, 1902. 44p. plates, front. folded map. (Bulletins of American Paleontology, vol.3,no.14)
                                                      8605

Kay, George Marshall. Stratigraphy and structure of eastern New York and western New England. 1939. 18 leaves, map. Page proof of a part of "Geologie der Erde, North America", v.2 which was to have been published by Borntrager, Berlin in 1939. Copy at Columbia University.   8606

Fountain, Lawrence F. Evolution of land utilization in the Adirondack massif. Ph.D. thesis, Clark University, 1941. 451p. Typescript.
                                                      8607

New York state geological association. Guidebook for the 26th annual field meeting at Plattsburg, N.Y. May 18-19. n.p. 1951. 26p. illus. maps. Reproduced from typewritten copy. With this is "Supplementary Guidebook to

Chazyan Stratigraphy" by Philip Oxley, 6 leaves.   8608

Walton, Matt Savage, jr. The geologic setting of Adirondack ore deposits. *In* American institute of mining and metallurgical engineers. Industrial mining division. 1954 fall meeting program, p.4-6. Citation taken from Berry thesis.   8609

Galloway, Jesse James and St. Jean, Joseph jr. The type of the stromatoporoid species *Stromatocerium rugosum* Hall. *Am Mus Nov,* May 11, 1955. no.1728. 11p. Fossil from Chazy.
                                                      8610

Graham, John Warren. Paleomagnetism and magneto-striction. *J Geophys Res,* Dec. 1956. 61:735-39. illus. Discussed in *Advances in Physics,* July 1957, 6:362-63.   8611

New York (state) State museum and science service. Geologic map of New York. Albany, 1961. (Map and chart series no.5) Consists of maps and text entitled "The Geology of New York State". Text available separately. Includes references to two unpublished studies:

Krieger, Medora (Hooper) Geology of the Indian lake quadrangle, New York (1:62,500) U.S. Geological survey, 1951; Rogers, C.L. Raquette lake quadrangle, (1:62,500). 1940-41.
8612

Isachsen, Y.William. Geological history of the Adirondack mountains. *NYS Con,* June-July 1962. 16:no.6:27-31. col. illus. table. The "Geological Paintings" illustrating this article are in the Whiteface Mountain Museum (*New York State Conservationist,* Oct.-Nov. 1962, 17:no.2:38)
8613

Geological society of America. Petrologic studies: a volume in honor of A.F. Buddington... N.Y. 1962. 660p. illus. port. maps (part folded, one col.) diagrs. tables. Includes "Progressive Metamorphism and Amphibolite, Northwest Adirondack Mountains, New York", by A.E.J. Engel and C.G. Engel.
8614

Simmons, Marvin Gene. Gravity survey of Adirondack area. Ph.D. thesis, Harvard University, 1962. 145p. maps, figures, tables. Typescript.
8615

Rowley, Elmer B. Geology and mineralogy of the Adirondack mountain region. Lake Placid, N.Y. Northland rock and mineral club, 1963. 34p. port. illus. map. "Rare-earth Pegmatite Discovered in Adirondack Mountain Area, Essex County, New York", p.20-34. Up to date, popular account with emphasis on minerals. A.N.
8616

Walton, Matt Savage, jr. and DeWaard, Dirk. ...Orogenic evolution of the precambrian in the Adirondack highlands, a new synthesis. Reprinted from Proceedings, Series B. 66:no.3, 1963. Konikl. Nederl. Akademie van Wetenschappen, Amsterdam. p.98-106. charts, maps.
8617

Ross, June Phillips. Champlainian cryptostome bryozoa from New York State, *J Paleontology,* Jan. 1964. 38:1-32. illus. tables, map. Includes the Adirondacks.
8618

Simmons, Marvin Gene. Gravity survey and geological interpretation, northern New York. *Geol Soc Am Bul,* Feb. 1964. 75:81-98. illus. tables.
8619

Hills, Allan and Gast, P.W. Age of pyroxene-hornblende granitic gneiss of the eastern Adirondacks by the rubidium-strontium whole-rock method. *Geol Soc Am Bul,* Aug. 1964. 75:759-66. Also in its Special Paper 76, 1963, p.80.
8620

Isachsen, Y. William. Extent and configuration of the precambrian in northeastern United States. *NY Acad Sci Tr,* May 1964. ser. 2:812-29. maps. Minor mention of the Adirondacks.
8621

Cantwell, T., Galbraith, J.N. jr. and Nelson, P. Deep resistivity results from New York and

Virginia. *J Geophys Res,* Oct. 15, 1964. 69: 4347-76. illus.
8622

Hoering, T.C. and Hart, R.A. A geochemical study of some Adirondack graphites. *In* Carnegie institution. Year book, 1963-64. Washington, 1964. 63:265-67. tables.
8623

New York state geological association. Guidebook, 36th annual meeting, Syracuse, 1964. N.Y. City college, Department of Geology, 1964. 124p. illus.
8624

Taylor, Hugh P. jr. Isotopic evidence for larger-scale oxygen exchange during metamorphism of Adirondack igneous rocks. *In* Geological society of America. Special paper 76, 1964. p.163-64. Abstract.
8625

THE CHAMPLAIN AND HUDSON VALLEYS

Arranged by date

Hitchcock, Charles Henry. Surfacial geology of the Champlain basin. *In* Vermont. State geologist. Report, 1909-10. p.199-212. illus.
8626

Stone, Donald Sherwood. Origin and significance of breccia along northwestern side of Lake Champlain. *J Geol,* Jan. 1957. 65:85-97. illus. incl. geol. map.
8627

Swain, Frederick M. Early middle ordovician ostracoda of the eastern United States. Part I-II... *J Paleon,* May 1957; July 1962. 31:528-70;36:719-44. illus. tables. Includes Champlain Valley specimens.
8628

Shaub, Benjamin Martin. Magnetite anomalies of the Ticonderoga N.Y. quadrangle. Albany, New York state science service, 1958. 13p. illus. (Report of Investigation no.5)
8629

Oxley, Philip and Kay, George Marshall. Ordovician Chazyan series of Champlain valley, New York and Vermont, and its reefs. *Am Ass Pet Geol Bul,* April 1959. 43:817-53. illus. maps.
8630

Ward, Richard F. Geology of the Hudson. *NYS Con,* June-July 1959. 13:no.6:16-19. col. illus. col. chart, col. maps. Abridged in *North Country Life,* Fall 1959, 13:no.4:44-47.
8631

New England intercollegiate geological conference. Stratigraphy and structure of west central Vermont and adjacent New York. Guidebook for the fifty-first annual meeting...October 17-18, 1959. Rutland, Vt. 1959. 87p. illus. maps. E-an Zen, editor.
8632

Berry, Richard Harry. Part I: Precambrian geology of the Putnam-Whitehall area, New York. Ph.D. thesis, Yale University, 1961. 60 leaves, col. photographs, chart, tables, map. Typescript. With this is bound: Part II: The origin of gneiss with anorthositic and charnockitic affinities, Putnam-Whitehall area, New York, by Richard H. Berry and Matt Walton. 1961. 42 leaves. photographs (part col.) chart, maps.
8633

OTHER LOCALITIES

Arranged by date

Diment, William Horace. A regional gravity survey in Vermont, western Massachusetts, and eastern New York. Ph.D. thesis, Harvard University, 1953. 176p. maps, diagrs. Typescript. 8634

Howd, Frank Hawver. Geology of the northwest quarter of the Bolton quadrangle, New-York. M.S. thesis, University of Rochester, 1953. 167 leaves, mounted illus. maps (one col. folded in pocket) Typescript. 8635

Buddington, Arthur Francis. Correlation of rigid units, types of folds and lineation in a Grenville belt. *Roy Soc Canada Proc,* 1955. 3d ser. 49:App.C45. Abstract. Meeting of June, 1955. 8636

Walton, Matt Savage, jr. Precambrian geology of the Paradox lake and Ticonderoga 15 minute quadrangles. *In* New England intercollegiate field conference. Field guide. Ticonderoga, 1955. p.3,4. Title from Berry thesis. 8637

Gillson, Joseph Lincoln. Genesis of titaniferous magnetites and associated rocks of the Lake Sanford district, New York. *In* American institute of mining engineers. Mining branch. Transactions, Mar. 1956. 205:296-301. illus. 8638

Brown, John S. and Engel, A.E.J. Revision of Grenville stratigraphy and structure in the Balmat-Edwards district, northwest Adirondacks, New York. *Geol Soc Am Bul,* Dec. 1956. 67:1599-1622. 8639

Buddington, Arthur Francis. Interrelated precambrian granitic rocks, northwest Adirondacks, New York. *Geol Soc Am Bul,* Mar. 1957. 68:291-306. plate. figures, tables. Twenty-one new chemical analyses of five major types of granitic rocks. 8640

Fisher, Donald W. Mohawkian (middle ordovician) biostratigraphy of the Wells outlier, Hamilton county, New York. Albany, University of the State of New York, 1957. 32p. plate, illus. maps (one folded) (New York State Museum and Science Service Bulletin no.359) 8641

Engel, Albert Edward John and Engel, Celeste G. Progressive metamorphism and granitization of the major paragneiss, Adirondack mountains, New York. Part 1: Total rock; Part 2: Mineralogy. *Geol Soc Am Bul,* Nov. 1958; Jan. 1960. 69:1369-1414; 71:1-58. charts (part fold.) maps, tables. 8642

Engel, Celeste G. and Engel, Albert Edward John. Progressive metamorphism of amphibolite, northwest Adirondack mountains, New York. *Geol Soc Am Bul,* Dec. 1958. 69:1559. Abstract. 8643

Putnam, George Wendell. The geology of some wollastonite deposits in the eastern Adirondacks, New York. M.S. thesis, Pennyslvania State University, 1958. 107 leaves. col.map in pocket. Typescript. 8644

Collins, Lorence Gene. Geology of the magnetite deposits and associated gneisses near Ausable Forks, New York. *Diss Abs,* Nov. 1959. 20:no.5:1739. 8645

Theokritoff, George. Taconic sequence in northern Washington county, New York. *Geol Soc Am Bul,* Dec. 1959. 70:1686-87. Abstract. 8646

Engel, Albert Edward John and Engel, Celeste G. Migration of elements during metamorphism in the northwest Adirondack mountains, New York. *In* U.S. Geological survey. Geological survey research, 1960. p.B465-70. charts. 8647

Buddington, Arthur Francis and Balsley, James Robinson jr. Micro-intergrowths and fabric of iron-titanium oxide minerals in some Adirondack rocks. *In* Krishna, M.S. ed. A collection of geological papers in commemoration... of Prof. C. Mahadevan. Hyderabad, India, 1961. p.1-16. 8648

DeWaard, Dirk. ...Tectonics of a metagabbro laccolith in the Adirondack mts. and its significance in determining top and bottom of a metamorphic series. Reprinted from Konikl. Nederl. Akademie van Wetenschappen, Amsterdam. Proceedings, series B. 1961. p.335-42. charts. 8649

Engel, Albert Edward John and Engel, Celeste G. Variations in properties of hornblendes formed during propressive metamorphism of amphibolites, northwest Adirondack mountains, New York. *In* U.S. Geological survey. Short papers in the geologic and hydrolic sciences. Articles 147-292. Washington, 1961. p. C313-16. tables, map. (U.S. Geological Survey Professional Paper 424C) Written jointly with R.G. Havens. 8650

Heyburn, Malcolm. Geologic mapping with the aid of magnetics, Tahawus area, New York. N.Y. 1961. (AIME Preprint no.61L13, Feb. 26, 1961) 8651

Engel, Albert Edward John and Engel, Celeste G. Hornblendes formed during progressive metamorphism of amphibolites, northwest Adirondack mountains, New York. *Geol Soc Am Bul,* Dec. 1962. 73:1499-1514. charts, tables, map. 8652

Buddington, Arthur Francis. Regional geology of the St. Lawrence county magnetite district, northwest Adirondacks, New York. Washington, 1962. 145p. illus. plates, maps in pocket. Written jointly with B.F. Leonard. 8653

DeWaard, Dirk ...Structural analysis of a precambrian fold: the Little Moose mountain syncline in the southwestern Adirondacks. Reprinted from Konikl. Nederl. Akademie van Wetenschappen, Amsterdam. Proceedings, series B. 1962. p.404-17. charts (one folded)   8654

Buddington, Arthur Francis, Fahey, J.J. and Vlisdis, A.C. Degree of oxidation of Adirondack iron oxide and iron-titanium oxide minerals in relation to petrogeny. *J Pet* (eng) 1963. 4:no.1:138-69.   8655

Davis, Brian Thomas Canning. Geology of the St. Regis quadrangle, New York, Ph.D. thesis, Princeton University, 1963. 196 leaves. maps and charts in pocket. Typescript.   8656

Eckelmann, F. Donald. Preliminary zircon data bearing on the origin of alaskite phacoliths, northwest Adirondacks. *Am Geophys Union Tr,* Mar. 1964. 45:127-28. Abstract.   8657

Theokritoff, George. Taconic stratigraphy in northern Washington county, New York. *Geol Soc Am Bul,* Mar. 1964. 75:171-90. illus. map.   8658

Denny, Charles S. and Postel, A. Williams. Rapid method of estimating lithology of glacial drift of the Adirondack mountains, New York. *In* U.S. Geological survey. Professional paper 501B. Washington, 1964. p.143-45. tables.   8659

DeWaard, Dirk. Metamorphic grade of the Adirondack highlands - the Sillimanite-mangerite subfacies. *In* Geological society of America. Special paper 76. N.Y., 1964. p.44. Abstract.   8660

----. Notes on the geology of the south central Adirondack highlands. *In* New York state geological association. Guidebook, 36th annual meeting. N.Y. 1964. p.3-17. charts, maps.   8661

Leonard, Benjamin Franklin 3d and Buddington, Arthur Francis. Ore deposits of the St. Lawrence county magnetite district, northwest Adirondacks, N.Y. Washington, U.S. Geological survey, 1964. 259p. plates in separate case. (Professional Paper 377)   8662

MINERALOGY

Altmann, Heinz C. To the editor. *Adirondac,* Jan.-Feb. 1964. 28:15. Iron spring on Giant Mountain.   8663

Aye, Tin. X-ray study of biotite from the Scott mine, Sterling lake, New York. Ph.D. thesis, University of Illinois, 1958. 60p. Microfilm. In *Dissertation Abstracts,* November 1958. 19:1053.   8664

Balsley, James Robinson jr. and Buddington, Arthur Francis. Iron-titanium oxide minerals, rocks and aeromagnetic anomalies of the Adirondack area, New York. *Econ Geol,* Nov. 1958. 53:777-805. illus. Discussion by W.J. Bichan in May 1959 issue, 54:512-15.   8665

----. Magnetic susceptibility, anistropy and fabric of some Adirondack granites and orthogneisses. *Am J Sci,* 1960. 258A:6-20. map, diagrs. tables.   8666

Balsley, James Robinson jr. and Buddington, Arthur Francis. Remanent magnetism of the Russell belt of gneisses, northwest Adirondack mountains, New York. *Ad Phys,* July 1957. 6:317-22. illus.   8667

Balsley, James Robinson jr. Remanent magnetization and anistropic magnetic susceptibility of Adirondack rocks. Ph.D. thesis, Harvard University, 1960. "Thesis consists of five published articles by the author alone or in conjunction with other geologists". K.C. Elkins, Harvard College Archives.   8668

Balsley, James Robinson jr., Buddington, Arthur Francis and Fahey, Joseph John. Titaniferous hematite and ilmeno-hematite correlated with inverse polarization in rocks of the northwestern Adirondacks, New York. *Am Geophys Union Tr,* 1953. 33:320. Abstract.   8669

Bartholomé, Paul M. Structural and petrological studies in Hamilton county, New York. Ph.D. thesis, Princeton University, 1956. 211p. Microfilm. In *Dissertation Abstracts,* 1957. 17:598.   8670

Brown, John S. and Kulp, J. Laurence. Lead isotopes from Balmat area. *Econ Geol,* Jan.-Feb. 1959. 54:137-39.   8671

Brown, John S. Occurrences of jordanite at Balmat, New York. *Econ Geol,* Jan.-Feb. 1959. 54:136-37.   8672

Cole, G. Glyndon. Potsdam sandstone. *No Country Life,* Winter 1958. 12:no.1:11-16. illus.   8673

De Rudder, Ronald Dean, and Beck, Carl W. Clinozoisite from the Willsboro wollastonite deposit, New York. *In* Geological society of America. Special paper 76. N.Y. 1964. p.42-43. Abstract.   8674

De Rudder, Ronald Dean. Mineralogy, petrology and genesis of the Willsboro wollastonite deposit, Willsboro quadrangle, New York. Ph.D. thesis, Indiana University, 1962. 156 leaves. Typescript.   8675

Description of the iron mountain of New York... Albany, Weed, Parsons & co.1869. 12p. On Lake Champlain between Westport and Essex. 8676

DeWaard, Dirk and Romey, W.D. ...Boundary relationships of the Snowy mountain anorthosite in the Adirondack mountains. Reprinted from Konikl. Nederl. Akademie van Wetenschappen, Amsterdam. Proceedings, series B, 1963. 66:no.5:251-64. charts, map. 8677

DeWaard, Dirk. Garnet development and garnet isograds in the granulite facies terrane of the Adirondack highlands. *Am Geophys Union Tr,* 1964. 43:128. Abstract. 8678

----. Mineral assemblages and metamorphic subfacies in the granulite-facies terrane of the Little moose mountain syncline, south-central Adirondack highlands. *K N Akad Wet Proc,* series B, 1964. 67:344-62. chart, map. Also issued as a reprint. 8679

Doe, Bruce R. Distribution and composition of sulfide minerals at Balmat, New York. *Geol Soc Am Bul,* July 1962. 73:833-54. tables, maps. 8680

Engel, Albert Edward John, Engel, Celeste G. and Havens, R.G. Mineralogy of amphibolite interlayers in the gneiss complex, northwest Adirondack mountains, New York. *J Geol,* Mar. 1964. 72:131-56. illus. 8681

Engel, Albert Edward John and Engel, Celeste G. Variations in the properties of a paragneiss and its constituent minerals, biotite, garnet and feldspar, as a function of kind and degree of metamorphism. *Geol Soc Am Bul,* Dec. 1955. 66:1554. Abstract. 8682

Gillson, Joseph Lincoln. Genesis of titaniferous magnetites and associated rocks of the Lake Sanford district, New York. *Min Eng,* Mar. 1956. 8:296-301. illus. 8683

Gosse, Ralph C. A fabulous find of gem tourmaline in New York state. *Lapidary J,* Oct. 1962. 18:680-82. Adirondack site. 8684

----. Some notes on the Batchellerville, New York quarry. *Rocks & Min,* July-Aug. 1963. 38:no.7-8:402-403. 8685

Hagner, Arthur Feodor, Collins, Lorence Gene and Aye, Tin. Genesis of the Scott magnetite deposit, Sterling lake, New York. *Min Eng,* Dec. 1958. 10:1246. Abstract. 8686

Hagner, Arthur Feodor and Collins, Lorence Gene. Host rock as a source of iron, Ausable Forks magnetite district, New York. *Econ Geol,* Nov. 1959. 54:1352. Abstract. Also in the Geological Society of America *Bulletin,* Dec. 1959. 70:no.12,pt.2:1613-14. 8687

Hays, Walter Wesley. A statistical analysis of magnetic susceptibilities and ore content of the Sanford lake titaniferous magnetite deposit, New York. M.A. thesis, Washington University (St. Louis) 19⁵9. 53 leaves. illus. charts, maps. Typescript. 8688

Kays, Marvin Allan. Petrographic and modal relations, Sanford hill titaniferous magnetite deposit. *Econ Geol,* Sept.-Oct. 1965. 60:no.6: 1261-97. 8689

----. Petrography of the Sanford hill titaniferous magnetic deposit, Essex county, New York. Ph.D. thesis, Washington University (St. Louis) 1961. 127 leaves. illus. charts, map. Typescript. 8690

Leonard, Benjamin Franklin 3d and Buddington, Arthur Francis. Iron ores of St. Lawrence county, northwest Adirondacks, New York. *In* U.S. Geological survey. Short papers on geologic and hydrolic sciences. Articles 1-146... Washington, 1961. p.B76-80. map. (U.S. Geological Survey Professional Paper 424B) 8691

Levin, Samuel Benedict. Genesis of some Adirondack garnet deposits. Baltimore, 1950. p.519-65. illus. maps. Columbia University thesis reprinted from Geological Society of America *Bulletin,* June 1950, 61:519-65. 8691a

Lindberg, Marie Louise and Ingram, Blanche. Rare-earth silication apatite from the Adirondack mountains, New York. *In* U.S. Geological survey. Professional paper 501B. N.Y. 1964. p.B64-65. tables. 8692

Linehan, Edward J. Who says rock hounds are crazy? *Town Journal,* Aug. 1955. p.28,64-65. Includes description of trip to Gore Mountain. 8693

Luedke, Elaine M., Wrucke, Chester T. and Graham, John A. Mineral occurrences of New York state with selected references to each locality...contributions to economic geology. Washington, G.P.O. 1959. 44p. folded map in pocket. (U.S. Geological Survey Bulletin 1072-F) Arranged by mineral. 8694

McKeown, Francis Alexander and Klemic, Harry. Rare-earth-bearing apatite at Mineville, Essex county, New York... Washington, 1956. 23p. tables, charts (U.S. Geological Survey Bulletin 1046-B) 8695

The mineral industries of New York state. *Bus NY,* Nov. 1962. p.1-6. illus. Brief data on National Lead at Tahawus, Benson Mine at Star Lake and Cabot Mine at Willsboro. 8696

Postel, Albert William. Silexite and pegmatite in the Lyon mountain quadrangle, Clinton county, New York. Albany, University of the State of New York, 1956. 23p. (New York State Museum and Science Service Circular 44) 8697

Prucha, John James. A petrogenic study of the Hermon granite in a part of the northwest Adirondacks. Ph.D. thesis, Princeton University, 1950. 113p. In *Dissertation Abstracts,* 1955, 15:no.4:561. 8698

Romey, William D. and De Waard, Dirk. Evoluation of anorthosite and associated rock suite in the Snowy mountain dome, Adirondack highlands. *In* Geological society of America. Special paper 76. N.Y. 1964. p.140. Abstract.
8700

Rowley, Elmer B. Epidote and allanite at Schroon lake, N.Y. *Rocks & Min,* Sept.-Oct. 1957. 32:451-61. illus.   8701

----. Huge tourmaline crystals discovered. *Min Mag,* Feb. 1942. 10:47-48,63-64.   8702

----. Monazite and cyrtolite crystals at Day, N.Y. *Rocks & Min,* July-Aug. 1960. 35:328-30. illus.   8703

----. Rare-earth pegmatite discovered in Adirondack mountain area, New York. *Rocks & Min,* July-Aug. - Sept.-Oct. 1962. 37:341-47, 453-60. illus.   8704

Schaller, Waldemar Theodor and Hildebrand,

Fred A. A second occurrence of the mineral sinhalite (2MO.Al$_2$O$_3$B$_2$O$_3$) *Am. Min;* May-June 1955. 40:453-57. illus. tables. Warren county.   8705

Silver, Leon T. Isotope investigations of zircons in precambrian igneous rocks of the Adirondack mountains, New York. *In* Geological society of America. Special paper 76. N.Y. 1964. p.150-51. Abstract.   8706

Stivers, Van W. Sacandaga river (N.Y.) labradorite. *Rocks & Min,* July-Aug. 1961. 36: 364-65.   8707

Van Wie, Adin W. Something new added... *Rocks & Min,* Sept.-Oct. 1960. 35:481. Overlook collecting area on the eastern shore of the Sacandaga Reservoir.   8708

Wentorf, Robert H. jr. The formation of Gore mountain garnet and hornblende at high temperature and pressure. *Am J Sci,* July 1956. 254:413-19. illus. tables.   8709

PLANT SCIENCE

Ketchledge, Edwin H. Checklist of the mosses of New York state. Albany, New York state Museum and science service, 1957. 55p. map. (Bulletin 363) Includes Adirondack area. 8710

Luther, Herbert S. Bushy bears. *NYS Con,* Oct.-Nov. 1962. 17:no.2:45. Asks identification of small trees with berries, attractive to bears.   8711

New York (state) State museum and science service. Symposium on botanical exploration in New York state...October 28, 1960. Albany, 1962. 26p. mimeographed.   8712

New York (state) State university college of forestry, Syracuse. Nature trail on the Archer and Anna Huntington wildlife forest, Newcomb, N.Y. n.p. 195-? unpaged (16p.) figures. Reproduced from typewritten copy. Preface signed by William L. Webb and Earl F. Patric.
8713

Phelps, Orra A. Some Adirondack ferns. *Adirondac,* July-Aug. 1960. 24:74,76.   8714

Saxton, Stanley E. Daylilies in the Adirondacks.

Herbertia, 1945. 12:151-54.   8715

----. Northern New York daylily evaluations. *Herbertia,* 1948. 15:32-37.   8716

Sayles, John M. Big pines. *NYS Con,* Aug.-Sept. 1959. 14:no.1:44. illus. A stand of giant pine in southeastern St. Lawrence county.
8717

Townsend, Mrs. Winfield A. Birdsfoot trefoil... *Gard Club,* Jan. 1957. 45:no.1:25.   8718

Virgil, Erwin E. Yew. *NYS Con,* Feb.-Mar. 1959. 13:no.4:43. Letter with answer by Earl A. Westervelt.   8719

Willsboro garden club. Wild flowers of Essex county, N.Y. found and identified by the members...1933 and 1934. n.p. n.d. 13 leaves, folded. mimeographed. Copy in the Keene Valley Public Library.   8720

Woodin, Howard E. Establishment of a permanent vegetational transect above timberline on Mt. Marcy, New York. *Ecology,* April 1959. 40:320-22. diagr. table. Also issued as a reprint.
8721

ZOOLOGY

GENERAL

Gibbs, Robert H. The chorus frog, Psuedacris nigrita, at Plattsburgh, New York. *Copeia,* Dec. 19, 1957. no.4:311-12.
8722

FISH

Bean, Tarleton Hoffman. Fish planting in public waters. A guide for stocking the inland waters of New York state with food and game fish. Albany, J.B. Lyon, 1916. 24p.   8723

Bieber, C.K. "Worms" *NYS Con,* April-May 1959. 13:no.5:45. Brief letter with reply by C. W. Green, on leeches as parasites on Lake Champlain smelt.   8724

Brigham, R.W. Lake Colden trout. *NYS Con,* Dec. 1957-Jan. 1958. 12:no.3:46. Letter with comment by R.G. Zilliox.   8725

Creaser, Edwin P. Adirondack jellyfish. *NYS Con,* June-July 1960. 14:no.6:31. illus. At Loon Lake.   8726

Cross, Elvin W. Schooling. *NYS Con,* Dec. 1959-Jan. 1960. 14:no.3:45. Letter on migration of fish in Lake Champlain with reply by John R. Greeley.   8727

Deuel, Charles L. Splake in New York. *NYS Con,* June-July 1958. 12:no.6:13. illus.   8728

Fish leeches. *NYS Con,* Oct.-Nov. 1958. 13:no.2:44. Letter from Harold S. Moore with reply by John R. Greeley.   8729

Flick, William A. and Webster, Dwight A. Comparative first year survival and production in wild and domestic strains of brook trout, *Salvelinus fontinalis. Am Fish Soc Tr,* Jan. 1964. 93:58-69. Also issued as a reprint.   8730

----. Problems in sampling wild and domestic stock of brook trout... *Am Fish Soc Tr,* April 1962. 91:140-44. tables. Also issued as a reprint.   8731

Greeley, John R. Landlocking Atlantic salmon. *NYS Con,* June-July 1956. 10:no.6:28-30. col. illus. Followed by a short article entitled: And Speaking of Salmon...Fish Taken in Lake George.   8732

Green, David M. jr. A comparison of stamina of brook trout from wild and domestic parents. *Am Fish Soc Tr,* Jan. 1964. 93:96-100. Also issued as a reprint.   8733

Greene, Robert L. Blue perch. *NYS Con,* Feb.-Mar. 1958. 12:no.4:45. Letter describing fish caught in Lake Champlain, with reply by John R. Greeley.   8734

Hatch, Richard W. Regular occurrence of false annuli in four brook trout populations. *Am Fish Soc Tr,* Jan. 1961. 90:6-12. At East Lake, Panther Lake, Upper and Lower Sylvan Ponds. Also issued as a reprint.   8735

Hatch, Richard W. and Webster, Dwight A. Trout production in four central Adirondack mountain lakes. Ithaca, Cornell university, 1961. 81p. charts, tables. (Cornell University Agricultural Experiment Station Memoir 373)   8736

Lake Champlain smelt. *NYS Con,* Feb.-Mar. 1959. 13:no.4:38.   8737

Lalime, Wendell. Lake Champlain's mysterious walleyes. *Ver Life,* Spring 1954. 8:no.3:48-52. illus. map.   8738

Miller, Roland B. 1957 - record year for Lake George landlocks. *NYS Con,* Oct.-Nov. 1957. 12:no.2:38.   8739

Pearce, William A. Fulton chain salmon. *NYS Con,* Feb.-Mar. 1960. 14:no.4:27. illus.   8740

Peters, F. Northern pike. *NYS Con,* Dec. 1958-Jan. 1959. 13:no.3:46. Letter with answer by Robert G. Zilliox.   8741

Schofield, Carl L. jr. Water quality in relation to survival of brook trout, *Salvelinus fontinalis* (Mitchill) *Am Fish Soc Tr,* July 1965. 94:227-35. charts.   8742

VanDercook, C.E. Lake George salmon. *NYS Con,* June-July 1960. 14:no.6:46. Letter with reply by John R. Greeley.   8743

Zilliox, Robert G. and Youngs, William D. Further studies on the smelt of Lake Champlain. *NY Fish & Game J,* July 1958. 5:164-74. illus. charts, diagrs. map.   8744

Zilliox, Robert G. Old acquaintance renewed. *NYS Con,* June-July 1958. 12:no.6:36. Tagged fish.   8745

----. Raquette patriarch. *NYS Con,* Dec. 1958-Jan. 1959. 13:no.3:37. illus. Lake trout.   8746

----. Splake. *NYS Con,* Dec. 1956-Jan. 1957. 11:no.3:47. In answer to a letter from Harry A. Hosley.   8747

----. The walleyes of Lake Champlain. *NYS Con,* April-May 1962. 16:no.5:10-11,34. illus. map.   8748

BIRDS

Bagg, Egbert. Nesting of *Certhia familiaris. Nutt Orn C Bul,* July 1879. 4:183. At Moose Pine, Hamilton County.   8749

Benson, Dirck and Foley, Donald D. Hatching dates of waterfowl in New York. *NY Fish & Game J,* July 1962. 9:73-92. charts, tables, map. Includes central Adirondacks.   8750

Delafield, Harriet L. Blue grosbeak at Port Kent. *Kingbird,* Oct. 1964. 14:215-16.   8751

----. Region 7 - Adirondack-Champlain. *Kingbird,* Jan., May, July, Oct. 1964; Jan., May, July, Oct. 1965. 14:48-51,112-13, 175-78,232-34; 15:45-48,119-21,181-84,224-28. Editor of bird reports.   8752

Foley, Donald D. and Benson, Dirck. Ringnecks in the Adirondacks. *NYS Con,* Dec. 1959-Jan. 1960. 14:no.3:29-30. col. illus. See also letter from Stan B. Wade in the February-March issue, p.47.   8753

Hutchinson, Jane. Adirondack chickadee; or, The case of the missing Sailor. *NYS Con,* Feb.-Mar. 1959. 13:no.4:22,36. illus.   8754

Lesperance, Thomas A. ed. Region 7 - Adirondack-Champlain. *Kingbird,* Oct., Dec. 1960; May, July, Oct. Dec. 1961; May, July Oct. Dec. 1962; Jan. May, July, 1963, 10:113-15,195-97;   11:61-64,116-19,170-72,224-26;12:

48-49,103-105,158-60; 13:45-47,117-18,173-75. The report appeared in 13:222-23 with no official editor. In the Oct. 1963 issue Harriet L. Delafield is announced as future editor.   8755

Merriam, Clinton Hart. The olive-sided fly-catcher. *Am Nat,* Dec. 1873. 7:750. In Lewis, Herkimer and Hamilton counties.   8756

Murphy, Robert William. The peregrine falcon, illustrated by Teco Slagboom. Boston, Houghton, Mifflin, ©1963. 157p. illus. The Adirondacks, p.64-71.   8757

New York (state) State museum and science service. Preliminary annotated checklist of New York state birds, by E.M. Reilly and K.C. Parkes. Albany, 1959. 42p. mimeographed.
                                                                                    8758

Pettingill, Olin Sewall. Bird finding in the Adirondacks. *Aud Mag,* May-June 1963. 65:138-41. port. map.   8759

Pettingill, Olin Sewall and Hoyt, Sally F. Enjoying birds in upstate New York... Ithaca, N.Y. Cornell university laboratory of ornithology, 1963. 89p. illus. tables, map. Includes Adirondack sites.   8760

Sheffield, Robert and Sheffield, Mary. Nesting of the Philadelphia vireo in the Adirondacks. *Kingbird,* Oct. 1963. 13:204-205.   8761

MAMMALS
General

Adirondack grays. *NYS Con,* Dec. 1957-Jan. 1958. 12:no.3:33. Gray fox.   8762

Beaver, otter, fisher harvest. *NYS Con,* Oct.-Nov. 1959. 14:no.2:41. Summary.   8763

Bromley, Albert W. ...Adirondack coyotes. *NYS Con,* Feb.-Mar. 1956. 10:no.4:8-9. illus. map.   8764

----. Aerial beaver survey. *NYS Con,* Feb.-Mar. 1956. 10:no.4:34-35. map.   8765

Cats. *NYS Con,* Oct.-Nov. 1958. 13:no.2:44. illus. Two letters on bobcats.   8766

Chased by a panther. *Sport NY,* Mar. 25, 1876. 6:no.146:16. illus. Photostat at the Adirondack Museum.   8767

Cook, David B. and Hamilton, William J. The forest, the fisher and the porcupine. *J For,* Oct. 1957. 55:719-22. illus. map.   8768

Curtiss, Arthur Leslie Byron- My last visit with John Burroughs. *Aud Mag,* Sept.-Oct. 1959. 61:222-24. ports. Beaver in the Adirondacks.   8769

Dauphine, T. Charles jr. Biology and ecology of the muskrats on a central Adirondack area. M.S. thesis, State University College of forestry, 1965. 141p. illus.   8770

Haines, Elijah. A panther fight. *NY Mirror,* July 15, 1837. 15:23. Brief note.   8771

Hamilton, William J. jr. Late fall, winter and early spring foods of 141 otters from New York. *NY Fish and Game J,* July 1961. 8:106-109. table.   8772

Hamilton, William J. jr. and Cook, David B. A note on the fisher. *J For,* Dec. 1958. 56:913. Trapping statistics.   8773

Harper, Francis. The ways of chipmunks. *In* Boston society of natural history. Bulletin. April 1927. 43:3-9. illus.   8774

Jacob, C. Albert jr. Mink-watching at Stumpville. *NYS Con,* June-July 1960. 14:no.6:12-14. illus. Loon Lake, Warren County.   8775

Martin, John Stuart. Behold the peripatetic coyote. *Sports Illus,* Mar. 23, 1959. 10:no.12: 40-41. illus. Includes the Adirondack area. See also article entitled "Coy-dog" in *New York State Conservationist,* June-July 1958, 12:no. 6:36, illus.   8776

Mech, David. The coyote comes east. *Adirondac,* May-June 1959. 23:52-53.   8777

Morehouse, Frank. Coyotes. *NYS Con,* June-July 1959. 13:no.6:46. Letter to the editor.   8778

Mowery, William Byron. America's newest wild animal. *Sat Eve Post,* Mar. 16, 1957. 29: no.37:51,137-141. illus.   8779

"Otterly" fantastic. *Tahawus Cloudsplitter,* May 1964. 5:no.5:13. illus. Brief note on otter caught in Indian Lake.   8780

Palmer, Ralph Simon. The moose, our largest deer. *Bul Schools,* Mar. 1955. 41:260-61. map.   8781

Panther. *NYS Con,* Feb.-Mar. 1957. 11:no.4: 43. Letters from the Rev. Harry F. Smith and Leonard Wright. See also letter from Mabon Kingsley in the June-July issue, p.46-47.   8782

Panther season opens. *NYS Con,* Oct.-Nov. 1958. 13:no.2:43. Letter from A.M. Curran.   8783

Patric, Earl F. Reproductive characteristics of red-backed mouse during years of differing population densities. *J Mam,* May 1962. 43: 200-205. illus. Study made in central Adirondacks.   8784

Poison, unlimited. Broadside reprint from the Ticonderoga *Sentinel,* Aug. 2, 1962. Raccoons poisoned at Schroon Lake.   8785

Seagears, Clayton B. ...The fisher, et al. *NYS Con,* Oct.-Nov. 1958. 13:no.2:48-49. illus.   8786

Sleicher, Charles Albert. Is the panther on the way back? *Trailmarker,* May-June 1962. 1:no. 1:22-24. Reprinted from his "The Adirondacks".   8787

Snyder, Robert G. Black cat of the forest. *Aud Mag,* Mar. 1954. 56:62-63. Reprinted in "The Audubon Book of True Nature Stories", 1958, p.205-11.   8788

Zippy, the raccoon. Photos by Dick Millais, North Hudson. *No Country Life,* Summer 1961. 15:no.3:26-30. Brief account of pet raccoon at Schroon Lake. 8789

Bear

Betts, Charles E. All about bears. *Adirondac,* Nov.-Dec. 1963. 27:87,95. 8790

Haddad, Elsie (Tisch) Ursus Americanus - Loj chapter. *Adirondac,* Sept.-Oct. 1961. 25: 104. Bear at Heart Lake. 8791

Mech, L. David. Bear facts. *Am For,* May 1959. 65:no.5:15, 48-49. illus. Cornell experiment. 8792

Merritt, Edison J. Letter to the editor. *Con,* Dec.1963-Jan.1964. 18:no.3:43. Bears at dumps. 8793

Nuisance black bears. *NYS Con,* Oct.-Nov. 1959. 14:no.2:40. 8794

Randall, Willet. Cold storage bear. *Con,* Feb.-Mar. 1963. 17:no.4:7-8. 8795

Waddell, William R. New York's biggest bear, as told to Ted Jones. *Outd Life,* May 1956. 117:no.5:48-49,68-69. illus. (part col.) 8796

Young, Mrs. Howard. Campmate. *NYS Con,* Dec. 1957-Jan. 1958. 12:no.3:44. 8797

Deer

Clay, Cecil. Freaks of nature in deer. *For & Stream,* Feb. 11, 1875. 4:5. Letter about doe with horns, killed by John Cheney. Signed: Tahawus. 8798

De Sormo, Maitland C. Lake Tear's curious doe. *Adirondac,* July-Aug. 1961. 25:78-79. 8799

Hatch, A.B. Deer - facts and fancies. *NYS Con,* Oct.-Nov. 1959. 14:no.2:26-30. illus. col. chart. 8800

Hays, W.J. Spike horns. *Am Nat,* May 1870. 4:188-89. "Adirondack's Reply", p.189-90. 8801

Hooks 'n bullets. *Tahawus Cloudsplitter,* Nov. 1965. 17, i.e.16:no.6:8. Quotes letter by Tahawus, pseud. Jan. 26, 1875 from *Forest and Stream,* on spike horn deer and deer hunting. See Clay, Cecil, no.8798 above. 8802

P., F.W. Spike horned bucks. *Am Nat,* Feb. 1871. 4:762-63. Information from H.H. Bromley of the Chasm House, Keeseville. 8803

Read, B.W. Deer ked. *NYS Con,* Feb.-Mar. 1958. 12:no.4:44. Letter about deer ticks with answer by E.L. Cheatum. 8804

Saber-toothed deer. *NYS Con,* April-May 1958. 12:no.5:42. Letter from A.B. Hatch. See also letter in the Aug.-Sept. issue, p.44. 8805

SOCIAL AND ECONOMIC HISTORY

COMMERCE AND INDUSTRY

GENERAL

Animal land. *No Country Life,* Summer 1957. 11:no.3:13-17. illus. On Route 9, four miles south of Lake George. 8806

Brownell, Catherine J. Fine's oar factory. *Quar,* April 1964. 9:no.2:20. Brief note. 8807

----. The old tannery at Fine. *Quar,* Oct. 1963. 8:no.4:7. 8808

Bulletin! Digest of business transacted by Adirondack civic interests...August 21, 1924. n.p. n.d. Folio broadside printed on yellow paper. 8809

A business and professional manual of the principal cities and towns of Vermont and cities and towns of north-eastern New York in the vicinity of Lake Champlain. Providence, Colonial advertising co. 1904. 214p. Copy at the Plattsburgh Public Library. 8810

Crockett, Walter Hill. Concerted action in the Champlain valley. *Vermonter,* Jan. 1930. 35:5. Champlain Valley Council. 8811

The Enchanted forest of the Adirondacks. *No Country Life,* Summer 1957. 11:no.3:15-22. illus. At Old Forge. 8812

The Fowler livery and transfer co...Saranac Lake, N.Y. Saranac Lake, N.Y. Adirondack enterprise, n.d. unpaged (8p. incl. covers) illus. Copy at the Adirondack Museum. 8813

A general storekeeper and his merchandise. *No Country Notes,* Mar. 1961. no.3:3. Records of a Champlain store, from the McLellan Collection. 8814

Ice harvest, 1890. *York State Trad,* Winter 1964. 18:no.1:17-18. 8815

Lee, Brian. The greatest flood in sixty years. *No Country Notes,* May 1965. no.23:3. Saranac River flood of 1892. 8816

Leonard, W.C. & co. Adirondack outfittings. Furnishings for the outdoor life. Saranac Lake, N.Y. 1912. 36p. illus. Copy at the Adirondack Museum. 8817

Myers, Delia Jenks. Grandfather was known as a "born kiln burner". *Reveille,* Sept. 1957. 2:no.10:2-3. Charcoal industry. 8818

New York (state) Commerce, department of. Business and industry tell: Why the north country area. Albany, n.d. 11p. ports. 8819

New York (state) Commission against discrimination. Newsletter. Albany, v.d. The issue for November 1958, volume 2, number 1, p.3, contains note of "Catskills and Adirondack resort survey". "The findings are being analyzed and will be released shortly". 8820

New York (state) Hudson river valley commission. Population report for the Hudson river valley commission, prepared by the Office for regional development of the State of New York. Iona Island, Bear Mountain, N.Y. 1965. 43p. charts. Adirondacks, regions 5 and 6. 8821

New York (state) Legislature. Joint committee on the winter tourist business. Public hearing, Lake Placid, New York, September 11, 1962. n.p. 1962. 63p. typescript. 8822

----. Report, 1956/57 - 1963/64. Albany, 1957-1964. v.p. Title varies: 1960, Staff report. 8823

New York (state) Office for regional development. Change/Challenge/Response: a development policy for New York state. Albany, 1964. 164p. figs. maps. Planning for New York State for the next sixty years. 8824

Olds, C.B. Old mills of the north country. *No Country Life,* Fall 1956. 10:no.4:4-10. illus. 8825

Operation toylift. *No Country Life,* Summer 1956. 10:no.3:34-40. illus. Includes description of North Pole, N.Y. Reprinted from *The Lamp,* Nov. 1954. Also in *Recreation,* Dec. 1956, 49:472-73. 8826

Oval wood dish sold to Adirondack plywood corporation. *N Logger,* July 1964. 13:no.1:9, 31. illus. 8827

Palmer, Jeanne. Early industries. *Cloud Splitter,* July-Aug. 1958. 21:no.4:1-2. Essay by 11th grade student, Roth's Pond, town of North Hudson. Hudowalski Annual Essay Contest, Schroon Lake. Reprinted in *Reveille,* Sept. 1958. 8828

The paper industry today in northern New York. *N Logger,* April 1964. 12:no.10:20-21, 66-67. illus. See also "Paper Making in Northern New York" in *Northeastern Logger,* May 1956, 4:no.11:10-11,58-61, illustrated. 8829

Rawlins, Brenda. Tanning:Schroon Lake's first industry. *No Country Life,* Winter 1960. 14:no.

1:58-59. Winner in the 1959 Hudowalski Essay Contest. 8830

Slade, Bertha. Rabbits. *Trailmarker,* Summer 1963. 2:no.1:9,31. 8831

Story book characters come to life at Enchanted kingdom. *No Country Life,* Spring 1958. 12:no.2:49-53. illus. 8832

Trumbull, Mrs. E.E. In berry land. *Fr Track News,* Aug. 1905. 9:144. illus. Berry picking. 8833

Underwriters' association of New York state. Tariff of rates for Adirondack summer camps... to take effect January 15, 1916. n.p. n.d. 61p. Lists owners and buildings. Copy at the Adirondack Museum. 8834

U.S. Commerce department. Area redevelopment administration. Tourist and recreation potential: Lake Champlain - Adirondack area... n.p. 1964. 99p. illus. maps (part folded). Reproduced from typewritten copy. 8835

Upper Hudson and Champlain valley business directory... Newburgh, N.Y. L.P. Waite and co. v.d. v.p. Title varies. Incomplete files at the Plattsburgh Public Library and at the State University College Library at Plattsburgh. 8836

Wild, Seargent P. Life and labor. *Ver Life,* Summer 1959. 13:no.4:48-53. illus. 8837

ARTS AND CRAFTS

Adirondack architecture...off to a fresh start. *Trailmarker,* May-June 1962. 1:no.1:25. illus. 8838

Cole, G. Glyndon. The Adirondack store. *No Country Life,* Summer 1957. 11:no.3:57-60. illus. Store near Saranac Lake, specializing in Adirondack craftwork. 8839

Hall, Robert. The miracle at Westcott Hill: the story of crystal wood... Broadside reprinted from the Elizabethtown *Valley News,* April 5, 1957. The work of Vesta and Robert Stearn. 8840

LaMora, Mrs. David. Redford glass. *No Country Notes,* Nov. 1963. no.15:2-3. 8841

Williams, Timothy. A native craft. *Trailmarker,* Oct.-Nov. 1962. 1:no.3:29,34. Balsam pillows painted by Julia Preston of Piseco. 8842

FORESTRY AND LUMBERING

Armstrong, Dick. More efficient skidding and yarding methods. *Northeast Log,* Aug. 1960. 9:no.2:24-25. illus. 8843

Armstrong, George R. The forest resources of New York state. *Northeast Log,* May 1956. 4:no.11:24-25,74-75. illus. 8844

Baar, C.F. Opportunities for forest land owners. *NYS Ranger Sch,* 1964. p.5-8,23. figures. 8845

Barrett, John W., Farnsworth, C. Eugene and

Rutherford, William. Logging effects on regeneration and certain aspects of microclimate in northern hardwoods. *J For,* Sept. 1962. 60: 630-39. charts, tables. Includes central Adirondacks. 8846

Blue, Ernest W. North country logging. *NYS Con,* June-July 1956. 10:no.6:46. illus. Letter to the editor. 8847

Braden, Leo and Reed, Frank A. Early lumbering in northern New York. *N Logger,* April 1964. 12:no.10:14-15,62-63. illus. 8848

Broderick, Ernie. Lumber industry conditions in the northern Adirondacks and south central New York. *Northeast Log,* Oct. 1956. 5:no.4: 36. 8849

Brown, Nelson C. Empire state forest products association. *Northeast Log,* June 1959. 7:no. 12:18-19,40-41. illus. 8850

Brown, Ralph Adams. The lumber industry in the state of New York, 1790-1830. M.A. thesis, Columbia University, 1933. 135p. Microfilm at the Adirondack Museum. 8851

Community seeking pulp mill engages consulting forester. *J For,* Aug. 1955. 53:624. Tupper Lake. 8852

Connola, David P. and others. Insect damage and its prevention in withdrawn saw timber. Albany, University of the State of New York, 1956. 36p. illus. charts, tables. (New York State Museum and Science Service Bulletin 352) Study made in blowdown areas near Stratford, Fulton County. 8853

Corbett, Edward S. Soil moisture storage as affected by varying intensities of cutting in a northern hardwood forest of the Adirondacks. M.S. thesis, State University College of Forestry, 1960. 80p. illus. 8854

Currier, Alfred W. The great tree. Saranac Lake, N.Y. Currier press, 1962? unpaged (24p.) illus. port. Growing white pine at Lincoln Brook Farm, Essex County. 8855

Curry, John R. and Rushmore, F.M. Experiments in killing northern hardwoods with sodium arsenite and ammonium sulfamate. *J For,* Aug. 1955. 53:575-80. tables. Experiments at the Adirondack Research Center, Paul Smiths. 8856

----. Forestry and forest aesthetics. *Northeast Log,* Nov. 1961. 10:no.5:26,36-37. illus. port. Includes Paul Smiths. 8857

Curry, John R. The management of Whitney park. *Northeast Log,* July 1957. 6:no.1:20-22, 48-49,71. illus. ports. 8858

Curtis, Robert O. and Rushmore, F.M. Some effects of stand density and deer browsing on reproduction in an Adirondack hardwood stand. *J For,* Feb. 1958. 56:116-21. illus. chart, tables. 8859

Davis, James Elwood and Ferree, Miles Joseph. Forest acreage and timber volume, Clinton county, New York. Syracuse, N.Y. State university college of forestry, 1956. 24p. (Bulletin 36) Bulletins 37 and 38 are similar reports on Essex and Franklin counties.   8860

Davis, James Elwood. Some observations on the forest resource of the Adirondack and Catskill regions. *Tappi*, Aug. 1955. 38:sup.141A-142A. Based on the Adirondack-Catskill forest survey.   8861

Day, O. Lovell. Lumbering at Days mills. *No Country Life*, Summer 1958. 12:no.3:46-47.   8862

Dinsdale, Evelyn. The lumber industry of northern New York, a geographical examination of its history and technology. Ph.D. thesis, Syracuse University, 1963. 166p. illus. Microfilm at the Adirondack Museum.   8863

Elwert, F.P. The Joseph Dixon memorial forest ...pictorial narrative. *Northeast Log*, April 1961. 9:no.10:30-31. illus. On the site of the old graphite mines between Hague and Brant Lake.   8864

Empire state forest products association. 50 years of forest management, 1906-1956. n.p. 1956. 12p. illus.   8865

----. Golden anniversary bulletin, History and summary of important events... n.p. 1956. 16p. Brief history of the Association and its accomplishments.   8866

Ferree, Miles Joseph and Hagar, Robert K. Timber growth rates for natural forest stands in New York state. Syracuse, N.Y. State university college of forestry, 1956. 56p. tables, map. (Technical Publication 78)   8867

Forest and acreage of northern New York: a symposium. Economic education council of northern New York, College of forestry in Syracuse, Teachers college at Plattsburg... April 18, 1956. n.p. 1956. 21p. Mimeographed.   8868

Foster, Clifford H. The importance of timber quality as a goal in silviculture. *J For*, July 1953. 51:487-90. Pack Forest, Warrensburg.   8869

Foster, Ralph W. A study of the growth and value of a high-quality eastern white pine tree. *J For*, Oct. 1957. 55:727-30. tables. Study made in Pack Forest.   8870

Frothingham, E.H. The northern hardwood forest; its composition, growth and management. Washington, 1915. 80p. illus. tables, maps. (U.S. Department of Agriculture Bulletin 285) Includes Adirondacks.   8871

Gadway, Rita Mary. Life in the south woods lumber camps. *No Country Life*, Fall 1958. 12: no.4:15-18.   8872

Good, Thomas, Recknagel, Arthur Bernard and Reed, Frank A. The growth of the paper industry in northern New York. *N Logger*, April 1964. 12:no.10:18-19, 50-51,56-59,64-65. Followed by unsigned illustrated article "The Paper Industry Today in Northern New York", p.20-21, 66-67.   8873

Hays, Douglas and Hays, Helen I. Brush and road monkey. *York State Trad*, Winter 1965. 19:no.1:39-40.   8874

Hochschild, Harold K. Lumberjacks and rivermen in the central Adirondacks, 1850-1950. Blue Mountain Lake, N.Y. Adirondack museum, 1962. 88p. illus. ports. facsims. chart, maps (including end papers) Revision of a chapter from his "Township 34".   8875

Holbrook, Stewart H. Yankee loggers... N.Y. International paper co. ©1961. 123p. illus.   8876

Illick, Joseph S. Recent developments in forestry. *In* New York (state) Legislature. Joint legislative committee on natural resources. Annual report, 1959. p.89-96.   8877

International paper co. Tupper lake tree farm: sportsman's map. n.p. n.d. Broadside printed on both sides and folded into 12p. illus. Maps on verso.   8878

Jackson, Harry F. Branding and driving in the Adirondacks. *No Country Life*, Spring 1960. 14:no.2:18-22. illus.   8879

Kerr, R.E. Lumbering in the Adirondack foothills. *Quar*, April 1964. 9:no.2:12-15. illus.   8880

Kingsbury, Corydon D. Cooperative forest management research project for state forests. *In* New York (state) Legislature. Joint legislative committee on natural resources. Annual report, 1957. p.53-55.   8881

Klaehn, F.U. Forest tree improvement in New York. *NYS Con*, June-July 1959. 13:no.6:20-21,35. illus. (part col.) Program of State University College of Forestry at Syracuse.   8882

----. Field trip for the 9th Northeastern forest tree improvement conference at State university college of forestry at Syracuse, N.Y. n.p. 1962. 98p. illus.   8883

Kling, Edwin M., Nelson, S.W. and Reed, Frank A. Growth of the lumber industry in northern New York. *N Logger*, April 1964. 12:no.10:16-17,46-47,52-55,60-61. illus. See also unsigned article "The Lumber Industry Today in Northern New York", p.22-23,68-69,76.   8884

Larson, Charles C. Forest economy of the Adirondack region. Syracuse, N.Y. State university college of forestry, 1956. 48p. illus. tables, charts, maps (one folded) (Bulletin 39)   8885

Littlefield, Edward Winchester. Further observations on Ponderosa pine in New York. *J For*, Oct. 1955. 53:731. 8886

----. Jack pine - poor relation or pioneer? *NYS Con*, April-May 1960. 14:no.5:6-7. illus. 8887

The logging operations of John E. Johnston. *Northeast Log*, May 1960. 8:no.11:10-13,60. illus. 8888

Lull, Howard W. Humus depth in the northeast. *J For*, Dec. 1959. 57:905-909. tables. Includes two stations at Paul Smith's. 8889

M. A lumber camp. *Univ Cynic*, Mar. 4, 1886. 3:121-22. 8890

Milligan, G. Lumber and rumors of war along Lake Champlain. *No Country Life*, Summer 1962. 16:no.3:42-44. Letter from Keeseville, Mar. 16, 1839 in the collection of Robert F. Hale. 8891

New York (state) State university college of forestry, Syracuse. Atlas of forestry in New York, by Neil J. Stout... Syracuse, N.Y. 1958. 95p. (Bulletin 41) 8892

----. The challenges of forestry; the addresses and technical papers presented on the occasion of the college's fiftieth anniversary celebration, April 12-14, 1961. Compiled by Richard E. Pentoney and William L. Webb. Syracuse, N.Y. 1961. 232p. illus. 8893

----. The Charles Lathrop Pack demonstration forest... n.p. n.d. Broadside printed on both sides and folded into 8p. illus. map. 8894

----. Forestry in the Adirondacks, by John W. Barrett...Edwin H. Ketchledge...Donald R. Satterlund...editors. Syracuse, N.Y. 1961. 139p. charts, tables, maps. Reproduced from typewritten copy. 8895

Niederheiser, Clodaugh M. Forest history sources of the United States and Canada. A compilation of the manuscript sources of forestry... St. Paul, Forest history foundation, 1956. 140p. New York, p.80-87. 8896

1956 northeastern logging shows. *Northeast Log*, Aug. 1956. 5:no.2:36-37. illus. Includes brief note on the 9th annual Woodmen's Field Day at Tupper Lake. See also note in December issue, 5:no.6:20-21. 8897

Olmsted, Norwood W. New York forester sees major changes in woodland management. *Northeast Log*, Nov. 1965. 14:no.5:10-11,30-31. port. illus. Woodlands manager of Finch, Pruyn & Co. Inc. predicts that more commercial woodlands will be open for recreation. 8899

Patterson, William. The Ward lumber co. tree farm. *Northeast Log*, Aug. 1957. 6:no.2:39-40. illus. 8900

Paul Smith's foresters take the woodsmen's trophy for the 7th straight victory. *N Logger*, July 1963. 12:no.1:35. 8901

Pesez, G.A. Forest management. *Northeast Log*, July 1957. 6:no.1:24-25,58-59,71. illus. By the woodlands manager of the International Paper Company. 8902

Petty, William. Woodmen's field day. *NYS Con*, Dec. 1958-Jan. 1959. 13:no.3:39. illus. Tupper Lake. 8903

Pope, Virginia. Planting great forests for posterity. *NY Times Mag*, Oct. 21, 1928. p.8-9. illus. 8904

Porter, Marjorie (Lansing) How logs were floated down the Glen in the 1890's. *Reveille*, Sept. 1957. 2:no.10:3. Logging between Keene and Upper Jay. 8905

----. Old time uses of wood. *Northeast Log*, June 1961. 9:no.12:20,55. illus. 8906

Recknagel, Arthur Bernard. How far have we come in industrial forestry? *Northeast Log*, May 1956. 4:no.11:18-19,72-73. illus. 8907

----. The pulp and paper industry in northern and central New York. *Northeast Log*, May 1960. 8:no.11:16-17,62. illus. Includes Adirondacks. 8908

Reed, Frank A. Forty-eight years in the north country. *NYS Ranger Sch*, 1964. p.9-11. Reminiscences of logging. 8909

Reynolds, Jeanne. "Emporium" was the word for lumbering. *Quar*, Oct. 1958. 3:no.4:6-8. Emporium Forestry Company. 8910

Rushmore, Francis M. The Adirondack research center. Upper Darby, Pa. Forest service, 1957. 18p. illus. (Northeastern Forest Experiment Station Research Paper 98) 8911

Rutherford, William A. jr. A test of plotless cruising in Adirondack hardwood. *Northeast Log*, April 1961. 9:no.10:16,42-44,54. port. tables. 8912

Sawmills of northern New York. *Northeast Log*, May 1960. 8:no.11:22-23,56-59. illus. 8913

Schick, Bruce A. Can international ¼″ rule volumes be obtained sawing eastern red spruce? *N Logger*, Oct. 1965. 14:no.4:20,40. illus. chart, tables. Laboratory tests at Paul Smith's College. 8914

Schreiner, Everett J., Littlefield, Edward Winchester and Eliason, E.J. Results of 1938 IV-FRO Scotch pine provenance test in New York. Upper Darby, Pa. 1962. 23p. illus. (Northeastern Forest Experiment Station Paper 166) 8915

Seminars on more intelligent bucking of hardwoods held at Old Forge. *N Logger*, June 1965. 13:no.12:14-15,34. 8916

Shelly, James N. Evaluation of a virgin island forest: a seminar report presented to the faculty of the Biology department, State university of New York, College of education, Albany, N.Y.

n.p. 1961. 28p. photographs, tables, map. Type-script. Vegetation survey of Dome Island, Lake George. See also "Dome Island Survey" in *Nature Conservancy News*, Winter 1962, 12:no. 4:11-12.   8917

Simmons, Fred C. The Reynolds lumber com-pany, Wells, N.Y. *Northeast Log*, May 1960. 8:no.11:24-25. illus.   8918

Society of American foresters. Annual meeting, Syracuse, N.Y. November 10-13,1957. Trip number 4. Forestry in the pine region of the Adirondacks. *J For*, Oct. 1957. 55:772. 8919

Society of American foresters. New York sec-tion. Forest plantations, the course ahead. Syracuse, N.Y. New York state college of for-estry, 1956. 22p. tables. Papers presented at the winter 1956 meeting.   8920

----. Committee on insects and diseases. A summary of current forest pest problems for New York state, 1956-58. Syracuse, N.Y. 1956. 21p.   8921

----. Same; supplement to the 1956-1959 re-port. Syracuse, N.Y. State university college of forestry, 1961. 6p.   8922

Stegeman, LeRoy C. The production of aspen and its utilization by beaver on the Hunting-ton forest. *J Wildlife Man*, July 1954. 18:348-58. tables.   8923

Stone, Earl L. and Baird, Guy. Boron level and boron toxicity in red and white pine. *J For*, Jan. 1956. 54:11-12. chart, table. On glacial outwash surrounding the Adirondack area.   8924

Stone, Earl L., Feuer, Reeshon and Wilson, Hugh M. Judging land for forest plantations in New York. Ithaca, N.Y. New York state college of agriculture, 1962. 15p. (Cornell Ex-tension Bulletin 1075)   8925

Stone, Flora Pierce, Reed, Frank A. and Wein, Bernard A. Some wood-using industries in northern New York. *Northeast Log*, May 1960. 8:no.11:20-21,32,44-45,47. illus.   8926

Twelfth annual woodsmen's field day. *North-east Log*, Dec. 1959. 8:no.6:34,71. illus. 8927

Von Ohlsen, Edward F., Coontz, Sydney H. and Compton, Kenneth C. Primary wood use in New York; a survey of industrial and nonin-dustrial use of roundwood. Syracuse, N.Y. State university college of forestry, 1958. 75p. maps, tables. (Bulletin 40)   8928

Warrensburg (N.Y.) News makes "outstanding contribution" to forestry. *Northeast Log*, July 1961. 10:no.1:41. Includes campaign against forest fires and the Washington Christmas tree.   8929

Webb, Jack. Adirondack logging with a wheel tractor. *Northeast Log*, Aug. 1956. 5:no.2:21-22. illus.   8930

Western, Florence E. The passing of the log drive... *No Country Life*, Spring 1961. 15:no. 2:21. illus.   8931

Where to get the wood? n.p. n.pub. 1952. Broadside reprint of article in Utica *Observer-Dispatch*, June 1, 1952.   8932

White, Donald P. Potash fertilizer improves growth in Adirondack plantation. *Northeast Log*, June 1956. 4:no.12:24-25. illus. Experi-ment at Pack Forest.   8933

Wilcox, Hugh. Some results from the chemi-cal treatment of trees to facilitate bark removal. *J For*, July 1954. 52:522-25. At Huntington Wildlife Forest.   8934

Wilcox, Hugh, Czabator, Felix and Girolami, Guido. Seasonal variations in bark-peeling characteristics of some Adirondack pulpwood species. *J For*, May 1954. 52:338-42. illus. charts.   8935

MINING
Arranged by date

Johnson, Walter R. Experiments on two vari-eties of iron, manufactured from the magnetic ores of the Adirondack iron works, Essex coun-ty N.Y. *Am J Sci*, July 1839. 36:94-105. 8936

New York (state) Supreme court. ...Albert Conro, Joseph M. Warren, William H. War-ren, Isaac B. Hart and George Lesley. The president, directors and company of the Bank of Vergennes, and Lucius A. Foote who sue as well, &c. against the Port Henry Iron company, Horace Gray, Ralph W. Crooker... Troy, N.Y. Johnson & Davis, 1848? 474,VIp.   8937

Advantages of the works and property of the Adirondac iron and steel co. for the manufac-ture of cast steel, of superior quality, on a large scale, and at a cheap rate. Philadelphia, Howell Evans, 1851. 10p. Copy at the Adirondack Mu-seum.   8938

St. Lawrence mining company. A report on the mines and lands... N.Y. Arthur A. Burnet, 1852. 11p. map. Prepared by F.B. Hough. 8939

Verrill, A.E. Report upon the property of the Essex and Lake Champlain ore and iron com-pany. Boston, Geo. C. Rand & Avery, 1865. 22p.   8940

Mennie, T. S. The mining and milling of gar-net for abrasive papers and cloths. *Min & Met*, May 1925. 6:226-28. Barton mine.   8941

Adirondack iron. *Essex Co*, May 1940. 23: no.5:12. Reprinted from the *DuPont Maga-zine*, May 1940.   8942

The MacIntyre development of National lead company, titanium division. In operation July 15, 1942. n.p. 1942? unpaged (4p.) illus. map.   8943

Allen, Paul W. The MacIntyre story. *Tah-awus Cloudsplitter*, Nov. 1951. 2:no.10:4-9. illus. port.   8944

Kearny, John H. and Lutjen, George P. E & M J visits the general superintendent at U.S.'s largest titanium mine. *Eng & Min J*, Dec. 1953. 154:no.12:83-88. illus. National Lead Company. 8945

Jones, F.R. More rock per dollar from the MacIntyre pit. *In* American institute of mining engineers. Transactions, May 1956. 205: 524-28. tables, figures. Also in *Mining Engineering*, 8:524-28. See also P.W. Allen's article "Dropball Cuts Blasting Costs at Tahawus" in *Mining Engineering* for April 1953, p.379. 8946

Ralph Moran Business Biographies, N.Y. Garnet abrasives: an 80-year history of the Barton mines corporation... North Creek, N.Y. 1956. 46p. front. illus. ports. 8947

Barker, Elmer Eugene. Mr. Hammond's iron towers. *No Country Life*, Spring 1957. 11:no. 2:33-39,52. Mining development of Charles Franklin Hammond. 8948

Bartholmé, Paul M. The Gore mountain garnet deposit, New York state; structure and petrography. Leopoldville, Congo Belge, Université Lovanium, 1958. 32p. Citation taken from *Science*, 20 March 1959. 8949

Carroll, Walter. Barton garnets of Gore mountain. Syracuse Post-Standard *Pictorial*, July 6, 1958. p.4-8. illus. incl. cover. 8950

Walker, Clifford. Rock pond. *NYS Con*, Oct.-Nov. 1959. 14:no.2:44. Letter on graphite mine with reply by Roger L. Borst. 8951

Bartholmé, Paul M. Genesis of Gore mountain garnet deposit, New York. *Econ Geol*, Mar.-April 1960. 55:255-77. illus. 8952

Lynd, Langtry E. Titanium. *In* American institute of mining, metallurgical, and petroleum engineers. Committe on industrial minerals volume. Industrial minerals and rocks. N.Y. 1960. p.851-80. Includes Lake Sanford. 8953

Templeton, Joseph P. Jersey City: early American steel center. *NJ Hist Soc Proc*, July 1961. 76:169-77. Early history of the mines at Adirondac. 8954

Hochschild, Harold K. The MacIntyre mine - from failure to fortune. Blue Mountain Lake, N.Y. Adirondack museum, 1962. 26p. illus. port. maps (including end papers) A revision of a chapter from his "Township 34". 8955

Jones & Laughlin steel. New York ore division. General information. n.p. 1962? 10p. illus. diagram, tables. Includes history of the Benson Mine. 8956

Mineral industry notes. *Emp State Geo*, Fall 1964. 3:no.1:12. Includes note on the Adirondack Development Corporation. 8957

Burnham, Koert D. and Warner, Eugene. Potential uses of wet processed wollastonite. n.p. 1964? 14p. (AIME Preprint 64H331) 8958

Carpenter, F. Scott jr. Wollastonite - its uses and its potential. n.p. 1964? 15p. (AIME Preprint 64H328) 8959

Choate, Lauren W. Evolution of wollastonite as an industrial mineral. n.p. 1964? 4p. (AIME Preprint 64H304) 8960

Mining in the north country. *York State Trad*, Spring 1965. 19:no.2:38-41. illus. Reprinted from the Albany *Times-Union*, Mar. 14, 1965. 8961

Cornwall, John H. Garnet - gem, rock-builder and abrasive. *Lapidary J*, Sept.-Oct. 1965. 19:650-58,662-63,750-60. illus. 8962

National lead company. The story of National lead company. N.Y. n.d. 33p. illus. (part col.) col. map. Booklet for employees. 8963

Republic steel corporation. Iron ore mining on Lake Champlain. n.p. n.d. Broadside printed on both sides and folded into 6p. illus. 8964

AGRICULTURE

Arnold, R.W. and Cline, Marlin G. Origin of a surficial deposit in soils of eastern Fulton county, New York. *Soil Sci Soc Proc*, May-June 1961. 25:240-43. Study made at Mayfield, west of the Sacandaga Reservoir. 8965

Burrell, A.B. The effect of irrigation on the occurrence of a form of cork disease and on the size of apple fruits. *Am Soc Hort Sci*, 1933. 30:415-20. 8966

----. Effectiveness and safety of fungicide - arsenical spray combinations in apples in the Champlain valley of New York. *Am Soc Hort Sci*, 1933. 30:87-94. 8967

----. Further pollination studies of the McIntosh apples in the Champlain valley of New York. *Am Soc Hort Sci*, 1930. 27:374-85. L.H. MacDaniels is joint author. 8968

----. Immediate and residual effects of sodium nitrate upon yield and growth of McIntosh apple trees. *Am Soc Hort Sci*, 1928. 25:258-62. Champlain valley. 8969

----. Pollination of the McIntosh apple in the Champlain valley; third progress report. *Am Soc Hort Sci*, 1931. 28:78-84. Written jointly with R.G. Parker. 8970

----. A response of apple trees to potash in the Champlain valley of New York. I-III. *Am Soc Hort Sci,* 1941-1943. 38:1-7; 40:8-12; 42:61-64. tables. Part II is written jointly with J.C. Cain and L.A. Brinkerhoff, Part III with Damon Boynton.   8971

Conklin, Howard E. and Lucas, Broder F. An economic classification of farm areas, Lewis county, New York. Ithaca, N.Y. New York state college of agriculture, 1954. 9p. col. map. (Cornell Economic Land Classification Leaflet 4)   8972

Davis, Darius Alton. The story of Davis hill: pioneer life in the Adirondacks. n.p. Privately printed, ©1963. 48p. illus. ports. Farm near Skerry, N.Y.   8973

Fynmore, Jim. Sign of spring: smoke and steam. *No Country Life,* Winter 1961. 15:no. 1:9-13. illus. Photographs of sugaring on farm of E.L. Varney near Harrisville, Lewis County.
8974

Howe, Frank Bonar. Classification and agricultural values of New York soils. Ithaca, N.Y. Cornell university, 1935. 83p. maps. (Cornell University Agricultural Experiment Station Bulletin 619)   8975

Logging operators run sugar bushes. *Northeast Log,* April 1958. 6:no.10:18-19. illus.
8976

MacDaniels, L.H. and Burrell, A.B. Pollination studies with the McIntosh apple in the Champlain valley fruit district. *Am Soc Hort Sci,* 1930. 26:65-73.   8977

Marschner, Francis Joseph. Land use and its pattern in the United states. Washington, G.P. O. 1959. 277p. illus. maps. (one folded in pocket) (U.S. Department of Agriculture Handbook 153) Includes Adirondacks.   8978

New York (state) State college of agriculture, Cornell university. Department of agricultural economics. 1954 census of agriculture. Ithaca, N.Y. 1958. v.p. mimeographed. Includes Clinton County, 21p.; Essex County, 15p.; Franklin County, 15p.; Fulton County, 15p.; Herkimer County, 16p. and Lewis County, 15p.
8979

New York (state) State college of agriculture,

Cornell university. 1954 census of agriculture. Ithaca, N.Y. 1957. v.p. Includes Clinton, Essex, Franklin, Fulton, Herkimer, Lewis, St. Lawrence, Saratoga, Warren and Washington counties. Prepared by C.A. Bratton.   8980

----. Department of agricultural economics. Census of agriculture, 1959. Ithaca, N.Y. 1962. v.p. Includes Clinton, Essex, Franklin, Fulton, Herkimer, Lewis, Oneida, St. Lawrence, Saratoga, Warren and Washington counties. Prepared by C.A. Bratton.   8981

----. Clinton county farm business summary, group vii, 1961 by C.W. Loomis and Richard Eschler. Ithaca, N.Y. 1962. 22p. mimeographed. Similar summaries are issued for the other Forest Preserve counties.   8982

----. Farming areas in Lewis county, a statistical summary of economic land classification... by Howard E. Conklin and Broder F. Lucas. Ithaca, N.Y. 1954. 23p.   8983

Nobe, Kenneth C. and Conklin, Howard E. An economic classification of farm areas, St. Lawrence county, New York. Ithaca, N.Y. New York state college of agriculture, 1957. 12p. col.map. (Cornell Economic Land Classification Leaflet 5)   8984

Peters, Ruth E. Maple sugarin' time in 'Liz'-bethtown. *No Country Life,* Winter 1958. 12: no.1:24-25. Quoted in *Reveille,* March 1958, p.1.   8985

Pomeroy, Allen. Diversified farming on Norman Ridge. *NE Home,* Jan. 28, 1961. p.6-7. illus. Near Saranac Lake.   8986

Potatoes. *No Country Notes,* Nov. 1963. no. 15:4.   8987

Rist, Iva Braley. Huntley's modern sugar making. *Tahawus Cloudsplitter,* Dec. 1965. 17, i.e.16:no.7:2,11. Letter describing maple sugar operation at Newcomb sixty years ago. 8988

Walker, Lawrence C. The low-potash soils in the Adirondack forests. *Bet Crops,* Feb. 1956. 40:no.2:24-26,50. illus. diagrs.   8989

Wilson, Mrs. Albert Frederick. The good earth of Essex county. *Gard Club,* Jan. 1957. 45: no.1:27.   8990

RESORTS AND HOTELS

The Adirondack company. Whiteface inn, Lake Placid, N.Y. Adirondacks... N.Y. Amsterdam press, 191-? 16p. illus.   8991

The Adirondacks. Albany? 191-? 22p. Schroon Lake and Edgewater Park. Copy at New York State Library.   8992

Adirondack house, Keene Valley, Essex co.

N.Y.... S. Kelley, proprietor. N.Y. C.H. Clayton & co. n.d. unpaged (16p.) illus. Also another edition printed by the Troy Times Art Press. In Keene Valley Library.   8993

...Adirondack lodge... N.Y. Mayor & Knapp, n.d. unpaged (4p.) illus.   8994

The Albedor. Fabulous Albedor is truly fabulous. n.p. n.d. unpaged (4p.) History of inn on Fourth Lake between Old Forge and Inlet. 8995

The Algonquin and cottages on Lower Saranac lake... Troy, N.Y. Troy times art press, n.d. unpaged (16p.) illus. John Harding, Manager. 8996

The Algonquin hotel and cottages on Lower Saranac lake... Saranac Lake, N.Y. Currier press, n.d. Broadside printed on both sides and folded into 8p. illus. map. 8997

...Altavista lodge, Saranac Lake, N.Y. n.p. n.d. Yellow broadside printed on both sides and folded into 6p. illus. maps. 8998

Ampersand hotel and cottages on Lower Saranac lake in the Adirondacks. Providence, Boston and N.Y. Livermore & Knight co. n.d. unpaged (12p. incl. covers) illus. maps. 8999

Anderson, Robert. Destination: Brown's tract. *York State Trad,* Winter 1963. 17:no.1:3-8. Notes from the guest register of Lawrence's Hotel at Moose River. 9000

Bradley's at the foot of the great range...St. Hubert's, Essex county, New York. n.p. 1940. 4p. Mimeographed. 9001

Broadwell, Andrew B. ...A tavern on the turnpike. *York State Trad,* Winter 1965. 19:no.1: 25-30. illus. Robinson's Tavern. 9002

Brownell, Catherine J. Fine's St. Nicholas hotel. *Quar,* Oct. 1965. 10:no.4:5. illus. 9003

Carman, Gayle. This was Paul Smith. *York State Trad,* Spring 1965. 19:no.2:32-37. illus. Taken from an article in the April 1933 *Club Dial* published by the Women's Club of White Plains. 9004

Carman, Gayle and Blahut, Brenda. An historic Plattsburgh hostelry. *No Country Notes,* May 1964. no.18:2. The Fouquet House. 9005

...Cascade lake house, Cascadeville, Essex county, New York. Glens Falls, N.Y.Possons, n.d. 8p. illus. E.M.Weston, proprietor. 9006

Cascade lakes club. Adirondacks. The Cascade lakes club, Cascade, N.Y. Troy, N.Y. Troy times art press, n.d. Broadside printed on both sides and folded into 16p. illus. 9007

The Clark-Wardner camps. For a healthful, wholesome vacation on Rainbow lake in the Adirondacks. n.p. n.d. unpaged (4p.) illus. map. 9008

Clawbonny in the Adirondacks, Keeseville, N.Y. Troy, N.Y. Troy times art press, n.d. unpaged (12p.) illus. 9009

The Cranberry lake club...Cranberry lake, New York. Syracuse, N.Y. Hillsberg press, n.d. unpaged (12p.) illus. 9010

Crescent bay camps. Located in New York state's forest reservation in the Adirondack mountains. n.p. n.d. Broadside printed on both

sides and folded into 6p. illus. On Lower Saranac Lake. 9011

Crown Point house... Crown Point, N.Y. 1901. unpaged (8p. incl. covers) illus. 9012

...The Deer's head inn, Elizabethtown, N.Y. Troy, N.Y. Troy times art press, n.d. unpaged (20p.) illus. Charles A. Ferriss, proprietor. Formerly the Mansion House. Also variant editions for 1902?, Benjamin Stetson, proprietor and for 1903, same title with different text and illustrations. 9013

Deer's head inn...Elizabethtown, New York... n.p. n.d. Broadside printed on both sides and folded into 8p. illus. map. E.J. Bastian and Stella Bastian, ownership-management. 9014

Delmarsh inn on Limekiln lake in the Adirondacks... Troy, N.Y. Troy times art press, n.d. unpaged (8p.) illus. map. 9015

The Deremo hotel on Cranberry lake... n.p. n.d. unpaged (8p.) illus. 9016

De Sormo, Maitland C. The Banner house. *York State Trad,* Fall 1965. 19:no.4:36-39. illus. On Lower Chateaugay Lake. 9017

----. Hotel Ayers on Lake Duane. *No Country Life,* Fall 1961. 15:no.4:21-24. illus. 9018

----. The three Macs of McCollom's. *No Country Life,* Winter 1962. 16:no.1:40-47. illus. Hotels near Meacham Lake run by Amiel G. McCollom, Clarence MacArthur and Earl MacArthur. 9019

Eagle bay hotel. Eagle Bay, New York, Adirondacks, Fourth lake, Fulton chain. Auburn, N.Y. Fenton press, n.d. unpaged (16p.) illus. map. 9020

Eagle bay hotel in the central Adirondacks on Fourth lake of the Fulton chain. Troy, N.Y. Troy times art press, 1931. 14p. illus. (part col.) map. Another edition, undated, 16p. 9021

Elk lake camps. Elk lake, southern gateway to the Adirondack peaks. n.p. n.d. Folded broadside, printed on green paper with illustrations and map. 9022

Elk lake camps on Elk lake, Blue Ridge, Essex county, New York. C.D. Davis, manager. Troy, N.Y. Troy times art press, 1933? unpaged (6p.) illus. 9023

Ella Lahey makes a find. *Quar,* April 1960. 5:no.2:14. illus. Stereoptican view of Blue Mountain House, 1879. 9024

Flume cottage, an Adirondack mountain resort in Keene Valley, Essex county, N.Y.... n.p. n.d. unpaged (4p.) folio. Martin Bahler, proprietor. 9025

Fonda, Johnstown and Gloversville r.r. co. Adirondack inn, Sacandaga park...New York. Gloversville, N.Y. n.d. unpaged (20p.) illus. One page of text. 9026

The Fouquet house: historic hostelry at Plattsburgh...H.C. Ricketson, proprietor. n.p. n.d. unpaged (4p.) illus. Also another undated and unpaged edition with slightly different title. 9027

Ga-ko-mas. A new hotel and club in the Adirondacks. n.p. 1915? 20p. illus. map. At northern end of Lower Saranac Lake. See also Ga-ko-mas in the Adirondacks: a prospectus. n.p. n.d. unpaged (20p.) illus. map. To be opened in 1916. 9028

Garondah lodge and cottages on Rainbow lake, N.Y....Clem and Gerry Collins, owners... n.p. n.d. Broadside printed on both sides and folded into 6p. illus. map. 9029

Greenough house and cottages, Ampersand park. n.p. n.d. unpaged (4p.) illus. 9030

Historic Royal savage inn, Plattsburg, N.Y... n.p. n.d. Broadside printed on both sides, folded into 6p. illus. map. 9031

Hochschild, Harold K. An Adirondack resort in the nineteenth century: Blue Mountain Lake, 1870-1900. Stagecoaches and luxury hotels. Blue Mountain Lake, N.Y. Adirondack museum, 1962. 99p. illus. plans, facsims. maps on end papers. Reviewed in the *Cloud Splitter,* July-August 1962, 25:no.4:10. A blanket review of the revised chapters of "Township 34" with the title "Yesteryears in the Adirondacks" appeared in the Fall 1962 issue of *North Country Life,* p.46-48. 9032

Hotel Ampersand, Lower Saranac lake, Adirondacks. n.p. n.d. unpaged (12p.) illus. map. Eaton & Young, managers (rubber stamp covering Eaton & Harding) 9033

Hotel Ampersand and cottages on Lower Saranac lake... n.p. n.d. unpaged (16p.) illus. 9034

Hotel Ampersand and cottages...W.E. & N.S. Little, owners and managers. Saranac Lake, N.Y. Currier press, n.d. Broadside printed on both sides and folded into 8p. illus. 9035

Hotel Champlain. The leading resort of the Adirondacks and Lake Champlain. The season of 1894...O.D. Seavey, manager. n.p. 1894? unpaged (8p. incl. covers) illus. map. 9036

Hotel Champlain: the peerless lake and mountain resort of the Adirondacks... N.Y. and Pittsburgh, Chasmar-Winchell, 1900? unpaged (32p.) illus. E.L. Brown, manager. At Bluff Point, near Plattsburgh. Also a variant edition, undated, 28p. 9037

Hotel Champlain and its surroundings... n.p. n.d. unpaged (16p.) illus. map. Cover title: Hotel Champlain, O.D. Seavey, manager. The superb summer hotel of the north. 9038

Hotel Champlain, Bluff Point near Plattsburgh. O.D. Seavey, manager ...In the far famed Adirondacks. N.Y. and Pittsburgh, Chasmar-Winchell, n.d. unpaged (32p.) illus. Also a 36p. edition. 9039

Hotel Champlain, the superb Adirondack and Lake Champlain resort... N.Y. Fleming and Carnrick, n.d. 22p. illus. map. O.D. Seavey, manager. Another edition printed in Buffalo by Matthews-Northrup co. A broadside printed on both sides and folded into 12p. with illustrations and map. 9040

Hotel Crawford. Adirondack mountains, Keene Valley, N.Y. Troy, N.Y. Troy times art press, n.d. unpaged (8p.) illus. 9041

Hotel Cumberland. Helen I. Clark, proprietor, Plattsburgh, N.Y. Malone, N.Y. n.d. unpaged (8p.) illus. Also a circular with title "The Cumberland" printed in Malone by M.J. Donahue, 1923. 8p. illus. map. 9042

Hotel Saranac. Saranac Lake, N.Y. Currier press, n.d. unpaged (12p.) illus. 9043

Hotel Saranac, Saranac Lake, New York. The logical headquarters for those desiring to visit the Adirondacks... n.p. n.d. Broadside printed on both sides and folded into 8p. illus. 9044

Hotel Saranac situated in the center of the Adirondack mtn. playground... n.p. n.d. Broadside printed on both sides and folded into 6p. illus. (part col.) map. 9045

Hotel Witherell, Plattsburgh, New York...Wm. H. Howell, proprietor. n.p. n.d. Broadside printed on both sides and folded into 8p. illus. 9046

...Hunter's home in the Adirondack mountains...Laverty brothers, proprietors, Elizabethtown, Essex county, N.Y. n.p. n.d. Broadside printed on both sides and folded into 6p. illus. 9047

...Hunters rest camp...Raquette Lake, N.Y. n.p. n.d. unpaged (12p.) illus. 9048

Hurricane lodge in the Adirondacks, Hurricane, Essex co. N.Y. Troy, N.Y. Troy times art press, n.d. unpaged (16p.) illus. K. Belknap, manager. Another edition, for the 35th season, undated and unpaged (16p.) with mounted illustrations and map. Mrs. M.G. Pringle, manager. 9049

Indian carry cottages & camps, Coreys, New York... n.p. n.d. unpaged (4p.) illus. map. R.C. Freeman, proprietor. 9050

Interbrook lodge, Keene Valley, N.Y.... n.p. 1923. unpaged (24p.) illus. 9051

Interbrook lodge and camps... n.p. n.d. unpaged (4p.) illus. maps. 9052

Interbrook lodge and cottages. A vacation paradise...Keene Valley, N.Y. n.p. n.d. Broadside printed on both sides and folded into 6p. illus. Owner-Management: Hugh F. Morrison. G. Walton Travis. 9053

...Interbrook lodge, Keene Valley, N.Y. M.E. Luck, proprietor. Edition of 1923. n.p. 1923. unpaged (24p.) illus. Other editions, 16p. and 20p. 9054

...Keene Valley inn and cottages, Keene Valley, N.Y. Troy, N.Y. Troy times art press, n.d. unpaged (12p.) illus. map tipped in. Another edition (8p.) has letter dated June 14, 1922 laid in. 9055

...Keene Valley inn, Keene Valley, N.Y. Troy, N.Y. Troy times art press, 1920. unpaged (12p.) illus. Orlando Beede, proprietor. Another undated edition, 12p. A. Block, proprietor. 9056

Krows, Arthur E. Vacation on the warpath. *Travel,* July 1956. 106:no.1:48-50. illus. Alpine Valley, Lake George resort. 9057

Lake Champlain and the Adirondacks. N.Y. Press of Fleming & Carnrick, n.d. unpaged (8p.) illus. map. Advertisement for Hotel Windsor at Rouse's Point. 9058

Lake Clear inn, in the heart of the great Adirondacks. n.p. n.d. Broadside printed on both sides and folded into 6p. illus. map. Another edition, entitled "Lake Clear Is Vacation Perfection", 8p. illustrated. 9059

Lake Meacham hotel, Duane, N.Y. Season of 1903. Troy, N.Y. Troy times art press, 1903? unpaged (12p.) illus. Another edition, without printer, 12p. illus. 9060

Lake Placid house on lakes Placid and Mirror... n.p. n.d. unpaged (4p.) illus. 9061

...Lake view house, Star Lake, N.Y. Morris & Fenno, props. Gilbertsville, N.Y. Journal print, n.d. unpaged (8p.) illus. 9062

Land of the lakes: Kushaqua in the Adirondacks... Buffalo, N.Y. Courier co. ©1896. unpaged (12p.) illus. Advertisement for Forge House, at Old Forge. 9063

The Leland house, Schroon Lake, N.Y. Warrensburgh, N.Y. Press of the News, n.d. unpaged (8p.) illus. 9064

The Lodge on beautiful Lake Clear... n.p. n.d. Broadside printed on both sides and folded into 4p. illus. map. Mrs. Fred Jarvis, owner and manager. 9065

"McCollom's" in the Adirondacks. n.p. n.d. unpaged (12p.) illus. Seven miles from Paul Smiths, on Rice Lake, Franklin County. 9066

McKenney, Clara (Bush) Cranberry hotels. *Quar,* April 1963. 8:no.2:5. illus. 9067

Mansion house, Elizabethtown, New York... n.p. 1888. unpaged (8p.) illus. 9068

Maplewood inn, Adirondacks, Elizabethtown, N.Y... Troy, N.Y. Troy times art press, n.d. 24p. illus. Another edition, printed by the Essex County Publishing Company, undated and unpaged (8p.) G.W. Jenkins, proprietor. Similar edition, printed in 1893. 9069

Miller, Roland B. Adirondack hotels. *NYS Con,* Dec. 1955-Jan. 1956. 10:no.3:8-10. illus. See also letters about this article in Feb.-Mar. and April-May issues, p.44 and p.41-42 in regard to the Blue Mountain Lake House and the Tupper Lake House. 9070

The New Columbian park hotel: the sportsmans paradise...located on Cranberry lake. 1905. Carthage, N.Y. Brownell, n.d. unpaged (12p.) illus. 9071

The New hermitage, David Scanlon, prop. Lake Bonaparte in the Adirondack mountains. Carthage, N.Y. Carthage republican job print, n.d. unpaged (20p.) illus. map. 9072

...New pond inn, Underwood, Essex county, N.Y. M. Sherman, prop. n.p. n.d. unpaged (8p. incl. covers) illus. 9073

Northbrook lodge in the Adirondacks near Paul Smiths, New York. n.p. n.d. Broadside printed on both sides and folded into 8p. illus. map. Another edition without map. 9074

Nunn's inn, Cranberry lake... Watertown N.Y. Lodge record press, n.d. unpaged (12p.) illus. 9075

Owls head hotel... *No Country Life,* Winter 1958. 12:no.1:53. Brief note on razing of old hotel in Keene. 9076

...Panorama lodge. A mountain retreat in the heart of the beautiful Adirondacks. n.p. n.d. Broadside printed on both sides and folded into 6p. illus. map. 9077

Paul Smith's hotel and cottages... n.p. n.d. Broadside printed on both sides and folded into 6p. illus. map. Also a variant edition with note: Operated by the Hotel Management Department of Paul Smith's College. 9078

Paul Smith's hotel co. Paul Smith's Adirondack park. Paul Smiths, N.Y. n.d. 24p. illus. map (dated 1898) Another edition, undated, 36p. 9079

----. Same. Paul Smiths, N.Y. n.d. unpaged (28p.) illus. (part col.) col. map, folded. Map is dated 1900. 9080

----. Same; ten lakes, twenty-three miles of waterway...Camp, cottage, casino and hotel life in the Adirondacks. Troy, N.Y. Troy times art press, 1927? Broadside printed on both sides and folded into 12p. illus. map. 9081

The perfect vacation spot. Indian rock camps on Lake Flower, Saranac Lake, N.Y. n.p. n.d. Broadside printed on both sides and folded into 6p. illus. 9082

Pine grove cottage, Jay, Essex county, New York. n.p. n.d. unpaged (6p.) illus. 9083

...Pine ridge cottage, North Hudson, Essex county, N.Y. L.A. Chaffey, proprietor... n.p. n.d. unpaged (8p. incl. covers) illus. 9084

Pinehurst in the Adirondacks; on Lower Saranac lake. n.p. n.d. Broadside printed on both sides in green ink, folded into 8p. illus. map. Rate schedule laid in. 9085

Prospect house. *No Country Life,* Summer 1960. 14:no.3:4-7. illus. Reprinted from *Ziyara Bugle.* Blue Mountain Lake. 9086

...Pyramid lake house...Orrin Harris, proprietor. P.O. Paradox, Essex county, N.Y. Ticonderoga, Sentinel press, n.d. unpaged (4p.) illus. 9087

Raquette lake, Adirondacks as a summer resort. Season of 1909... N.Y. Leverick co. 1909. unpaged (32p.) illus. Issued by C.H. Bennett, proprietor of The Antlers. 9088

Reilly, Mrs. John. The Merrill house: an old hotel on Upper Chateaugay lake. *York State Trad,* Fall 1964. 18:no.4:24-28. illus. ports. See also letters from Ralph Bellows about steamboats on Chateaugay Lake in the Winter 1965 issue, p.50-51. Includes brief note about the Lake House. 9089

...Riverside inn, Saranac Lake, N.Y. n.p. n.d. unpaged (16p.) illus. 9090

Rocky point inn and cottages...Inlet, New York. Troy, N.Y. Troy times art press, n.d. unpaged (16p.) illus. A.G. Delmarsh, proprietor. 9091

Rogers rock hotel. ...Rogers rock on Lake George. n.p. n.d. 11p. Accompanied by twelve loose plates. 9092

Rustic lodge. *NYS Con,* Oct.-Nov. 1956. 11: no.2:43. Letters from Warder H. Cadbury and I.W. Williams about famous lodge on Upper Saranac Lake. 9093

The Sagamore, Lake George. Season 1895. Philadelphia, 1895? 32p. illus. 9094

The Sagamore, Green island, Lake George, N.Y. n.p. 190-? 25p. illus. folded map. 9095

The Sagamore, south end of Green island, Lake George. Philadelphia, Ketterlinus printing house, 1890. 32p. illus. Also another edition for 1894, printed by Possons, Glens Falls, N.Y. 9096

"St. Hubert's" Keene Heights P.O., Beede's N.Y. Glens Falls, N.Y. S.R. Stoddard, n.d. unpaged (16p.) illus. map. Also another edition, 24p., Orlando Beede, proprietor. 9097

St. Hubest's inn, Keene Heights (Adirondacks) New York. Glens Falls, N.Y. S.R. Stoddard, n.d. unpaged (20p.) illus. maps. "A new and handsome hotel on the site of the old Beede House". Beede and Houghton, proprietors. 9098

St. Jermain's hotel. *Weekly Novelette,* June 23, 1860. 7:240. illus. At Chazy Lake. 9099

St. Jermain's hotel, Chazy lake, New York. *Ballou,* April 3, 1858. 14:209. illus. 9100

The St. Regis, one of the leading hotels of Saranac Lake, N.Y... English & Murnane, proprietors. Saranac Lake, N.Y. Currier press, n.d. Broadside printed on both sides and folded into 12p. illus. map. On yellow paper. 9101

Saranac inn on picturesque Upper Saranac lake... n.p. n.d. unpaged (8p. folded) col. illus. Sharp Ltd. Hotels. 9102

Saranac inn on Upper Saranac lake...M.B. Marshall, manager... n.p. n.d. Broadside printed on both sides and folded into 24p. illus. map. Another edition, 8p. illus. (Kirkeby Hotel) 9103

Sekon lodge on beautiful Upper Saranac lake in the Adirondacks. n.p. n.d. Broadside printed on both sides and folded into 6p. col. illus. 9104

...Sekon lodge on Fish rock, Upper Saranac lake, N.Y. America's finest mountain lodge resort. n.p. n.d. Broadside printed on both sides and folded into 16p. illus. map. At head of title "Robert Dellevie's" 9105

The Shaw house, Long Lake, N.Y. n.p. n.d. unpaged (4p.) illus. Date stamped on first page: July 8, 1902. 9106

Star lake and its environs, and the new Star lake house; Foley & Lyman, proprietors. n.p. 1896. 20p. illus. 9107

...Stevens house, Lake Placid, N.Y. n.p. n.d. unpaged (12p.) illus. Also a variant edition, 16p. undated. 9108

The Stevens house overlooking Lake Placid and Mirror lake. Troy, N.Y. Troy times art press, n.d. unpaged (20p.) illus. maps (one folded) Folded into red cover. Cover title: Lake Placid, Adirondacks. 9109

The Tahawus house, Geo. W. Egglefield, proprietor...n.p. n.d. unpaged (12p.) illus. At Keene Valley. 9110

Tahawus house in the Adirondacks, Keene Valley. n.p. n.d. Broadside printed on both sides and folded into 10p. illus. 9111

Tahawus house in the Adirondacks, Keene Valley. W.B. Egglefield & co. proprietors. n.p. n.d. unpaged (12p.) illus. Also an unpaged 8p. leaflet without name of preprietor and a 9p. undated edition in gray folder, with cover title "In the Heart of the Adirondacks. Tahawus House..." 9112

...Taylor house and cottages...Taylor's-on-Schroon, Warren co., N.Y. Glens Falls, N.Y. Glens Falls printing co. n.d. unpaged (4p.) illus. 9113

...Taylor house and fifteen cottages. Lake view point, Schroon lake... Glens Falls, N.Y. S.R. Stoddard, 1890? unpaged (16p.) illus. 9114

Tormey's cabins & cottages. The perfect vacation... n.p. n.d. Broadside printed on both sides and folded into 12p. illus. Laid in is 3p. supplement, with plans and maps, mimeographed. Includes "The Legend of Onchiota". 9115

Tormey's deluxe cottages, Onchiota, New York ... n.p. n.d. 16p. incl. covers. map. Mimeographed in green ink. 9116

Trail's end, Keene Valley, New York... n.p. 1961? Folded broadside printed on both sides, with illustrations. Green paper, "A small family inn and hikers' lodge"   9117

...Trembleau hall, inc. on Lake Champlain, Port Kent, N.Y. Troy, N.Y. Troy times art press, n.d. 30p. illus, map.   9118

Undercliff on Lake Placid... n.p. 1903. unpaged (12p. incl. covers) illus.   9119

Undercliff on Lake Placid: the pearl of the Adirondacks. n.p. n.d. unpaged (16p. incl. covers) illus. Also a variant undated edition, 16p. with different text and illustrations.   9120

Wardner farm, Rainbow lake, Franklin county, New York. The Adirondacks in their inspiring splendor... n.p. n.d. Broadside printed on both sides and folded into 8p. illus. 9121

...Wawbeek hotel and cottages... n.p. n.d. Broadside printed on both sides and folded into 8p. col. illus. map. On Upper Saranac Lake. Harry and Terry Purchase, proprietors.   9122

...Wawbeek lodge. N.Y. Ronalds press, n.d. Broadside printed on both sides and folded into 8p. illus. map.   9123

Weld's on Lake Clear in the heart of the Adirondacks. n.p. n.d. Broadside printed on both sides and folded into 8p. illus. map.   9124

Wessels, William L. Ghost hotel. *Trailmarker,* Mar. 1963. 1:no.4:10-12. illus. Prospect Hotel at Blue Mountain Lake.   9125

The Westport inn...gateway to the Adirondacks. n.p. n.d. unpaged (12p.) illus.   9126

The Westport inn. H.P. Smith. n.p. n.d. unpaged (20p.) illus. Cover title: Adirondacks, Westport, Lake Champlain.   9127

The Westport inn, Lake Champlain...H.P. Smith. Troy, N.Y. Troy times art press, n.d. unpaged (24p.) illus. Another undated edition printed by the Troy Times Art Press, 20p. 9128

The Westport inn, Westport-on-Lake Champlain, New York. n.p. n.d. unpaged (8p.) illus. Mrs. O.C.Daniell, manager.   9129

The Westport inn, Westport-on-Lake Champlain, New York. H.P. Smith. n.p. n.d. unpaged (20p.) illus.   9130

Westport inn. What to do at the Westport inn. Buffalo, Matthews-Northrup, n.d. unpaged (16p.) illus. maps. Also a similar edition without illustrations entitled "What One Can Do at Westport".   9131

...Whiteface cottage. Mrs. John W. Fletcher, prop. n.p. n.d. unpaged (8p.) illus. At Bloomingdale.   9132

Whiteface inn. A few words about Whiteface inn, Lake Placid, N.Y... The Adirondack company, owner. N.Y. Amsterdam press, n.d. unpaged (18p.) illus. Harrington Mills, manager.   9133

Whiteface inn, Lake Placid, N.Y...Adirondack co., owner, Edwin H. Lee, manager. N.Y. Amsterdam press, n.d. unpaged (20p.) illus. 9134

Whiteface inn, Whiteface, N.Y. Located on the shore of beautiful Lake placid. Henry W. Haynes, managing director... n.p. n.d. Broadside printed on both sides and folded into 6p. col. illus.   9135

Whiteface mountain house and the Homestead, Wilmington, N.Y. Troy, N.Y. Troy times art press, 1932. unpaged (12p.)   9136

The Windsor. What one can do... n.p. n.d. unpaged (12p.) illus. At Elizabethtown.   9137

...The Windor...Elizabethtown, N.Y. n.p. n.d. unpaged (4p.) illus.   9138

The Windsor, Elizabethtown, N.Y. n.p. n.d. unpaged (24p.) illus. Orlando Kellogg & Son, proprietors.   9139

The Windsor, Elizabethtown, N.Y. Glens Falls, N.Y. C.H. Possons, n.d. unpaged (16p. incl. covers) illus. Orlando Kellogg, proprietor. 9140

The Windsor. Adirondacks. Elizabethtown, N.Y. Orlando Kellogg & son. n.p.n.d. unpaged (32p.) illus. Also a variant edition printed by the Troy Times Art Press, 28p. and two other editions, without printer, 24 and 20p.   9141

Witherill hotel. Witherill hotel in historic Plattsburgh on Lake Champlain, New York. The Howell collection of Americana and antiques. n.p. n.d. 13p. illus. Also their "Weathervanes", undated and unpaged (12p.) illustrated.   9142

COMMUNICATIONS, TRANSPORTATION AND PUBLIC WORKS

GENERAL

Cone, Gertrude E. Development of commerce on Lake Champlain. *No Country Life,* Winter 1960. 14:no.1:40-43,45. From her master's thesis (no.4392)   9143

----. Improvements in transportation. *No Country Life,* Spring 1960. 14:no.2:34-37. From the thesis noted above.   9144

----. Travel in the Champlain valley in pioneer times. *No Country Life,* Summer 1959. 13:no. 3:40-42. From the thesis noted above.   9145

Jacob, C. Albert jr. The Riverside stage. *NYS Con,* June-July 1960. 14:no.6:46. illus. Letter with picture of the stage in front of the Wells House, Pottersville.   9146

New York (state) Laws, statutes, etc. Laws of the State of New York respecting navigable communications between the great western and northern lakes and the Atlantic ocean. N.Y. T.&W. Mercein, 1817. 14p.   9147

Rist, Leslie. Autos. *Tahawus Cloudsplitter,* May 1964. 15:no.5:14. illus. Notes on early autos in Newcomb. See also his "More about Autos" in the Summer 1964 issue, 15:no.6:10.
9148

A stage robbery. *Reveille,* Sept. 1962. 7:no.7:4. Tally-ho held up near North River.   9149

CANALS
Arranged by date

New York (state) Canal commissioners. Report...on the canals from Lake Erie to the Hudson river, and from Lake Champlain to the same. Presented...17 February 1817. Albany, J. Buel, 1817. 90p.   9150

New York (state) Laws, statutes, etc. Acts passed at the forty-third session of the Legislature...respecting the canals from Lake Erie to the Hudson river and from Lake Champlain to the same. Albany, Websters and Skinners, 1820. 20p.   9151

New York (state) Legislature. Assembly. Report...relative to the construction of the Black river canal. Albany, 1829. v.p. maps. Assembly, March 9, 1829.   9152

----. Report...on a resolution...relative to the cost of canals and railroads. Albany, 1835. 44p. folded plates. (Assembly Document 1835 no. 296) Includes rates on the Champlain Canal.
9153

New York (state) Legislature. Assembly. Canal commissioners. Report...in answer to a resolution...relative to contracts on the canals. Albany, 1841. 42p. tables. (Assembly Document 1841 no.203) Black River Canal, p.26-30. 9154

New York (state) Legislature. Senate. Canal commissioners. Report...on the several canals other than the Erie. Albany, 1850. 13p. (Senate Document 1850 no.83) Locks on the Champlain Canal, p.11-12.   9155

New York (state) Attorney-general. Report... on the bill to provide for the enlargement of the state canals. Albany, 1851. 22p. (Senate Document 1851 no.68) Black River Canal.   9156

New York (state) State engineer and surveyor. Report...relative to the cost of finishing the canals. Albany, 1853. 4p. (Senate Document 1853 no.64) Includes Black River Canal.   9157

New York (state) Legislature. Senate. ...Report on survey of Hudson river to Fort Edward and of Champlain canal enlargement from tidewater to Whitehall. Washington, 1867. 111p. (Senate Document 1867 no.37)   9158

New York (state) Canal investigating commission. Report...transmitted to the Legislature Feb. 28, 1899. N.Y. Wynkoop, Hallenbeck, Crawford co. 1899. 209p. tables. Includes enlarging and improving the Champlain Canal.
9159

New York (state) State engineer and surveyor. Rules governing construction... Albany, 1905? 42p. Barge canal.   9160

----. Laws and regulations for the improvement of the Erie, Oswego and Champlain canals... Albany, J.B. Lyon, 1906. 75p. diagrs. tables.
9161

Hall, C. Eleanor. The opening of the northern canal. *No Country Life,* Summer 1956. 10: no.3:41-44. Champlain Canal.   9161a

Willoughby, William R. The inception of the Erie and Champlain canal projects. *Niag Front,* Winter 1957. 3:no.4:105-15.   9162

RAILROADS
General

Hochschild, Harold K. Adirondack railroads, real and phantom. Blue Mountain Lake, N.Y. Adirondack museum, 1962. 21p. illus. maps. Selections, with revisions from his "Township 34".   9163

Miller, Roland B. Iron horses in the Adirondacks: an account of the early railroads. *NYS Con,* Oct.-Nov. 1956, April-May 1957. 11:no.2:18-19; 11:no.5:9. illus.   9164

The Adirondack Company

Adirondack company. Addendum: The Adirondack railway and its relation to through traffic. n.p. n.d. 9 leaves. Proof sheets, printed after 1871. W.C. Copy at the Adirondack Museum.
9165

----. The Adirondack company. n.p. n.d. 17p. Publicity brochure probably published in 1864. W.C. Copy at the Adirondack Museum. 9166

----. Adirondack company's amended articles of association. N.Y.? 1871? 9p.   9167

----. Proposals are invited for $1000,000 of construction bonds... N.Y. 1864. 3p. Signed by G.T.M. Davis, president, Nov. 10, 1864. Copy at the Adirondack Museum.   9168

Hochschild, Harold K. Doctor Durant and his iron horse. Blue Mountain Lake, N.Y. Adirondack Museum, 1961. 17p. illus. maps (incl. end papers) A revised extract from his "Township 34"   9169

New York (state) State engineer and surveyor. Annual report...for the year ending Sept. 30, 1875. Albany, Jerome B. Parmenter, 1876. 1175p. (Assembly Document no.132) p.421-33 Adirondack railroad report.   9170

Northern Railroad

Allen, C. F. H. Notes on the Ogdensburg and

Lake Champlain r.r. *Rail & Loc,* April 1960. 102:49-50.   9171

Gile, Frank L. A history of the Northern railroad company of New York. 149 leaves. maps. Master's thesis, University of Nebraska, 1960. Typescript.   9172

Hayward, James. Report of surveys and estimates for the Northern railroad in New York. Boston, S.N. Dickinson & co. 1847. 27p. tables, folded map. Cover title: Ogdensburgh & Lake Champlain Railroad. Engineer's Report.   9173

New York (state) Legislature. Assembly. Report of Edwin F. Johnson, chief engineer, in relation to the survey of the Ogdensburgh and Champlain rail-road. Albany, 1839. 57p. (Assembly Document 1839 no.133)   9174

Sacket's Harbor and Saratoga Railroad

Clarke, Charles Ezra. ...An address before a meeting of the Sackets Harbor & Saratoga railroad company...November 13, 1850... Boston, N.S. Dearborn, 1851. 12p. At head of title: To the Capitalists of Boston. Another edition, published in 1850, by J.H. Jennings, N.Y. has 16p.   9175

----. An argument on the expediency of constructing a railroad from Sacket's Harbor to Saratoga. Boston, Bazin & Chandler, 1851. 25p.   9176

Edwards, Abraham Franklin. Report of A.F. Edwards, chief engineer of the Sacket's Harbor and Saratoga rail road, in reply to certain resolutions of the board of directors with respect to the weight of different kinds of lumber, cord wood, charcoal, etc. and the cost of transportation... N.Y. Wm. E. and J. Sibell, 1854. 16p.   9177

----. Second annual report and report of the consulting engineer of the Sacket's Harbor and Saratoga rail road. N.Y. Sibell, 1854. 40p. Copy owned by Warder Cadbury.   9178

Ellis, Samuel. Facts concerning the bonds and stock, the railroad and lands of the Sacket's Harbor and Saratoga rail road, N.Y. Wm. E. and J. Sibell, 1854. 12p.   9179

New York (state) Legislature. Senate. Committee on railroads. Report...on memorial of the Saratoga and Sackets Harbor railroad. Albany, 1856. 21p. (Senate Document 1856 no. 93)   9180

Sacket's Harbor and Saratoga railroad co. Specifications. n.p. n.d. 6p. Construction details. Copy at the Adirondack Museum.   9181

Other Railroads

Allen, Richard Sanders. Better late than never. *Trains,* Jan. 1959. 19:no.3:40-47. illus. map. The Delaware and Hudson to Tahawus.   9182

----. The Carry railroad. *York State Trad,* Spring 1965. 19:no.2:between p.28 and 29. illus.

Six-page article on unnumbered pages.   9183

Delaware and Hudson railroad corporation. Board of managers. Inspection of lines, June 2, June 5, 1927. Albany, 1927. 126p. illus. tables. Cover title: Passenger, freight and work equipment on the Delaware and Hudson. Cleveland's trip to the Adirondacks, p.71-72.   9184

----. Inspection of lines. June 7th to June 10th, 1928. Albany, 1928. 360p. illus. Cover title: Passenger and Freight Stations. Report compiled by H.S. Clarke. Copy at the Plattsburgh Public Library.   9185

----. Inspection of lines. June 4th to June 7th, 1936. Albany, 1936. 126p. illus. tables. Cover title: Power Motive, Passenger, Freight and Work Equipment 1926-1936. Copy at the Adirondack Museum.   9186

The golden chariot. *Trailmarker,* July-Aug. 1962. 1:no.2:4-6. port. W. Seward Webb's railroad (Adirondack and St. Lawrence).   9187

Lake Ontario & Hudson river railroad company. Lake Ontario and Hudson river railroad. n.p. n.d. 3p. Published between 1857 and 1860. W.C. Copy at the Adirondack Museum.   9188

----. Report, with minutes of proceedings and evidence, as taken before Commission appointed to examine all the facts relating to the estates and privileges possessed by the company, September 1858. London, Metchim & Burt, 1858. v.p. folded col. maps, folded diagr. Copy at the Adirondack Museum.   9189

Palmer, Richard. Adirondack train has last toot. *Empire,* Nov. 7, 1965. p.9-11. illus. New York Central East Syracuse to Tupper Lake run sponsored by the Central New York Chapter, National Railway Historical Society. 9190

Railroadians of America. Book no.3: an illustrated record of the motive power and growth of the Delaware and Hudson railroad... N.Y. 1941. 128p. illus. maps. Based on the D&H's "Motive Power..." 1926 and "Motive Power, Passenger, Freight..." 1936. Copy at the Adirondack Museum.   9191

Train wreck at Cheever. *Reveille,* April 1962. 7:no.25:1-3. illus.   9192

ROADS AND BRIDGES

Bridge over the Ausable river. *Weekly Novelette,* Sept. 28, 1861. 10:48. illus.   9193

Crown Point road. 200 years. *Ver Life,* Autumn 1959. 14:no.1:19. Anniversary of building the Crown Point military road.   9194

Kimball, Francis P. The open road of the empire state. *NY Times Mag,* Feb. 19, 1928. p.10-11. illus.   9195

LaDuke, John T. Travel: route 9N. *Trailmarker,* July-Aug. 1962. 1:no.2:21-22. map.   9196

Lane, Duane J. A giant crumbles: the Saranac river plank road. *No Country Notes,* May 1965. no.23:2.   9197

Myers, Delia Jenks. Early road conditions in the north country. *Reveille,* Mar. 1958. 2:no.11: 1,3.   9198

New York (state) Lake Champlain bridge commission. Annual report, 1959. Albany, 1960. 8p., appendix. Mimeographed.   9199

----. Same, 1960. Albany, 1961. 10p., appendix. Mimeographed.   9199a

Ticonderoga chamber of commerce. Before the Champlain bridge commissions. Memorandum. Ticonderoga, 1926. 13p. tables, map. Plea for bridge at Ticonderoga.   9200

Travel: the Adirondack trail. *Trailmarker,* May-June 1962. 1:no.1:3,30,32. map. Brief description of Route 30, officially designated as the Adirondack Trail.   9201

Williams, Timothy. Travel: the Nick Stoner trail. *Trailmarker,* Summer 1963. 2:no.1:15-17. illus. map. Portion of Route 10.   9202

STEAMBOATS AND OTHER CARRIERS

Burch, Barbara J. A re-evaluation of early nineteenth century business ethics: the Champlain transportation company. 117p. Typescript of economics honors project at Middlebury College, April 1959.   9203

Cone, Gertrude E. First boats on Lake Champlain. *No Country Life,* Fall 1959. 13:no.4:37-39. Extract from her master's thesis (no.4392)   9204

Dickens, Charles. Thru the eyes of Charles Dickens. *No Country Life,* Fall 1962. 12:no.4:42-43. An extract from his "American Notes" praising the Lake Champlain steamer *Burlington.*   9205

Dobson, John A. The "Ti" sails again. *Ver Life,* Autumn 1950. 5:no.1:40-43. illus.   9206

Hill, Ralph Nading. The one and only Ti. *Ver Life,* Summer 1961. 15:no.4:2-7. illus.   9207

----. Sidewheeler saga: a chronicle of steamboating. N.Y. Rinehart & co. inc. ©1953. 342p. front. illus. ports. Part II on lakes George and Champlain.   9208

----. Spirit of the lake. *Ver Life,* Summer 1948. 2:no.4:6-9. plates, figs. Steamboats on Lake Champlain.   9209

----. Two centuries of ferry boating. The colorful story of the carryalls of Lake Champlain. n.p. Shelburne museum, n.d. unpaged (10p.) illus. (part col.) folded map. Reprinted from *Vermont Life.*   9210

Hochschild, Harold K. Adirondack steamboats on Raquette and Blue Mountain lakes. Blue Mountain Lake, N.Y. Adirondack museum, 1962. 34p. illus. ports. facsims. maps (including end papers). A selection with revisions, from his "Township 34".   9211

Hodges, Frederick. Steamboats on the Fulton chain: from the notebooks of Fred (Adirondack) Hodges; (edited by his son-in-law, Maitland C. De Sormo) *York State Trad,* Winter 1965. 19:no.1:34-38. illus.   9212

Pictures from the past: steamboats on Lake Champlain and Lake George. *No Country Life,* Winter 1962. 16:no.1:25-30. illus.   9213

Raquette lake transportation company. Articles of incorporation and by-laws. Saratoga Springs, N.Y. Saratogian print, 1901. 15p. Copy at the Adirondack Museum.   9214

Rushlow, George. Steam navigation on Lake Champlain. *Vermonter,* Oct. 1898. 4:33-41. plates, maps.   9215

Seaman, Frances (Boone) 'Little Buttercup'. *No Country Life,* Summer 1961. 15:no.3:4-10. illus. Recovery, at Long Lake, of Durant steamboat sunk in 1885.   9216

Tuttle, Charles Henry. The first steamboats on Lake George. *Top o' the World,* June 1937. 1:no.8:1-2.   9217

LIFE AND MANNERS

GENERAL

Camp Uncas in the Adirondacks opens. Former home of J. Pierpont Morgan. *Northeast Log,* Aug. 1957. 6:no.2:62.   9218

Childwold, N.Y. Childwold memorial presbyterian church in the Adirondacks. Cook book produced by Ladies aid society... Kansas City, Mo. North American press, 1954. 42p.   9219

The Champlain valley book of recipes. Collected by young ladies of Trinity church, Plattsburgh... Plattsburgh, N.Y. Telegram printing house, 1890. 185p.   9220

Dewey's tavern. *No Country Notes,* Sept. 1965. no.24:3. Town of Champlain.   9221

Emerson, Joseph W. Inscriptions from Williams street cemetery in Whitehall, N.Y. *New Eng Hist & Gen Reg,* April 1952. 106:106-10.   9222

Essex county Adirondack garden club. Essex county Adirondack garden club. n.p. 1928. unpaged (10p.) Constitution, etc. Copy in the Keene Valley Public Library.   9223

Eyes on the sky at Lake Placid... *Rotarian,* July 1955. 87:no.1:40-42. Pictorial report on

International Assembly of 1955. 9224

Gronemeijer, Carl F. Names of lecturers and their topics at the Lake Placid, N.Y. convention & show of the Eastern federation, June 20,21, & 22, 1963. *Rocks & Min,* May-June 1963. 38:248-49. 9225

Hay, William. A history of temperance in Saratoga county; containing biographical sketches of Billy J. Clark...and all other original members of the Union Temperate Society of Moreau and Northumberland... Saratoga Springs, N.Y. G.M. Davison, 1855. 153p. 9226

Hochschild, Harold K. Life and leisure in the Adirondack backwoods. Blue Mountain Lake, N.Y. Adirondack museum, 1962. 122p. illus. ports. facsims. maps (including end papers). Selection, with revisions, from his "Township 34". 9227

Keeseville, N.Y. Baptist church. The little gem. A family cook book compiled by the ladies... AuSable Forks, N.Y. Adirondack record, 1916. 232p. Copy at the Adirondack Museum. 9228

Keith, Marion G. comp. I'll tell you a story. Choice recipes from the Royal savage inn, Plattsburg, New York... Lake Placid, N.Y. Litho Placid printing service, inc. ©1950. 180p. illus. ports. Revised edition published March 1957. 9229

Kreuger, Henry E. The last prison camp. *Con,* Feb.-Mar. 1963. 17:no.4:2-5,36. illus. Situated on the east slope of Dannemora Mountain. 9230

Lawlessness in the Adirondacks. *For & Stream* June 22, 1876. 6:322. The St. Germain brothers. 9231

The Liberty, an adventure in eating. *No Country Life,* Spring 1958. 12:no.2:54-59. illus. At Whitehall. 9232

Lowrie, Sarah D. History of the Essex county Adirondack garden club: 1941. n.p. n.d. 4 leaves. mimeographed. Copy in the Keene Valley Public Library. 9233

----. 1939-1940. History of the Essex county Adirondack garden club. n.p. 1940. 4 leaves. mimeographed. Copy in the Keene Valley Public Library. 9234

MacDougal, Harry M. They danced until daylight. *Reveille,* April 1957. 1:no.9:1,4. The Clark Brothers orchestra. 9235

Myers, Delia Jenks. Social life of the north country. *Reveille,* Sept. 1958. 2:no.13:1-2. 9236

Order of the eastern star. Mt. Morris chapter no.361. Tupper taste tempters...recipes contributed by the people of Tupper Lake... Tupper Lake, N.Y. 1951. unnumbered pages. mimeographed. Second issue, 1953. 9237

Pell, John H. G. "The oldest flower garden

in America". Elizabethtown, N.Y. Essex county historical society, 1956. 8p. Address at the dedication of the Colonial Garden at the Adirondack Center. Describes the Jardin du Roi at Fort Carillon. 9238

Plattsburgh, N.Y. First Methodist episcopal church. Ladies' association. The centennial cook book... Plattsburgh, N.Y. Sentinel publishing co. 1914. 128p. illus. 9239

Plattsburgh, N.Y. Trinity church. Dorcas club. Tried and true recipes. Plattsburgh, N.Y. 1936. 118p. In ring binder. 9240

Porter, Marjory (Lansing) comp. The Liberty eatery and antique emporium; Katherine Leddick, proprietor. Whitehall, N.Y. n.d. 122p. At Whitehall. Title from Mrs. Porter. 9241

Saranac Lake, N.Y. Federation of churches. The unvarnished truth about Saranac Lake. n.p. 1917? unpaged (12p.) illus. Election pamphlet on prohibition. 9242

Saranac Lake, N.Y. Methodist church. Methodist cook book... Saranac Lake, N.Y. Paul's mimeograph service, 1954. 78p. Reproduced from typewritten copy. 9243

Shannon, Martin J. The summer of the big story. *Trailmarker,* Summer 1963. 2:no.1:4-7, 18. illus. ports. The Gillette murder case. 9244

Simmons, Julia (Gardelphe) The house on Culver hill. *York State Trad,* Summer 1964. 18: no.3:52-54. 9245

Smith, Howard M. Early dances of the north country. *Our Town,* Spring 1963. 2:no.1:3-6. 9246

Stickney, Edward E. First Masonic lodge in Essex county, *Reveille,* April 1956. 1:no 5: 2-3. See also letter by E. Eugene Barker in the September issue, p. 1,3. 9247

Temperance in Clinton county. *No Country Notes,* Feb. 1963. no.12:1. 9248

True. A treasury of True: the best from 20 years of the man's magazine; ed. by Charles N. Barnard. Greenwich, Conn. Fawcett publications. ©1958. 319p. illus. Includes "The Search", by Carl Kaufman. 9249

Tupper Lake, N.Y. Grace methodist church. Tupper Lake's treasure of personal recipes; compiled by the W.S.C.S... Kansas City, Mo. Bev Ron publishing co. 1952. 40p. 9250

United community funds and councils of America. A new look at government and voluntary services - Proceedings, Adirondack workshop, August 10-14, 1953, Silver Bay, N.Y... N.Y. 1953. 22 leaves. 9251

The W.C.T.U. *No Country Notes,* Nov. 1963. no.15:3. Meeting at Ellenburg Depot, June 11, 1897. 9252

Wikoff, Climena M. comp. Placid eating; 2d ed. N.Y. Radio magazines, inc. 1959. 152p. illus. (part col.) 9253

Willard, Cyrus Field. First American military lodge. *NY Mas Outlook,* Dec. 1938. 15:76. Brief note on Lodge at Crown Point. 9254

A world unique and magnificent, photographed by Alfred Eisenstaedt. *Life,* Nov. 5, 1965. 59: no.19:54-72A. col. illus. col. port. Includes description of the Adirondack home of Mrs. Marjorie Merriweather Post, Camp Topridge on Upper St. Regis Lake. 9255

FOLKLORE AND BALLADS

Aber, Ted and King, Stella (Brooks). Tales from an Adirondack county. Prospect, N.Y. Prospect books, 1961. 208p. illus. Reviewed in *North Country Life,* Fall 1961, 15:no.4:30. Hamilton county. 9256

Adirondack miscellany. *Yorker,* Mar.-April 1961. 19:no.4:15. 9257

Bill Nye and his Matilda story. *York State Trad,* Summer 1963. 17:no.3:18-22. port. Nye's story as told by S.R. Stoddard in the *Northern Monthly,* Nov. 1907, with a brief biography. 9258

Clough, Benjamin Clough, ed. The American imagination at work. Tall tales and folk tales. N.Y. Knopf, 1947. 707p. Includes: Adirondack Anecdotes by Edith E. Cutting (from AB 4688); Adirondack Fauna by H.W. Thompson (from AB 4731); Captain Carver's Narrative of Ethan Allen's Captivity (from AB 134) 9259

Cutting, Edith E. Whistling girls and jumping sheep; sketches by Erwin S. Austin. Cooperstown, N.Y. Farmer's museum, 1951. 85p. illus. Includes north country tales. 9260

Drew, Hazel C. Tales from Little Lewis. Lyons Falls, N.Y. author, ©1961. 56p. illus. 9261

Drew, Mary Derby. Some old sayings. *Reveille,* Dec. 1956; April 1957. 1:no.8:4; 1:no. 9:3. 9262

Franz, Eleanor (Waterbury) Jerusha Maria and her songs... *No Country Life,* Winter, Spring, Fall 1956: Winter, Spring, Fall 1957; Winter 1958. 10:no.1:52-53,55; 10:no.2:47-51; 10:no.4:48-50; 11:no.1:40-42; 11:no.2:55-56; 11:no.4:44-46; 12:no.1:48-51. 9263

Gordon-Cumming, Constance Frederica. A legend of Inverawe. *Atlan,* Sept. 1884. 54:333-38. 9264

Huguenin, Charles A. The ghost of Ticonderoga. *NY Folk Q,* Spring 1959. 15:4-24. 9265

Jagendorf, Moritz Adolf. Upstate, downstate: folk tales of the middle Atlantic states... N.Y. Vanguard press, 1949. 299p. "A New Way of Tamin' Wolves", p.60-63; "Adirondack Sketters", p.37-39. 9266

Larson, Mildred R. The taller the better. *NY Folk Q,* Winter 1961. 17:271-87. Includes tales about Nick Stoner. 9267

Lauder, Sir Thomas Dick. Tales of the highlands... London, Hamilton, Adams & co. 1881. 376p. plates. "The Legend of the Vision of Campbell of Inverawe", p.330-76. 9268

Morton, Doris (Begor) Great-grandfather and the panther. *York State Trad,* Winter 1964. 18:no.1:19-20. 9269

Porter, Marjorie (Lansing) The Adirondack saga. *No Country Life,* Spring 1961. 15:no. 2:19-20. Reprinted from the booklet (10p.) accompanying Folkways Record "Champlain Valley Songs" from the Marjorie L. Porter Collection of North Country Folklore. Mrs. Porter also wrote the text accompanying the Stinson record "Adirondack Folksongs". 9270

Reynolds, James. Ghosts in American houses. N.Y. Farrar, Straus and Cudahy, 1955. 229p. illus. "The Smile that Broke the Widow's Heart", p.84-88. Mad Anthony Wayne at Ticonderoga. 9271

Rice, Dorothy Pitt. The Union soldier. *York State Trad,* Winter 1965. 19:no.1:45,49. Ghost at Crown Point. 9272

Rogers, Frank D. Folk-stories of the northern border. Clayton, N.Y. Thousand Island publishing co. 1897. 273p. illus. ports. The French settlers, p.218-28. 9273

Samuels, Charles E. Folklore in *Eben Holden. NY Folk Q,* Summer 1957. 13:100-103. 9274

Seagears, Clayton B. The great white stag of Whiteface mountain. *NYS Con,* Aug.-Sept. 1957. 12:no.1:48-49. illus. Comments on littering as well as folklore. 9275

Seaman, Ruth. Tales our fathers told us. *NY Folk Q,* Dec. 1963. 19:275-78. illus. Snakes on Diamond Island, Lake George, etc. 9276

Side hill clinchers. *NYS Con,* April-May 1958. 12:no.5:43. Letter from Watson G. Harding. 9277

Stiles, Fred T. Legends of Furnace Hollow. *No Country Life,* Spring, 1959. 13:no.2:24-26. 9278

----. Welch Hollow. *NY Folk Q,* Mar. 1963. 19:19-26. 9279

Street, Alfred Billings. The white jack of the Upper Saranac. *Beadles M,* July 1866. 2:65-69. Phantom deer. 9280

----. Wild Joe, a tale of Indian Lake. *Beadles M,* Sept. 1866. 2:211-15. Locale is Brown's Tract. 9281

Thomas, Howard. Folklore from the Adirondack foothills... Prospect, N.Y. Prospect books, 1958. 150p. illus. Reviewed by G.C. in *North Country Life,* Winter 1959, 13:no.1: 56-57. 9282

---- Tales from the Adirondack foothills.

Sketches by John Mahaffy. Prospect, N.Y. Prospect books, 1957. 150p. illus. Reviewed by Dorothy A. Plum in *Adirondac,* November-December, 1957, 21:116.   9283

The three Indians: a tradition of Raquette lake. *Am Misc,* July 1, 1865. 1:no.13:202.   9284

Warner, Frank M. A salute and a sampling of songs. *NY Folk Q,* Autumn 1958. 14:202-23. port. Includes music and words by John Galusha.   9285

PRINTING AND PUBLISHING

PERIODICALS RELATING TO THE ADIRONDACKS

The Adirondack enterprise. Carnival edition. Saranac Lake, N.Y. 1915. 32p. illus. Issue dated Feb. 4, 1915.   9286

----. Special issue, July 3, 1902. Saranac Lake, N.Y. 1902. 24p. illus. ports. Featuring Saranac Lake.   9287

----. Special real estate and builders' section, May 25, 1911. Saranac Lake, N.Y. 1911. 8p. illus.   9288

Adirondack life, 1960-date. Warrensburg, N.Y. Robert Hall, 1960-date. Originally a magazine supplement to north country newspapers; now a supplement to the *Warrensburg - Lake George News.* Contains many articles of Adirondack interest. Irregular in publication. Files in the Richards Library, Warrensburg and the Adirondack Museum, Blue Mountain Lake.   9289

Adirondack mountain club, inc. Conservation committee. ...Newsletter, no.1- n.p. Nov. 1960-date. Issued irregularly. Reproduced from typewritten copy. The first issue included "Basic Conservation Policies of the Adirondack Mountain Club".   9290

Adirondack peeks: Forty-sixer newsletter. v.1- , 1963- n.p. 1963-date. Mimeographed. First issue dated Fall-Winter 1963-1964.   9291

The Adirondack scout, v.1-? Utica, N.Y. 1960-? Published in June, July and August. Travel and trail information; recreation. Ceased publication.   9292

Adirondack travel news, v.1, no.1 - n.p. Adirondack attractions association, 1959- illus. maps. Designed for the tourist. Issues 2 and 3 are for July-August and August-September 1959.   9292a

The Aurora borealis, no.1- April 1964-. Lake Placid, N.Y. Northland rock & mineral club, 1964-date.   9293

Backwood's journal, v.1, no.1 - July-August 1957-. Paradox, N.Y. 1957-date. Reproduced from typewritten copy. Originally published at Old Forge, N.Y. with title *Log Cabin Life.* Absorbed *Birch Bark News* in 1963.   9294

Bolton conservation club news, 1948- Bolton Landing, N.Y. 1948-date. Monthly.   9295

Champlain valley guide. Plattsburgh, N.Y. Henry J. Demary, pub. Monthly. Issue for August 1924 in the Plattsburgh Public Library.   9296

The Champlain valley news; sponsored by New York - Vermont interstate commission on Lake Champlain basin. Ticonderoga, N.Y. 1959. Three issues, May, June and July 1959 (v.1 nos.1-3) Publicity in newsletter form. 9297

Clinton county historical association. North country notes, no.i- Nov. 1960- Plattsburgh, N.Y. 1960-date. Quarterly.   9298

Conservation council comments, v.1, no.1- April-May 1961-Kingston, N.Y. New York state conservation council, 1961-date. Frequency and place of publication vary. Preceded by its *Bulletin.*   9299

Essex co. republican. Supplement: Oct. 20, 1905. n.p. 1905. unpaged (4p.) illus. port. Issue devoted to Crown Point. Edited by A.A. Young.   9300

----. Same: Nov. 3, 1905. n.p. 1905. unpaged (4p.) illus. Issue devoted to Port Henry. Edited by A.A. Young.   9301

----. Same: Nov. 17, 1905. n.p. 1905. unpaged (4p.) illus. Issue devoted to Essex. Edited by A.A. Young.   9302

The Fortnightly: a bulletin issued during the summer covering activities in the Town of Keene. v.1, no.1- July 1-15, 1956- Keene Valley, N.Y. 1956-date. Reproduced from typewritten copy. Robert Denniston, editor. 9303

Franklin historical review. v.1- 1964- Malone, N.Y., Franklin county historical society, 1964-date. Annual.   9304

George Fuller Golden journal, v.1- Saranac Lake, N.Y. Adirondack enterprise print shop, 1907-? Issued ten times a year. Volume 1 number 2 in the Saranac Lake Free Library. 9305

Historical society of the town of Chester. Bulletin, 1962- Chestertown, N.Y. 1962-date. mimeographed.   9306

Hotel Saranac quarterly; published by the Hotel Saranac... Saranac Lake, N.Y. 1931-1932. File at Paul Smith's College Library.   9307

John Thurman historical society. Quarterly, v.1- August 1963- Athol, N.Y. 1963-date. mimeographed. 9308

Lake George historical association. Bulletin, no.1- 1964- Lake George, N.Y. 1964-date. Annual. 9309

Lake George mirror, devoted to the interests of the queen of the American lakes. Assembly Point, Lake George, N.Y. W.H. Tippetts, 1895-? Issued weekly, June-September. 9310

Lake George park commission. Newsletter, no.1- July-Aug. 1962- Ticonderoga, N.Y. 1962-date. Quarterly. Under the Conservation Department. 9311

Lake Placid club. Lake Placid club life. First issue - pre-winter - 1959. Lake Placid Club, N.Y. 1959-date. illus. Revival of an older publication with the same title. Issued seasonly. 9312

Lake Placid villager, 1958/59- Lake Placid, N.Y. Jack Barry, 1958-date. Issued annually. Free distribution through the Lake Placid Chamber of Commerce. 9313

Meet the town. Lake Placid edition. Saranac Lake, N.Y. Sheridan advertising service, 1929-1962. illus. maps. Annual; irregular in publication. 9314

The Mountain book lover, v.1- Lake Placid, N.Y. 1906-? Volume 1, season 1906 at the Adirondack Museum. 9315

Nelson's American lancet. Plattsburgh, N.Y. 1850-1856. 12v. Volumes 1-3 have title *Northern Lancet*. 9316

New York (state) Conservation department. Conservation bulletin from Commissioner Harold G. Wilm, v.1, no.1- 1959- Albany, 1959-? Issued irregularly. The first eight issues are undated. Volume 2, number 1 is dated February 1960. 9317

New York state historical association. Bulletin from Headquarters house. Ticonderoga, N.Y. 1932-1946. 14v. Title varies. Last issued was v.14, no.2. 9319

Northeastern forest fire protection commission. Compact news, no.1- Oct. 1, 1952- Chatham, N.Y. 1952-date. Quarterly. mimeographed. 9320

Northweek, no.1- June 1961- Gouveneur, N.Y. 1961-date. Unpaged monthly regional magazine for northern New York state. First issue included illustrated article on the Adirondack Museum. 9321

Our town: the story of Diana, Lewis county, New York. v.1- Dec. 1962- Natural Bridge, N.Y. 1962-1965. mimeographed. Quarterly. Edited by Glen Hawkins. Suspended with the winter 1964/65 issue. 9322

The Researcher. v.1,no.1- Fall, 1964- Saranac Lake, N.Y. Trudeau foundation, inc. 1964-date. The first issue is devoted to the dedication of the new research laboratories. 9323

Saranac Lake, N.Y. Board of health. Bulletin, 1916- Saranac Lake, N.Y. 1916-? Published bi-monthly. Cartoons and text by Dr. C.C. Trembley. Issues for May 1916 and May 1917 in the Saranac Lake Free Library. 9324

The Service letter. Indian Lake, N.Y. 1943-1946. 3v. For members of the armed forces. Issued irregularly. Revived during the Korean War; 5 letters, Dec. 17, 1951 - Mar. 20, 1953. File at the Adirondack Museum. 9325

This Adirondack week. Lake Placid, N.Y. Garfield Jones, 1948-1963. Weekly; irregular. First issue, Christmas week 1948 had title *This Week in Lake Placid*. 9326

The Tower. v.1, no.1- Sept. 1956- Ticonderoga, N.Y. International paper company, 1956-date. Monthly. The May 1959 issue, volume 3, number 5 was a special issue on Lake George and included "Champlain Valley Profile", "Ticonderoga Mills Festive Exhibit and Float" and "Ticonderoga Yesterdays". 9327

The Trailmarker, the magazine of the Adirondacks. Utica, N.Y. Trailmarker corporation, 1962-1963. 2v. Bimonthly. Suspended with volume 2, number 1, Summer 1963. Reviewed in *North Country Life,* Fall 1962, 16:no.4:52. 9328

Trotty Veck messenger, 1916- Saranac Lake, N.Y. 1916-date. Annual. Files at the Paul Smith's College Library and the Saranac Lake Free Library. 9329

Valley news. Special anniversary edition, Mar. 8, 1962. Elizabethtown, N.Y. 1962. unpaged (32p.) illus. Contains: More than a newspaper - a community service, by Marjorie Lansing Porter; Essex county's most famous murder (Henry Debosnys case), etc. 9330

"We, the patients". News of Will Rogers hospital and O'Donnell memorial research laboratories. v.1,no.1- Mar. 1, 1962- Saranac Lake, N.Y. 1962-date. Published monthly. 9331

NEWSPAPER COLUMNS AND PERIODICALS ON THE ADIRONDACKS

Carson, William R. Billsbord: monthly column in *New York State Medicine,* May 1, 1962-date. 9332

Mason, Howard C. Backward glances. Glens Falls, N.Y. Webster mimeoprint service, 1963-1965. 3v. ports. plates. map. Originally issued as a newspaper column in the Glens Falls dailies. Reproduced from typewritten copy. Reviewed in *York State Tradition* Spring and Fall 1964, 18:no.2:58-59 and 18:no.4:60-61. 9333

Plum, Dorothy Alice. ADK in the news. *Adirondac,* Jan.-Feb. 1957. 21:24. Newspaper columns on the Adirondacks.   9334

Porter, Marjorie (Lansing) Upstate things 'n stuff. In the Plattsburgh *Press Republican,* 1963-date. A weekly column. The author has also contributed a series "See Clinton County First" to the *Press Republican* in addition to

"The History of Keeseville" to the *Essex County Republican,* 1944-1946.   9335

Roden, William M. Adirondack sportsman. In the *Warrensburg News,* May 5, 1955-date. A weekly column. Also in the *Adirondack Enterprise* (Saranac Lake), Mar. 8, 1955- and in the *Glens Falls Post-Star,* February 17, 1955 - date. In other north country papers from time to time.   9336

HEALTH AND MEDICINE

GENERAL

The Adirondacks as a winter resort. *Harper W,* Jan. 7, 1888. 32:19.   9336a

American Trudeau society. Membership roster issued September, 1942... N.Y. n.d. 219p. 9337

Brown, Lawrason. Osler and Trudeau. *Am Rev Tub,* June 1925. 11:374. Editorial.   9338

Clinton county, N.Y. Health department. Annual report, 1959. Plattsburgh, N.Y. 1959. unpaged. mimeographed. Issues for 1962, 1963, 1964 and 1965 are in the Plattsburgh Public Library.   9339

Cole, G. Glyndon. The monster of epidemy. *York State Trad,* Winter 1964. 18:no.1:4-8, 52-55. Cholera epidemic.   9340

Essex county health association, inc. Annual report, April 1st, 1960 -- March 31st, 1961. Keene Valley, N.Y. 1961. unpaged (8p.) 9341

History of the Town of Moriah ambulance squad, inc. n.p. 1965. unpaged (4p.) Laid in the 1965 program of the Essex County Agricultural Fair.   9342

Michele, Sister Mary. Personalized care of the aged and chronically ill. *Health News,* June 1965. 42:no.6:4-11. illus. Sanitorium Gabriels institutes a new service.   9343

Munro, David Colin. Man alive; you're half dead! Revised ed. N.Y. Bartholomew house,

1952. 255p. Author was medical director at the Lake Placid Club, 1929-1943.   9344

National tuberculosis association. Program of the thirty-first annual meeting, June 24, 25, 26 and 27, 1935, Saranac Lake, N.Y. N.Y. 1935. 28p. col.illus.   9345

Saranac Lake society for the control of tuberculosis, inc. Saranac Lake, New York, in the Adirondacks. Pioneer health resort. Saranac Lake, N.Y. n.d. unpaged (4p.) illus.   9346

Trudeau, Edward Livingston. History of the tuberculosis work at Saranac Lake. *J Outd Life,* May 1931. 28:269-79. illus. ports. 9347

Trudeau foundation, inc. Annual report...1959-Saranac Lake, N.Y. 1959-date. The first in the report series since 1951.   9348

----. ...Dedication of the Trudeau foundation research laboratories, August 1st, 1964. Saranac Lake, N.Y. 1964. unpaged (4p.) Program with brief historical note.   9349

Trudeau school of tuberculosis, Saranac Lake, N.Y. Outline of proposed schedule of the course of study. Saranac Lake, N.Y. 1916. unpaged (6p.) Laid in is "List of Lecturers Invited for the First Session".   9350

White, William Chapman. A permanent cure for TB? *Womans H C,* Feb. 1952. p.44,52,54.   9351

HOSPITALS AND SANATORIA

Heise, Fred H. Trudeau sanatorium after 1903. *J Outd Life,* May 1931. 28:280-84. illus. 9352

Independent order of foresters. Thirteenth and fourteenth annual report of Rainbow sanatorium for tuberculosis, January 1925. n.p. n.d. 47p. illus. ports. tables. At Rainbow Lake.   9353

Keene Valley hospital, inc. To friends of the Keene Valley hospital. Keene Valley, N.Y. 1956. unpaged (4p.) Annual report announcing new building.   9354

----. To members and friends of the Keene Valley hospital. Keene Valley, N.Y. 1964. unpaged (4p.) Annual report.   9355

Plattsburgh, N.Y. Physicians hospital. Cere-

monies for placing marker stone for nurses' residence...August 6, 1952. n.p. n.d. unpaged (24p.) illus.   9357

----. Medical and surgical yearbook, no.1-2. Plattsburgh, N.Y. 1929-1930. v.p.   9358

----. The Physicians hospital of Plattsburgh. Plattsburgh, N.Y. 1929. unpaged. front. illus.   9359

The Will Rogers hospital and O'Donnell memorial research laboratories. Saranac Lake, N.Y. N.Y. 1964? unpaged (8p.) illus. 9360

Will Rogers hospital and O'Donnell memorial research laboratories. The story of Will Rogers memorial hospital fund... Saranac Lake, N.Y. 1965. 30p. illus. ports.   9361

RELIGIOUS HISTORY

Allen, Cornelia (Hagar) and Esden, Joan (Cruikshank) comp. History of methodism in Plattsburgh. Plattsburgh, N.Y. 1965. unpaged (16p.) illus. ports.   9362

Allen, Stanton P. A summer revival and what it brought about. N.Y. Hunter & Eaton, ©1894. 200p. plates. At Lyon Mountain. Copy in the Plattsburgh Public Library.   9363

Brayton, D. Religious intelligence of Plattsburgh circuit. *Chr Advocate*, May 21, 1831. 4:149-50.   9364

Brown, George S. Letter...on West Fort Anne. *Chr. Advocate*, Nov. 9, 1839. 13:46.   9365

----. Revival at Warrensburg. *Chr Advocate*, Oct. 19, 1838. 13:34.   9366

Bulkley, E.A. Historical sketch of the Presbytery of Champlain, with outlines of the histories of the churches under its care. Plattsburgh, N.Y. Tuttle, 1877. 16p. Copy in the Keene Valley Public Library.   9367

Chazy, N.Y. Presbyterian church. Memorial service for Mrs. Alice T. Miner...April 1, 1950. n.p. 1950. unpaged, port.   9368

Chestertown, N.Y. Community church. The community church, Chestertown, N.Y. Lake George, N.Y. Adirondack resorts press, n.d. 23p. illus. port. Cover title: Dedication program (June 30, 1946)   9369

Colman (i.e. Coleman?) Seymour. Warren circuit. *Chr Advocate*, Oct. 30, 1829. 4:34. Another article with same title in issue for May 21, 1830, 4:150.   9370

Ellenburg, N.Y. Methodist church. The one hundredth anniversary...August 22, 1943. Ellenburg, N.Y. 1943. 12p. mimeographed. 9371

Essex and Champlain Baptist association. Minutes of the fiftieth anniversary...September 3d, 4th and 5th, 1884. Including a history of the first fifty years, 1834-1884... Plattsburgh, Tuttle, 1884. 44p. illus. front.plates. ports.   9372

Frazier, Jno. Jay circuit. *Chr Advocate*, Feb. 20, 1835. 9:102.   9373

Gilbert, William. The Church of the good thief. *York State Trad*, Fall 1965. 19:no.4:32-35. illus. At Clinton Prison, Dannemora. 9374

Gorrie, Peter Douglas. Black River and northern New York conference memorial, second series... Watertown, N.Y. Charles E. Holbrook, 1881. 472p. port.   9375

----. The Black River conference memorial: containing sketches of the life and character of the deceased members of the Black River conference of the M.E. church... N.Y. Carlton & Phillips, 1852. 356p. ports.   9376

Graham, Henry. History of the Troy conference of Methodist episcopal church. Albany, J.B. Lyon, 1908. 321p. tables. Includes Plattsburg and Champlain districts.   9377

H. Warren circuit. *Chr Advocate*, Sept. 1845. 20:1.   9378

Hogue, Roswell A. Centennial. 1853-1953. St. Peter's roman catholic church, Plattsburgh, N.Y. Plattsburgh, N.Y. 1953. 192p. illus. ports.
                                        9379

Johnstone, Margaret Blair. When God says "No": faith's starting point. N.Y. Simon & Schuster, 1954. 311p. Experiences of a minister's wife at Wadhams, N.Y.   9380

Jones Mrs. Mabel (Merryfield). History of the Minerva Baptist church - in pageant form. n.p. n.pub. 1957. 12p. mimeographed.   9381

Keene Valley, N.Y. First congregational church. A manual... n.p. n.d. Folio broadside, printed on one side.   9382

Keeseville, N.Y. Methodist episcopal church. Souvenir booklet - 125th anniversary...1827-1952. Keeseville, N.Y. Essex county republican, n.d. unpaged.   9383

Kingsley, W.L. An Adirondack church. *Christ Union*, Oct. 13, 1880. 22:302. Dedication of the Keene Valley Congregational Church.   9384

Klauder, Alexander L.A. Historical sketches of Franklin county, by Frederick J. Seaver, Malone, N.Y. A criticism...and a refutation of erroneous and libelous statements made concerning him and his parish at Tupper Lake. n.p. n.d. 8p.   9385

Lake Placid club. The great challenge. n.p. n.d. unpaged (8p.) illus. port.   9386

Lusk, William B. St. Regis Presbyterian church, Paul Smith's, N.Y. Some memories of its beginning. n.p. n.pub. 1949. 24p. illus. ports. unpaged. Cover title: Memories of the early days of St. Regis Presbyterian church. 1899-1949.   9387

McLeister, Ira Ford. History of the Wesleyan methodist church in America... Syracuse, N.Y. Wesleyan methodist publishing association, 1934. 347p. 50pl. (incl. front. ports.) Nathan

Wardner, p.117-20; Champlain conference, p.255-58. 9388

Maddox, Aaron W. The lumber camp parish of the Adirondacks: a brief account of the work carried on by the Presbyterian synod of New York in the north woods. N.Y. Synodical home missions, 1915. 12p. illus. ports. 9389

Marvin, B. Letter from West Poultney, Vt. *Chr Advocate,* Nov. 16, 1838. 13:50. Schroon circuit. 9390

Methodist episcopal church. Conferences, Troy. The one hundred twenty-fifth anniversary celebration...May 23, 1957... Glens Falls, N.Y. n.d. unpaged (6p.) illus. ports. 9391

New properties spur four Adirondack missions. *Alb Church,* Nov. 1957. 2:no.6:7. illus. 9392

New windows portray auxiliary and Indian themes. *Alb Church,* Jan. 1958. 3:no.1:8. illus. 9393

North Chester, N.Y. Baptist church. 100th anniversary... n.p. 1960. 23p. illus. Near Olmstedville. 9394

Olmstedville, N.Y. Methodist church. The Methodist church, Olmsteadville (sic) New York, 1848-1948. n.p. n.d. unpaged leaflet. Program for centennial commemoration service, September 26, 1948. Contains brief history by the Reverend Leonard C. Russell. 9395

Parks, Stephen. Troy conference miscellany... Albany, J. Lord, 1854. 423p. illus. ports. tables. Includes Warren County. Part 2, "Reminiscences of Deceased Members". 9396

Parmalee, Ashabel. Pioneering in northern New York. Reprinted from *Journal* of the Presbyterian historical society, v.24, no.4, Dec. 1946. p.223-235. 9397

Paul Smiths, N.Y. St. John's in the wilderness. St. John's in the wilderness. Paul Smiths, N.Y. n.d. Broadside printed on both sides and folded into 6p. 9398

Peru, N.Y. First congregational church. Centennial, 1822. 1922... n.p. n.d. unpaged (8p.) illus. 9399

Plattsburgh, N.Y. Beth Israel congregation. Seventy-fifth anniversary...1861-1936. n.p. n.d. 84p. ports. 9400

Plattsburgh, N.Y. First Baptist church. Fortieth anniversary, May 16, 1878 - May 16, 1918. n.p. 1918. unpaged (20p.) illus. ports. 9401

Plattsburgh, N.Y. First methodist church. Facing our opportunity... Plattsburgh, N.Y. n.d. unpaged oblong leaflet (8p.) illus. Fund-raising publicity. 9402

Plattsburgh, N.Y. First presbyterian church. 1814-1914. Commemoration service held in observance of the centenary of the Battle of Plattsburgh and the beginning of one hundred years of peace between English-speaking peoples. Plattsburgh, N.Y. 1914. unpaged. illus. Program with brief historical notes. 9403

----. One hundred fiftieth anniversary, 1797-1947. n.p. n.d. 32p. illus. port. Includes brief history. 9404

----. Proceedings at the centennial anniversary... 1897. n.p. n.d. 127p. plates, ports. 9405

Plattsburgh, N.Y. St. John's church. St. John's church...1868-1943. Plattsburgh, N.Y. 1943. unpaged (28p.) illus. facsims. ports. 9406

Plattsburgh, N.Y. St. Peter's church. ...Catalogue... Plattsburgh, N.Y. 1903. 32p. List of English and French books in the church library. 9407

----. Year book and church directory. Plattsburgh, N.Y. 1931? unpaged. illus. ports. 9408

Plattsburgh, N.Y. Trinity church. Year book... November 1st, 1898 to November 1st 1899. n.p. n.d. 8p. illus. 9409

Pomeroy, Benjamin. Schroon circuit. *Chr Advocate,* Nov. 16, 1838. 13:50. 9410

Port Henry, N.Y. Presbyterian church. Ladies' aid society. Souvenir book, Port Henry, N.Y. 1902. Port Henry, N.Y. Essex county publishing co. 1902. unpaged. illus. ports. 9411

Prudon, John J. History: second methodist episcopal church, South Plattsburg, New York, 1855-1955. n.p. n.d. unpaged (12p.) illus. 9412

Reed, Frank A. Lumberjack sky pilot. Old Forge, N.Y. North country books, ©1965. 155p. illus. ports. maps. Based partially on his "Sky Pilot's Page" which started in the February 1939 issue of *Lumber Camp News* and was continued through the May 1966 number of the *Northern Logger.* 9413

St. Dismas, the good thief, patron of Clinton prison chapel, Dannemora, N.Y. n.p. n.pub. n.d. 54p. illus. A collection of articles and poems on building the Church of the Good Thief. 9414

Saranac Lake, N.Y. Church of St. Luke the beloved physician. The parish record. Saranac Lake, N.Y. 1912. v.p. Issues for February, May and December contain articles on the church and Saranac Lake, as well as obituaries for Paul Smith and Dr. Albert Henry Allen. 9415

Saranac Lake, N.Y. First methodist church. 125th anniversary...1838-1963... n.p. n.d. unpaged (44p.) illus. ports. Includes the history of the church. 9416

Saranac Lake, N.Y. First presbyterian church. Yearbook and church directory...the forty-second anniversary number, 1890-1932... n.p. 1932? 76p. illus. ports. Includes an article "Saranac Lake in the Nineties". 9417

Schuyler Falls, N.Y. Methodist episcopal church. Re-dedication services...Nov. 7-14, 1926. n.p. n.d. unpaged (4p.) illus. Brief history of the church. 9418

Stead, Henry. Revival of work of God on Saratoga circuit. *Chr Advocate,* Oct. 21, 1831. 6:30. 9419

Sullivan, Mrs. Nell B. ...A short history of the Presbyterian church of Chazy, New York, 1805-1955... Champlain, N.Y. Moorsfield press, 1955. 8p. 9420

Summer chapels in vacationland. *Alb Church,* Aug. 1956. 10:no.4:7. illus. Includes picture of the Church of the Transfiguration at Blue Mountain Lake, N.Y. 9421

Thomas, Robert B. The Peru plan. "A next step in church unity..." Peru, N.Y. Community church, 1945? unpaged (16p.) 9422

Ticonderoga, N.Y. First methodist church. One hundred and fifty years of Methodism in Ticonderoga. Ticonderoga, N.Y. 1961. 19p. illus. 9423

Tupper Lake, N.Y. St. Thomas church. The 1932 year book... Tupper Lake, N.Y. 1932. unpaged (36p.) illus. port. Copy at the Adirondack Museum. 9424

Webster, Katharine M. and Webster, George A. A history of the First methodist church of Sanford's Ridge. Glens Falls, N.Y. 1960. 42p. illus. ports. Reproduced from typewritten copy. 9425

Wessels, William L. The story of the twin churches. *Trailmarker,* July - Aug. 1962. 1:no. 2:10-12,25. illus. Identical construction of the Church of the Good Shepherd, St. Hubert's Island, Raquette Lake and the Church of Our Saviour, Mandarin, Fla. 9426

Wild, A.W. A hundred years of congregationalism in the Champlain valley. Burlington, Vt. Free press association, 1891. 19p. 9427

Wood, John W.B. The northern avalanche. *Chr Advocate,* June 15, 1832. 6:165:col.2-3. Effect of the flood of 1830 upon a church family. 9428

Woodbury, G.F. Colportage wagon work; or, How Adirondack colporter missionary does his work. n.p. American baptist publication society. n.d. 9p. illus. Preaching and distribution of religious books. Copy at the Adirondack Museum. 9429

Worman, E. Clark. The Silver Bay story, 1902-1952. Silver Bay, N.Y. Silver Bay association, 1952. 133p. front. illus. tables. 9430

EDUCATION

GENERAL

Adirondack girl scout council. *Tahawus Cloudsplitter*, Sept. 1965. 17(1.e. 16) :no.5:10. 9431

Angell, George W. "Education in the Champlain valley" Ticonderoga, N.Y. New York - Vermont interstate commission on the Lake Champlain basin, 1961. 16p. port. illus. Address given Sept. 27, 1961. 9432

Becker, Howard I. ed. Early school reports, 1842-1864, town of Long Lake, Hamilton county, N.Y. Rexford, N.Y. ? 1957? 9 leaves, tables. mimeographed. Cover title. 9433

Beckman, H.C. Camp Dudley celebrates its fiftieth birthday. *Camp Mag,* Feb. 1935. p.19, 27. illus. port. 9434

Boroff, David. Dancers in the Adirondacks. *Dance Mag,* Aug. 1958. 32:no.8:42-44,72-73. illus. At Green Mansions, adult summer camp near Warrensburg. 9435

Camp Riverdale in the Adirondacks. n.p. 1926? 31p. illus (part folded). At Long Lake. 9436

Clark, Ted. Camp on sightly Adirondacks lake nets "invaluable" data for chapters. *Deke Q,* Dec. 1961. 79:147-55. Delta Kappa Epsilon Camp on Silver Lake. 9437

Clinton county historical association. Implementing our historical association. The constitution and by-laws... Plattsburgh. N.Y. 1962. 7p. Reproduced from typewritten copy. Proposed revisions. 9438

Cooper, Frank Albert. The Plattsburgh idea in education, 1889-1964. Plattsburgh, N.Y. Plattsburgh college benevolent and educational association, inc. 1964. 175p. illus. ports. facsims. 9439

Doty, Richard S. The character dimension of camping. N.Y. Association press, 1960. 192p. illus. Based on research at Camp Chingachgook, Lake George. 9440

Doty, Richard S. and Stettner, John. Growth toward attitude objectives in a summer camp as indicated by two sociometric devices. *Union Coll St,* July 1954. 1:no.8:79-100. figures. At Camp Chingachgook, Lake George. Reprinted in Union College's "Methods of Character Development", 1960. 9441

Doty, Richard S. A study of relationship of boys' wishes to their sociometric status. *Union Coll St.* Mar. 1955. 1:no.12:153-61. Also issued as a reprint. 9442

Early Clinton county school records. *No Country Notes,* May 1961, no.4:2. Excerpts from Town of Peru records. 9443

Hall, Ruth C. Address commemorating the 65th anniversary of the first Lake Placid Conference on home economics. *J Home Econ,* Jan. 1965. 57:no.1:17-21. illus. 9444

Jones, Louis Clark. Hancock house. *N Y Hist,* July 1958. 39:280. Transfer to Fort Ticonderoga Association. The library, noted in the preface of the *Adirondack Bibliography,* p.vi, was transferred to Cooperstown. 9445

Kaighn, Raymond P. Camp Dudley. *Assn Boys,* June 1905. 4:109-24. illus. port. 9446

New York (state) State university, Albany. Atmospheric sciences research center. Whiteface mountain summer program, 1963. Albany, 1963. 194p. illus. map. Reproduced from typewritten copy. Title page reads: Summer program, 1964. The following papers are included: Benton, Allen H. The siphonaptera of Whiteface Mountain, p.4-14; Klein, Harold G. The intra-and interspecific social and agonistic behavior *Peromyscus leusopus* and *Clethrionomys gapperi,* p.15-20; Reilly, Richard W. A general ecological study of the moss flora on Whiteface Mountain, p.21-83; Hart, Thomas C. Forest tree ecology studies on Whiteface Mountain, p.84-89; Falconer, Raymond E. Tests with mobile iron-nuclei measuring equipment at Whiteface Mountain, p.92-105; Randers-Pherson and others. Seismic motion in the one-second period range in the northeastern United States, p.106-120; Roark, Terry P. Whiteface Mountain as a possible astronomical observatory site, p.121-31. Gokhall, Narayan, R. Dependence of freezing temperatures of supercooled water drops on rate of cooling, p.132-48; Dingledy, David. Photosenstive glasses for ultraviolet and visible radiation detection, p.149-55; Bradfield, Walter S. On electrodynamic modeling of planetary atmospheres, p.156-86. 9447

----. Whiteface mountain summer program, 1964. n.p. n.d. 18p. Reproduced from typewritten copy. 9448

78

Pierce, Francis P. Early history of Wadhams old log schoolhouse that burned in 1845. *Reveille*, Sept. 1956. 1:no.7:1,4. 9449

Robinson, Anthony. Downstate teacher enjoys profitable summer workshop in the Adirondacks. *NYS Ed*, May 1961. 48:no.8:29-30. illus. Science camp at Twin Valleys. 9450

Rose, Hubert D. Ideas for the Deke operating practices handbook are discussed profitably at conference camp. *Deke Q*, Dec. 1961. 79: 155-56. Camp at Silver Lake. 9451

Rothschild, Maurine. A laboratory summer. *No Country Life*, Summer 1962. 16:no. 3:16-18. Camp at Lewis, directed by Dr. Phillip Walker of the State University College,

Plattsburgh. 9452

Saranac Lake rehabilitation guild. Vocational training division. Bulletin of the business education department... Saranac Lake, N.Y. n.d. 28p. Oblong folder. mimeographed. 9453

Schoolmarms of 1850. *Reveille*, Mar. 1958. 2:no.11:1-3. 9454

Stebbins, Henry M. Longshore treasure. *NYS Con*, April-May 1956. 10:no.5:10-11. Life at a camp operated by the Conservation Department. 9455

Ward, Ruth. Camp treetops. Master's thesis, School of Social Work, Columbia University, 1947. 83 leaves, maps. Typescript. Summer camp near Lake Placid. 9456

SCHOOLS AND COLLEGES

NEW YORK STATE COLLEGE
OF FORESTRY, CORNELL

Horner, Harlan Hoyt. History of forest education in the state of New York. *In* New York (state) State university college of forestry, Syracuse. Dedication of the Louis Marshall memorial. Syracuse, N.Y. 1933, p.30-42. Includes the history of the College of Forestry at Cornell and the founding of the New York State College of Forestry at Syracuse. 9457

Hosmer, Ralph Sheldon. Cornell university - early education in professional forestry. *Northeast Log*, May 1956. 4:no.11:14,62-65. illus. See also articles by Hosmer entitled "Cornell Foresters 1902-03" and "Cornell Foresters 1922-23" in the December issue, p.44-45, 83. 9458

Schenck, Carl Alwin. The Biltmore story; recollections of the beginning of forestry in the United States. Edited by Ovid Butler. St. Paul, Minn. American forest history foundation, Minnesota historical society, 1955. 224p. front. plates, ports. Fernow's operations on Cornell college of forestry tract, p.106-10. Visit to forests of the Adirondacks, p.185-86. 9459

UNIVERSITY COLLEGE,
SYRACUSE UNIVERSITY

Applegate, Howard Lewis. The story of Minnowbrook. Syracuse, N.Y. University college of Syracuse university, 1962. 10p. illus. Number 27 of a series of papers on adult education. Blue Mountain Lake camp used by Syracuse University as a conference center.
9460

----. The story of Pinebrook. Syracuse, N.Y. University college of Syracuse university, 1962. 8p. illus. Camp on Upper Saranac Lake now used as university conference center. 9461

----. The story of Sagamore. Syracuse, N.Y.

University college of Syracuse university, 1961. 15p. illus. map. History of the lodge on Sagamore Lake built by William West Durant, now used by Syracuse University. Third edition, revised was published in 1962. 9462

NEW YORK STATE UNIVERSITY
COLLEGE OF FORESTRY, SYRACUSE

College of forestry at Syracuse university. *N Logger*, Aug. 1963. 12:no.2:30-31. Resume of activities. 9463

Coufal, James E. School the students built. *Am For*, May 1962. 68:no.5:34-35,53-54. illus. The New York State Ranger School at Wanakena. 9464

Hoyle, Raymond J. Syracuse & Wanakena - State university college of forestry. *Northeast Log*, May 1956. 4:no.11:15, 66-69. illus. 9465

Irving, Roy. The Ranger school at Wanakena. *NYS Con*, Dec. 1956-Jan. 1957. 11:no.3:10-11. illus. 9466

New York (state) State university college of forestry, Syracuse. Alumni association. Forestry college: essays on the growth and development of New York state's College of forestry, 1911-1961... George R. Armstrong, editor; Marvin W. Kranz, associate editor. Syracuse, N.Y. 1961. 360p. illus. ports. "The Cornell College of Forestry - 1898 to 1903", p.7-9; "The Ranger School", by James F. Dubuar, p.279-308. 9467

Patric, Earl F. The Huntington wildlife forest. *NYS Con*, Oct.-Nov. 1960. 15:no.2:16-17. illus. 9468

Ranger school grows. *NYS Con*, Oct.-Nov. 1962. 17:no.2:35. 9469

Volmes, Peter B. N.Y. state ranger school marks 50th birthday by dedicating new wing. *Northeast Log*, Dec. 1962. 11:no.6:23,66. illus. 9470

----. Syracuse forestry college celebrates 50th birthday. *Northeast Log,* July 1961. 10:no.1: 8-9,32. illus.   9471

OTHER SCHOOLS AND COLLEGES

Camp Mas-sa-we-pie. The summer school of Saint John's school... Manlius, N.Y. 1921. 24p. illus. Between Cranberry and Tupper lakes.   9472

Catholic summer school of America. Tercentenary celebration - Champlain assembly; Cliff Haven, Lake Champlain, New York. n.p. 1909? 64p. tables.   9473

The Champlain summer school - historical and descriptive. *Moshers,* July 1899. 14:no.3: 142-214. This is the entire issue, except for four pages of advertising in the back. Included is not only history and description of the Summer School, but also much history of Lake Champlain. G.C.   9474

Chazy, N.Y. Chazy central rural school. Chazy central rural school... n.p. 1921. 105p. illus. plans.   9475

Faculty changes at Paul Smith's college. *J For,* June 1961. 59:485-86.   9476

Freedom or chaos? *Newsweek,* June 29, 1964. 63:noj26:83. illus. Lewis-Wadhams School.   9477

Lake Placid club. Lake Placid club boys' school. Lake Placid Club, N.Y. n.d. 4p. "The Club was founded 31 years ago." Copy at the Adirondack Museum.   9478

New York (state) State University. Champlain college. ...Champlain college at Plattsburgh. n.p. 1948? 16p. illus.   9479

New York (state) State university college, Plattsburgh. Alumni association. The twenty-fifth anniversary of the State normal school at Plattsburgh, N.Y... Plattsburgh, N.Y. 1915. 38p. illus. ports.   9480

Northwood school. The Epitome, published by the junior class. Lake Placid Club, N.Y. v.d. Volume 5, June 1931 is dedicated to Harry Wade Hicks. 138p. illus. ports. Copy in the Saranac Lake Free Library.   9481

----. The Northwood school; established 1905.

Lake Placid Club, New York... Boston, Mass. Vincent-Curtis, n.d. unpaged (32p.) illus. Copy at the Adirondack Museum.   9482

Paul Smith's add faculty members. *J For,* Dec. 1958. 56:963-64.   9483

Rutherford, William A. Paul Smith's college - forestry education. *Northeast Log,* May 1956. 4:no.11: 16-17,57. illus.   9484

----. Safety training at Paul Smith's college. *J For,* July 1961. 59:514-15.   9485

----. Wood - and Paul Smith's college. *Northeast Log,* July 1959. 8:no.1:10-11,32. illus.   9486

Saranac Lake, N.Y. Union school. Catalogue... 1892-1893. Saranac Lake, N.Y. n.d. 38p. Union Free School District no.1, Town of Harrietstown, Franklin County.   9487

Siau, John F. A history of Paul Smith's college. *Adirondac,* Mar.-April 1960. 24:30-31,35. map.   9488

Tupper Lake, N.Y. Public schools. Catalogue of the Tupper Lake public schools with courses of study...September, 1916. Tupper Lake, N.Y. Herald press, n.d. 20p. illus.   9489

The Union academy. *No Country Notes,* Sept. 1965. no.24:4. Founded by The Union, Peru.   9490

U.S. Forest service scientists at Paul Smiths to be transferred. *Northeast Log,* July 1961. 10:no.1:33. Research center discontinued.   9491

University given Saranac Lake camp. *St. Law Univ Bul,* April 1965. 33:no.4:14. illus.   9492

Westport, N.Y. High school. Prospectus of Westport high school... Keeseville, N.Y. Essex county publishing co. 1901. unpaged (16p.) front.   9493

Willsboro, N.Y. Union school. Catalogue and course of study...1901-1902. Port Henry, N.Y. Essex county publishing co. 1901. unpaged (16p.)   9494

Woodsmen's weekend at Paul Smith's college. *Northeast Log,* May 1961. 9:no.11:73. Collegiate. See also similar article in the August 1961 issue, 10:no.2:24-25, illustrated. 9495

LIBRARIES

Berry, R. Edwin and Leggett, Mary G. The Clinton-Essex-Franklin library, first multi-county system in the state. *Bookmark,* Feb. 1965. 24:141-45. illus.   9496

Carter, Robert L. The North country library system - fifteen years young. *Bookmark,* Mar. 1964. 23:163-70. illus.   9497

Clifford, E.B. ...Historical sketch of the Lake

Placid public library. Lake Placid, N.Y. 1902. unpaged (32p.) illus.   9498

Cole, G. Glyndon. Saranac Lake free library. *No Country Life,* Fall 1956. 10:no.4:21-25. illus.   9499

Harshe, Florence E. A profile of the Southern Adirondack library system. *Bookmark,* Oct. 1963. 23:no.1:8-11. illus. plans.   9500

Keene Heights library club. Catalogue. Library...together with the library rules and regulations. n.p. 1892. 29p. Situated at Beede's (later St. Hubert's) Essex County. Another edition, including first supplement, 36p. 1893?. Copy at the Adirondack Museum. 9501

----. Constitution, adopted Sept. 6, 1892. n.p. n.d. unpaged (8p.) Copy at the Adirondack Museum. 9502

Keene Valley library association. Building committee. Keene Valley library association, 1891-1962. n.p. 1962. unpaged (4p.) illus. plan. On proposed new wing. 9503

Miller, Roland B. Library at Paul Smith's. *NYS Con*, April-May 1959. 13:no.5:37. illus. Paul Smith's College. 9504

New York (state) State library. Division of library extension. Profiles of some public library systems in New York state, reprinted from *The Bookmark*, 1963-64. Albany, 1964. 45p. illus. Reproduced from typewritten copy. Southern Adirondack, p.1; North Country, p.25. 9505

North country library system formed. *Bul Schools*, Nov. 1958. 45:137. Brief note on cooperative system for St. Lawrence, Lewis and Jefferson counties. 9506

Saranac Lake, N.Y. Free library. A catalog of books...fiction and nonfiction. Saranac Lake, N.Y. Enterprise press, 1922. 70p. 9507

Southern Adirondack library system. In review: book reviews by teenagers of member libraries. Ballston Spa, N.Y. 1962. 27 leaves. mimeographed. 9508

Three cooperative library systems. *Bul Schools*, Sept. 1958. 45:40-41. illus. Brief note on formation of Southern Adirondack Library System covering Saratoga, Warren and Washington counties. 9509

Van Brakle, Donald. Callboard. *In* Saranac summer theatre, inc. Program, July 14-19, 1958, p.4. Column on the Adirondack Collection of the Saranac Lake Free Library. 9510

MUSEUMS

Adirondack museum. *No Country Life*, Spring 1958. 12:no.2:17-23. illus. At Blue Mountain Lake. 9511

Adirondack museum features boat exhibit. *Hist News*, Sept. 1965. 20:no.9:188. 9512

Adirondack museum opens. *Mus N*, Sept. 1, 1957. 35:no.5:1. illus. Brief description of museum founded by the Adirondack Historical Association. 9513

Arthur, Helen. The colonial garden pays tribute to the craftsmen in lead. *Reveille*, Sept. 1958. 2:no.13:2,4. Description of lead cistern and dolphin at the Colonial Garden in Elizabethtown. 9514

Barrow, Howard J. Six nations Indian museum. *No Country Life*, Spring 1958. 12:no.2:43-48. illus. 9515

Cadbury, Warder H. An Adirondack museum. *Adirondac*, Jan.-Feb. 1956. 20:2. At Blue Mountain Lake. 9516

Elizabethtown chamber of commerce. Elizabethtown: its Adirondack center museum and colonial garden. Elizabethtown, N.Y. 1964? Broadside printed on both sides and folded into 24p. illus, maps. Includes "Adirondack Tours... in Essex County and Environs." 9517

Essex county historical society. The colonial garden... Elizabethtown, N.Y. ©1959. unpaged. col.illus. Brief review in *Adirondac*, Sept.-Oct. 1959, 13:102,107. See also "Elizabethtown's Colonial Garden" in *North Country*

Life, Spring 1959, 13:no.2:22-23. 9518

----. Wild flowers of the Colonial garden... Elizabethtown, N.Y. 1959. 34 leaves. mimeographed. Brief review in *Adirondac*, Sept.-Oct. 1959, 13:102,107. 9519

Franklin county historical and museum society. The Franklin house of history. n.p. n.d. Broadside printed on both sides and folded into 4p. illus. map. 9520

Fynmore, Jim. Relics of 1890 travel in the central Adirondacks. *No Country Life*, Fall 1957. 11:no.4:36-41. illus. At the Adirondack Museum. 9521

Inverarity, Robert Bruce. The Adirondack museum. *NY Hist*, July 1958. 39:261-67. illus. See also his article with same title in the *Yorker*, Mar. 1961, 19:no.4:10-11, illus. 9522

----. Thoughts on the organization of museums. *Curator*, Nov. 1959. 2:293-303. Adirondack Museum. 9523

Lawrence, Richard W. jr. The Adirondack center. *NY Hist*, July 1958. 39:256-60. At Elizabethtown. Also in the *Yorker*, March-April 1961, 19:no.4:14. 9524

----. A colonial garden in the north country. *Con*, April-May 1965. 19:no.5:18-19. illus. (part col.) At the Adirondack Center, Elizabethtown. 9525

Miller, Roland B. Adirondack museum. *NYS Con*, Dec. 1955-Jan. 1956. 10:no.3:37. illus. See also his articles with same title in issues for Dec. 1956-Jan. 1957 and Dec. 1957-Jan. 1958, 11:no.3:4 and 12:no.3:9-10, illus. The December 1957-January 1958 article is on the dedication of the Museum.   9526

----. Adirondack museum publications. *Con,* Dec. 1962-Jan. 1963. 17:no.3:39.   9527

----. The Adirondack museum - revisited; an institution with exciting and ever-changing display of Adirondackana. *NYS Con,* Dec. 1961-Jan. 1962. 16:no.3:12-13. illus. Reprinted in *North Country Life,* Summer 1962, 16:no.3:38-41.   9528

Roseberry, C.R. New Adirondack attractions: museum to open doors Aug. 4. Albany, 1957. illus. Broadside, printed on both sides, from the Albany *Times-Union,* July 21, 1957. Adirondack Museum.   9529

Seaman, Frances (Boone) The Adirondack museum. *Cloud Splitter,* Jan.-Feb. 1957. 20:no.1:8-10.   9530

Showers, Paul. Holiday museum. N.Y. 1957. Broadside reprint, with illustrations and map, from the *New York Times,* July 21, 1957. The Adirondack Museum.   9531

Vars, Nancy. Adirondack museum. *In* Syracuse Post Standard *Pictorial,* Feb. 1, 1959. p.5, 7. illus. Also illustration on front cover. 9532

Whitehill, Walter Muir. The virtuoso's collection. *Mus N,* Jan. 1963. 41:no.5:22-29. Includes the Adirondack Museum and Fort Ticonderoga Museum.   9533

RECREATION IN THE ADIRONDACKS

GENERAL

Adirondack chamber of commerce. Vacationing in the Adirondacks. Auburn, N.Y. Fenton press, n.d. 70p. illus. map.   9534

Adirondack enterprise. Special sportsman's show edition, Feb. 20, 1908. 23p. illus. Contents: The Adirondacks...canoe trip; Mountain roads; Mountain peaks; Lakes well stocked; Deer increasing.   9535

Adirondack golf debate, 1900. *Reveille*, Dec. 1959. no.17:4. Reprinted from the *Elizabethtown Post*, May 10, 1900. Comparison of Whiteface Golf Links at Lake Placid with Cobble Hill Links at Elizabethtown.   9536

Adirondack mountain club, inc. Trails committee. Standards of trail construction. Albany, N.Y. 1923. 6 leaves. mimeographed.   9537

Adirondack resorts association. Recreation in the Adirondacks. N.Y. Richardson press, n.d. unpaged (16p.) illus. map. Another edition, undated, same place and publisher. 12 folded pages, illustrations and map.   ·   9538

Babcock, Richard. Thunder on the left. *Adirondac*, July-Aug. 1957. 21:74,77. Struck by lightning.   9539

Blanchard, Fessenden Seaver. An outboard cruising guide to New England, eastern New York state and adjacent Canadian waters. N.Y. Dodd, Mead, 1958. 167p. illus. The Champlain Canal, Lake Champlain and Lake George, p. 32-62.   9540

Braman, Wallace J. Bark-eater bowmen hold grand finale. *Archery*, Nov. 1957. 29:no.11: 24. illus. AuSable Forks archery club.   9541

Burton, Harold B. Holiday handbook of escape. *Holiday*, July 1962. 32:no.1:101-106. col. illus. Includes climb up Marcy from Heart Lake.   9542

Carroll, Hanson. Skin diving. *Ver Life*, Summer 1960. 14:no.4:43-46. illus.   9543

Chestertown, batter down...another nor'easter's bound your way. *Tahawus Cloudsplitter*, Mar. 1964. 15:no.3:6-11. illus. North-eastern Corvette Owners' Club weekend at Chestertown.   9544

Conroy, William Brown. The changing recreational geography of the Adirondack mountain area. Thesis for degree of Doctor of So-

cial Science, Graduate School of Syracuse University, 1963. 279 leaves, tables, map. Typescript. See also his article based on the thesis, "The Case of the Adirondacks" in *Recreation*, Jan. 1965, 58:no.1:15-16. illus.   9545

Davis, Wynn. Family funland. *Redbook*, Jan. 1957. 108:no.3:48-50,80-81. illus.   9546

----. Hudson river secret. *Outdoor Life*, June 1959. 123:no.6:40-43,127,143-46. illus. col. map. Rubber life rafts used to float the Hudson.   9547

Doig, Herbert E. Stillwater tree farm. F.W. M.A. again opens private lands. *Con*, Aug.-Sept. 1964. 19:no.1:13. map.   9548

Fulling, Edmund H. Holiday reminiscences in the Adirondacks. *Gard J*, Nov.-Dec. 1963. 13:225,238. Botanizing. Refers to Orra Phelps and Edwin Ketchledge.   9549

Healy, Trudy (Besag) First PSOC Adirondack expedition. *Adir Peeks*, Fall 1964. 1:no.2:12-14. illus.   9550

Hooker, Mildred Phelps (Stokes) Camp chronicles; with an introduction and notes by Paul F. Jamieson. Blue Mountain Lake, N.Y. Adirondack museum, 1964. 60p. front. illus. map. Reviewed by Roland B. Miller in the *Conservationist*, April-May 1965, 19:no.5:40. Also reviewed in *York State Tradition*, Fall 1964, 18:no.4:61.   9551

Hoyt, Murray. Away-outdoors. *Ver Life*, Summer 1959. 13:no.4:54-60. illus. map.   9552

Hudowalski, Grace (Leach) The "Adirondack" experience. Your vacation guide. Adirondack, N.Y. Adirondack attractions association, 1962. 16p. col. illus.   9553

Knox, J. Armoy, A [devil] of a trip; or, The log of the yacht Champlain... N.Y. National literary bureau, ©1888. 128p. illus. Author, accompanied by "Adirondack" Murray sailed from Lake Champlain to the St. Lawrence.   9554

Lange, Willem Maurits III. Crazy mixed-up nuts - the wonderful history of GORP. *Summit*, June 1957. 3:no.6:6-7,24. Food concoction invented at the Winter Mountaineering School in 1954.   9555

Loope, P. Fay. Spring and the seven carries, by

Old Adirondacker, pseud. *Adirondac,* May-June 1961. 25:54. Fishing and canoeing. 9556

Lost child. *NYS Con,* Oct.-Nov. 1958. 13: no.2:39.   9557

M., '86. A summer recollection. *Univ Cynic,* April 1, 1885. 2:135. Trip to an Adirondack lake.   9558

Manning, Gordon. P. Lake George. *Outdoors,* Aug. 1960. 2:no.3:14-17. illus.   9559

Moody, Howard. Adirondack paradise. *Trailmarker,* Summer 1963. 2:no.1:27-29,33. illus.   9560

Mulholland, William D. Forest recreation in New York. *In* Society of American Foresters. Proceedings, 1957. Washington, 1958, p.18-20.   9561

----. Recreation...in the Forest preserve region. *Northeast Log,* July 1957. 6:no.1:28-29, 60-63. illus. map.   9562

New York (state) Commerce department. New York state vacationlands. Albany, 1956-date. v.p. col. illus. maps. Issued annually. Includes the Adirondacks.   9563

New York (state) Conservation department. New York state parks. Albany, 1935. 82p. illus. maps (one folded) Adirondack region, p.44-53.   9564

----. Now or never. A bold new program for outdoor recreation. n.p. 1960. 24p. illus. (part col.) col. charts, col. maps.   9565

----. Your outdoor recreation map. Albany, 1962. Large broadside map with text on the reverse, folded into 24 sections. illus.   9566

New York (state) Conservation department. Division of lands and forests. Lake George. Albany, 1961. 12p. illus. folded map. Also issued in 1963.   9567

New York (state) State university college of forestry, Syracuse. When you are in the woods. Albany, J.B. Lyon, n.d. 16p. illus. Includes "What Do You See in Trees", by Gurth Whipple and "Campfires" by A.V.S. Pulling.   9568

Norton, Mortimer. Fun under the Adirondack sun. *Trailmarker,* Summer 1963. 2:no.1:10-14,34-35. illus.   9569

Our great summer playground. *Munsey,* June 1896. 15:258-84. illus.   9570

Phelps, Orra A. The old beaver trail. *Adirondac,* Mar.-April 1962. 26:32-33. Nature trail at Adirondak Loj.   9571

Running the rapids of the upper Hudson. *Scrib M,* April 1881. 21:857-70. illus. 9572

Saranac boat and waterways club. Constitution and by-laws. Saranac Lake, N.Y. 1931. 12p. Copy in the Saranac Lake Free Library. 9573

Sears, George Washington. The Adirondack letters of George Washington Sears, whose pen name was "Nessmuk." With explanatory notes and a brief biography by Dan Brenan. Blue Mountain Lake, N.Y. Adirondack museum, 1962. 177p. illus. Reviewed by D.A. Plum in *New York History,* Jan. 1963, 44:88-90; other reviews in *York State Tradition,* Winter 1963, 17:no.1:60 and in *Adirondac,* Nov.-Dec. 1962, 26:98.   9574

Thorp, George B. A day of adventure. *Adirondac,* May-June 1960. 24:53,56-57,59. Exploration by seaplane.   9575

Trevor, John B. jr. Adirondack sailors. *Adirondac,* July-Aug. 1960. 24:68-69,83. illus. Sailboats on St. Regis and Spitfire lakes. 9576

----. Upper St. Regis lake, yachting capital of the Adirondacks. *No Country Life,* Summer 1957. 11:no.3:39-41. illus.   9577

Wachtung field archers. The fastest growing sport. n.p. n.d. Illustrated broadside, printed before 1960, advertising archery club at Saranac Lake.   9578

Ward, Mrs. Mary L. 1914 ADK motor trip. *Adirondac,* May-June 1958. 22:59-61. illus.   9579

Welch, Fay. Make an Adirondack pack basket. *Camp Mag,* May-June 1943. p.14-15. illus.   9580

----. 12 pointers on woods courtesy. *Camp Mag,* Jan. 1951. p.21. illus. Extract from his "When You Are in the Woods", 1950 edition.   9581

Wells, Fred L. Adirondack vignettes. *Adirondac,* Sept.-Oct. 1961. 25:98-100.   9582

Why fees. *Con,* Dec. 1964-Jan. 1965. 19:no.3:45. Objection to parking fee. See also letters in the following issues: June-July 1965, p.44; October-November 1965, p.45.   9583

Wildland research center, University of California. ...Wilderness and recreation - a report on resources, values and problems. Report to the Outdoor recreation resources review commission...Washington, 1962. 362p. illus. tables, maps. (ORRRC Study Report 3) Sierra Club edition. Mt. Marcy tract included in survey.   9584

Williams, Earl W. Champlain voyage. *Ver Life,* Summer 1952. 6:no.4:3-7,53. illus. Small boats on Lake Champlain.   9585

Wilm, Harold G. Recreation development: now or never. *NYS Con,* Feb.-Mar. 1960. 14: no.4:16-20. col. illus. Includes Adirondacks.   9586

GUIDES AND EQUIPMENT

Adirondack guide boat: how good is the modern version of this useful little craft? *Con Repts,* May 1962. 27:233. illus. Rating of modern glass fiber reinforced plastic boat.   9587

Boone, Frank. The Adirondack guide boat. *No Country Life* Winter 1958. 12:no.1:12-28. illus.   9588

Durant, Kenneth, comp. Guide-boat days and ways; gathered and edited by Kenneth Durant, with seven sketches by Frederick B. Allen. Blue Mountain Lake, N.Y. Adirondack museum, 1963. 267p. plates, maps. Reviewed in *York State Tradition,* Winter 1964. 18:no.1:58-59.   9589

Gardner, John. ...An authentic guideboat. *Maine Coast Fish,* Oct. 1965. 46:no.7:8-9. illus. Constructed by Laurence Babcock. 9590

----. Collection of rare small craft makes Adirondack museum 'boat show' of historic value. *Nat Fish,* Sept. 1965. 46:no.6:8-9. illus. 9591

----. Death rode the river. *Outdoor Maine,* Oct. 1960. 11:no.10:6-7. illus. Lumberman's bateau. Includes account of boats sunk in Lake George.   9592

----. First lines of Adirondack guide boat. *Outdoor Maine,* Aug. 1960. 9:no.8:8,9,11. illus.   9593

----. Guide boat. *Outdoor Maine,* Sept. 1960. 9:no.9:8-9. illus. diagr.   9594

----. A Maine wherry for the Adirondacks: marine and woodland boat-building joined in mountain museum. *Maine Coast Fish,* Oct.

1959. 14:no.3:8-9,16. illus. diagrs. The Adirondack Museum adds a salmon wherry. 9595

----. Plastic may bring rebirth of traditional craft. Adirondack boat good move in right direction. *Nat Fish,* April 1963. 44:no.1:8-9 illus. Fiber glass boats built by Thomas T. Bissell at Long Lake.   9596

----. A young man shows the way to use modern materials in an authentic guideboat. *Nat Fish,* Oct. 1965. 46:no.7:8. illus. The work of ADKer Laurence Babcock.   9597

Gucker, Colba F. Raising a cabin at Camp Lincoln. *Camp,* Sept. 1927. 2:9.   9598

Hart, Merwin Kimball. To the editor. *Adirondac,* Mar.-April 1961. 25:40. Merits of the guide boat.   9599

The old and the new. *NYS Con,* Oct.-Nov. 1958. 13:no.2:46. illus. Letter from Fox B. Conner, with comment on the Adirondack guide boat by Roland B. Miller.   9600

Rice, Fred M. Fred M. Rice, builder of Adirondack row boats... Saranac Lake, N.Y. Adirondack enterprise, n.d. unpaged (8p. incl. covers) illus. Cover title: F.M. Rice. Catalogue. Adirondack Boats.   9601

Stumpp, Edwin A. Of guides and boats. *NYS Con,* Feb.-Mar. 1959. 13:no.4:46. Query about the Sabattis family with answer by Roland B. Miller.   9602

Three guides. *NYS Con,* Oct.-Nov. 1958. 13: no.2:43. illus. Brief note on picture taken in 1894.   9603

CANOEING

Canoe capers. *Harper W,* Sept. 10, 1887. 31: 647. illus. p.653. American Canoe Association at Lake Champlain, August 12-17. Describes S.R. Stoddard's "Atlantis".   9604

Canoeing in the Adirondacks. *Harper W,* Sept. 22, 1888. 32:718. Full-page illustration by W.A. Rogers, p.709. Canoe shown is the "Psyche" owned by C. Kirk Monroe.   9605

Delaware and Hudson railroad corporation. Canoe cruising in a summer paradise. Albany, n.d. 24p. illus. maps. Complied by Borden H. Mills sr. Listed as unlocated in Adirondack Bibliography, p.295. Also issued in its "A Summer Paradise", 1913. Copy at Adirondack Loj.   9606

Grinnell, Lawrence I. Canoeable waterways of New York state and vicinity. N.Y. Pageant press, ©1956. 349p. illus. tables, folded map. Excellent manual including many Adirondack trips.   9607

Jamieson, Paul F. The waterways then and now. *Adirondac,* Sept.-Oct. 1960. 24:88-90,94. Canoe trip to the site of the Philosophers' Camp at Follensby Pond.   9608

Lesure, Thomas B. Adventure by canoe. *Travel,* June 1962. 117:no.6:47-48,50,52. illus. Includes Adirondacks.   9609

Loope, P. Fay. Rainbow lake to Lake Kushequa, by Old Adirondacker, pseud. *Adirondac,* Mar.-April 1961. 25:38.   9610

Loveday, Lydia. Hudson highway. *Appalachia,* Dec. 1957. no. 31:532-33. From Newcomb to North River.   9611

McAneny, Herbert. Whitney ponds. *Adirondac,* May-June 1960. 24:50-52,59. Camp Riverdale trip, Long Lake, Tupper and the Whitney Preserve.   9612

Mills, Borden H. sr. Following the trail. *Four Tr News,* Sept. 1905. 9:197-200. illus. 9613

----. Old Forge to Tupper, 1904. *Adirondac,* Nov.-Dec. 1961 - Mar.-April 1962. 25:110-112,115; 26:14-18, 34-35.   9614

----. Rondax to Big Wolf. *Adirondac,* July-Aug. - Sept.-Oct. 1960. 24:77-82, 95-99. illus.   9615

Mohn, G. Frederick. Canoeing the Oswegat-chie. *Adirondac,* July-Aug. 1965. 29:50-51. illus.   9616

Norton, Charles Ledyard. The canoe convention on Lake George. *Can Mo,* Oct. 1881. 20: 426-29. Reprinted from the *Christian Union.* American Canoe Association camp on a Lake George island.   9617

Peters, Pete. Top canoe route. *Saga,* Jan. 1955. 9:no.4:7. Part of the "Ask the Experts" column is devoted to an Adirondack canoe route. 9618

Seagears, Clayton B. ...Canoe craft. *NYS Con,* April-May 1958. 12:no.5:48-49. illus.   9619

Woodford, A.J. Canoe routes. *No Country Life,* Spring 1958. 12:no.2:61-64. illus. Condensed from an article in the *New York State Conservationist.*   9620

HIKING, CLIMBING, CAMPING

GUIDEBOOKS

Adirondack mountain club, inc. Guide to Adirondack trails; high peak region and Northville-Placid trail; 6th ed. Gabriels, N.Y. 1957. v.p. plate, folded maps. Edited by L. Morgan Porter. Reviewed by Ruth Gillette Harvey in *Living Wilderness,* Summer-Fall 1957, no.61, p.22 and by Muir Dawson in *Summit Magazine,* November 1957, 3:no.11:20.   9621

----. Same: 7th ed. Gabriels, N.Y. 1962. v.p. illus. maps (folded) Edited by L. Morgan Porter. Reviewed in *Appalachian Trailway News,* May 1963, 24:25.   9622

Adirondack trail improvement society, inc. New abridged guide to Adirondack trails, St. Huberts and Keene Valley regions, New York. n.p. 1960. Folded broadside printed on both sides. Prepared by Harold Weston.   9623

Davis, Arthur K. Notes on Santanoni and Panther. *Adirondac,* Nov.-Dev. 1956. 20:109. Trail notes supplementing R. Strobel's "After the Blowdown" in the May-June issue. 9624

Fenichel, Robert R. To the editor. *Adirondac,* July-Aug. 1963; Sept.-Oct. 1964. 27:62; 28:77. Northville-Placid trail.   9625

Jamieson, Paul F. Who maps paradise? *Con,* April-May 1963. 17:no.5:45. Requesting trail guide to Cranberry Lake - Oswegatchie region, with reply by Victor Glider.   9626

Jessen, Robert L. The long path. *County Gov,* July 1961. 11:no.4:22-25. illus. Trail, planned by the Ramapo Ramblers, from New York City to Wilmington, N.Y. See also "The Long Path" in the *Conservationist* for October-November 1962, 17:no.2:33.   9627

MacNaughton from Henderson leanto. *Ad-irondac,* Mar.-April 1959. 23:39,41. Detailed trail description.   9628

New York (state) Conservation department. Division of lands and forests. Trails in the Lake George area. Albany, 1965. Broadside printed on both sides and folded into 8p. illus. map.   9629

The Northville-Placid trail. *Sup News,* Jan. 1963. 13:no.1:12,40,45.   9630

Porter, Lewis Morgan. Trail notes. *Adirondac,* Nov.-Dec. 1963 - Jan.-Feb. 1964; May-June 1964; Mar.-April 1965. 27:94; 28:9,39; 29:29.   9631

Shorey, Archibald Thompson. Random scooters find new trails. *Adirondac,* Jan.-Feb. 1958. 22:18. Knapp estate, east side of Lake George.   9632

Trails in the Saranac lake area. Reprinted from the *Adirondack Daily Enterprise,* July 1956. n.p. 1956. 6 leaves. mimeographed. (ADK Corner, by P.F. Loope)   9633

HIKING AND CLIMBING

General

Allen, Herbert C. jr. Between seasons. *Adirondac,* May-June 1958. 22:56-57. Tahawus to Flowed Lands in the early spring.   9634

Atkinson, Suzie. Trip from Au Sable club to Elk lake. *Adirondac,* Nov.-Dec. 1959. 23:115, 123. Excerpt from letter.   9635

Bach, Bryce. With the scouts in the high peaks. *Adirondac,* Sept.-Oct. 1962. 26:80-81. 9636

Bayle, Francis L. Ten days on Adirondack trails. *Adirondac,* Sept.-Oct. 1956. 20:84-87.   9637

Bear brook trail. *NYS Con*, Oct.-Nov. 1957. 12:no.2:34. New trail at Carry Falls reservoir. 9638

Birge, Vincent. Climbing the high peaks. *Trailmarker*, Summer 1963. 2:no.1. Special unpaged insert (8p.) continued on p.30. 9639

----. Hiking - Northville-Placid trail. *NYS Con*, Oct.-Nov. 1962. 17:no.2:28-29. map. Other articles by Birge on the Northville-Placid trail appeared in the *Trailmarker*, Oct.-Nov. 1962, 1:no.3:2-5,20-21, illus. map, with title "A Naturalist Hikes the Long Trail" and in *Adirondac*, Sept.-Oct. 1962, 26:72-73,82, illus. with title "Ten Days on the Northville-Placid Trail." 9640

Blackmar, Abel Edward. Sewards in summer... *Adirondac*, May-June 1962. 26:48,51. 9641

----. The wonderland of the north. *Adirondac*, May-June 1961. 25:48-51,54. From Duck Hole to Indian Face. 9642

Bliss, Robert Newell, comp. Three days on the Northville-Placid trail. *Adirondac*, July-Aug. 1964. 28:60-63. illus. 9643

Bowker, Lee H. High peaks in May...drawings by Trudy Healy. *Adirondac*, Mar.-April 1965. 29:20-23. illus. Nine-day pack trip. 9644

Chrenko, Richard M. Savage Sewards succumb. *Adirondac*, May-June 1958. 22:63-64. 9645

Clarke, Charles. Adirondack adventure. *Mt Club Md*, April-May-June 1959. 25:no.4:7-17. Marcy, Algonquin, etc. 9646

Cotter, Rev. Lawrence E. The Sewards by way of Calkins brook... *Adirondac*, July-Aug. - Sept.-Oct. 1963. 27:60,78. 9647

Crandall, Carl. H. Dear Harry. *Adirondac*, May-June 1956. 20:50-51. Hiking for juniors. 9648

Davis, Arthur K. Two climbs from Cold river. *Adirondac*, Nov.-Dec. 1957. 21:118-19. illus. 9649

de Chadenedes, Eleanor. Autumn in the Adirondacks. *Pot App Trail Club*, Oct.-Dec. 1964. 33:75-80. illus. 9650

De Sormo, Maitland C. Over the range with Hazel... *Adirondac*, July-Aug. 1962. 26:61, 68. Hiking in a hurricane. 9651

----. The saga of the four blunders; or, Prowling along the Panthers. *Adirondac*, July-Aug. 1959. 23:76-79. 9652

----. The saga of the shirt; or, Sky-men in the mountains. *Adirondac*, Sept.-Oct. 1959. 23: 103-105. Paratroopers at Duck Hole. 9653

Dickinson, Don. How many miles to cover the forty-six? *Adirondac*, July-Aug. 1959. 23:82-85. Redfield, etc. 9654

----. A mountain mishap. *Adirondac*, Jan.-Feb. 1959. 23:16-18. port. Disappearance of Leslie A. Wiggs, known as Howard Gilroy. 9655

Figiel, Richard. There's a fire on the ledge! *York State Trad*, Spring 1963. 17:no.2:4-8. Marooned on Rogers' Rock. 9656

Fleming, Howard C. 46/23 - new record? *Adirondac*, Jan.-Feb. 1959. 23:10-13. illus. Climbing the 46. 9657

Fun on foot. *Tel Rev*, Oct. 1960. 51:no.10:12-15. Pictures with brief text featuring Arthur Beach and James Stankard. Includes some Adirondack trips. 9658

Germond, Henry. On favorite mountains. *Cloud Splitter*, May-June 1957. 20:no.3:2-3. 9659

----. The Sewards aren't so tough; or, If at first you don't succeed. *Cloud Splitter*, Nov.-Dec. 1959. 22:no.6:6-9. illus. 9660

A glimpse of the Adirondacks. *Cath World*, Nov. 1876. 24:261-69. 9661

Glover, William B. Climbs with Walter Lowrie. *Adirondac*, Nov.-Dec. 1956. 20:110-12, 119. illus. 9662

Goodwin, James A. Clearing Keene valley trails. *Adirondac*, Mar.-April 1958. 22:38-39. illus. 9663

----. Paths on the trailless peaks. *Adir Peeks*, Fall 1964. 1:no.2:6. illus. 9664

Gulbis, Mrs. Ingrid. Bienvenue, Canadiens! *Adirondac*, Nov.-Dec. 1961. 25:108-109. illus. 9665

Healy, Trudy (Besag) On your own two feet... *Better Camping*, Sept.-Oct. 1964. 5:no.5:20-23. illus. 9666

----. A solitary ramble. *Adirondac*, May-June 1962. 26:44-46. illus. Overnight trip on the Range. 9667

Hiscock, L. Harris. Strange events in 1950. *Adirondac*, Mar.-Apr. 1957. 21:41-42. Climbing Baxter and Spread Eagle. 9668

Hudowalski, Grace (Leach) I climbed my forty-sixth peak. *Adirondac*, Nov.-Dec. 1956. 20: 116-17. 9669

Jamieson, Paul F. A state of mind, Brisbane. *Adirondac*, Sept.-Oct. 1958. 22:100-103. Climbing Emmons, Couchie and East Dix, with Larry Babcock as guide. 9670

Loope, P. Fay. Swamps, bogs and marshes, by Old Adirondacker, pseud. *Adirondac*, July-Aug. 1961. 25:76-77. 9671

----. Trails. *Adirondac*, Jan.-Feb. 1956. 20:16, 19. Trail making. 9672

M. "Old Slide", I-II. *Univ Cynic*, Dec. 3, 24, 1885. 3:86-87, 100-101. 9673

McAneny, Herbert. On Bullhead mountain. *Adirondac*, Sept.-Oct. 1957. 21:95-97. illus. Hikers search for lost plane.   9674

Miller, Clinton H. jr. Free-wheeling on the N/P trail... *Adirondac*, May-June 1965. 29:36-42,45. illus.   9675

----. Kingdom of bushwack; or, Conquest of the mighty Seward range. *Adirondac*, Nov.-Dec. 1956, Jan.-Feb. - Mar.-April 1957. 20:105-108,114; 21:16-20, 32-35. Comment by F. L. Stone, p.23.   9676

----. Recollections of the Northville-Placid trail. *Adirondac*, Nov.-Dec. 1958; Mar.-April 1959. 22:114-18; 23:34-38. illus.   9677

Plum, Eleanor Mary. Albany chapter climbs. *Adirondac*, Sept.-Oct. 1958. 22:107. Seward range.   9678

Pringle, Larry. The Sargent pond overnight. *NYS Con*, Dec. 1957 - Jan. 1958. 12:no.3:17, 34. illus. (part col.) Trip taken by a New York State conservation camp.   9679

Shorey, Archibald Thompson. On not getting lost. *Cloud Splitter*, Jan.-Feb. 1963. 26:no.1: 5-6.   9680

----. My favorite mountains... *Adirondac*, Mar.-April 1963. 27:27.   9681

----. New trail shelters ready. *Adirondac*, May-June 1962. 26:47.   9682

Strain, Paula. Southerners invade high peaks. *Adirondac*, May-June 1965. 29:44-45. Potomac Appalachian Trail Club based at Adirondak Loj.   9683

Strobel, Rudolph W. After the blowdown. *Adirondac*, May-June 1956. 20:48-49,56. Climbing Santanoni, Panther and Couchsachraga.   9684

Trent, George D. High peak country. *Adirondac*, July-Aug. 1956. 20:64-69. illus. New York Chapter trip.   9685

Weld, Paul W. On the trail of the forty-six. *Adirondac*, Nov.-Dec. 1964. 28:90-93. illus. Macomb and East Dix.   9686

----. Our trailless heritage. *Adir Peeks*, Spring 1965. 2:no.1:2-3. Danger of herd paths on unmarked peaks.   9687

Welles, Peter. The forty-six in eleven days. *Adir Peeks*, Spring 1965. 2:no.1:7-10. illus. Extracts, compiled by Trudy Healy, from articles published in Camp Pok-o-Moonshine's "Those Elysian Fields."   9688

Individual Mountains

Chrenko, Richard M. MacNaughton in the fall. *Adirondac*, May-June 1958. 22:53-54. illus.   9689

The Colden trapdyke. *Adirondac*, July-Aug. 1959. 23:79-80. illus. See also editorial in the May-June issue, 23:50.   9690

Cronkhite, Eric. A March ascent of Mount Skylight. *Cloud Splitter*, May-June 1958. 21: no.3:8-10.   9691

Dickinson, Don. Donaldson from the west... *Adirondac*, Nov.-Dec. 1962. 26:90-92,97. illus.   9692

----. Raspberry country. *Adirondac*, May-June 1964. 28:36-39. illus. A new route through the Cold River country up Couchsachraga. Author's first name given incorrectly as John.   9693

Friend, Eleanor. Climbing Seymour... *Adirondac*, Sept.-Oct. 1964. 28:73-74,79.   9694

Goodwin, James A. The Giant slides. *Adir Peeks*, Fall-Winter 1963-1964. 1:no.1:6-7. map.   9695

Grahame, Fred. The Giant question mark... *Adirondac*, Nov.-Dec. 1963. 27:86,95.   9696

Hudowalski, Grace (Leach) Adirondack forty-sixers climb Hoffman. *Adirondac*, Nov.-Dec. 1957. 21:106-107.   9697

Jamieson, Paul F. The wart of Iroquois. *Adirondac*, Jan.-Feb. 1958. 22:5-8 illus. Climbing Marshall via the ridge from Iroquois. 9698

Lange, Willem Maurits III. The dyke. *Adirondac*, May-June 1956. 20:52-53. Colden.   9699

Loope, P. Fay. Cascade via the falls. *Adirondac*, Jan.-Feb. 1961. 25:15. Signed: Old Adirondacker.   9700

Mount Marcy popular climb in the east. *Summit*, June 1960. 6:no.6:16-17. illus. Brief note. See also letter in the November issue, p.21.   9701

Nash, Duane H. III My forty-sixth - Allen! *Adirondac*, Jan.-Feb. 1956. 20:14-15. Signed: Dan Nash.   9702

Nash, Nancy Robertson. Let's keep going, dad! *Adirondac*, July-Aug. 1957. 21:70-72. illus. Becoming a 46er on Couchsachraga.   9703

Raymond, Lyle jr. Allen from Skylight. *Adirondac*, Sept.-Oct. 1961. 25:90,95.   9704

----. The wind blew west. *Adirondac*, Mar.-April 1959. 23:40-41. Climbing Giant in a storm.   9705

Read, W. Ascent of Ampersand mountain... *Old & New*, Sept. 1874. 10:342-51. Ascent made with W.W. Ely. Includes words and music of "The Lumberman's Song."   9706

Roessler, Alice and Roessler, Dick. Adirondack weekend. *Mt Club Md*, Jan.-Feb.-Mar. 1957. 23:no.3:12-14. Algonquin from Heart Lake.   9707

S. A day's tramp. *Univ Cynic*, Oct. 21, 1885. 3:61-63. To the summit of Whiteface.   9708

Schaefer, Mary. Fire, rain and a cloud. *Adirondac*, Sept.-Oct. 1956. 20:92-95. Gothics.   9709

Shorey, Archibald Thompson. More Mac-Naughton for random scooting. *Adirondac,* Sept.-Oct. 1958. 22:98. 9710

Sondheimer, Henry and Ginandes, Peter. Mission on Wright. *Adirondac,* Mar.-April 1960. 24:32,35. Boys from Camp Lincoln help disabled climbers. 9711

Train, Cuthbert R. August day on Rocky peak... *Adirondac,* Sept.-Oct. 1965. 29:70-73. illus. 9712

----. To the editor. *Adirondac,* Jan.-Feb. 1957. 21:22-23. Climbing Haystack with Walter Lowrie. 9713

Rock Climbing

Dienel, Gerry. Those ADK's *Alpenhorn,* Feb. 1965. 2:1-4. 9714

Goodwin, James A. Rock climbing school at the Loj. *Adirondac,* Sept.-Oct. 1965. 29:81. 9715

Healy, Trudy (Besag) Adk'ers on the rocks: the story of the ADK Rock climber's guide. *Adirondac,* Nov.-Dec. 1965. 29:86-89. illus. 9716

Lawrence, Paul A. First ascent of north face of Gothic mountain. *Adirondac,* Nov.-Dec. 1957. 21:115-16. illus. 9717

Turner, J.M. Climbing at Poke-o-Moonshine. *Appalachia,* Dec. 15, 1960. no.131:248-49. illus. 9718

Weissner, Fritz. Adirondack rock climbs: Chapel pond area. *Adirondac,* July-Aug. 1965. 29:56. 9719

CAMPING

Atkinson, James P. Camping in the Cold river country in the nineties. *Adirondac,* Jan.-Feb. 1956. 20:5-9. Biographical note, p.4. 9720

Autumn campsites. *NYS Con,* Oct.-Nov. 1958. 13:no.2:38. The 1959 list is in the Oct.-Nov. 1959 issue, 14:no.2:34. Sites scheduled to remain open. 9721

Bartholf, Benjamin A. sr. Campsite record book. *NYS Con,* April-May 1959. 13:no.5:47. Statistics of the Sacandaga campsite. 9722

Camping out as a fine art. *Harper W,* Nov. 17, 1883. 27:731. illus. 9723

Dean, Larry. Burlington mountain climbers August camp popular. *Long Tr News,* Nov. 1959. 19:no.4:3. Sharp Bridge campsite. 9724

De Morgan, John. Golden hours authors' camping out club in the Adirondacks; or, Writers on a racket. *Gold Hours,* July 21 - Sept. 22, 1900. Nos. 651-660. Keene, Whiteface and Marcy regions. Copy at the Adirondack Museum. 9725

Dempsey, David. Ah, wilderness! (Milkman: Pls 1v 2 qts) *NY Times Mag,* June 30, 1957. p.12-13. illus. Paradox Lake campsite. 9726

Eggleston, Edward. Camping on the Raquette. *Christ Union,* Sept. 22, 1875. 12:233. 9727

Hammond, Henry D. Breakfast a la coon. *Cloud Splitter,* July-Aug. 1956. 19:no.4:7-9. Camping near Johns Brook Lodge. 9728

Harte, Jessamy. A camp in the Adirondacks. *Ladies HJ,* July 1892. 9:no.8:3. illus. Long Lake. 9729

Jamieson, Paul F. Camping on state lands through the years: the Adirondack lean-to and the Forest preserve. *Con,* Feb.-Mar. 1965. 18: no.4:3-7. illus. 9730

----. The lean-to then and now. *Adirondac,* Nov.-Dec. 1960. 24:111-15, 121. 9731

Kelsey, Paul M. Camp trash disposal. *Con,* Dec. 1964-Jan. 1965. 19:no.3:40. illus. See comment by A. Booth in the April-May issue, p.45. 9732

Liell, Edward N. Autumn camping. *Four Tr News,* Jan. 1906. 10:43-45. illus. Caughnawauga Club at Catlin Lake. 9733

McAneny, Herbert. A night at Hathaway's camp. *Adirondac,* Mar.-April 1962. 28:27, 32. illus. 9734

Menz, William F. jr. and McMullen, Donald. An early spring camping trip. *Cloud Splitter,* May-June 1962. 25:no.3:9-10. Saddleback. 9735

Milton, Kirby M. Campsite litter. *NYS Con,* April-May 1960. 14:no.5:46. Letter with reply by W.D. Mulholland. 9736

Murray, William Henry Harrison. How to spend the summer. Camping out. *Christ Union,* June 20, 1877. 25:552. Reprinted in *Golden Rule,* June 27, 1877. 9737

Nabonor, T. The first night in camp. *Woods & Wat,* Summer 1899. 2:no.2:11. 9738

New and rebuilt leantos. *Adirondac,* Jan.-Feb. 1959. 23:4. Conservation Department announcement. See also "New Open Camps Built during Summer 1959" in the November-December issue, 23:116. 9739

New York (state) Conservation department. Camping in the Adirondack and Catskill Forest preserve. Albany, 1956. unpaged (4p.) illus. Rules and list of campsites. Also published in 1961. 9740

New York (state) Conservation department. Division of lands and forests. New York state public campsites. Albany, 1961. Broadside printed on both sides and folded into 6 sections. illus. (part col.) map. 9741

Norton, Robert B., Gregory, Peter T. and English, John E. Forest recreation in New York state. *Con,* June-July 1963. 17:no.6:18-21. illus. (part col.) 9742

Parry, Don. ...Tent and trailer campers' guide

to New England and New York state. 11th ed. Rocky Hill, Conn. Outdoor publishers, 1964. 66p. illus. Lake George islands, p.48; Adirondack Forest Preserve, p.49-57.   9743

Pearson, Jonathan. Wilderness barbarians. *NYS Con,* June-July 1959. 13:no.6:43. Letter protesting litter at Terrill Pond and Spruce Lake. Answer by W.D. Mulholland. See also letter from Robert Plumb in the October-November issue, p.47.   9744

Shafer, Elwood L. jr. and Stout, Neil J. Socioeconomic characteristics of Adirondack camper (abstract) *In* New York (state) Legislature. Joint legislative committee on natural resources. Annual report, 1964. p.56-64.   9745

Signs for campers. *NYS Con,* Oct.-Nov. 1959. 14:no.2:37. Signs, for leantos, given by the Adirondack Mountain Club.   9746

State parks and campsites. *No Country Life,* Spring 1958. 12:no.2:65-66. illus. List of those in northern New York.   9747

Weekend camping at Mt. Marcy. *Tahawus Cloudsplitter,* June 1965. 17(i.e.16): no.4:4,8. Two letters on camping in South Meadows.   9748

HUNTING AND FISHING

Balsam, pseud. Adirondacks. *Rod & Gun,* Oct. 28, 1876. 9:55. At Fenton's, No.4.   9749

----. Fall notes from the wilderness. *Rod & Gun,* May 13, 1876. 8:97-98. From Fenton's.   9750

----. Smith's lake, North woods, N.Y. June 18. *Rod & Gun,* July 3, 1875. 6:217.   9751

----. Wilderness sketches. *Am Sportsman,* Dec. 5, 1874 - Mar. 13, 1875. 5:150-51,196-97, 278,374-76. Continued in *Rod & Gun* April 24 - May 29, 1875, 6:54-55, 134.   9752

Bowes, Anne La Bastille. Big Moose and the F.W.M.A. *NYS Con,* Dec. 1961-Jan. 1962. 16:no.3:16-18. illus. map. Hunting.   9753

Burden, William Douglas. Look to the wilderness. Boston, Little, Brown, 1960. 251p. illus. Chapter 6, "The Still-Hunter" reprinted from *Atlantic Monthly,* November 1956. Whitney Preserve.   9754

Colles, James. Journal of a hunting expedition to Louis lake, 1851. Blue Mountain Lake, N.Y. Adirondack museum, 1961. 79p. illus. facsims. Reviewed by Per E. Guldbeck in *New York History,* January 1963, 44:86-88. Review also in *North Country Life,* Winter 1962, 16: no.1:58-59.   9755

Crannell, C.M. Experienced observation. *NYS Con,* Feb.-Mar. 1960. 14:no.4:43. Letter on hunting.   9756

D'Orr. Adirondack memories. *Rod & Gun,* Jan. 6, 1877. 9:209. Newcomb area.   9757

Finch, Pruyn opens Adirondack tract to hunters and fishermen. *Northeast Log,* Jan. 1960. 8:no.7:23,49. illus.   9758

Fishing and hunting areas extended in Adirondacks. *Am For,* May 1934. 40:222.   9759

Grahame, Arthur. Carried out on a blind. *Outdoor Life,* Sept. 1954. 114:no.3:34-35,64-65, 124-25. illus.   9760

Heath, Mrs. Aneita Strife. Fall 1960 cover photo. *No Country Life,* Spring 1961. 15:no. 2:53-54. illus. Identifies some of the hunters shown in photograph taken early in 1900's at Number Four.   9761

Holland, Raymond Prunty. My gun dogs... Boston, Houghton, 1929. 182p. front. plates. Includes "Game Shooting in the Adirondacks with John Burnham," p.124-26 and "Game Shooting near Willsboro," p.135.   9762

Lesser, George H. Old hunter's secret: time out. *Con,* Oct.-Nov. 1965. 20:no.2:10. illus.   9763

Murdoch, Allan. Get the most out of your duck decoys. *Outdoor Life,* Oct. 1950. 106:no. 4:42-44, 90-91. illus.   9764

The night before, we had been over to Holland's... *Vassar Misc,* Dec. 1880. 10:109-114. Anonymous account of loon-hunting at Blue Mountain Lake.   9765

Norton, Mortimer. ...An autumn blend of outdoor sports. *Trailmarker,* Oct.-Nov. 1962. 1: no.3:15-17,21. Hunting.   9766

Now and Then, pseud. Among the Adirondacks. *Rod & Gun,* Oct. 16, 1875 - Feb. 26, 1876. 7:39, 122, 340-41. Fulton Chain and the Saranacs.   9767

Porter, William T. Sporting expedition to Hamilton co., N.Y. *Spirit Times,* Sept. 5, 1840. 10:319.   9768

R., F.J. A strange bedfellow. *Rod & Gun,* Jan. 27, 1877. 9:257-58. Panther story. Jack Featherly of Chateaugay, the guide.   9769

Roden, William M. A hunter's Adirondack afternoon. *Ad Life,* Dec. 1962. p.6,11. illus.   9770

Royal, pseud. Drowning a parson. *Rod & Gun,* Feb. 3, 1877. 9:281. Duck shooting at St. Regis. 9771

Saranac Lake fish and game club. Constitution and by-laws. Saranac Lake, N.Y. Enterprise press, 1923. unpaged (8p.) 9772

Smith, John Talbot. A little duck-shooting. *Woods & Wat,* Winter 1899-1900. 2: no.4:4. Lake Champlain. 9773

Stallknecht, F.S. Sporting tour in August, 1858, of F.S. Stallknecht and Charles E. Whitehead: being Stallknecht's account of it, with Whitehead's illustrations. *Leslies Illus,* Nov. 13-20, 1858. 6:378-80, 394-96. illus. ports. "This is the article referred to in H. Perry Smith's 'The Modern Babes in the Wood,' p.221-22." W.C. Includes picture and account of the Philosopher's Camp. 9774

Trembley, Charles C. Life is not so bad. *Am Wood,* Nov. 1951. 1:no.5:4-5,36-37. illus. Shooting woodcock. 9775

Wulff, Lee. Adirondack fireball. *Outdoor Life,* Sept. 1953. 112:no.3:42-43,102-104. illus. Hunting. 9776

Y. The north woods. *Rod & Gun,* Aug. 7, 1875. 6:283. 9777

HUNTING
Deer

Balsam, pseud. Jack shooting. *Rod & Gun,* May 13, 1876. 8:97-98. 9778

Danaher, Dan. ...Packtrain hunt in New York. *Outdoor Life,* Oct. 1965. 136:no.4:36-39,112-16. illus. 9779

Deer hunters - travel. *NYS Con,* Oct.-Nov. 1959. 14:no.2:42. Summary of information from checking stations. 9780

Hard, Josephine Wilhelm. My first deer: the story of a sportswoman in the Adirondacks. *Fr Track News,* Sept. 1904. 7:149-51. illus. 9781

Miller, Seaver Asbury. Deer-hunting in the Adirondacks. *Am Field,* Nov. 27, 1897. 48:no. 22:449. 9782

Potter, Frederick A. Adirondack deer trails of 1908... *For & Stream,* Nov. 1924. 94:594-95,625-26. illus. 9783

Tahawus, pseud. Jacking in the north woods. *For & Stream,* June 22, 1876. 6:317. Author is Cecil Clay. 9784

Tall deer shooting. *West World,* April 29, 1871. 13:no.17:3. Raquette River. 9785

Other Game

Erickson, Albert W. Technique for live-trapping and handling black bears. *In* North American wildlife conference. Transactions, 1957. 22:520-43. 9786

Free, Stuart. "There goes a bear!" *NYS Con,*

Oct.-Nov. 1960. 15:no.2:32-33. illus. map. 9787

An incident of the woods. *In* Dr. Brandreth's almanac, 1861. p.29-32. illus. Humorous account of a bear hunt at Brandreth Lake. Photostat at the Adirondack Museum. 9788

Thornton, Marty. Barrel of bruin... *Outdoor Life,* June 1949. 103:no.6:41,84. illus. 9789

FISHING
General

An angling story around the Adirondacks. *Trailmarker,* Summer 1963. 2:no.1:12-13. Brief directory. 9790

Bassett, Percy E. The score on the Ausable. *Outdoor Life,* May 1946. 97:no.5:26-28, 80, 83-84. 9791

Beardslee, Lester A. The Adirondacks - fishing at Piseco lake, by Piseco, pseud. *For & Stream,* June 17, 1876. 6:302. 9792

Brown, Henry Kirke, and Sylvester, ----. The wilderness and its waters. *Crayon,* Mar. 14 - July 4, 1855. 1:163-65, 180-81, 194-95, 227-28, 242-43, 258-59, 275-76, 291-92, 307-308, 324-25, 338-39, 355-56, 387-88; 2:5-6. Published anonymously; authors identified on p.188 of the issue for Mar. 21, 1855. 9793

Cheney, Albert Nelson. Smelts. *For & Stream,* Mar. 2, 1876. 6:55. Brief letter. See also comments in issues for April 6 and May 18, 6:131, 234. 9794

Dagles, Frank J. Lake George fishing. *NYS Con,* April-May 1959. 13:no.5:42-43. Letter with comment by Robert G. Zilliox. 9795

Dean, Howard J. Fishing Fourth lake. *NYS Con,* Feb.-Mar. 1959. 13:no.4:44-45. Letter with answer by William A. Pearce. 9796

Drahos, Nicholas. Adirondack sequel. *Outdoor Life,* Dec. 1957. 120:no.6:56-59,113, 117-20. illus. (part col.) Sequel to John Keats's "Adirondack Adventure" listed below. 9797

An 1842 fishing trip to Moose river. *York State Trad,* Spring 1963. 17:no.2:48-50. 9798

Frost, Charles Hubbard. My summer vacations. Chelsea, Mass. Author, 1890. 234p. Includes descriptions of fishing trips in the Adirondacks in 1884 and 1885. 9799

Keats, John. Adirondack adventure; illustrated by Morris Gollub. *Outdoor Life,* July 1955. 116:no.1:56-57, 103-107. Fishing a little-known lake in the southern Adirondacks. 9800

Lenahan, J.M. North country fishing. *NYS Con,* Dec. 1959-Jan. 1960. 14:no.3:42-43. Letter with reply by Robert G. Zilliox. 9801

M. A fishing trip in the Adirondacks. *Univ Cynic,* May 20, 1885. 3:15-16. 9802

McCluskey, Ross C. Fishing when America was young. *Outdoor Life,* July 1948. 102:no.1: 36-39,70-71. illus. 9803

Norton, Mortimer. The miracle of Mars... *Trailmarker,* May-June 1962. 1:no.1:12-14, 26-28. illus. New lures for fishermen.   9804

O'Brien, Don. They fish from trees. *Outdoor Life,* May 1952. 109:no.5:35. illus. Fishing with guns.   9805

Rush, Bob. Sacandaga. *No Country Life,* Summer 1948. 2:no.3:30-31,45.   9806

Schott, Hal. Budget wilderness. *Travel,* Mar. 1960. 113:56-58. Cedar Lakes region.   9807

Silent intruder... *Trailmarker,* May-June 1962. 1:no.1:4-6,26. illus. Attack by an eagle while fishing.   9808

Williams, Ann. Ladies in camp. *Rod & Gun,* July 8-29, 1876. 8:228, 260-61, 277. Fishing club from Schoharie. Saranac region.   9809

Trout

Anderson, Robert V. Fishing Piseco - 1850. *No Country Life,* Summer 1960. 14:no.3:16-19. Piseco Trout Club.   9810

B., W.G. Trouting on Boreas river. *Rod & Gun,* Sept. 30, 1876. 8:419.   9811

Davis, Wynn. To catch trout on opening day. *Outdoor Life,* April 1957. 119:no.4:56-57,84, 97. illus.   9812

----. We go native in New York. *Outdoor Life,* June 1955. 115:no.6:50-53,82-84. illus.   9813

Heacox, Cecil E. The brown trout: a success story. *Sports Illus,* April 30, 1956. 4:no.18: 42-45. illus. (part col.)   9814

Judd, Larry. Raquette trout. *NYS Con,* Dec.

1958-Jan. 1959. 13:no.3:47. Letter, with answer by Robert G. Zilliox. See also letter from John F. Woodhull, in the April-May issue, p.44.   9815

McNulta, John. The trout and the Indian. *Field & S,* Nov. 1955. 60:no.7:94-95,171-72. col. illus. Reprinted from the May 1900 issue.   9816

Miller, C. Blackburn. I'll take that trout cure any time. *Outdoor Life,* June 1946. 97:no.6:36-37, 90-93. illus.   9817

Norton, Mortimer. ...In spring, it's trout time. *Trailmarker,* May-June 1962. 1:no.1:7-9. illus.   9818

Porter, William T. Trout-fishing in Hamilton county, N.Y. *In* Brinley, Francis. Life of William T. Porter. N.Y. Appleton, 1860. p.224-39.   9819

Webber, Charles Wilkins. Trout on Jessup's river. *Godey,* Oct. 1851. 43:204-207.   9820

Other Fish

Davis, Wynn. Best time for bass... *Outdoor Life,* Sept. 1956. 118:no.1:42-43,97-101. illus. St. Regis River and Saranac Lake.   9821

----. Fish walleyes right. *Outdoor Life,* June 1956. 117:no.6:46-47,84-89. illus.   9822

Jeliffe, Ely. The red salmon - how to catch him. *NYS Con,* April-May 1958. 12:no.5:16-18. illus. (part col.) Includes Adirondack waters.   9823

Latham, Sidney. A flyer in bass. *Outdoor Life,* Aug. 1943. 92:no.2:22-23,70-71.   9824

Norton, Mortimer. ...Summer time is bass time. *Trailmarker,* July-Aug. 1962. 1:no.2:30-31,34,36. illus.   9825

TRAPPING

Gibson, William Hamilton. Camp life in the woods and the tricks of trapping and trap making... N.Y. Harper, 1881. 300p. illus. plates.   9826

Maunton, Ed. Beaver trapper's diary: a professional's account of his experiences last season. *NYS Con,* June-July 1956. 10:no.6:12-16. illus. map.   9827

Next case, please. *NYS Con,* April-May 1958. 12:no.5:33. Trapping dispute.   9828

WINTER SPORTS

GENERAL

Adirondack life...Dec. 1962. Magazine supplement to the Lake Placid *News.* 14p. illus. Special winter sports issue. See also Warrensburg edition, same date, 20p. illus.   9829

Adirondack mountain club, inc. Winter activities committee. The Adirondack winter mountaineering manual. Gabriels, N.Y. 1957. 28p. illus. Comment by Vilhjamur Stefansson in *Adirondac,* November-December, 1957, p.113. Brief review in *Appalachia,* June 1958, no. 126:143.   9830

----. ...Winter activities committee announces the third annual winter mountaineering school...1956. n.p. 1956. Broadside printed on both sides. illus. Similar announcements for 1957-65. Reports on the school as follows: Barker, E. Gilbert. Winter mountaineering school, 1959. *Adirondac,* Jan.-Feb. 1960. 24: 15; Barker, E. Gilbert. To Reverend Peter A. Ward, editor... *Adirondac,* Jan.-Feb. 1959. 23:13-15. illus. Beede, Homer. 1956 winter mountaineering school... *Adirondac,* Jan.-Feb. 1957. 21:8; Beede, Homer. Winter mountaineering school at Adirondak loj. *Adirondac,* Mar.-April 1956. 20:29,33,35. illus.; Biddle, William W. The fifth annual Adirondack winter mountaineering school... *Appalachia,* June 1958. no.126:101-102; also in *Appalachian Trailway News,* Jan. 1958. 19:no.1:12: Healy, Trudy (Besag) WMS students slowed by slush. *Adirondac,* Jan.-Feb. 1965. 29:6; Healy, Trudy (Besag) Winter school: session II. *Adirondac,* Mar.-April 1965. 29:30. illus.; Shorey, A.T. Winter mountaineering school best ever. *Cloud Splitter,* Mar.-April 1958. 21:no.2:7-8; Van Dyke, Paul A. Mountaineering school big success. *Adirondac,* Jan.-Feb. 1964. 28:2; Van Dyke, Paul A. Winter mountaineering school... *Adirondac,* Jan.-Feb. 1963. 27:7. 9831

Bell, James Christy and others. Three winter days in the woods. *Adirondac,* Jan.-Feb. 1964. 28:10-11,15. JBL weekend in 1928. Other authors are William K. Dean, Lawrence I. Grinnell, Arnold W. Knauth, William J. Parker, Anna Lord Strauss, Marjorie Lord Strauss. 9832

Blaisdell, Harold F. Icetime angling. *Ver Life,* Winter 1959-60. 14:no.2:10-14. illus. 9833

Brown, Gladys R. Ice fishing in the Adirondacks. *No Country Life,* Winter 1958. 12:no. 1:4-7,10. illus. 9834

Carroll, George. Goosepimple gulch...madmen on Mt. Van Hoevenberg. *Lake Pl Club Life,* Mid-Winter 1961. p.16-17. illus. Signed: G.C. Bob sledding. 9835

Chase, Creta C. Dog sled racing: the snow country's newest sport. *No Country Life,* Winter 1958. 12:no.1:29-32. illus. 9836

Drahos, Nicholas. The Olympic bob-sled run at Mt. Van Hoevenberg. *NYS Con,* Dec. 1961-Jan. 1962. 16:no.3:28-29,34-35. illus. 9837

Hall, C. Eleanor. Ice fishing on Lake Champlain. *NY Folk Q,* Mar. 1965. 21:19-25. illus. 9838

----. Want to go to stove-pipe city? *Cloud Splitter,* Jan.-Feb. 1957. 20:no.1:4-6. Ice fishing on Lake Champlain. 9839

James, Stuart. Camping at thirty below. *Pop Mech,* Jan. 1964. 121:no.1: 128-32,210-12. illus. 9840

Levy, Robert. Winter camping and mountaineering in the Adirondacks. *In* Peterson, Gunnar, ed. The outing club handbook. Chicago, 1955. p.65-70. illus. 9841

Mech, L. David. Christmas night in the Adirondack wilderness. *Adirondac,* Nov.-Dec. 1958. 22:119-21. illus. 9841a

Midwinter carnival. Saranac Lake comes to the fore again with its hospital on ice. *J Outd Life,* Feb. 1907. 4:17-19. illus. 9842

Roden, William M. Cold facts about frosty fun. *Ad Life,* Jan. 31, 1963. p.6-7. illus. table. Ice fishing. 9843

Rolleston, Mrs. Ruth E. Rambling on snow shoes, Glens Falls ADK. *Adirondac,* Nov.-Dec. 1958. 22:126-27. 9844

Sad ice-boat accident. *Reveille,* June 1962. 7: no.26:1,3-4. 9845

Saranac Lake. Winter sports in the Adirondacks. Saranac Lake, N.Y. Currier press, n.d. Broadside printed on both sides and folded into 12p. illus. map. 9846

Souvenir program...Saranac Lake...winter carnival...1957. n.p. n.d. unpaged (20p.) illus. Includes history of the Winter Carnival. 9847

Terrell, Roy. The fastest run of all. *Sports Illus,* Feb. 27, 1961. 14:no.8:14-19. illus. ports. Mt. Van Hoevenberg. 9848

Thrills in ice-boating. *Vermonter,* Mar. 1941. 46:71. On Lake Champlain. 9849

Winter carnival. *No Country Life,* Winter 1956. 10:no.1:7-11. Pictures with brief text. Old Forge. 9851

Winter carnival. *No Country Life,* Winter 1957. 11:no.1:13-18. illus. Saranac Lake. 9852

Zilliox, Robert G. Trout fishing through the ice - pro and con. *NYS Con,* Feb.-Mar. 1960. 14:no.4:30-31. illus. 9853

OLYMPIC GAMES

Olympic games (winter) Lake Placid, 1932. General rules and program... n.p. n.d. 32p. plans. 9854

----. Official souvenir book... Andover, Mass. Andover press, n.d. 60p. illus. port. 9855

----. III Olympic winter games...February 4-13, 1932. n.p. n.d. unpaged (18p. incl. covers) illus. 9856

United States olympic bobsled committee. Official program... Olympic tryouts. n.p. 1947. 12p. illus. port. maps. 9857

WINTER MOUNTAIN CLIMBING

Chrenko, Richard M. MacNaughton in the winter. *Adirondac,* Sept.-Oct. 1958. 22:97-98. 9858

Frenette, William. The trap dike in winter.

Adirondac, Mar.-April 1961. 25:28-30. illus. 9859

Glover, William B. Winter climbs in the Adirondacks. *Adirondac*, May-June 1957. 21: 64-66,72. illus. 9860

Hart, Merwin Kimball. Tragedy on Marcy. *Adirondac*, Mar.-April, 1957. 21:26,40. 9861

Healy, Trudy (Besag) Calling all adventurers: winter climbing in the Adirondacks. *Better Camping*, Jan.-Feb. 1965. 6:1-26. illus. 9862

----. The Macomb adventure. *Adirondac*, Nov.-Dec. 1961. 25:114-15. illus. 9863

Huston, T.M. and Catelli, Armand. Winter mountaineering in the Sewards...drawings by Trudy Healy. *Adirondac*, Jan.-Feb. 1965. 29: 4-5,13. illus. 9864

Lawrence, Richard G. Sawteeth in winter. *Adirondac*, Nov.-Dec. 1956. 20:118. 9865

Mohawk valley hiking club. Yearbook. Schenectady, N.Y. 1932. 35p. illus. mimeographed. Contains "Tahawus in Winter". 9866

Schaefer, Mary. Schaefer expedition, December 1959. *Adirondac*, Jan.-Feb. 1961. 25:4-6, 13. Climbing Marcy and Haystack. Members of the expedition are named in letter on p.14-15. 9867

Shuley, J.H. Letter to Kim Hart. *Adirondac*, Jan.-Feb. 1958. 22:19. Winter climbs on Dix. 9868

Thomas, Dugal. North face of Gothics... a solo winter ascent. *Adirondack Peaks*, Spring 1965. 2:no.1:12. Appended is brief description "Giant from the East", via new slide. 9869

SKIING

Adirondack boom. *Skiing*, Nov. 1960. 13:no. 3:58. Big Tupper Ski Center. 9870

Adirondack ski area bolsters economy of nearby villages. *Skiing*, Jan. 1959. 11:no.4:11. Whiteface. 9871

Barrell, David. The people spoke - and New York becomes a world ski center. *Con*, Dec. 1963-Jan. 1964. 18:no.3:32-34. illus. (part col.) Gore Mountain Ski Center featured. 9872

Beetle, David Harold. We ski up Marcy - almost! *Adirondac*, Jan.-Feb. 1958. 22:9-10, 14. illus. Reprinted from the Utica *Observer-Dispatch*, April 13, 1952. 9873

Big improvements at Mt. Whitney ski area. *Lake Pl Club Life*, Mid-Autumn, 1961. p.18. illus. 9874

----. Whiteface: the inside story of how New York state's new $2.5 million ski area was built. *Ski Mag*, Nov. 1957. 22:no.2:100-103. See al-

Burton, Harold B. Placid's playgrounds. *Ski Life*, Feb. 1961. 3:no.5:28-31,54-55. illus. map. 9875

so "N.Y. Builds Giant Resort" in *Skiing*, Nov. 1, 1957, 10:no.1:25; "Whiteface Opens" in *Skiing*, Feb. 15, 1958, 10:no.8:2. 9876

----. Why do I ski? *Sat Eve Post*, Feb. 8, 1958. 230:no.32:36-37,110,112,115. col. illus. 9877

Carroll, George. It all started in 1932. *Ski Mag*, Feb. 1960. 24:no.5:48-50. 9878

Davis, Wynn. Skiing in private schools. *Am Ski Ann*, 1935-36. p.92-98. illus. Includes program of Northwood School, Lake Placid Club. 9879

Draper, Arthur G. Whiteface in the Adirondacks. *Am Ski Ann*, 1942-43. p.123-24. 9880

Duryea, Perry B. Whiteface mountain ski center. *Am Ski Ann*, 1945-46. p.207. 9881

Elkins, Frank, ed. The complete ski guide... N.Y. Doubleday, Doran, 1940. 286p. incl. front. illus. maps, tables. Includes Adirondacks. 9882

----. National cross country championships. *Am Ski Ann*, Nov. 1952. 37:no.1:126-27. Held at Paul Smith's. 9883

----. World championships - Nordic events at Lake Placid - Rumford. *Am Ski Ann*, Nov. 1950. 35:no.1:59-64. illus. 9884

Excitement at Placid. *Skiing*, Feb. 1961. 13: no.5:30. 9885

Flinner, Ira A. Junior skiing at Norwood (sic) *Am Ski Ann*, 1937-38. p.52. Northwood School, Lake Placid Club. 9886

Gifford, Bruce. Push from Placid. *Ski Mag*, Nov. 1963. 28:no.2:67,165-66. illus. 9887

Goldthwaite, George Edgar. Ski enthusiasts launch attacks on Article 14. *Adirondac*, Mar.-April 1957. 21:39. Comment by Hal Burton, p.40. 9888

Gusik, Ronnie. Westchester skiers wax merry at Whiteface. *Ski Mag*, Dec. 1959. 24:no.3:30-32. illus. 9889

A hill for Harriman. *Sports Illus*, Nov. 25, 1957. 7:no.22:39-41. map. Whiteface. 9890

Lake Placid bids. *Skiing*, Nov. 1962. 15:no.2: 35-37. IX Olympic Games. 9891

Lake Placid New Year's tournaments. *Am Ski Ann*, 1945-46. p.186-89. illus. 9892

Langley, Roger. The Olympic tryouts in cross-country racing and the classics combined. *Am Ski Ann*, 1948. p.90-91. At Lake Placid Club. 9893

Lift law for New York. *Skiing*, Dec. 1952. 15: no.3:11-12. 9894

McCluggage, Denise. Three upstate places. *Ski Mag*, Feb. 1965. 29:no.5:107. Snow Ridge, Old Forge, North Creek. 9895

Miss Rhinegold and Mr. Baseball ski Lake Placid. *Ski Mag,* Feb. 1956. 20:no.5:54-55. Brief text accompanying two pages of photographs by George Burns. 9896

Morgan, Donald Fair. Flying on skies. Broadside preprint of article in *Every Week Magazine,* Jan. 24, 1932. illus. 9897

New lodge and beginners slope at Whiteface mountain ski center. *Am Ski Ann,* Nov. 1951. 36:no.1:180. 9898

New upstate center approved in N.Y. by township voters. *Skiing,* Nov. 15, 1957. 10:no.2:29. McCauley Mountain, Old Forge. See also "New York Gives Nod on $85,000 Project for Old Forge Area" in *Skiing,* Dec. 15, 1957, 10: no.4:19; and "McCauley Mt. Plans Mid-Dec. Opening" in *Skiing,* Oct. 1958, 11:no.1:58. 9899

New York (state) Adirondack mountain authority. Annual report... Nov. 1, 1960 - October 31, 1961. Albany, 1963. v.p. mimeographed. Also issued for 1961/1962, Albany, 1963. 9900

New York (state) Commerce department. Let's go skiing in New York state. Albany, 1957. Folded broadside, illus. map. Includes description of new Whiteface development. The Department also issued "N Y Skier", Winter 1957-58, a 6p. leaflet reproduced from typewritten copy. Includes various Adirondack sites. 9901

----. Ski New York. Albany, 1956-1965. Large folded broadside with map and illustrations in color. Issued annually. 9902

----. Where to ski in New York state. Albany, 1958. Illustrated folder, unpaged. 9903

New York lists races. *Nat Skiing,* Dec. 1, 1956. 9:no.3:17. 9904

New Yorkers urge legislative ski action. *Nat Skiing,* Jan. 15, 1957. 9:no.6:18. 9905

Newell, Ed. 1956 New York winter sports forum. *Am Ski Ann,* Dec. 1956. 40:no.4:99. At Lake Placid. 9906

Nine ski meets scheduled for Whiteface mtn. *Skiing,* Dec. 1958. 11:no.3:73. 9907

Notes from Whiteface mountain. *Am Ski Ann,* Jan. 1952. 36:no.2:42. 9908

Old Forge carnival picks skiing queen. *Nat Skiing,* Feb. 15, 1957. 9:no.8:14. 9909

Old Forge hosts New York's first jr. race camp. *Skiing,* Jan. 1960. 12:no.4:14. 9910

Old Forge reaps ski benefits from local bond issue. *Skiing,* Nov. 1959. 12:no.2:7. 9911

Osborne, Lithgow. New York state's invitation to skiers. *In* Elkins, Frank, ed. Complete ski guide... N.Y. Doubleday Doran, 1940. p.108-13. 9912

----. What New York is doing to promote skiing. *In* Elkins, Frank. Ski guide for 1938. N.Y. Greenberg, 1937. p.47-52. 9913

Ostgaard, N.R. Meeting of the FIS council. *Am Ski Ann,* Feb. 1950. 34:no.3:20. At Lake Placid, Feb. 1, 1950. 9914

----. Opening address. *Am Ski Ann,* Feb. 1950. 34:no.3:19-20. At world ski championship, Lake Placid. 9915

Patnode, Luke. The ultra die-hards; a patch of snow on New York state's Mt. Marcy provides a powerful lure to parched skiiers on a hot summer day. *Ski Mag,* Mar. 1961. 25:no.6:30-31. 9916

Roden, William M. New Gore Mt. and the winter Olympics. *Ad Life,* Jan. 23, 1964. p.3. illus. The January 16th issue is on the Gore Mountain Ski Center. 9917

Seagraves, Van H. Whiteface mountain ski center... *NYS Con,* Dec. 1958-Jan. 1959. 13:no.3: 20-22. illus. (part col.) 9918

Ski resort planned for Kobl mt. at Lake Placid, N.Y. *Nat Skiing,* Nov. 15, 1956. 9:no.2:21. See also "Lake Placid Builds Poma" in *Skiing,* Nov. 1, 1957. 10:no.1:23. 9919

Ski trails in New York. *In* Elkins, Frank. Ski guide for 1938. N.Y. Greenberg, 1937. p.120-42. 9920

Wagner, Evelyn. Adirondack skiing on Whiteface mountain. *Ford Times,* Dec. 1959. 51: no.12:28-31. col. illus. 9921

Weekend tour to Whiteface. *Ski Life,* Mar. 1959. 1:no.4:30-33. illus. Photographs by Peter Schroeder. 9922

Where to ski - New York - Adirondack region. *In* Elkins, Frank, ed. Complete ski guide. N.Y. Doubleday Doran, 1940. p.123-26. 9923

Whiteface mtn. *Skiing,* Oct. 1960. 13:no.1:52. 9924

Whiteface mountain ready for another record-breaking season. *Am Ski Ann,* Nov. 1955. 40: no.1:31. 9925

Whiteface mt. ski center open. *Am Ski Ann,* Jan. 1953. 37:no.2:40. 9926

Whiteface patrol debunks dangers of skiing. *Skiing,* Mar. 1959. 11:no.6:41. 9927

Whiteface records minimum casualties. *Skiing,* Feb. 1960. 12:no.5:85. 9928

Whiteface ski center - one of the east's leading attractions. *Am Ski Ann,* Nov. 1950. 35:no.1: 202. 9929

CLUBS AND PRIVATE PRESERVES

GENERAL

Adirondack park association. The Adirondacks: the Adirondack park area. Adirondack, N.Y. 1965? Broadside printed on both sides in green ink and folded into 6p. illus. 9930

De Sormo, Maitland C. and De Sormo, Sylvia A. Mullin's Adirondack Shangri-la. *No Country Life,* Spring 1962. 16:no.2:36-39,41. 1600-acre preserve formerly owned by Lem Merrill, now operated by Velita and Francis Mullin. 9931

Wessels, William L. The Uncas estate, inc. *Adirondac,* July-Aug. 1957. 21:78. Former home of J. Pierpont Morgan, originally the home of William West Durant, now open to the public. 9932

INDIVIDUAL CLUBS

THE ADIRONDACK MOUNTAIN CLUB

Adirondack club holds mountaineering school Lake Placid, Dec. 27. *Skiing,* Dec. 1, 1957. 10:no.3:33. 9933

Adirondack mountain club, inc. Adirondack mountain club. Objectives. n.p. n.d. unpaged (6p.) illus. After 1925. 9934

----. The Adirondack mountain club welcomes you to Adirondak loj. Gabriels, N.Y. n.d. unpaged (4p.) printed in green. illus. Similar leaflets were issued, 1960-1962. The 1961 publication included Johns Brook Lodge. 9935

----. The Adirondack mountain club welcomes you to...Adirondak loj on Heart lake, and to Johns Brook lodge in the high peaks...Gabriels, N.Y. 1965. Broadside printed in green ink on both sides and folded into 8p. illus. 9936

----. Adirondak loj on its 700-acre wilderness tract...welcomes you... Gabriels, N.Y. 1963. Broadside, folded, printed in green on both sides. illus. With this is included the summer announcement for Johns Brook Lodge. 9937

----. Bunk in an ADK lodge in 1964... Gabriels, N.Y. 1964. Broadside printed on both sides and folded into 8p. illus. Advertising Adirondak Loj and Johns Brook Lodge. 9938

----. The committees. *Adirondac,* Nov.-Dec. 1959. 23:117. Officers and governors, p.111. 9939

----. Revised draft of constitution and by-laws... to be adopted...April 3, 1922. n.p. n.d. 8p. 9940

----. Treasurer's comparative report for 1929 and 1928. n.p. n.d. unpaged. (4p.) 9941

----. Treasurer's report. *Adirondac,* Oct.-Nov. 1959. 23:112. 9942

----. Treasurer's report for 1927. n.p. n.d. 4p. Preceded by statement on club activities by Arnold Knauth. Reports were also printed for 1928 (4p.) and 1930 (4p.) 9943

----. Welcome to Adirondak loj. n.p. 1959. Broadside printed on both sides. illus. Announcing the winter season. Also issued for 1963 and 1964. 9944

----. Welcome to the Adirondacks... Gabriels, N.Y. 1958. unpaged. illus. Also issued in 1959 (6p.) with slightly different title. The 1959 publication concerned mountaineering safety and was noted in *Adirondac,* Mar.-April 1959, 13:30. 9945

----. A winter welcome to Adirondak loj. n.p. 1962? Broadside printed on both sides. illus. map. Similar publications each year. 9946

Adirondack mountain club, inc. Adirondak loj chapter. Adirondak loj chapter...summer and winter rates. n.p. 1941. unpaged (8p.) 9947

Adirondack mountain club, inc. Adirondak loj fund committee. Memorandum, February 1960. n.p. 1960. Broadside, green paper. 9948

----. ...A progress report on Adirondak loj. n.p. 1959. 2p. illus. 9949

Adirondack mountain club, inc. Johns Brook lodge committee. A wilderness welcome. *Adirondac,* May-June 1957. 21:48-49,59. illus. Description of the Lodge. 9950

Adirondack mountain club, inc. New York chapter, inc. Handbook of information, 1964. N.Y. 1964. 42p. 9951

Anthony, Theodore Van Wyck. ...To all friends of the Adirondacks... Newburgh, N.Y. 1928. unpaged (3p.) Letter protesting proposal to name peak in honor of the Marshalls. Letter of Jan. 14 laid in. 9952

Bayle, Francis L. Glens Falls chapter history. *Adirondac*, Mar.-April, 1960. 24:28-29. 9953

Betts, Charles E. To the editor. *Adirondac*, Nov.-Dec. 1965. 29:93. illus. Describing the club's anti-trash signs. By chairman of the Clean Trailsides Committee. 9954

Branch, Lillian and Branch, Harvey. Those earliest days at JBL. *Adirondac*, May-June 1957. 21:50-51. illus. 9955

Burton, Harold B. More about Adirondak loj. *Adirondac*, May-June 1959. 13:56. 9956

Byrne, Wayne H. To the editor. *Adirondac*, May-June 1961. 25:58. Suggesting use of Adirondak Loj for intellectual pursuits. See also letter by D.A. Plum in the July-August issue, 25:83 and from Maitland De Sormo in the September-October issue, 25:101. 9957

Carson, Russell Mack Little. Adirondack mountain club policies and chapter activities. *Cloud Splitter*, July-Aug. 1956. 19:no.4:3-6. Excerpts from a talk to the Albany Chapter, December 8, 1928. 9958

Denniston, Robert. Crandall memorial leanto. *Adirondac*, Nov.-Dec. 1965. 29:89. At Johns Brook Lodge. 9959

----. Denniston states ADK position. *Adirondac*, Sept.-Oct. 1961. 25:89,102. On the Wilderness Area bill. 9960

----. Fall outing. *Adirondac*, Nov.-Dec. 1959. 23:116. 9961

----. Loj fund report. *Adirondac*, Mar.-April 1965. 29:27. 9962

----. President's message. *Adirondac*, Nov.-Dec. 1960. 24:107. 9963

----. The president's page. *Adirondac*, Jan.-Feb. - Nov.-Dec. 1961; Jan.-Feb. - Sept.-Oct. 1962. 25:3, 27,47,67,87,107,109; 26:3,23,39,51, 71,81. 9964

Distin, William G. Heart lake before the big fire. *Adirondac*, Mar.-April 1964. 28:24-25. illus. 9965

Dittmar, Adolph G. Project picnic tables... *Adirondac*, July-Aug. 1964. 28:56-57. illus. 9966

----. To the editor. *Adirondac*, May-June 1965. 29:46. illus. Activities of the Algonquin Chapter. 9967

Foster, Kenneth and Foster, Mrs. Nancy. Meet the Fosters. *Adirondac*, Sept.-Oct. 1965. 29: 64. port. Caretakers at Adirondak Loj. 9968

Goodwin, James A. A history of the Keene valley chapter. *Adirondac*, July-Aug. 1960. 24: 70,73. 9969

Hanmer, Mrs. Reeta W. Recollections of JBL in 1928. *Adirondac*, May-June 1957. 21:51-53. illus. 9970

Hicks, Harry Wade. Early days of Adirondak loj. *Adirondac*, Jan.-Feb. 1959. 23:5-7. With a footnote by his daughter, Harriet Hicks Smith. 9971

Johns brook lodge - 1925. *Cloud Splitter*, Nov.-Dec. 1962. 25:no.6:6-7. Report from the archives. 9972

Johnson, Theron C. The president's page. *Adirondac*, Nov.-Dec. 1964; Jan.-Feb. - Nov.-Dec. 1965. 28:83-84; 29:3,13, 19, 35, 49, 65,81, 85. port. 9973

Jones, Hollis Barlow. Hurricane chapter history. *Adirondac*, Sept.-Oct. 1960. 24:91,102. 9974

Kardys, John. Be an ADKer. *Cloud Splitter*, Jan.-Feb. 1965. 28:no.1:1. 9975

Leggett, Edward H. Ed Leggett recalls the good old days: Adirondak loj and the Lake Placid club. *Adirondac*, Jan.-Feb. 1963. 27:10-11,15. illus. 9976

Loope, P. Fay. Loj operating committee reports. Board approves three-year plan. *Adirondac*, May-June 1962. 26:40-42. illus. 9977

Miller, Clinton H. jr. The improved Adirondak loj. *Adirondac*, Mar.-April 1964. 28:20-22. illus. Other photographs on p.23. 9978

Mills, Borden H. sr. To the editor. *Adirondac*, Jan.-Feb. 1961. 25:14. Announcing organization of the Past Presidents Association. 9979

Mitchell, Robert B. ADK capital improvement fund... *Adirondac*, May-June 1963. 27:48. See also his "Loj Fund Report" in the May-June 1964 issue, 28:34. 9980

Mohn, G. Frederick. Finger lakes chapter formed. *Adirondac*, Jan.-Feb. 1963. 27:13. New chapter formed. 9981

Newkirk, Arthur Edward. The president says. *Adirondac*, Jan.-Feb. - Mar.-April, July-Aug., Sept.-Oct. 1956. 20:3-4,23,63,83. Comments on the defeat of the Panther Dam admendment and Forest Preserve legislation. 9982

O'Brien, Margaret (Goodwin) Report on JBL. *Adirondac*, Sept.-Oct. 1965. 29:73. Johns Brook Lodge. 9983

Observations of a JBL window washer. *Adirondac*, July-Aug. 1956. 20:77. Work weekend at Johns Brook Lodge. 9984

Perkins, Bernard. What the Adirondack mountain club means to me. III. *Adirondac*, Mar.-April 1958. 22:40. By the assistant hutmaster at Johns Brook Lodge, 1957. See also letter from Mrs. Louise Levy in the May-June issue, p.58,61 for further reminiscences. 9985

Phelps, Orra A. Birders' week end at Adirondak loj. *Adirondac*, July-Aug. 1965. 29: 61.   9986

Plum, Eleanor Mary. Letter to the editor. *Adirondac*, Nov.-Dec. 1957. 21:114. Appreciation of those who helped operate Johns Brook Lodge, especially George Kugler.   9987

Porter, Lawrence. What ADK has meant to me... *Adirondac*, Nov.-Dec. 1957. 21:117.
                                                        9988

Porter, Lewis Morgan. Maps and guidebooks. *Adirondac*, Jan.-Feb. 1962. 26:13. Committee report.   9989

----. The president says. *Adirondac*, 1959-1960. 23:3-4,27-28,58,75,91,111-12; 24:3,27,33,47,67, 87,104.   9990

Progress report - 1955. *Adirondac*, Mar.-April 1956. 20:24-27. Summary of committee reports.   9991

Reed, Mrs. Susan A. An open letter to President Denniston... *Adirondac*, May-June 1962. 26:49. Poking fun at "progress".   9992

Schaefer, Monica. The unforgettable cage. *Adirondac*, Nov.-Dec. 1958. 22:127. An episode at Johns Brook Lodge.   9993

Shorey, Anna (Snow) Albany chapter history: bare bones, veiled in verbiage with apologies to the MEN who have been most unfairly ignored. *Adirondac*, Jan.-Feb. 1960. 24:6-9. illus.   9994

Shorey, Archibald Thompson. Information for new members. *Adirondac*, May-June 1956. 20: 47. Reprinted from the *Cloud Splitter*, March-April 1956.   9995

Strobel, Rudolph W. The trails committee: past and present. *Adirondac*, Sept.-Oct. 1963. 27:75-78.   9996

Trent, George D. Annual meeting, 1959. *Adirondac*, Nov.-Dec. 1959. 23:114,122.   9997

Tyler, Alanson Ranger. Fund collecting: its perils and joys... *Adirondac*, Mar.-April 1962. 26:28-29. Raising money to purchase Adirondak Loj.   9998

----. No more Nubbins. *Adirondac*, May-June 1957. 21:56-57. illus. The burro of Johns Brook Lodge.   9999

----. What the Adirondack mountain club means to me. II. After a decade. *Adirondac*, Jan.-Feb. 1958. 22:17-18.   10000

Ward, Peter A. Personal recollections of Nubbins. *Adirondac*, May-June 1957. 21:57-59. illus. The burro.   10001

Waterhouse, Alice. - And there was light. *Adirondac*, May-June 1957. 21:53-55. illus. Taking a 250 pound lighting plant in to Johns Brook Lodge.   10002

With the chapters. *Adirondac*, Nov.-Dec. 1959; Jan.-Feb. - Sept.-Oct. 1960. 23:117; 24:19, 34,64,84,104. Chapter news.   10003

Young, Henry L. Adirondak loj: 1963... *Adirondac*, Mar.-April 1963. 27:23-26. illus. plans. Program for improving the club lodge at Heart Lake.   10004

----. The president's page. *Adirondac*, Nov.-Dec. 1962; 1963; Jan.-Feb. - Sept.-Oct. 1964. 26:87-88; 27:3,19,21,35,51,63,67,71,83,94; 28:3, 19,30,35,44,51,52,64,67,79.   10005

LAKE PLACID CLUB

The Adirondacks: a winter holiday out of the beaten paths. n.p. n.d. Broadside printed on both sides and folded into 12p. Reprint of article on the Lake Placid Club in Boston *Transcript*, Feb. 1, 1911.   10006

Adirondak loj club. To campers and trampers generally... Lake Placid Club, N.Y. 1932. One page letter, dated September 5, 1932, announcing opening.   10007

----. To campers and trampers who know Adirondak loj. Lake Placid Club, N.Y. 1932. One page letter dated September 6, 1932 announcing formation of Adirondak Loj Corporation.
                                                       10008

Barton, Rexford Wadleigh and others. A Christmas chronicle of the lame ducks. Cambridge, Mass. Privately printed, 1922. 109p. photographs tipped in. Lake Placid Club, Christmas 1921.   10009

Dewey, Godfrey. The Adirondak loj of long ago... *Adirondac*, July-Aug. 1963. 27:52-56. illus. port. Original lodge built by Henry Van Hoevenberg.   10010

----. Sixty years of Lake Placid club. Reprint of a talk given... August 4, 1955. n.p. n.d. 12p.
                                                       10011

Lake Placid club. Adirondak loj of Lake Placid club, Essex co., N.Y. Lake Placid Club, N.Y. Forest press, n.d. 12p. illus. After 1927.
                                                       10012

----. Another nest for the sno birds. Lake Placid Club, N.Y. 1925. 4p. illus. plan.   10013

----. The book of Christmas carols. n.p. n.d. 32p.   10014

----. Fall. Lake Placid Club, N.Y. 1929? 16p. illus. Copy at the Adirondack Museum. 10015

----. Information for conference guests. n.p. 1958. Broadside printed on both sides and folded into 6p. illus.   10016

----. Placid holidays. n.p. 1955. unpaged (16p.) illus. (part col.) Also published in 1958, 16p.
                                                       10017

----. Summer holidays. n.p. 1957. Broadside printed on both sides and folded into 8p. illus. Also issued in 1959 with title: "Summer Season."   10018

Lake Placid club education foundation. Vacation plan... Lake Placid Club, N.Y. 1957.

Broadside printed on both sides and folded into 6p. illus. 10019

A picture review of club improvement program. *Lake Pl Club Life,* Summer 1963. p.11-19. illus. 10020

Robert Earll McConnell foundation. A personal invitation... n.p. n.d. Broadside printed on both sides and folded into 8p. illus. Vacations at the Lake Placid Club. 10021

OTHER CLUBS AND PRESERVES

Adirondack farm and forest club, inc. The what, where, how, why and when... Lyons Falls, N.Y. 1921. unpaged (24p.) illus. 10022

Adirondack forty-sixers. The Adirondack forty-sixers... Albany, Peters press, 1958. 147p. illus. map on end papers. Members list kept up-to-date by loose sheets in pocket. Brief review in *Appalachia,* June 1958, no.126:143. 10023

----. Climbing the Adirondack 46. Adirondack, N.Y. 1963. unpaged (8p.) illus. Printed on green paper. Several editions issued, all undated; the 3d edition appeared in 1964. 10024

Adirondack league club. 75th anniversary, 1890-1965. n.p. 1965. 74p. illus. facsims. maps. Based on the Club Yearbooks; includes reproduction of part of the first Yearbook, 1891. Also "The A.L.C. Half a Century Ago", by Charles Hendee Smith. 10025

Adirondack mountain reserve. Ausable club: historical foreword by Robert W. de Forest. Officers, members and constitution, 1930. St. Huberts, N.Y. 1930. 39p. illus. map. 10026

----. Certificate of incorporation and by-laws of the Adirondack mountain-reserve and of the Ausable lake and mountain club as amended February 14, 1906. n.p. n.d. 26p. See also their "Season of 1904" (3p. plans) and "To the stockholders", 1905, 28p. 10027

Altamont club circular. N.Y. 1897. 4p. map. Letter dated April 13, 1897, signed by Frederic P. Wilcox, R.C. Alexander, O.L. Snyder, George H. Johnson and A. Romeyn Pierson. 10028

And now there are 155! (Adirondack forty-sixers, of course) *Adirondac,* Jan.-Feb. 1959. 23:18. List of new members and aspirants is in March-April issue, 23:31. 10029

Association for the protection of the Adirondacks. The Association for the protection of the Adirondacks... N.Y. 1921. 15p. illus. Date supplied from list of officers and trustees. 10030

Ausable club, St. Huberts, N.Y. The Ausable club...February 1, 1910. n.p. 1910. 64p. 10031

----. The Ausable club of the Adirondack mountain reserve, 1948-49. n.p. n.d. 12p. illus. 10032

----. Ausable club, St. Huberts, Essex county, N.Y. n.p. n.d. unpaged (24p.) illus. 10033

----. The Ausable club, St. Huberts P.O. Essex co. N.Y. n.p. 1909. 64p. 10034

----. Prospectus of the Ausable lake and mountain club. n.p. n.d. 16p. illus. map. Cover dated 1906. 10035

Balsam, pseud. Reminiscences of the C.A. club. *Rod & Gun,* Sept. 4, 1875. 6:347. Continued in the January 1, 1876 issue, 7:209,212. illus. 10036

Brown Swan club, Schroon Lake, N.Y. n.p. n.d. Folded broadside printed on both sides. illus. map. 10037

Cold river reminiscences of a hillbilly turning forty-sixer. *Adirondac,* May-June 1959. 23:63-66. illus. 10038

Custodian's camp, Morehouse lake, 1896. *NYS Con,* Aug.-Sept. 1956. 11:no.1:36. Picture with brief description of the Morehouse Lake Club. 10039

Cutler, Wolcott. On nature's level. *Wings of Love,* Autumn 1957. 30:no.1:1-6. illus. Includes description of two-week vacation at Back Log Camp. 10040

Eagle's nest country club. Certificate of incorporation, constitution and by-laws... n.p. n.d. 15p. Incorporated in 1901. 10041

Freedman, Estelle. To be or not to be a 46'er. *Cloud Splitter,* May-June 1965. 28:no.3:5-7. 10042

Goodwin, James A. Sandy Healy becomes youngest forty-sixer. *Adirondac,* Sept.-Oct. 1959. 23:106-107. Sandra Healy of the Hurricane Mountain Chapter. 10043

Hampson, Robert. Hooks 'n bullets. *Tahawus Cloudsplitter,* Mar. 1964. 15:no.3:12. Sanford Lake Rod & Gun Club. See also short article in the February 1965 issue, p.10. 10044

Healy, Trudy (Besag). Forty-sixers meet at Adirondak loj. *Adirondac,* July-Aug. 1962. 26:64. illus. 10045

Hudowalski, Grace (Leach) The Adirondack forty-sixers. *Appalachia,* June 1958. no.126:104-105. 10046

----. Forty-six New York mountains: a brief description of the Adirondack forty-sixers - the hardy souls who climb the peaks. *Con,* June-July 1964. 18:no.6:16-17. col. illus. See also letter from Mrs. Barbara J. Relyea in the December 1964-January 1965 issue, p.43. 10047

----. That magic number. *Adirondac,* May-June 1961. 25:56-57. Adirondack 46ers. 10048

----. Thirty more win forty-sixer patch... *Adirondac,* July-Aug. 1963. 27:58,61. 10049

----. Those amazing forty-sixers! *Adirondac,*

Jan.-Feb. 1958. 22:15-16. Followed by list of Aspiring Forty-Sixers.   10050

Irondequoit club. Irondequoit club in the southern Adirondacks, 1892/93. n.p. n.d. 4p. Framed copy at the Irondequoit Club, Lake Piseco.
10051

Johnson, Thomas Lynn. The early years of the Saturday club. Cleveland, O. Rowfant club, 1921. 69p. port. (Rowfantiana no.9, Nov. 1921) Includes material on the Adirondack Club.
10052

Lake George association. The Lake George association; 350th Champlain-Hudson festival edition. Its aims and accomplishments... Diamond Point, N.Y. 1959? unpaged (4p.) printed on yellow paper.   10053

Perkins, George F. Journeys to the Adirondacks... n.p. Privately printed, 1956. 20p. Extracts from diaries for 1879,1882,1883 and 1885 of president of the Hollywood Club. 200 copies printed. Copy in the Adirondack Museum.
10054

The Vilas game and fish preserve is for sale or to lease... n.p. n.d. Broadside printed on both sides. Signed: E.A. Carpenter.   10055

Whitney, H. LeRoy. The North woods club. *Anglers Club,* June 1964. 43:no.2:2-6. illus. map.   10056

Ward, Peter A. The call of the forty-sixers. Syracuse Post-Standard *Sunday Magazine,* April 4, 1965. p.4,6,8. illus. incl. cover. 10057

BIOGRAPHY

COLLECTIVE

Biographies in brief: Percy B. Eckhart; Herbert W. Molony: Edward L. Steininger. *Lake Pl Club Life*, Mid-Autumn 1961. p.12, 14. illus. Club members. 10058

Carroll, George. Adirondack tales... Mark Twain and other writers. *Lake Pl Club Life*, Mid-Autumn 1961. p.6,15. illus. Signed: G.C. Brief notes on writers who have stayed at the Lake Placid Club. 10059

De Sormo, Maitland C. Adirondack guides: four who were legends in their time: Cheney, Sabattis, Dunning and "Old Mountain" Phelps. *Ad Life*, July 16, 1964. p.2-3,15. ports. 10060

----. Meacham lake guides. *No Country Life*, Fall 1962; Winter 1963. 16:no.4:13-18; 17: no.1:25-29. illus. ports. 10061

Krueger, Henry E. Hermits of the north woods. *Con*, Aug.-Sept. 1965. 20:no.1:6-9. ports. 10062

Miller, Clinton H. jr. The new first family. *Adirondac*, Nov.-Dec. 1963. 27:95. The Hohmann family become 46ers. 10063

Newton, Earle Williams. Heritage of Vermont - Green mountain rebels. *Ver Life*, Autumn 1948. 3:no.1:24-37. Ethan Allen and Benedict Arnold. 10064

----. Same: redskins to redcoats. *Ver Life*, Winter 1948. 2:4-9, 48-53. plates, figures, maps. Jogues, Rogers, Champlain. Amherst, etc. This article and the one cited above were reprinted in Newton's "The Vermont Story", published by the Vermont Historical Society in 1949. 10065

Nichols, Leon Nelson. Bony of Wilmurt. St. Johnsville, N.Y. Enterprise and news, 1934. 19p. illus. (Tales of the Early Mohawk Region, no.3) Nick Spencer and Joseph Bonaparte. Copy at the Adirondack Museum. 10066

Porter, Marjorie (Lansing) ...The Davidson sisters. *No Country Life*, Summer 1960. 14: no.3:26-28. (Sons and Daughters of the Champlain Valley) Lucretia Maria and Margaret Miller Davidson. 10067

----. ...Lorenzo and Peggy Dow. *No Country Life*, Winter 1959. 13:no.1:36-39. 10068

Powell, Lewis N. ed. Out of the north country: Christian pioneers of northern New York; compiled and edited by Rev. Lewis N. Powell. Syracuse, N.Y. New York state council of churches, 1959? 64p. Published in honor of the 350th Champlain anniversary. Includes Jehudi Ashmun, Nathaniel Colver, Cyrus Comstock, Lorenzo Dow, Georgia Harkness, Elijah Hedding, Ira Manley, Ashabel Parmalee, Conant Sawyer, George Orlia Webster. 10069

Spectator, pseud. In a characteristic letter... *Outlook*, Sept. 19, 1908. 90:105-107. Stevenson, Aldrich, Emerson, Lowell, Warner and others. 10070

Steele, Vern. Two upstate characters of earlier times: Nick Stoner, Nat Foster. *No Country Life*, Winter 1956. 10:no.1:46-47. 10071

Taylor, Andrew Jackson, comp. One ancestral tree from Essex co. N.Y. n.p. n.pub. 1917? 24p. Ransom, Baker, Taylor and Fowler families. Title supplied by Louise Hargreaves. 10072

The Wells of Brandon, New York... Springfield, Mass. n.pub. 1962. 20 leaves. mimeographed. 10073

Wessels, William L. Adirondack profiles. Lake George, N.Y. Adirondack resorts press, 1961. 201p. illus. ports. Includes chapter on Adirondack churches. Third edition published in 1964. Reviews in *North Country Life*, Summer 1961, 15:no.3:54; *Northweek*, June 1961; *Supervisor's News*, June 1962, 12:no.2:41 (reprinted from *New York State Conservationist*); *York State Tradition*, Spring 1964, 18:no.2:59-60. Extract with title "Adirondack Literati" in *Cornell Plantations*, Autumn 1961, 17:40-43. 10074

West, Edith Willoughby (Goodman) The Goodmans of Bolton, New York: their ancestry and descendants. Glens Falls, N.Y. 1930. 100p. front. (col. coat of arms) 10075

Wilcox, Morris R. Men & mountains; with illustrations by Vera Bolton. Francestown, N.H. Golden quill press, ©1959. 138p. illus. Samuel de Champlain, the Green Mountain Boys, the Ballad of Samuel Beach, the Ballad of Ethan Allen, MacDonough of Champlain. 10076

INDIVIDUAL BIOGRAPHY

Arranged by biographee

Abbott, Karl P. Open for the season. Garden City, N.Y. Doubleday, 1950. 278p. Autobiography. —   10077

Aldrich, B. Cedric. Short shrift at "Ti." *Vermonter*, Dec. 1933. 38:315-17. illus. Ethan Allen.   10078

Brown, Slater. Ethan Allen and the Green Mountain boys... N.Y. Random house, 1956. 184p. illus. (Landmark Series no.66)   10079

Crockett, Walter Hill, ed. ...Vermonters: a book of biographies. Brattleboro, Vt. Stephen Daye press, 1931. 254p. (Green Mountain Series) Ethan Allen, p.15-19.   10080

Davis, Kenneth S. "In the name of the great Jehovah and the continental congress!" So bellowed Ethan Allen... *Am Heritage*, Oct. 1963. 14:no.6:65-77. illus.   10081

De Morgan, John. The hero of Ticonderoga; or, Ethan Allen and his Green mountain boys. Philadelphia. McKay, 1896. 233p.   10082

De Puy, Henry Walter. Ethan Allen and the Green mountain heroes of '76... Boston, Dayton & Wentworth, 1853. 428p. Another edition published in Buffalo by Phinney & Co., 1859 (©1855) Also issued in Boston, 1855 with title: The Mountain Hero and his Associates.   10083

Green mountain man. *Aramco*, July 1959. 10: no.7:3-6. illus. port. Ethan Allen.   10084

Hall, Henry. Ethan Allen: the Robin Hood of Vermont. N.Y. Appleton, 1892. 207p. Ticonderoga, p.61-80.   10085

Holbrook, Stewart H. Ethan Allen. N.Y. Macmillan, 1940. 283p. map. Ticonderoga, p.2-19.   10086

Fowler, Barnett. He set the stage for better conservation. *Adirondac*, July-Aug. 1961. 25: 70-71. port. John S. Apperson.   10087

John S. Apperson. *Nature Con News*, Spring 1963. 13:no.1:9-10.   10088

John Samuel Apperson, 1878-1963. *Adirondac*, Mar.-April 1963. 27:29.   10089

LeMaire, Amy. In memoriam. *Fed Gard Clubs NY*, April-June 1963. 35:no.2:15. John S. Apperson.   10090

...Spends $10,000 to save islands... n.p. 1957. unpaged (4p.) Reprint of article from the Albany *Knickerbocker News*, August 27, 1917. John S. Apperson works to preserve the Lake George islands.   10091

Deck, Malcolm. Benedict Arnold: son of the Havens. N.Y. Antiquarian ltd. press, 1961. 534p.   10092

Wallace, Willard Mosher. Traiterous hero: the life and fortunes of Benedict Arnold. N.Y.

Harper, 1954. 394p. ports. maps, facsims.   10093

De Sormo, Maitland C. ed. Ed Arnold, oldtime Adirondack guide; from the notebooks of the late Fred (Adirondack) Hodges. *York State Trad*, Winter 1964. 18:no.1:30-36. illus. port.   10094

Blankman, Edward J. Irving Bacheller: regional voice of America. *Quar*, Oct. 1959. 4:no.4:1-7. illus. port.   10095

Jakobson, Albert. Hollywood - the Racquette river and one of America's first fifth columnists. *Quar*, Jan. 1960. 5:no.1:1-5. Jabez Bacon's acquisition of one half of the town of Hollywood.   10096

Porter, Marjorie (Lansing) ...Theodorus Bailey. *No Country Life*, Summer 1959. 13:no.3:27-28.   10097

Hammond, Henry D. Robert Balk, 1899-1955. *Adirondac*, Jan.-Feb. 1956. 20:13.   10098

----. To the editor. *Adirondac*, Mar.-April 1956. 20:40. Proposal to name promontory near Plateau in memory of Robert Balk. 10099

Eugene Barker. *Cloud Splitter*, May-June 1964. 27:no.3:4.   10100

Porter, Marjorie (Lansing) ...Dr. William Beaumont. *No Country Life*, Spring 1959. 13: no.2:29-31.   10101

Ida Beede. *Adirondac*, Mar.-April 1964. 28:22. Brief obituary.   10102

Cole, G. Glyndon. Nathan Beman, boy hero of Ticonderoga. *York State Trad*, Fall 1963. 17: no.4:44-46. illus.   10103

Bement, William Barnes. Catalogue of the works of art, with illustrations and descriptions; also views of the summer and winter homes... Philadelphia, Lippincott, 1884. 145p. front. (port.) plates. Text by Charles M. Skinner; illustrations by F. Gutekunst.   10104

Stan Benham, fearless bobsledder. *Gr Mom*, Mar. 1960. 2:no.9:42-46. illus. Native of Lake Placid.   10105

Bennett, Cora L. Floyd Bennett; foreword by rear admiral Richard E. Byrd. N.Y. Payson, 1932. 168p. illus. Citation from the Warrensburg Public Library.   10106

In memoriam. *Adirondac*, Nov.-Dec. 1960. 24:122. Nellie Bingham, member of the New York Chapter of the Adirondack Mountain Club.   10107

Bishop, Ira Elmore, comp. ...Basil Bishop of Essex county. *Yesteryears*, Dec. 1965. 9:no. 34:75-78. Part of series: Descendants of James Bishop.   10108

----. ...Elijah Bishop of Essex county. *Yesteryears*, Sept. 1965. 9:no.33:34-37. Part of series:

Descendants of James Bishop. 10109

Schevill, Ferdinand. Karl Bitter: a biography... Chicago, University of Chicago press, ©1917. 68p. front. (port.) plates. Noted sculptor a summer visitor to Raquette Lake. 10110

The Bonaparte enigma. *Our Town,* Fall 1963 - Winter 1964. 2:no.3:91-94; 2:no.4:173-75; 3: no.1:29-32; 3:no.2:57-60; 3:no.3:117-20; 3:no. 4:157-59. Joseph Bonaparte. 10111

Brown, George S. Brown's abridged journal containing a brief account of the life, trials and travels... Troy, N.Y. Prescott & Wilson, 1849. 392p. Describes his ministry in Warren County. 10112

In memoriam. George Walter Brown. *Sup News,* June 1963. 13:no.2:13. port. 10113

Brown, Grace. Grace Brown's love letters. Read in the Herkimer court house, November 20, 1906, at the trail of Chester E. Gillette charged with her murder. Herkimer, N.Y. Citizen pub. co. n.d. 23p. Copy at the State University College Library, Plattsburgh. 10114

Burt, Olive (Woolley) American murder ballads and their stories... N.Y. Oxford university press, 1958. 272p. Grace Brown, p.32-34. 10115

Hynd, Alan. The American tragedy murder. *True,* Feb. 1961. 42:no.285:68, 105-110. col. illus. Grace Brown. 10116

Balch, David A. Marching on! *Villager,* Dec. 1960. 33:no.3:22,55. John Brown, abolitionist. 10117

Cunningham, Anna K. John Brown's farm is historic site. *Bul Schools,* Feb. 1956. 42:188-89. illus. Reprinted in *North Country Life,* Summer 1956, 10:no.3:21-22. 10118

The death of John Brown. *Reveille,* Dec. 1959. no.17:1-2,4. Extracts from articles in the *Elizabethtown Post,* Dec. 10, 1859 and Mar. 2, 1899 and from George Brown's "Pleasant Valley." 10119

Eastman, Ed. The grave where John Brown sleeps. *Am Agric,* Sept. 19, 1959. 156:594. illus. 10120

Gee, Clarence S. The stone on John Brown's grave. *NY Hist,* April 1961. 42:157-68. illus. 10121

Hall, Robert. John Brown's Sunday at Elizabethtown. *Ad Life,* Dec. 1962. p.14. illus. ports. 10122

John Brown, 1800-1859: a brief story of his life. Watertown, N.Y. Santway, ©1921. 36p. Copyright by G.W. Hughes. 10123

The John Brown farm, Lake Placid, New York... n.p. n.d. 6p. folder. illus. "Printed and distributed by the Office of the Town Historian, Town of North Elba, Lake Placid, N.Y." 1962? 10124

The life, trial and execution of Captain John Brown, known as "Old Brown of Ossawatomie"... N.Y. Robert M. DeWitt, ©1859. 108p. illus. port. 10125

Lockwood, Ida. John Brown's life at North Elba. *Reveille,* April 1956. 1:no.5:1,4. 10126

Myers, John Platt. John Brown - the unconquerable... *Bul Schools,* Sept. 1959. 46:16-17. port. Speech at dedication of the restoration of the John Brown farm, July 12, 1959. See also p.26. 10127

Nelson, Truman. Memo to politicians: John Brown revisited. *Nation,* Aug. 31, 1957. 185: 86-88. illus. Thought evoked by the ceremony at John Brown's grave, 1957. 10128

New York (state) University of the state of New York. Historic sites of New York state. Albany, 1960. 56p. illus. ports. maps. Includes John Brown farm. 10129

----. The John Brown farm at North Elba... Albany, 1961. unpaged (4p.) illus. map. 10130

David Buck, early settler in Peru, New York. His direct ancestry; a partial listing of his descendants and some related families. n.p. n.pub. n.d. 16 leaves. mimeographed. Copy in the Saranac Lake Free Library. 10131

Miller, Roland B. Raymond J. Burke. *NYS Con,* April-May 1962. 16:no.5:36. Former game protector at Raquette Lake. 10132

Wildlife news. *Am Wildlife,* Nov.-Dec. 1939. 28:243-45. Obituary of John B. Burnham. See also George O. Webster's "Essex county resident pays tribute to John B. Burnham" in *Lumber Camp News,* January 1940. 10133

Ham, Dale S. He sells lily smells. *Time,* Jan. 1962. p.46-50,80-81. Also in *True,* Jan. 1962. The story of Okey Butcher who has a camp on the Boreas River road. 10134

Bennett, Leonard. Manhunt for an AWOL major... *Mast Detect Mag,* Feb. 1960. 59:no. 5:52-56,83-85. illus. ports. James Arlon Call. See also Norman Carlisle's "Wilderness wager with death" in *True,* April 1965, p.31-33, 96- 10135

Bayle, Francis L. Russell M.L. Carson. *Adirondac,* Jan.-Feb. 1961. 25:18. 10137

Honors for Russ Carson. *Adirondac,* Jan.-Feb. 1960. 24:27. illus. Brief note of award by the New York State School Boards Association. 10138

Forbes, Allan and Cadman, Paul F. France and New England... Boston, State street trust co. 1929. 3v. Champlain, volume three. 10139

Paltsits, Victor Hugo. A critical examination of Champlain's portraits. *Acadiensis,* 1904. 4:306-11. ports. 10140

Steele, Vern. ...Samuel de Champlain. *No Country Life,* Fall 1958. 12:no.4:40-41. port. 10141

Talman, James J. Champlain as an explorer in inland North America. *Ver Hist*, Jan. 1960. 28:no.1:22-32.   10142

Prindle, Cyrus. Memoir of the Rev. Daniel Meeker Chandler. Middlebury, Vt. Ephraim Maxham, 1842. 114p. Biography of son of pioneer settlers of Pendleton, now Newcomb. Copy in the Adirondack Museum.   10143

De Sormo, Maitland C. Mrs. Chase of Loon lake house: a colorful personality of another era. *No Country Life*, Winter 1960. 14:no.1: 24-32. illus. ports. Mary H.H. Chase. 10144

----. More about the 'Mrs.' ... *No Country Life*, Spring 1961. 15:no.2:34-39. port. Mary H.H. Chase.   10145

Mrs. Chase, owner of the Loon lake house, expires. Broadside reprint from *Troy Times*, Jan. 19 and 20, 1933. illus.   10146

Hill, William H. A.N. Cheney and his gun. *NYS Con*, Feb.-Mar. 1956. 10:no.4:42. Letter on his death.   10147

A panther story, by our guide. *Weekly Novelette*, Jan. 12, 1861. 8:279. John Cheney. 10148

Hall, B.M. The life of Rev. John Clark... N.Y. Carlton & Porter, 1856. 276p. port. Warren circuit, Plattsburgh district.   10149

Wessels, William L. Moses Cohen, peddler to capitalist: an Adirondack pioneer merchant. Lake George, N.Y. Adirondack resorts press, ©1963. 35p. illus. ports. Reviewed in *York State Tradition*, Spring 1964. 18:no.2:59.

10150

McHale, John F. The amazing Glyndon Cole. *Trailmarker*, Oct.-Nov. 1962. 1:no.3:7-8,22-23. port. History of *North Country Life* and its editor.   10151

Miller, Roland B. Verplanck Colvin and the great land survey. *No Country Life*, Spring 1956. 10:no.2:22-26. Reprinted from *New York State Conservationist*.   10152

Schaefer, Paul. Adirondack trails. *Liv Wild*, Autumn 1965. no.90:36-37. Reprinted from *Conservation Council Comments*, April 1964. On Verplanck Colvin.   10153

Cone, Gertrude E. Peter Comstock. *No Country Life*, Fall 1961. 15:no.4:8-9. From her master's thesis, Adirondack Bibliography 4392.
10154

Blankman, Lloyd G. Henry Conklin. *York State Trad*, Fall 1965. 19:no.4:47-48. illus. (North Woods Profile)   10155

Adams, Joseph H. The big scoop. *Ed & Pub*, Aug. 14, 1926. 59:no.12:41. Coolidge plagued by mosquitoes and black flies at the Summer White House in the Adirondacks.   10156

French, David P. James Fenimore Cooper and Fort William Henry. Reprinted from *American Literature*, Mar. 1960, 32:28-38.   10157

Covey, Frances (Alden) The Earl Covey story: a biography. N.Y. Exposition press, ©1964. 164p. illus. ports. Reviewed in *York State Tradition*, Fall 1964, 18:no.4:59-60 and *Conservationist*, June-July 1965. 19:no.6:42.   10158

J.R. Curry appointed general manager of Whitney industries. *J For*, June 1954. 52:470. port.
10159

Rev. A.L. Byron-Curtiss. *Northeast Log*, Jan. 1960. 8:no.7:52. Notice of death, October 30, 1959.   10160

Fillmore, Mrs. Susan F. Teaching in the Plattsburgh academy. *No Country Notes*, Jan. 1965. no.21:3. Brief note about Lucretia Davidson.   10161

Davidson, Margaret (Miller). Selections from the writings...with a preface by Miss C.M. Sedgwick. Philadelphia, Lea & Blanchard, 1843. 272p. "The Events Of a Few Eventful Days in 1814," p.17-88, describes the Battle of Lake Champlain.   10162

Irving, Washington. Biography and poetical remains of the late Margaret Miller Davidson... Philadelphia, Lea & Blanchard, 1841. 359p.
10163

Davidson, Thomas. Autobiographical sketch. *J Hist Ideas*, Oct. 1957. 18:531-36.   10164

Lataner, Albert. Introduction to Davidson's "Autobiographical sketch." *J Hist Ideas*, Oct. 1957. 18:529-31. Brief allusion to Glenmore.   10165

Shorey, Archibald Thompson. Albert Tatum Davis, woodsman and surveyor. *Adirondac*, Mar.-April 1961. 25:36,38.   10166

West, Edward G. Albert T. Davis. *NYS Con*, Feb.-Mar. 1960. 14:no.4:8-9. illus. ports.
10167

Major-General Henry Dearborn. *Reveille*, Sept. 1963. 8:no.31:1-2.   10168

Ravitz, Abe C. Philander Deming: Howell's Adirondack prodigy. *NY Hist*, Oct. 1955. 36: 404-12.   10169

Lake Placid club. To Lake Placid club members. n.p. n.pub. 1905? 47p. Petition to remove Melvil Dewey as state librarian, with Dewey's reply to the Regents, Isidor Singer's letter to *The Sun*, etc. Copy at the Adirondack Museum.   10170

Charles L. Dickert, 1867-1942... n.p. 1961? unpaged (4p.) "The master taxidermist and naturalist" of Saranac Lake.   10171

Meade C. Dobson, 1880-1961. *Adirondac*, Sept.-Oct. 1961. 25:102.   10172

Porter, Marjorie (Lansing) ...Daniel Dodge. *No Country Life*, Fall 1959. 13:no.4:23-24.
10173

Rockwell, Landon G. A new friend for the Adirondacks: Justice Douglas meets the ADK. *Adirondac*, July-Aug. 1962. 26:56-57,63. illus. William O. Douglas. 10174

Arthur G. Draper. *Ski Mag*, Dec. 1960. 25:no. 3:4. Other articles appeared in *Skiing*, Nov. 1960, 13:no.2:11 and *Ski Life*, Dec. 1960, 3: no.3:25. 10175

James F. Dubuar to retire from New York state ranger school. *J For*, Oct. 1956. 54:739,741. 10176

Porter, Earl. James Francis Dubuar: a man and a school. *J For*, Aug. 1955. 53:590-91. port. Includes history of the Ranger School. 10177

Samuel Dunning, Adirondack guide. *Reveille*, Dec. 1959, Mar. 1960. no.17:4; no.18:3. Reprinted from the *Elizabethtown Post*, June 4, 1896. 10178

The life, confessions, writings and execution of Edward Earl... Hanged at Sageville, Hamilton county, N.Y. October 14, 1881. Amsterdam, N.Y. Amsterdam Recorder hydralic print, n.d. 15p. Copy owned by Warder H. Cadbury. 10179

Jamieson, Paul F. Emerson in the Adirondacks. *NY Hist*, July 1958. 39:215-37. plate. 10180

Hosmer, Ralph Sheldon. Dr. Fernow's life work... *J For*, April 1923. 21:321-23. 10181

"Bill" Foss retires. *NYS Con*, Aug.-Sept. 1960. 15:no.1:26. port. 10182

C.H. Foster retires from Pack forest, Potter appointed. *J For*, Sept. 1959. 57:698. 10183

Atwell, Charles and Rapp, Marvin A. Nat Foster: hunter. *NY Folk Q*, Autumn 1960. 16: 174-79. 10184

Franz, Eleanor (Waterbury) Hunting the hunter: Nat Foster today. *NY Folk Q*, Dec. 1964. 20:270-75. illus. 10185

----. Who was Nat Foster? *No Country Life*, Summer 1959. 13:no.3:20-22. 10186

Wiltsey, Norman B. Backwoods shooting match. *Am Gun*, Spring 1961. 1:no.2:46-48. illus. Transcript of a soldier's diary giving an eye-witness account of shooting match with Nat Foster at Manheim in 1814. 10187

Forster, Herman. Founder of N.Y. state council dies. *Con Council Com*, May 1963. 2:no.2: 1-2. port. Karl T. Frederick. 10188

Sachs, B. Dr. Gerster; as man and scholar. *Char Club*, 1925. 6:37-42. port. Brief mention of the Adirondacks. Also issued as a reprint. Following this article is "Tribute to the Memory of Arpad G. Gerster," by Lewis S. Pilcher, p.43-49. 10189

Sparse Grey Hackle, pseud. Doctor John of Long Lake: a once-over of John C.A. Gerster, M.D. *Anglers Club*, Oct. 1954. 33:no.3:11-12. illus. Author is Alfred W. Miller. 10190

Rukeyeser, Muriel. Willard Gibbs. Garden City, N.Y. Doubleday, Doran, 1942. 465p. front. (port.) ports. plate, facsims. Keene Valley, p.183-84, 191-94, 299. 10191

Meet Mr. Tupper Lake. *Trailmarker*, July-Aug. 1962. 1:no.2:23-24. port. Moses Ginsberg. 10192

George E. Goldthwaite, 1889-1960. *Adirondac*, Jan.-Feb. 1960. 24:4,12. 10193

George E. Goldthwaite (1890-1960) *Appalachia*, June 15, 1960. no.130:128-29. 10194

Swiftest of all. *Adirondac*, Sept.-Oct. 1964. 28:66. Memorial to George E. Goldthwaite. 10195

Spargo, John. With Maxim Gorky in the Adirondacks. *Craftsman*, Nov. 1906. 11:148-55. port. At East Hill, Keene. 10196

Seth Green. *Harper W*, Sept. 1, 1868. 32:655. Obituary. 10197

Millard, Eugenia. "Big Shot" Bill Greenfield. *NY Folk Q*, Autumn 1965. 12:216-21. 10198

Hackett, Allen. Quickened spirit: a biography of Frank Sutliff Hackett. N.Y. Riverdale country school, 1957. 212p. port. illus. Chapter 9, "Peace of the Woods" describes Camp Riverdale on Long Lake. Reviewed by A. Ranger Tyler in *Adirondac*, July-Aug. 1957. 21:76. 10199

Dorothy Haeusser. *Cloud Splitter*, Mar.-April 1963. 26:no.2:10. 10200

Henry D. Hammond. *Adirondac*, Jan.-Feb. 1964. 28:14. 10201

Miller, Roland B. Requiem for a craft. *Con*, Dec. 1962-Jan. 1963. 17:no.3:27. Death of Willard J. Hanmer closes last shop making guideboats. 10202

Schultz, Ed. Ted Hanmer, builder of Adirondack guide boats. *No Country Life*, Spring 1957. 11:no.2:23-25. port. illus. 10203

Porter, Marjorie (Lansing) ...Georgia E. Harkness. *No Country Life*, Spring 1960. 14:no.2: 43-44. (Sons and Daughters of the Champlain Valley) 10204

Edwin A. Harmes (1880-1962) *Adirondac*, Nov.-Dec. 1963. 27:93. port. 10205

Award for Harpp. *NYS Con*, Aug.-Sept. 1959. 14:no.1:15. illus. Noble H. Harpp of Warrensburg cited for work in white pine blister rust control. 10206

President Harrison at Loon Lake and Plattsburgh. *York State Trad*, Fall 1963. 17:no.4: 19-24. News stories from the *Plattsburgh Republican*, summer of 1892. 10207

Herbert, Henry William. Life and writings of Frank Forester... edited by David W. Judd... N.Y. Orange Judd co. 1882. 2v. fronts. plates.

Volume 1, p.110-265, "The Wigwam in the Wilderness; or, 'Ky Sly and his Companye.' "
                                                    10208

Hibbard, Billy. Memoirs of the life and travels of B. Hibbard...containing an account of his experience of religion and of his call to and labours in the ministry for nearly thirty years... N.Y. J.C. Totten, 1825. 368p. Copy at Union Theological Seminary. A later edition was published by Piercy & Reed, New York, 1843.
                                                    10209

Harry Wade Hicks. *Adirondac*, May-June 1960. 24:61.   10210

Porter, Marjorie (Lansing) Lucy B. Hobbs. *No Country Life*, Fall 1960. 14:no.4:23-24. (Sons and Daughters of the Champlain Valley)
                                                    10211

De Sormo, Maitland C. Adirondack Hodges. *York State Trad*, Spring 1964. 18:no.2:36-48. illus. port.   10212

Charles Fenno Hoffman. *Harper W*, Mar. 10, 1883. 27:147. See also obituary in the June 28, 1884 issue, 28:407.   10213

Smith, Mrs. E. Oakes. ...Charles Fenno Hoffman. *Beadles M*, June 1867. 3:538-49.   10214

Ralph S. Hosmer. *Con*, Dec. 1963-Jan. 1964. 18:no.3:40. Brief obituary.   10215

Shirley, Hardy L. Ralph Sheldon Hosmer. *J For*, May 1957. 55:380-81. port.   10216

Brandis, D. The late Franklin B. Hough. *Indian Forester*, Sept. 1885. 11:426-31.   10217

Randall, Charles Edgar. Hough: man of approved attainments. *Am For*, May 1961. 67: no.5:10-11,41-42,44. port.   10218

Littlefield, Edward Winchester. Bill Howard — an appreciation. *Adirondac*, Mar.-April 1958. 22:33-34. port. Reprinted from the *Journal of Forestry*, April 1949. Preceded by Editor's note that the name of Witchhopple has been officially changed to Mount Howard.   10219

Welcome back, Gracie! *Adirondac*, May-June 1963. 27:34. Grace L. Hudowalski.   10220

Chester C. Jackson. *NYS Con*, Dec. 1959-Jan. 1960. 14:no.3:41. port. Brief obituary.   10221

Prindle, Cyrus. Life of Rev. Richard Jacob. *Chr Advocate*, May 20, 1836. 10:153.   10222

Hoffman, Elmer Owen. Adirondack hermit: Ferdinand Jenson. *No Country Life*, Winter 1956. 10:no.1:12-17.   10223

Brown, William Adams. Morris Ketchum Jesup: a character sketch. N.Y. Scribner, 1910. 247p. port.   10224

Risteen, Frank B. sr. The man Canada forgot... Sir John Johnson, loyalist. *Staff*, Oct. 1962. p.6-8,49. illus.   10225

Carr, Joseph D. Death of Mother Johnson.

For & Stream, Feb. 4, 1875. 3:410. Lucy A. Johnson.   10226

Boswell, Charles and Thompson, Lewis. The man who built Buffalo Bill. *True*, July 1956. 36:no.230:32-33,96-108. illus. (part col.) Ned Buntline (E.Z.C. Judson) Includes a little material on the Adirondacks.   10227

Edward Zane Carroll Judson. *Camp News*, Sept. 1, 1886. 19:193-95. Obituary of Ned Buntline.   10228

A memoir of Catharine R. Keese, late of Peru, N.Y. comprising extracts from her letters and other sketches... N.Y. Egbert, 1866. 76p. Copy at the State University College Library, Plattsburgh.   10229

Porter, Marjorie (Lansing) ...Catherine R. Keese. *No Country Life*, Winter 1960. 14:no.1: 52-53. (Sons and Daughters of the Champlain Valley)   10230

Kellogg, David S. The journals of Dr. Kellogg. *No Country Notes*, Mar. 1964. no.17:2-3,4. This issue also includes a description of visit of William D. Howells and an account of a Clinton County murder.   10231

Adirondack mountain club, inc. Resolution of the Board of governors. *Adirondac*, Nov.-Dec. 1957. 21:109. On the death of Frederick T. Kelsey.   10232

In memoriam. Charles S. Kenwell. *Sup News*, Jan. 1961. 11:no.1:12,29. port.   10233

Radford, Harry V. A youthful Adirondack guide. *Woods & Wat*, Summer 1899. 2:no.2:13. Frederick E. King of North Hudson.   10234

Noxon, Paul. A character study. *Cloud Splitter*, Sept.-Oct. 1957. 20:no.5:5-7. Howard Kretz.   10235

Betts, Charles E. Adirondack boulders. *Adirondac*, May-June 1962. 26:51. On Noah LaCasse's stone rolling parties.   10236

Orrin ("Ott") Lamphear. *Con*, June-July 1964. 18:no.6:39. Brief obituary.   10237

Dedication of George H. LaPan memorial highway...Saranac Lake, N.Y. 1958. Broadside folded into 4p. port. Includes tribute to La Pan.   10238

Hays, Helen I. Pants Lawrence in New York. *York State Trad*, Winter 1963. 17:no.1:14. Frank Lawrence.   10239

Nichols, Leon Nelson. Ann Lear. St. Johnsville, N.Y. Enterprise and news, 1933. 24p. illus. (Tales of the Early Mohawk Region, no. 2). Nick Spencer and Herkimer County. Copy at the Adirondack Museum.   10240

Shorey, Archibald Thompson. Elizabeth Weare Coffin Little. *Adirondac*, May-June 1961. 25: 53,59.   10241

Norton, Mortimer. Old Lobb of Piseco lake.

Fur-Fish-Game, July-Aug. 1958. 53:no.7:12-13,22-23; no.8:28-32. illus. Floyd Ferris Lobb.
10242

John T. Carr Lowe. *Adirondac*, Nov.-Dec. 1963. 27:93. Brief obituary.   10243

Cadbury, Warder H. "Forestry laws are God's laws." *Adirondac*, May-June 1958. 22:65. Historical note on a manuscript sermon by the Reverend John P. Lundy. Includes bibliographical data on Lundy's "The Saranac Exiles."
10244

Cranker, Clifford. The tragedy of Jane McCrea. *York State Trad*, Summer 1965. 19:no.3:35-37.   10245

Blankman, Lloyd G. Johnny McCullen. *York State Trad*, Summer 1965. 19:no.3:45-46. illus. (North Woods Profile)   10246

Biographical sketch of Captain Thomas Macdonough. *Anal Mag*, Mar. 1816. 7:200-15. illus. port. This issue also includes "Anecdote of the Action on Lake Champlain", p.224. See also "Commodore Macdonough" in the July 1818 issue, 12:88.   10247

Darling, Charles H. Commodore Macdonough. *Ver Hist Soc Proc*, 1903-1904. p.57-89.   10248

Feinberg, Benjamin F. "Commodore Thomas Macdonough...the man." An address delivered ...Sept. 11, 1958. Plattsburgh, N.Y. Battle of Plattsburgh day commission, 1958. 8p.   10249

Kehoe, Harry P. "Macdonough at Plattsburgh." An address delivered ...Sept. 11, 1957. Plattsburgh, N.Y. Clinton county historical society and Battle of Plattsburgh day commission, 1958. unpaged (4p.)   10250

Macdonough, Rodney. Life of Commodore Thomas Macdonough, U.S. navy. Boston, Fort Hill press, ©1909. 313p. front. (port.) plates, ports. maps (part folded) facsim.   10251

Macdonough centennial at Vergennes and Fort Cassin. September...1914. n.p. n.pub. 1914. 32p. Cover title: 1814-1914. Souvenir program.   10252

Macdonough's victory; McComb's victory. *Niles*, Oct. 1, 1814. 7:41-45.   10253

Muller, Charles G. Hero of Champlain. N.Y. John Day, 1961. 192p. illus. Thomas Macdonough.   10254

Rigdon, Walter B. Close-up: Harry MacDougal. *County Gov*, Aug. 1962. 3:no.5:22. port.   10255

Francis I. McGuirk. *Adirondac*, Nov.-Dec. 1965. 29:97. Brief obituary.   10256

Manley, Atwood. The little-known Alexander Macomb: a biographical sketch. *Quar*, Jan. 1959. 4:no.1:1-8. map.   10257

Smithers, Nina W. Alexander Macomb - land speculator. *No Country Life*, Winter 1956. 10:noj1:31-33. map.   10258

Goetze, Klaus. Herbert L. Malcolm... *Appalachia*, June 1959. n.s.25:431-32.   10259

In memoriam. *Adirondac*, Jan.-Feb. 1958. 22:14. Isabel (Smith) Malmstrom.   10260

Streeter, Edward. ...Frail conqueror. *Family Weekly*, Mar. 10, 1963. p.4-6. port. Isabel (Smith) Malmstrom.   10261

Curry, John R. Rev. C.W. Mason, 1868-1957. *Northeast Log*, Jan. 1958. 6:no.7:16-17,42-43, 49. ports.   10262

Welch, Fay. Sharon J. Mauhs - a dedicated conservationist. *Con Council Com*, May-June 1965. 4:no.3:6-7. illus. port. Also in *Adirondac*, Sept.-Oct. 1965, 29:66-69, port.   10263

Memorial service for Mr. William H. Miner at the Chazy central rural school, Chazy, New York...Apr. 6, 1930. n.p. n.d. unpaged. port.
10264

William H. Miner. October 22, 1862 - April 3, 1930. n.p. n.d. unpaged (16p.) port. 10265

Fort Ticonderoga museum. Bulletin (North American review) 1957-1958. vol.10, nos. 1-2. Number one is devoted to Brig. General Richard Montgomery. Number two includes articles on the semi-centennial of the restoration of Fort Ticonderoga; La ville de Carillon, by Serge Gagne; Investigations at the French village, by J. Duncan Campbell.   10266

Heacox, Cecil E. Dr. Emmeline Moore. *Con*, Dec. 1963-Jan. 1964. 18:no.3:47.   10267

Lewis Henry Morgan... Schenectady, N.Y. Union college, 1946. 23p. port. (Union Worthies, no.1) Includes contributions by Leslie A. White, Arthur C. Parker and Bernhard J. Stein.
10268

Put their names in lights... *Fortune*, Sept. 1938. 18:no.3:67-73. illus. ports. Biography of William Morris, Sr. Includes Camp Intermission at Lake Colby.   10269

Adirondack Murray memorial association. Prospectus. Organized Aug. 3, 1906. n.p. n.pub. n.d. unpaged (12p.) port.   10270

Cole, G. Clyndon. ...Adirondack Murray. *No Country Life*, Spring 1958. 12:no.2:10-12,67. See also letter from W.J. Griffin, Sr. in the Summer issue, p.52.   10271

Shorey, Archibald Thompson. Adirondack Murray. *Adirondac*, Sept.-Oct. 1958. 22:104.
10272

An old guide gone. *For & Stream*, Mar. 23, 1876. 6:98. William Nash.   10273

LaDuke, John T. Royal (Red) Nedeau: beatnik or neatnik... *Ad Life*, Jan. 31, 1963. p.4. illus. ports. Folk singer from Chateaugay.   10274

Geneology of Daniel Newcomb. *Tahawus Cloudsplitter*, Jan. 1965. 16:no.1:6-7. illus. port. Compiled by Mrs. Mary Breen, Helen Shevlin and Leslie Rist.   10275

Johnson, Theron C. Nice going, Dave. *Adirondac,* May-June 1965. 29:34. Appreciation of David L. Newhouse as chairman of the Adirondack Mountain Club's Conservation Comittee.   10276

Carroll, George. Anna Newman: an Adirondack story retold for Heaven hill farm. Saranac Lake, N.Y. Currier press, 1962. unpaged (8p.) illus.   10277

Caleb Nichols, intelligence agent. *No Country Notes,* Nov. 1964. no.20:2-3.   10278

Northup, Soloman, b.1808. ...Twelve years a slave... Auburn, N.Y. Derby & Miller, 1853. 336p. front. plate. Autobiography of a free negro born at Minerva, N.Y.   10279

In memoriam. *Trailmarker,* Summer 1963. 2: no.1:24-25. port. Brief tribute to Mortimer Norton.   10280

Seaman, Ruth. The Indian preacher: Samuel Occum, Mohegan presbyterian. *Yester,* Dec. 1963. 7:75-79.   10281

Wishard, Luther Deloraine. Silas H. Paine at Silver Bay: an appreciation. Montclair, N.J. New era pub. co. n.d. 29p. front.   10282

Parkman, Francis. Journals, ed. by Mason Wade. N.Y. Harper, 1947. 2v. illus. ports. maps. Includes Lake George and Lake Champlain.   10283

Demere, Philippe. L'amiral du Lac Champlain: Joseph Payant dit St. Onge... Montreal, G. Ducharme, 1929. 16p. front. illus. (Chroniques du Haut-Richelieu no.3) First pilot of Lake Champlain.   10284

Huden, John Charles. The admiral of Lake Champlain. *Ver Hist,* Jan. 1962. 30:66-69. Payant.   10285

Pearse, James. A narrative of the life of James Pearse, in two parts. Rutland, Vt. Printed by William Fay for the author, 1825. 144p. Part 2 contains the account of his imprisonment at Plattsburgh. Pertinent poems written while imprisoned, p.142-44.   10286

Lowrie, Sarah D. In memory of Sarah Thompson Pell... Part II: Garden club history, 1938-1939. n.p. 1939. 3,3 leaves. mimeographed. Copy in the Keene Valley Public Library. 10287

Clifford R. Pettis. *J For,* Mar. 1927. 25:257-59.   10288

Miller, Roland B. W.E. Petty. *NYS Con,* Aug.-Sept. 1956. 11:no.1:35. Brief obituary.
                                          10289

Jaffee, Mrs. Elizabeth B. To the editor. *Adirondac,* Sept.-Oct. 1962. 26:83. In appreciation of Doctor Orra Phelps and the Nature Museum at Adirondak Loj.   10290

Grahame, Arthur. Father of conservation. *Outdoor Life,* Jan. 1948. 101:no.1:9-11,95-97. illus. Gifford Pinchot.   10291

Pinkett, Harold T. Gifford Pinchot, consulting forester, 1893-1898. *NY Hist,* Jan. 1958. 39:35-49.   10292

Place, Marian (Templeton) Gifford Pinchot: the man who saved the forests, by Dale White, pseud. N.Y. Messner, ©1957. 192p. Includes brief account of his work in the Adirondacks.
                                          10293

Coolidge, Louis Arthur. Orville H. Platt of Connecticut, an old-fashioned senator. N.Y. Putnam, 1910. 655p. front. plates, ports. facsims. Orville Hitchcock Platt, summer resident of Long Lake.   10294

L.P. Plumley heads Ranger school at Wanakena. *J For,* May 1957. 55:413.   10295

The north country's Johnny Podres: hero of the 1955 world series. A sympsoium of press comment. *No Country Life,* Winter 1956. 10:no.1: 24-27. illus.   10296

Marjorie L. Porter and her "Champlain valley songs." *No Country Life,* Spring 1961. 15:no.2:18. Announcement of publication by Folkways Records of an album of songs and ballads from the Porter Collection.   10297

Major, Nettie Leitch. C.W. Post - the hour and the man. A biography with genealogical supplement... Washington, Judd & Detweiler, inc. 1963. 318p. illus. (part col.) facsims. ports. (part col.)   10298

Blankman, Lloyd G. ...Bill Potter. *York State Trad,* Fall 1964. 18:no.4:49-50. illus. (North Woods Profile)   10299

Stories of Mike Rafter. *Reveille,* April 1962. 7:no.25:3. Notorious criminal.   10300

Brown, George Levi. ...The story of William Ray... *Reveille,* Dec. 1962; Mar., June 1963. 7:no.28:1-4; 8:no.29:1-4; 8:no.30:1-3. From his "Pleasant Valley."   10301

Ross, Donald G. jr. Martha Reben. *Con,* Oct.-Nov. 1964. 19:no.2:46.   10302

For A.B. Recknagel. *Con,* June-July 1965. 19: no.6:40. Memorial forest.   10303

Friends present Frank Reed with retirement purse. *N Logger,* Feb. 1965. 13:no.8:18. illus.
                                          10304

Rev. Frank Reed retires as senior editor of the *Northern Logger. In* New York state ranger school 1964 alumni news. Wanakena, N.Y. 1964. p. 22-23.   10305

Blankman, Lloyd G. Grotus Reising. *York State Trad,* Spring 1965. 19:no.2:42-43. illus. port. (North Woods Profile)   10306

Stiles, Fred T. Pioneer doctor of upstate New York. *NY Folk Q,* Winter 1960. 16:279-86. Nathaniel Rhoades of Washington County.
                                          10307

Ernest Rist. *Northeast Log,* April 1960. 8: no.10:52-53. Brief obituary of "Mr. Adirondack." 10308

In memoriam. Ernest D. Rist, 1894-1959. *Sup News,* Jan. 1960. 10:no.1:8. port. Followed by poem "Mr. Adirondacks," by Alan F. Bain, dedicated to Ernest D. Rist. 10309

Wildlife after dark - meet one of our greatest amateur photographers, a man whose pictures of animals at night have won wide critical acclaim. *Outdoor Life,* June 1943. 91:no. 6:38-45. illus. Hobart V. Roberts. 10310

Bill Roden manager of Rondack Mt. authority. *Con Council Com,* April-May 1961. 1:no. 1:6. William Roden. 10311

Cuneo, John R. Robert Rogers of the rangers. N.Y. Oxford university press, 1959. 308p. illus. Reviewed by Ellis A. Johnson in *New York History,* January 1960, 41:89-92. 10312

Rogers, Robert. Journals...reprinted from the original edition of 1763... Introduction by Howard H. Peckham. N.Y. Corinth books, 1961. 171p. port. maps. 10313

Stiles, Fred T. Tales of Rogers and his rangers. *No Country Life,* Fall 1959. 13:no.4:25-28. 10314

Walker, Joseph Burbeen. Life and exploits of Robert Rogers, the ranger: a paper read...November 5, 1884. Boston, J.N. McClintock, 1885. 15p. 10315

Gebo, Tom. Noah Rondeau, "Mayor" of Cold river. *York State Trad,* Fall 1965. 19:no.4:43-46. 10316

Breen, Mrs. Mary ed. Theodore Roosevelt. n.p. n.d. 12p. port. Reproduced from typewritten copy. Prepared by the pupils of the Newcomb Central High School for the Tahawus Sportsmen's Show, 1951. 10317

Carroll, George. Adirondack tales: Rough rider's ride. *Lake Pl Club Life,* Jan. 1961. p.6,11. illus. Signed: G.C. Theodore Roosevelt. 10318

Harmes, Edward A. 2:15 a.m. T.R.'s ride from Tahawus to North Creek. *Adirondac,* Nov.-Dec. 1963. 27:88-92. 10319

Paine, Hugh. I always called him Ted. *Reveille,* June 1958. 2:no.12:3,4. Reprinted from the *Masonic Outlook of N.Y. State,* Dec. 1938. Noah LaCasse's reminiscences of Theodore Roosevelt. 10320

Steele, Vern. ...Theodore Roosevelt. *No Country Life,* Spring 1958. 12:no.2:60,67. Celebration at Newcomb. 10321

Townsend, George Washington. Our martyred president...Memorial life of William McKinley... n.p. n.pub. 1901. 512p. illus. ports. Pages 467 through 480 on Theodore Roosevelt and his Adirondack trip. 10322

Adirondack center, Elizabethtown, N.Y. James N. Rosenberg. August 1959. Elizabethtown, N.Y. 1959. unpaged (4p.) illus. Brief biographical note accompanying exhibition catalog. 10323

Rosenberg, James Naumberg. Painter's self-portrait; edited with an introduction by Milton S. Fox. N.Y. Crown publishers inc. 1958. 203p. illus. (part mounted, part col.) ports. 10324

Smith, Terence. Retrospective: Rosenberg. Plattsburgh, N.Y. State university college at Plattsburgh, 1964. 25p. illus. Reproduction of several Adirondack landscapes. 10325

Rosenbluth, Robert. The many lives of Robert Rosenbluth: excerpts from his autiobiography. *For Hist,* Spring-Summer 1964. 8:17-21. illus. port. The complete text unpublished, is in the New York State Library. Includes account of the State of New York vs. Chateaugay Ore and Iron Company. 10326

In memory of General Henry H. Ross, who died at Essex, Essex county, N.Y. on the 13th day of Sept. 1862. n.p. n.pub. n.d. 27p. Portrait tipped in opposite title page. 10327

Manley, Atwood. J. Henry Rushton - famous boat builder. *Quar,* April 1958. 3:no.2:1-7. illus. ports. 10328

Ryder, William. The superannuate; or, Anecdotes, incidents and sketches of the life and experiences of William Ryder...related by himself. George Peck, editor. N.Y. G. Lane & B.C. Tippett for the Methodist episcopal church, 1845. 160p. 10329

Brenan, Dan. Mitchell Sabattis. *NYS Con,* Aug.-Sept. 1959. 14:no.1:44. Followed by letter from Lloyd Sabattis, great grandson of Mitchell. 10330

Headley, Joel Tyler. The St. Regis Indians. *In* Christian parlor book. N.Y. 1848. 4:251-59. Character sketch of Mitchell Sabattis. Early version of part of his "The Adirondack", 1848. 10331

Smith, Mrs. Hartwell. Sabattis at Newcomb. *NYS Con,* Aug.-Sept. 1950. 6:no.1:37. See also letter from Charles E. Lewis "More on Sabattis" in the October-November issue, 6: no.2:36. 10332

Porter, Marjorie (Lansing) ...Peter Sailly. *No Country Life,* Fall 1958. 12:no.4:25-27. First article in the series "Native Sons and Daughters of the Champlain Valley." 10333

Otto Schniebs, a way of life. *Skiing,* Mar. 1959. 11:no.6:23-26. port. illus. 10334

De Sormo, Maitland C. Lord of Debar pond: Robert Schroeder... *No Country Life,* Fall 1959. 13:no.4:29-36. illus. port. 10335

Bacheller, Irving. From stores of memory...
N.Y. Farrar & Rinehart, 1938. 306p. Philo
Scott, p.127-33.   10336

Bill Severinghaus. *Con Council Com*, July
1963. 2:no.3:4,12. port. C.W. Severinghaus.
                                         10337

William H. Seward. Schenectady, N.Y. Union
college, 1951. 26p. port. (Union Worthies no.
6). Contributors: Douglas W. Campbell, Dex-
ter Perkins, Philip C. Jessup.   10338

Blankman, Lloyd G. Henry Shepard. *York
State Trad*, Summer 1964. 18:no.3:13. (North
Woods Profile)   10339

Green, Seth. Panther shooting in the north
woods. *Country*, Mar. 2, 1878. 1:262. Brief
letter about Jack Sheppard.   10340

Selma M. Shultz. *Adirondac*, May-June 1958.
22:54. Obituary of a member of the New York
Chapter, Adirondack Mountain Club.   10341

Rickard, Chauncey. Jeptha R. Simms...auth-
or. *Sch Co Hist Rev*, Oct. 1954. 18:no.2:23-26.
illus.   10342

Morton, Doris (Begor) Philip Skene of
Skenesborough. Bicentennial issue. Granville,
N.Y. Grastorf press, 1959. 84p. front. port.
illus. maps. Reviewed in *North Country Life*,
Fall 1959, 13:no.4:56-57.   10343

Smith, Adeline "Pat" (Rielly) I will look unto
the hills. Keeseville, N.Y. Essex county republican co. inc. 1958? 17p. Biography of Doctor
John Smith.   10344

Smith, Kate. Upon my lips a song. N.Y. Funk
& Wagnalls, ©1960. 213p. illus. ports. 10345

----. Living in a great big way... N.Y. Blue rib-
bon books, ©1938. 230p. front. (port.) plates.
                                         10346

Collins, Geraldine. The biography and funny
sayings of Paul Smith. Paul Smiths, N.Y. Paul
Smith's college, 1965. 55p. illus. ports. Cover
title: Paul Smith. Taken from E. Long's "Funny sayings of Paul Smith" (AB 7114)   10347

----. Paul Smith. *Franklin Hist R*, Aug. 1965.
2:4-11. illus. port.   10348

Tetu, Robert A. Paul Smith: pioneer in the Adirondacks. Typescript of research paper, Paul
Smith's college, May 1965. 11 leaves. Copy in
the Saranac Lake Free Library.   10349

The Adirondack hermit. *Reveille*, Sept. 1962.
7:no.27:3. port. William Smith. Reprinted
from the *Essex County Republican*.   10350

Moore, Howard Parker. A life of General
John Stark of New Hampshire. N.Y. author,
1949. 539p. Includes Robert Rogers.   10351

Stark, Caleb. Memoir and official correspondence of Gen. John Stark... Concord, N.H. Ed-
son C. Eastman, 1877. 495p. front. Memoir of
Robert Rogers, p.388-486.   10352

Balch, David A. The teller of tales. *Villager*,
Mar. 1961. 33:no.6:19,39-42. Stevenson at Saranac Lake.   10353

Brickner, Samuel M. Stevenson at Saranac
Lake. *NY Times Mag*, Oct. 24, 1915. p.9. illus.   10354

Caldwell, Elsie (Noble) Last witness for Robert Louis Stevenson. Norman, Okla. University
of Oklahoma press, ©1960. 384p. illus. ports.
Saranac Lake, p.25-27.   10355

Chapman, Livingston. Stevenson in the Adirondacks. *J Outd Life*, June 1935. 32:210-12. illus.   10356

Cole, G. Glyndon. RLS in Saranac Lake. *No
Country Life*, Winter 1959. 13:no.1:21-24. illus. Robert Louis Stevenson.   10357

Henry James and Robert Louis Stevenson. A
record of friendship and criticism. Ed...by Janet Adam Smith. London, R. Hart-Davis, 1948.
Includes letters to and from R.L.S. during his
Saranac Lake winter, 1887/88.   10358

Adirondack guide. *NYS Con*, Dec. 1959-Jan.
1960. 14:no.3:41. port. Brief note on Harry
Stickney.   10359

Stickney, John R. Memoirs of John R. Stickney. Bolton Landing, N.Y. 1965. 64p.   10360

Mason, Howard C. The vanishing American.
York State Trad, Fall 1964. 18:no.4:6-8. From
his "Backward Glances", v.2. Fred Stiles and
his family.   10361

Everson, Ida G. William J. Stillman: Emerson's "gallant artist." *NE Quar*, Mar. 1958.
31:32-46.   10362

Richardson, Edgar P. William J. Stillman:
artist and art journalist. *Union Worthies*, 1957.
12:9-15. Minor reference to the Adirondacks.
                                         10363

William James Stillman, 1828-1901. *In* Jones,
Agnes (Halsey) comp. Rediscovered painters
of upstate New York, 1700-1875. Cooperstown,
N.Y. New York state historical association,
1958. p.70-71. illus. Reproduction of Stillman's
painting, "The Philosophers' Camp in the Adirondacks."   10364

De Sormo, Maitland C. Stoddard of Glens
Falls. *Ad Life*, Jan. 31, 1963. p.8-9. illus. Seneca Ray Stoddard.   10365

Seneca Ray Stoddard. *York State Trad*, Spring
1963. 17:no.2:14-23,42. illus. Text accompanied
by "A Pictorial Record of the Past Made by a

Pioneer Photographer - Seneca Ray Stoddard".
(Stoddard Album 1) Album 2 appears in the
Fall 1963 issue, 17:no.4:13-18. 10366

Hays, Helen I. Nick Stoner. *No Country Life,*
Spring 1960. 14:no.2:30. 10367

Leach, Frederic B. The man whose praise we
sing. *Am Heritage,* April 1965. 16:no.3:62-63,
97-99. illus. port. Nick Stoner. 10368

Brown, Lawrason. Trudeau. *J Outd Life,* May
1931. 28:285-89. illus. Edward Livingston Trudeau. 10369

----. Trudeau's family tree. n.p. n.pub. 1934.
11p. illus. Reprinted from the *Journal of the
Outdoor Life,* Oct. and Nov. 1934. 10370

Harrod, Kathryn E. Man of courage: the story
of Dr. Edward L. Trudeau... N.Y. Julian Messner, ©1959. 192p. Reviewed in *North Country
Life,* Spring 1960. 14:no.2:53-54. 10371

Knopf, Sigard Adolphus. The statue of Edward Livingston Trudeau. n.p. 1918. 5p. illus.
Reprinted from the *New York Medical Journal,* Aug. 24, 1918. 10372

Krause, Allen Kramer. Trudeau, the physician.
Nat Tub Assn Tr, 1935. 31:40-46. 10373

Pattison, Harry A. Trudeau, the churchman.
Nat Tub Assn Tr, 1935. 31:29-39. 10374

Trembley, Charles C. Trudeau, the sportsman.
Nat Tub Assn Tr, 1935. 31:19-28. 10375

Trudeau, Francis B. Boyhood recollections.
J Outd Life, May 1931. 28:296-97. illus. 10376

A. Ranger Tyler. *Adirondac,* Mar.-April 1963.
27:18,26. See also "Resolution Passed by the
Board of Governors", on p.41 of the May-June
issue. 10377

...A. Ranger Tyler. *NYS Ed,* Mar. 1963. 50:
no.6:14. port. The April issue carries letters on
Tyler's death, p.4. 10378

Benedict, Darwin. A. Ranger Tyler. *Cloud
Splitter,* Mar.-April 1963. 25:no.2:3. 10379

Carroll, George. Man in the leather suit...
Lake Pl Club Life, June 1960. p.7,10. illus.
port. Henry Van Hoevenberg. 10380

Piro, Tony. Jumping's junior miss. *Ski Life,*
Mar. 1960. 2:no.6:47. Sandra Vitvitsky of Lake
Placid. She was also featured in *America Illustrated,* the Polish language magazine issued by
the U.S. Information agency for distribution
abroad. 10381

Cole, G. Glyndon. Edgar P. Wadhams, first
bishop of Ogdensburg. *York State Trad,* Summer 1964. 18:no.3:38-44. illus. port. 10382

In memoriam. Margaret Wagar. *Sup News,*
June 1961. 11:no.2:23. port. 10383

Spargo, John. Lieutenant Colonel Joseph Wait
of Rogers' rangers and the continental army:
freemason and pioneer Vermont settler. n.p.
1942. 21p. Copy in the Rutland Free Library.
10384

Alice Waterhouse: a tribute. *Cloud Splitter,*
Jan.-Feb. 1964. 27:no.1:4. 10385

Porter, Marjorie (Lansing) ...Elkanah Watson.
No Country Life, Winter 1959. 13:no.1:34-36.
10386

----. ...Smith Mead Weed. *No Country Life,*
Winter 1961. 15:no.1:37-39. (Sons and Daughters of the Champlain Valley) 10387

Thorpe, Thomas Bangs. Lynde Weiss; an autobiography...by George H. Throp... Philadelphia, Lippincott, 1852. 188p. illus. Incorrectly
attributed by the publisher to George H.
Throop. 10388

William Chapman White, '23. *Princeton Alum,*
Feb. 3, 1956. 56:no.15:27. Brief obituary. 10389

Worthington, Ruth (Drake) William Chapman
White. *Adirondac,* Mar.-April 1956. 20:36-37.
10390

Miller, Roland B. Alvin G. Whitney. *NYS
Con,* Aug.-Sept. 1960. 15:no.1:35. Brief obituary. 10391

Plum, Eleanor Mary. In memoriam. Anna Williams. *Adirondac,* Mar.-April 1958. 22:35.
Member of the Albany Chapter of the Adirondack Mountain Club. 10392

Harkness, J. Warren. Eleazer Williams. *No
Country Life,* Summer 1960. 14:no.3:42-48.
In the battles of Plattsburgh and Cumberland
Bay. 10393

Pew, William A. Colonel Ephraim Williams,
an appreciation; with a foreword by General
Leonard Wood. Williamstown, Mass. Williams
college, 1919. 29p. map. Battle of Lake George,
Sept. 8, 1755. 10394

Harold G. Wilm (editorial) *Con Council Com,*
Jan.-Feb. 1962. 1:no.4:2. Urging appointment
as Conservation Commissioner. 10395

Meet Dr. Harold G. Wilm, Conservation commissioner... *NYS Con,* Feb.-Mar. 1959. 13:
no.4:3. port. 10396

Porter, Marjorie (Lansing) Andrew Wither-
spoon. *No Country Life,* Winter 1962. 16:no.
1:48-49. His trial at Methodist Church conference in Keeseville, 1838. 10397

Cuddeback, Elizabeth. Paul Austin Wolfe.
N.Y. Brick presbyterian church, 1964? unpaged (8p.) 10398

Bowerman, Edith Z. A famous fisherman.
Four Tr News, Sept. 1905. 9:184. illus. Monu-
ment to Reuben Wood, Cranberry Lake. 10399

Wescott, R. Obituary of Isaac Woodward of Warrensburg. *Chr Advocate,* Jan. 24, 1834. 8:88.   10400

Blankman, Lloyd G. Jonathan Wright, trapper. *Fur-Fish-Game,* Mar. 1961. 56:no.3:14-15,38-41,48-50. illus.   10401

New skipper. Welcome aboard, Henry! *Adirondac,* Nov.-Dec. 1962. 26:88,100. port. Henry L. Young, President of the Adirondack Mountain Club. See also "Thank you, Henry" in the November-December 1964 issue, 28:82. Accomplishments of the club under Young's leadership.   10402

Carroll, George. Adirondack tales...The Reverend Joshua Young. *Lake Pl Club Life,* Mid-Winter 1961. p.6,15. illus. Signed: G.C.

                                                    10403

Howard Zahniser. *Adirondac,* July-Aug. 1964. 28:50.   10404

THE ADIRONDACKS
IN ART AND LITERATURE

GENERAL

A. Fitzwilliam Tait, Adirondack artist. *No Country Life,* Winter 1957. 11:no.1:23-25. illus. 10405

Adirondack museum. Winslow Homer in the Adirondacks: an exhibition of paintings... Blue Mountain Lake, N.Y. ©1959. 81p. illus. Introduction by Lloyd Goodrich. "Winslow Homer and the Adirondacks", by James W. Fosburgh; "Some of Homer's Adirondack Models", by John R. Curry. Brief review in *Adirondac,* Sept.-Oct. 1959, 23:102,107. Also reviewed in *North Country Life,* Winter 1961, 15:no.1:51. 10406

Cadbury, Warder H. Sketches by Frederick B. Allen. *Adirondac,* July-Aug. 1959. 23:72-73. illus. Footnote on Allen's sketches of Lower Ausable Lake and Gothic Mountain. 10407

Carmer, Carl Lamson, comp. The tavern lights are burning... N.Y. David McKay company inc. ©1964. 567p. "The Adirondacks", p.167-210. Anthology. Reviewed in *York State Tradition,* Fall 1964. 18:no.4:54-55. Another review on p.56. 10408

Deerwood music camp, Saranac inn, N.Y. Season of 1956... n.p. n.d. unpaged (24p.) illus. map. Published annually. 10409

Edgerton, Samuel Y. jr. The murder of Jane McCrea: the tragedy of an American *tableau d'histoire. Art Bul,* Dec. 1965. 47:481-92. illus. 10410

Frederic Remington art memorial museum. Frederic Remington. Ogdensburgh, N.Y. n.d. Broadside printed on both sides and folded into 6p. illus. map. 10411

Goodrich, Lloyd. Winslow Homer. *Perspect USA,* Winter 1956. no.14:44-54. 10412

Huth, Hans. Nature and the American: three centuries of changing attitudes. Berkeley, Cal. University of California press, ©1957. 250p. col.front. illus. plates. Includes a number of Adirondack views and comments on Thomas Cole, the Philosophers' Camp and the Forest Preserve. 10413

Jacobson, Robert. Lake George opera festival at Diamond Point. *Mus Am,* Aug. 1963. 83: no.8:7. 10414

Jamieson, Paul F. ed. The Adirondack reader; the best writings on the adventurous and contemplative life in one of America's most loved regions. N.Y. Macmillan, 1964. 494p. illus. Reviewed by D.A. Plum in *Adirondac,* Nov.-Dec. 1964, 28:95; by Robert Newell Bliss in *Appalachia,* Dec. 1965, 35:no.4:785; by William B. Conroy in *New York History,* April 1965, 46:194-96; by Paul H. Oesher in *Living Wilderness,* Spring 1965, 29:31-33; and in *York State Tradition,* Winter 1965, 19:no.1:5-7. 10415

Manley, Atwood. Some of Fredᵃric Remington's north country associations, prepared for Canton's Remington centennial observance, 1961. Ogdensburgh, N.Y. 1961. 47p. ports. illus. Cover title: Frederic Remington in the Land of his Youth. Reviewed in *North Country Life,* Winter 1962, 16:no.1:56-58. 10416

...Painted reveries from long ago. *Life,* Nov. 27, 1964. 57:no.22:129-30. illus. (part col.) Reminiscences of Edna A.W. Teall. 10417

Peach, Arthur Wallace, ed. Vermont prose: a miscellany; edited by Arthur Wallace Peach and Harold Goddard Rugg. Brattleboro, Vt. Stephen Daye press, ©1931. 256p. Includes selections by Champlain, Ethan Allen and others. 10418

Plum, Dorothy Alice. The Adirondack bookshelf. *Adirondac,* Sept.-Oct. 1959-date. 23:no. 4-date. 10419

Spectorsky, Auguste C. ed. The book of the mountains, being a collection of writings about the mountains in all their aspects. N.Y. Appleton-Century-Crofts, 1955. 492p. illus. Includes Carl Carmer's essay on Tongue Mountain. 10420

Stow, Millicent. History in prints... Ticonderoga, N.Y. 1938. 6p. front. Written to accompany a special exhibition of prints at Headquarters House, Ticonderoga. New York State Historical Association. 10421

Stutler, Boyd B. Glory, glory, Hallelujah! The story of "John Brown's body" and "Battle hymn of the republic". Cincinnati, O.C.J. Krehbiel co. 1960. 47p. front. ports. facsims. 10422

Willis, Nathaniel Parker. Mountain, lake and river: a series of twenty-five steel engravings from Bartlett and others. The descriptive text by N.P. Willis and others... Boston, Estes & Lauriat, 1884. 96p. front. plates. Selections from his "American Scenery." 10423

ESSAYS

Carson, William R. Random thoughts while riding through the western Adirondacks. Reprinted from *New York State Medicine*, Feb. 1, 1964, 64:no.3.   10424

Challis, Mary J. Look again! "the forest... stretching in unbroken miles." *Adirondac*, Sept.-Oct. 1963. 27:72-73. Beauty of the Forest Preserve.   10425

Chrenko, Richard M. Adirondack explorative research. *Adirondac*, Jan.-Feb. 1962. 26:11. See also the September-October 1961 issue, 25:103, "S.C.G.S. Assails ADK Lassitude".   10426

Cornwell, George. Adirondack summer: observations in poetic and prose form. N.Y. Vantage press, 1964. 64p.   10427

Fosburgh, Hugh. One man's pleasure: a journal of the wilderness world; illustrated by Walter W. Ferguson. N.Y. Morrow, 1960. 191p. illus. Brief review in *North Country Life*, Winter 1961, 15:no.1:5; reviewed by Leonard Lee Rue III in *Audubon Magazine*, Nov.-Dec. 1960, 62:300-301. See also P. Schuyler Miller's "A Brace of Fosburghs" in *Adirondac*, July-Aug. 1960, 24:71-72 for a review of this volume and Pieter Fosburgh's "The Natural Thing".   10428

Loope, P. Fay. Adirondack boulders, by Old Adk'er, pseud. *Adirondac*, Mar.-April 1963. 27:20-21.   10429

----. Adirondack snow - sunny zero mornings offer rare visions, by Old Adirondacker, pseud. *Adirondac*, Jan.-Feb. 1962. 26:12.   10430

----. Four seasons of a mountain, by Old Adirondacker, pseud. *Adirondac*, July-Aug. 1962. 26:62-63. Mount Marcy.   10431

----. Frost on the mountain, by Old Adirondacker, pseud. *Adirondac*, Sept.-Oct. 1962. 26:77. Frost formations.   10432

---. ...The murmuring pines & the hemlocks, by Old Adirondacker, pseud. *Adirondac*, Sept.-Oct. 1961. 25:97,103.   10433

----. North country winter, by Old Adirondacker, pseud. *Adirondac*, Nov.-Dec. 1961. 25:117.   10434

Newman, Burt. Peace of mind thru nature. Paradox, N.Y. Backwoods journal, 1962. unpaged (52p. incl. cover) illus. Reproduced from typewritten copy.   10435

Nixon, Edgar Burkhardt. The armchair mountaineer. *Adirondac*, Nov.-Dec. 1956-date. 20:no.6-. Essays on a variety of Adirondack topics including climbing, Johns Brook Lodge, Scott Pond.   10436

The peace of an Adirondack winter. *No Country Life*, Winter 1957. 11:no.1:38. illus. Reprint of an editorial from the *Lake Placid News*.   10437

Plum, Dorothy Alice. Living with the Adirondack bibliography. *Cloud Splitter*, May-June 1957. 20:no.3:4-5.   10438

Reiser, Milton. The eternal hills: an appreciation of the earth's mountain ranges. n.p. 1940? unpaged (8p.) illus. Copy at the Adirondack Museum.   10439

Schaefer, Paul. Adirondack trails. *Con Council Com*, April-May 1964. 3:no.2:3; 3:no.3:3. Includes Verplanck Colvin.   10440

White, William Chapman. Just about everything in the Adirondacks; introd. by Alfred S. Dashiell. Blue Mountain Lake, N.Y. Adirondack museum, 1960. 101p. illus. Oblong octavo. Selection of Bill White's columns from the *New York Times* and the *New York Herald Tribune*. Reviewed in *North Country Life*, Winter 1960, 14:no.:46-47, and in *Adirondac*, Sept.-Oct. 1960, 14:no. 1.   10441

----. Yon icy peak. *Adirondac*, Jan.-Feb. 1962. 26:6,12. Marcy in winter. Reprinted from the *New York Herald Tribune*,©1953.   10442

Young, Henry L. Random mental scoot. *Adirondac*, May-June 1959. 23:61-62. illus.   10443

FICTION

Adams, Samuel Hopkins. The corpse at the table. *No Country Life*, Winter 1962. 16:no.1: 5-8. Condensed from the *Saturday Review of Literature*, Sept. 5, 1942, 25:13-15. Also in *Readers' Digest*, Aug. 1942. Locale is north country.   10444

Allen, Merritt Parmelee. The flicker's feather. N.Y. Longmans, Green, 1953. 220p. French and Indian wars in the Lake Champlain region.   10445

Bentley, Phyllis. Miss Phipps discovers America. *Ellery Queen*, Mar. 1963. 41:no.3:88-104.   10446

Brainard, John Gardiner Calkins. ...Fort Braddock letters; or, A tale of the French and Indian wars... Worcester, Mass. Dorr & Howland,

1827. 98p. Originally published in the *Connecticut Mirror*. For other editions see Wright's "American Fiction". 10447

Blechman, Burt. The war of Camp Omongo. N.Y. Random house, 1963. 215p. 10448

Churchill, Winston, 1871-1947. The title-mart. A comedy in three acts. N.Y. Macmillan, 1905. 215p. 10450

Cooper, James Fenimore. The last of the Mohicans: a narrative of 1757. By the author of "The pioneers"... Philadelphia, H.C. Carey and I. Lea, 1826. 2v. Fort Edward, Glens Falls, Fort William Henry and Lake George area. For historical accuracy see David P. French's "James Fenimore Cooper and Fort William Henry" in *American Literature*, March 1960, 32:28-38. 10451

----. Satanstoe; or, The Littlepage manuscripts. A tale of the colony. N.Y. Burgess, Stringer & co. 1845. 2v. Chapters 22-24, the attack on Montcalm at Ticonderoga. 10452

Craine, E.J. The air mystery of Isle La Motte. Cleveland, O. World syndicate pub. co. ©1930. 246p. 10453

Downes, Anne Miller. No parade for Mrs. Greenia. Philadelphia, Lippincott, 1962. 350p. Lake George area. 10454

Edmonds, Walter Dumaux. The Boyds of Black River. N.Y. Dodd, Mead, 1953. 248p. 10455

Fleming, Ian. The spy who loved me. N.Y. Viking, 1962. 211p. 10456

Fosburgh, Hugh. The drowning-stone. N.Y. Morrow, 1958. 198p. 10457

Hamilton, Carson C. Jeff Utter. N.Y. Exposition press, ©1964. 192p. 10458

Hammond, William Alexander. Doctor Grattan: a novel. N.Y. Appleton, 1885. 417p. Keene-Elizabethtown area. 10459

Haun, Frances Ledyard. The French lovers: a tale of Lake Bonaparte. Buffalo, Matthews-Northrup works, n.d. 21p. 10460

Heald, Aya. Shadows under Whiteface. N.Y. Vantage press, 1956. 264p. Reviewed in *Adirondac*, May-June 1956, 20:60. Based on an unsolved murder at St. Regis Falls. 10461

Longstreth, Thomas Morris. Trouble guaranteed. N.Y. Macmillan, 1960. 185p. 10462

Morgan, M.J. Playing Indian. *Four Tr News,* Jan. 1910. 10:65-67. illus. 10463

Muller, Charles G. The proudest day: Macdonough on Lake Champlain. N.Y. John Day, 1960. 373p. illus. Reviewed in *North Country Life,* Winter 1961. 15:no.1:50-51. 10464

Murray, William Henry Harrison. How Deacon Tubman and Parson Whitney celebrated New Years. *In* his The busted ex-Texan and other stories. Boston, DeWolfe, Fiske & co. 1890. p.55-83. plates. 10465

O'Quill, Maurice, pseud. The lake outlaw: a tale of the Lake Champlain waters... Plattsburgh, N.Y. A.C. Nelson, 1851. 68p. Copy at the Hammond Library, Crown Point. 10466

Queen, Ellery, pseud. The hunt for the phantom gunman. *Am Weekly,* Jan. 4, 1959. p.8-9. col. illus. 10467

Reben, Martha, pseud. (Rebentisch, Martha Ruth) A sharing of joy. N.Y. Harcourt, Brace & World, inc. ©1963. 183p. 10468

Remington, Frederic. Pony tracks...with an introduction by J. Frank Dobie. Norman, Okla. University of Oklahoma press, ©1961. 176p. illus. "Black Water and Shallows", p.85-92 describes a canoe trip in the Cranberry Lake region. 10469

Roberts, Jesse David. Bears, Bibles and a boy: memories of the Adirondacks. Illustrated by Gil Walker. N.Y. W.W. Norton, 1961. 256p. illus. Warren County near Brant Lake. Reviewed in *North Country Life,* Fall 1961, 15:no.4:31-32. 10470

Roberts, Kenneth Lewis. Northwest passage. Garden City, N.Y. Doubleday, Doran & company, 1937. 709p. maps on endpapers. Includes Crown Point and trip by canoe up Lake Champlain. 10471

----. Rabble in arms: a chronicle of Arundel and the Burgoyne invasion. Garden City, N.Y. Doubleday, Doran & company, 1933. 870p. maps on endpapers. Includes preparation for the Battle of Valcour Island. 10472

Robinson, Rowland Evans. A Danvis pioneer: a story of one of Ethan Allen's Green mountain boys. Boston, Houghton, 1900. 214p. Ticonderoga and scouting on Lake Champlain. 10473

----. Hero of Ticonderoga. Burlington, Vt. Shanley & co. 1898. 187p. Reprinted in his "Danvis Folk", centennial edition, Rutland, Tuttle, 1934. 10474

Sokoloff. Like flipping a coin. *Ellery Queen,* Oct. 1963. 42:no.4:41-53. 10475

Soraci, Carmelo. The convict and the stained glass windows. N.Y. John Day, 1961. 253p. illus. Clinton Prison at Dannemora. Review, from New York Herald-Tribune *Books,* in *North Country Life,* Fall 1961, 15:no.4:32-33. 10476

Stevenson, Robert Louis. The master of Ballantrae: a winter's tale. N.Y. G. Munro, 1889. 192p. (Seaside Library. Pocket Edition no. 1228) "Two journeys through the eastern part of the Adirondacks are described in this romance, with eighteenth century setting...This book was planned and partially written at Saranac Lake". P.J. 10477

Stiles, Showell. Gentleman Johnny. N.Y. Macmillan, 1963. 243p.   10478

Street, Alfred Billings. The pirate of the lower Saranac. *Fr Leslies Pop Mo,* Oct. 1876. 2:434-35. illus. Baker's at Saranac Lake.   10479

Taylor, Frank Hamilton. Camp idleways: a story of Raquette Lake (Adirondacks) *Demorest,* Aug. 1887. 23:601-609. illus.   10480

Terhune, Albert Payson. The fighter. N.Y. F.F. Lovell co. ©1909. 386p. Raquette Lake is the scene of the latter half of this novel. 10481

Trombley, Della. The hermit of the Adirondacks. Boston, Sherman, French & company, 1915. 264p.   10482

Van de Water, Frederic Franklyn. Reluctant rebel. N.Y. Duell, Sloan & Pearce, 1948. 442p. Ticonderoga.   10483

White, Rhoda Elizabeth (Waterman). Jane Arlington; or, The defrauded heiress, by Uncle Ben of Rouse's Point. Rouse's Point, N.Y. D. Turner, 1853. 48p. Cover title. Wright's "American Fiction" locates a copy at the University of Virginia Library. Listed as unlocated in. Adirondack Bibliography, p.295.   10484

White, Stewart Edward. Blazed trail; illustrated by Thomas Fogarty. N.Y. Grosset & Dunlap, ©1902. 527p. front. plates. Ferris J. Meigs in his ms. "The Santa Clara Lumber Company" gives locale as Raquette River not far above Tupper. W.C.   10485

POETRY

Allen, Herbert C. jr. A cloud to share. *Cloud Splitter,* July-Aug. 1960. 23:no.4:5.   10486

----. Modern lumbering needs. *Adirondac,* May-June 1959. 23:55.   10487

----. Scenic wilderness area. *Adirondac,* May-June 1959. 23:55.   10488

Appleton, Thomas Gold. Faded leaves. Boston, printed for the author, 1872. 150p. 10489

Bain, Alan F. "Mr. Adirondacks". *Sup News,* Jan. 1960. 10:no.1:8. Dedicated to Ernest D. Rist.   10490

Burnham, John B. My mountain home. n.p. n.pub. n.d. 16p.   10491

Byrne, Margaret H. (Myers) For those who spoof, a new porch roof. *Adirondac,* Nov.-Dec. 1957. 21:112. Verse by Peggy on Johns Brook Lodge controversy.   10492

Cameron, Gene. Ballad of the ancient packbasket. *NYS Con,* Oct.-Nov. 1959. 14:no.2:44.   10493

Carman, Bliss. ..."An open letter"... *York State Trad,* Winter 1963. 17:no.1:55. Extract from a poem written at Saranac Lake in the winter of 1919.   10494

Carver, Jonathan. The New-Hampshire ranger. *Knick Mag,* April 1845. 26:146-48. Robert Rogers. Reprinted in Farnham, Charles Haight. "A Life of Francis Parkman", 1901, p.365-73 and in Parkman's "Representative Selections", 1938.   10495

Clark, Arthur B. Joe's bear. *NYS Con,* Oct.-Nov. 1959. 14:no.2:38. Dialect poem about Joe Bolio.   10496

Coates, Walter John. ed. ...Vermont verse: an anthology; edited by Walter John Coates & Frederick Tupper. Brattleboro, Vt. Stephen Daye press, ©1931. 256p. front. illus. (ports.)

(Green Mountain Series) Includes "Ethan Allen" by Rufus Wilmot Griswold; "The Armorer's Errand", by Julia C.R. Dorr; "Champlain and Lake Champlain" by Daniel L. Cady.   10497

Cobane, Orville N. 'There ain't no road up Marcy'. *Adirondac,* July-Aug. 1963. 27:50.   10498

Cole, Anna Matthews. Adirondack journey. *No Country Life,* Winter 1958. 12:no.1:21.   10499

Cook, Joseph. Overtones: a book of verse. N.Y. Knickerbocker press, 1903. Includes "At John Brown's Grave", "An Exile's Return to the Adirondacks", "Suns and Souls at Lake George", "Ticonderoga and Montcalm." 10500

Coxe, Arthur Cleveland. St. Sacrement: a legend of Lake George. *In* his Christian ballads, Philadelphia, 1864, p.19-34. First published in 1847.   10501

Crapsey, Adelaide. Verse; new edition. N.Y. Knopf, 1934. 132p. Includes poems written at Saranac Lake in 1914.   10502

Davidson, Lucretia Maria. Amir Khan and other poems...with a biographical sketch by Samuel F.B. Morse... N.Y. Carvill, 1829. 174p.   10503

----. Poetical remains...collected and arranged by her mother; with a biography by Miss Sedgwick...new edition, revised. Philadelphia, Lea and Blanchard, 1846. 248p. With this is bound: Irving, Washington. Biography and poetical remains of the late Margaret Miller Davidson...new edition, revised. Philadelphia, Lea and Blanchard, 1847. 248p.   10504

Dunham, Harvey Leslie. Some day, perhaps. *No Country Life,* Winter 1956. 10:no.1:45.   10505

Fowler, Albert Vann. The fish god. Rosemont, Pa. 1961. 34p. illus. Reprinted from *Approach, a Literary Quarterly,* Spring 1961. 10506

Gile, Blanche F. Champlain sunset. *Vermonter,* June 1920. 25:80. 10507

Goldmark, Josephine. Climbing Giant at night, by J.G. - 1902. In her Poems, n.p. n.d. p.8-12. 10508

Goldmark, Susan. A mountain vista. *Adirondac,* May-June 1956. 20:47. 10509

Grant, Roll. Tebo: a log driver's chantey of the early days on the Raquette river... *Box Mark,* Mar. 1926. 2:no.10:inside back cover. 10510

Hall, Florence E. Banners unfurled; with illustrations by Judith Van Amringe. Vineyard Haven, Mass. Seven seas press, 1965. 35p. 10511

Harbaugh, Thomas Chalmers. By the shores of Lake Champlain. *Four Tr News,* Jan. 1906. 10:71. 10512

Havens, Palmer E. My maple tree: reminiscences of childhood. Albany, Weed, Parsons & co. 1883. 35p. illus. 10513

Haynes, William, comp. Camp-fire verse, chosen by William Haynes and Joseph Leroy Harrison; with introduction by Stewart Edward White. N.Y. Duffield and company, 1917. 244p. Includes "North Woods Living", by Florence E. Pratt and "Boating up the Oswegatchie" by Lewis V. Randolph. 10514

Hays, Helen I. Early June (in the Adirondacks) *Adirondac,* Mar.-April 1960. 24:44. 10515

Hemenway, Mark. North land rhymes. n.p. n.pub. ©1962 unpaged. Copy in the Lake Pacid Club Library. 10516

Hines, Edna Green. In the north country. *No Country Life,* Winter 1958. 12:no.1:22. 10517

Jacobs, Patricia. Adirondack swamp. *No Country Life,* Winter 1956. 10:no.1:44-45. 10518

Johnson, Ellen (Adkins) Homespun: views of persons and places. Ticonderoga, N.Y. 1960. unpaged. Reproduced from typewritten copy. Accompanied by her "Explanation of the Streetroad Anthology: 'Homespun'..." 8 leaves, reproduced from typewritten copy. 10519

Johnson, Ellen M. To Fort Ticonderoga: our fortress. *Ft Ti Mus Bul,* 1956. 9:131, 133. 10520

Judson, Edward Zane Carroll. Another woods idyl, by Ned Buntline. *For & Stream,* Sept. 4, 1879. 3:no.4:1. 10521

Larned, Augusta. To the Upper Ausable lake. *In* her In woods and fields. N.Y. Putnam, 1895. p.31-33. 10522

Lauffer, Paul. Our forest. *Adirondac,* Dec. 1945. 9:no.6:12. 10523

Leggett, Benjamin Franklin. Outdoor poems. N.Y. Raeburn book co. 1906. 221p. front. (port.) Includes "Mt. Tahawus" and "Loon Lake". 10524

Longstreth, Thomas Morris. Mount Donaldson. *Adirondac,* Dec. 1957. 21:108. See also letter from Longstreth on the same page. 10525

----. The sky through branches. N.Y. Century, ©1930. 81p. Includes "The Guide" (Jed Rossman) and "Mount Donaldson". 10526

MacDougal, Harry M. Pete Pequoix of Pea Soup lake. Elizabethtown, N.Y. author, ©1949. 56p. Fiction. 10527

Mackaye, Percy Wallace. Poems. N.Y. Macmillan, 1909. 189p. "Ticonderoga", p.3-15. 10528

Makin, Elizabeth Francesca. JBL. *Adirondac,* Sept.-Oct. 1945. 9:no.4:3. 10529

Nelson, Stan. Stanzas for sophistocrats. Saranac Lake, N.Y. 1962. 20 leaves. 10530

Nixon, Edgar Burkhardt. Editor's report. *Adirondac,* July-Aug. 1964. 28:64. 10531

North country poets. *No Country Life,* Winter, Spring 1956; Fall 1957; Summer-Fall 1958. 10:no.1:54-55; 10:no.2:45-46; 11:no.4:53; 12: no.3:36,39; 12:no.4:60-62. 10532

An old timer (Written about 1883 or '84) Reprinted for Xmas 1960 by B.H. Gray. n.p. 1960. 3p. Title of poem: Wardner's Rainbow Hall. 10533

Partello, E. Dan. Trees in winter. *NYS Con,* Oct.-Nov. 1959. 14:no.2:46. 10534

Pelton, Effie Sophronia. Spring is coming to the north country. *No Country Life,* Winter 1959. 14:no.1:41-42. 10535

Peters, Ruth E. I'm on a sabbatical... *No Country Life,* Spring 1959. 13:no.2:41-42. illus. 10536

Plaisted, Edgell R. Nightfall on Lake Champlain. *Vermonter,* Summer 1931. 36:149. 10537

Ranney, Archie C. Contentment; composed by Archie C. "Bobcat" Ranney, June 1947. n.p. n.pub. n.d. Broadside, illustrated. 10538

Rice, W.C. To a hermit thrush. *York State Trad,* Fall 1963. 17:no.4:43. By the Hermit of Ampersand. 10539

Roberts, Harry. Minerva creek in autumn. *No Country Life,* Fall 1961. 15:no.4:11. 10540

Rondacarry, pseud. Not the Wabash. *Woods & Wat,* Autumn 1900. 3:no.3:13. 10541

Ross, Barbara L. To Lake Champlain. *Vermonter,* Sept. 1936. 41:146. 10542

Scopes, Helen M. The cycle of the year. Poems; privately printed for my friends. Saranac Lake, N.Y. Currier press, ©1958. 35p.   10543

Shaw, Rev. Clemons. Our own northland and other poems. Oswegatchie, N.Y. 1905. 128p. illus. Includes "Cranberry Lake", "The Guide", and other poems.   10544

----. Poetical portraits. Oswegatchie, N.Y. 1903. 200p. front. ports.   10545

Simmons, Julia (Gardelphe) Rhymes from a rural school. N.Y. Exposition press, 1962. 64p. Written by a teacher of English at the Saranac Central School. Her "Company - Uninvited" appeared in *York State Tradition*, Spring 1963, 17:no.2:26.   10546

Snow, Thomas H. Sporting among the Adirondack hills in the autumn of 1858... Boston, 1863. 12p. Cover title.   10547

Speare, E. Ray. Verses in French Canadian patois. Boston, 1957. 104p. Part I: "Doings at the Hollywood Club..."   10548

Speuf, William, pseud. Two roofs are better than one! *Adirondac*, May-June 1958. 22:51. More verse about the roof at Johns Brook Lodge.   10549

Stone, William Leete, comp. Ballads and poems relating to the Burgoyne campaign. Annotated... Albany, Joel Munsell's sons, 1893. 359p. front.   10550

Street, Alfred Billings. At night in the woods. *Appleton*, Nov. 21, 1874. 12:656. illus.   10551

----. Burgoyne. A poem written for the centennial celebration... 17th of October 1877, of Burgoyne's surrender. Albany, Weed, Parsons & co. 1877. 66p.   10552

Strube, Janet. October 12-14, 1956. *Cloud Splitter*, Nov.-Dec. 1956. 19:no.6:7-8. ADK fall outing.   10553

Sussdorf, Agnes. Wings over Whiteface: victory verse. Illustrations in pen and ink by Princes Olga Shirinsky after photographs and original sketches by the author. N.Y. Paebar company, 1944. 45p. illus.   10554

Taber, Edward Martin. Stowe notes, letters and verses. Boston, Houghton, 1913. 335p. The Adirondacks, p.132-48.   10555

Tindall, Mrs. William J. Rock Dunder. *Vermonter*, Autumn 1916. 21:220.   10556

Torrance, Fred A. The kiln. Troy, N.Y. Prout printers, 1959. 62p. "Old Whiteface"; "Mountain Twilight"; "Tonight and Tomorrow".   10557

Van Brakle, John. Dependence. *No Country Life*, Fall 1958. 12:no.4:28. illus.   10558

----. Fort Ticonderoga. *No Country Life*, Spring 1959. 13:no.2:2. illus.   10559

----. Sea gulls in the Adirondacks. *No Country Life*, Summer 1960. 14:no.3:28.   10560

----. Sunset at Blue mountain lake. *No Country Life*, Spring 1961. 15:no.2:7.   10561

Wilkins, Elsie. Adirondack summer. *Trailmarker*, Summer 1963. 2:no.1:26. See also same title in *Trailmarker* for July-Aug. 1962. 1:no.2:28.   10562

----. The doe. *York State Trad*, Winter 1964. 18:no.1:2.   10563

----. Holiday time. *No Country Life*, Spring 1958. 12:no.2:1.   10564

----. Mountain height. *No Country Life*, Fall 1958. 12:no.4:2. illus.   10565

----. The northern hills. *Trailmarker*, May-June 1962. 1:no.1:27.   10566

----. Summer nocturne. *No Country Life*, Summer 1958. 12:no.3:2.   10567

----. West Canada creek. *No Country Life*, Spring 1956. 10:no.2:20-21. illus.   10568

----. Winter's silver hands. *No Country Life*, Winter 1958. 12:no.1:23.   10569

Wilson, Grace Warner. Champlain valley. *No Country Life*, Fall 1959. 13:no.4:53.   10570

----. Lake George. *No Country Life*, Spring 1959. 13:no.2:17.   10571

----. Path of freedom (Lake Champlain). *No Country Life*, Winter 1959. 13:no.1:8.   10572

Woods, Thomas Francis. Three waters; with illustrations by Edward P. Buyck... Albany, Argus press, 1933. 98p. incl. plates, illus. "At Buel", p.27-32.   10573

DIME NOVELS

Note: The titles listed in this section may be found at the Adirondack Museum, Blue Mountain Lake, N.Y. Citations from Warder H. Cadbury.

Arnold, Allan. Jack, Jerry and Joe; or, Three boy hunters in the Adirondacks. N.Y. Frank Tousey, 1909. 32p. col. wrappers. (Pluck and Luck, no.588, Sept. 8, 1909) Locale - Wilmington and Jay.   10574

Bellwood, Herbert. Rivals of the pines; or, The hunt for the great white stag. N.Y. Street & Smith, 1907. 32p. (Brave and Bold Weekly, no.244)   10575

Diamond Dick and Pard Jimmy; or, The mystery of Cranberry cove. N.Y. Street & Smith, 1909. 32p. col. wrappers. (Diamond Dick Jr. Boys Best Weekly, no.663, June 26, 1909)   10576

Diamond Dick in the Adirondacks; or, The man with the scarred face, by the Author of "Diamond Dick". N.Y. Street & Smith, 1909. 32p. col. wrappers. (Diamond Dick Jr. Boys Best Weekly, no.662, June 19, 1909)   10577

Diamond Dick's last eastern trail; or, The chase after Craig. N.Y. Street & Smith, 1909. 32p. col.wrappers. (Diamond Dick Jr. Boys Best Weekly, no.664, July 3, 1909)   10578

Harbaugh, Thomas Chalmers. The hidden lodge. Cleveland, Arthur Westbrook co. n.d. 32p. wrappers. (Western Weekly no.58) First published in Beadle's Half Dime Library, N.Y. 1878.   10579

Little, C. Jack, Jerry and Joe; or, Three boy hunters in the Adirondacks. *Happy Days,* Sept. 19-Oct. 31, 1896. nos. 101-107.   10580

Norris, Stanley. Phil Rushington's friends; or, The Springvale boys in a lumber camp. N.Y. Street & Smith, 1900. 32p. col. wrappers, pictorial cover. (Do and Dare, no.7, Mar. 31, 1900)   10581

Patten, Gilbert. Dick Merriwell in the wilds; or, The call of the woods, by Burt L. Standish, pseud. N.Y. Street & Smith, 1908. 32p. col. wrappers. (Tip Top Weekly, no.646, Aug. 29, 1908) For reprint, see note for "Dick Merriwell's Inspiration".   10582

----. Dick Merriwell's inspiration; or, The boys of Loon lodge, by Burt L. Standish, pseud. N.Y. Street & Smith, 1908. 32p. col. wrappers. (Tip Top Weekly, no.644, Aug. 15, 1908) With nos. 645-47 reprinted as "Dick Merriwell in the Wilds", New Medal Library no.702 (Dec. 1912) and Merriwell Series no. 167 (May 1927)   10583

----. Dick Merriwell's red comrade; or, The messenger from the west, by Burt L. Standish, pseud. N.Y. Street & Smith, 1908. 32p. col. wrappers. (Tip Top Weekly, no.647, Sept. 5, 1908) Locale for numbers 644-647 is Blue Mountain Lake. See note for "Dick Merriwell's Inspiration".   10584

----. Dick Merriwell's shooting; or, The gun club in the woods, by Burt L. Standish, pseud. N.Y. Street & Smith, 1908. 32p. col. wrappers. (Tip Top Weekly, no.645, Aug. 22, 1908) See notes for the two titles above.   10585

----. Frank Merriwell's athletic team; or, Sport in the Adirondacks, by Burt L. Standish, pseud. N.Y. Street and Smith, 1900. 32p. col. wrappers. (Tip Top Weekly, no.222, July 14, 1900) With nos. 223 and 224 reprinted in "Frank Merriwell's Faith", New Medal Library, no. 392 and Merriwell Series no.60 (April 1923)   10586

----. Frank Merriwell's camp; or, Yale athletes in the great north woods, by Burt L. Standish, pseud. N.Y. Street & Smith, 1900. 32p. col. wrappers. (Tip Top Weekly, no.223, July 21, 1900) See note for title above.   10587

----. Frank Merriwell's jeopardy; or, The wolves in the woods, by Burt L. Standish, pseud. N.Y. Street & Smith, 1904. 32p. col. wrappers. (Tip Top Weekly, no.449, Nov. 19, 1904) See note for following title.   10588

----. Frank Merriwell's magic spectacles; or, Peril in the Adirondacks, by Burt L. Standish, pseud. N.Y. Street & Smith, 1904. 32p. col. wrappers. (Tip Top Weekly, no.447, Nov. 5, 1904) With nos.448 and 449 reprinted in "Frank Merriwell's Peril", New Medal Library no.557 and the Merriwell Series no.115 (July 1925)   10589

----. Frank Merriwell's woodcraft; to the rescue of Old gripper, by Burt L. Standish, pseud. N.Y. Street & Smith, 1904. 32p. col. wrappers. (Tip Top Weekly, no.448, Nov. 12, 1904). See note for title above.   10590

----. Frank Merriwell's wrist; or, The nerve of iron, by Burt L. Standish, pseud. N.Y. Street & Smith, 1900. 32p. col. wrappers. (Tip Top Weekly, no.224, July 28, 1900) See note for "Frank Merriwell's Athletic Team."   10591

Shackleford, H.K. The winning nine; or, Batting for a fortune. N.Y. Frank Tousey, 1911. 32p. wrappers. (Pluck and Luck, no.685, July 19, 1911)   10592

Shea, Cornelius. Two weeks in the woods: the boy hunters of the Adirondacks. *Happy Days,* Oct. 11-Nov. 1, 1913. illus. Locale is Aden Lair and Hoffman Mountain.   10593

----. The young deer hunters; or, Trapped in the Adirondacks. *Happy Days,* Feb. 17-Mar. 9, 1912.   10594

Sheridan, Frank. In the woods; or, The adventures of four young campers. N.Y. Street & Smith, 1908. 32p. wrappers. (Brave and Bold Weekly, no.283, May 23, 1908)   10595

Standish, Hal. Fred Fearnot and his guide; or, The mystery of the mountain. N.Y. Frank Tousey, 1901. 28p. col. wrappers. (Work and Win, no.141, Aug. 16, 1901) Reprinted July 16, 1915 as no.867. Locale is Blue Mountain. Sequel to "Fred Fearnot's Camp Hunt".   10596

----. Fred Fearnot and Jumping Jack; or, The boy wonder of the athletes. N.Y. Frank Tousey, 1909. 32p. wrappers. (Work and Win, no.549, June 11, 1909)   10597

----. Fred Fearnot at hunter's home; or, Six days in the woods. N.Y. Frank Tousey, 1911. 32p. wrappers. (Work and Win, no.671, Oct. 13, 1911)   10598

----. Fred Fearnot's camp hunt; or, The white deer of the Adirondacks. N.Y. Frank Tousey, 1901. 28p. col. wrappers. (Work and Win, no. 140, Aug. 9, 1901) Reprinted as no.866, July 9, 1915.   10599

----. Fred Fearnot's duel in the dark; or, Fighting an unseen foe. N.Y. Frank Tousey, 1909. 32p. wrappers. (Work and Win, no.550, June 18, 1909)   10600

Thompson, Maurice. Threshold of the gods. Springfield, Mass. 1880. 32p. (Good Company, v.4 no.6)   10601

JUVENILE WORKS

The Adirondacks... Schuylerville, N.Y. Screen process printers, n.d. unpaged (24p.) illus. Cover title: Souvenir Coloring Book of the Adirondacks. Cover and page art by James E. Palmer. Copy in the Saranac Lake Free Library. 10602

Alderman, Clifford Lindsey. Joseph Brant: chief of the Six nations. N.Y. Messner, ©1958. 192p. 10603

Averill, Henry K. A new geography and history of Clinton county, New York; comp. from original manuscripts, surveys and other reliable sources; 2d ed. rev. and enl. Plattsburgh, N.Y. 1885. 32p. illus. maps. 10604

Bacheller, Irving. The house of the three ganders. Indianapolis, Bobbs Merrill, 1928. 315p. Locale, the Saranac region. 10605

Best, Herbert. Gunsmith's boy; illustrated by Erick Berry, pseud. Chicago, Philadelphia, Winston, 1942. 220p. col. front. illus. 10606

----. Ranger's ransom: a story of Ticonderoga; illustrated by Erick Berry, pseud. N.Y. Aladdin books, 1953. 192p. illus. (American Heritage) 10607

Clark, Margaret (Goff) Adirondack mountain mystery. N.Y. Funk & Wagnalls, ©1965. 158p. illus. Locale is Keene, N.Y. See note in *Adirondack Peeks,* Spring 1965, 2:no.1:11. 10608

Cooper, Frank Albert. Mr. Teach goes to war. N.Y. McGraw, 1957. 187p. (Whittlesley House Book) War of 1812, Champlain region. Brief review in *North Country Life,* Spring 1957, 11:no.2:60. 10609

Corner stones of America: Ticonderoga. *Open Road,* April 1941. 23:no.3:10-11,31. illus. 10610

Crownfield, Gertrude. Joscelyn of the forts. Decorations by George M. Richards. N.Y. Dutton, ©1929. 282p. front. plates. Ticonderoga. 10611

De Morgan, John. The hero of Ticonderoga; or, Ethan Allen and his Green mountain boys. Philadelphia, McKay, 1896. 223p. 10612

Edmonds, Walter Dumaux. Two logs crossing: John Haskell's story. Illustrated by Tibor Gergely. N.Y. Dodd, Mead, 1943. 82p. illus. Scene laid at Moose River. 10613

Edwards, Cecile Pepin. Champlain: father of New France... N.Y. Abingdon press, ©1956. 127p. illus. map. 10614

Geary, Clifford N. Ticonderoga: a picture story. N.Y. McKay, ©1953. unpaged. col. illus. 10615

Guernsey, Clara Floreda. Oliver's prisoner. Philadelphia, A. Martien, 1871. 222p. illus. 10616

Henty, G.A. With Wolfe in Canada; or, The winning of a continent. N.Y. A.L. Burt, 189-. 401p. incl. maps. Lake George, Ticonderoga, Lake Champlain, Fort William Henry. 10617

Johonnot, James. Neighbors with claws and hoofs and their kin. N.Y. Appleton, 1886. 256p. (Natural History Series, Book 4) 10618

Jones, Louis Clark. Spooks of the valley. Ghost stories for boys and girls... Boston, Houghton, 1948. 111p. illus. Ticonderoga, p.86-96. 10619

Kay, Ross. The Go ahead boys in the island camp. N.Y. Goldsmith pub. co. ©1916. 251p. 10620

Kellen, Konrad. Battle in the wilderness. N.Y. Walker, 1961. 103p. illus. (Companion Book Series) Fort William Henry and Ticonderoga. 10621

Kent, Louise (Andrews) He went with Champlain. Illustrated by Anthony D'Adamo. Boston, Houghton, 1959. 259p. illus. 10622

Knox, Thomas Wallace. The young nimrods in North America: a book for boys. N.Y. Harper, 1881. 299p. illus. Adirondacks, p.163-87. 10623

Lancaster, Bruce. Guns in the forest. Boston, Little, 1952. 259p. illus. Revised edition of his "Guns of Burgoyne." 10624

----. Guns of Burgoyne. N.Y. Grosset & Dunlap, 1939. 424p. 10625

----. Ticonderoga: the story of a fort; il. by Victor Mays. Boston, Houghton, 1959. 181p. illus. maps. (North Star Books) Reviewed in *North Country Life,* Winter 1960, 14:no.1:61-62. 10626

Lincoln, Andrew Carey. Motorcycle chums in the Adirondacks. Chicago, M.A. Donohue & co. ©1913. 248p. front. 10627

Norman, Charles. Orimha of the Mohawks: the story of Pierre Esprit Radisson among the indians... N.Y. MacMillan, 1961. 94p. illus. 10628

Parker, Arthur Caswell. Rumbling Wings and other Indian tales...illustrated by Will Crawford. Garden City, N.Y. Doubleday, Doran & co. 1928. 279p. col.front. illus. plates (part col.) 10629

----. Skunny Wundy and other Indian tales... illustrated by Will Crawford. Garden City, N.Y. Doubleday, Doran &co. 1928. 262p. incl. col.front. illus. col. plates. 10630

Pier, Arthur Stanwood. The Plattsburgers... Boston, Houghton, 1917. 185p. front. 10631

Rathborne, St. George. The young fur takers. Chicago, M.A. Donohue & co. 1912. 258p. Fiction. Title from Warder H. Cadbury. 10632

Ridle, Julia Brown. Mohawk gamble. N.Y. Harper & Row, 1963. 200p. illus. Title from Robert Livingston. 10633

Rossman, Jerry. Don't get stuck in our chimney! Humorous, intimate and profound letters to...Santa's workshop... N.Y. Exposition press, ©1965, 91p. illus. facsims. 10634

Spicer, Marianne. Wonderful adventure with

Samuel de Champlain. Lake George, N.Y. Adirondack resorts press, 1959? 24p. Biography. 10635

Syme, Ronald. Champlain of the St. Lawrence... N.Y. Morrow, 1952. 189p. front. illus. 10636

Tomlinson, Everett Titsworth. Scouting on Lake Champlain: the young rangers. N.Y. and London, Appleton, 1925. 351p. illus. (American Scouting Series) 10637

----. Two young patriots; or, Boys of the frontier, a story of Burgoyne's invasion... N.Y. Grosset and Dunlap, ©1898. 366p. illus. 10638

----. With flintlock and fife: a tale of the French and Indian wars... Boston and Chicago, W.A. Wilde, ©1903. 356p. front. illus. 10639

Vetter, Marjorie (Meyn) Champlain summer. N.Y. Funk & Wagnalls, 1959. 183p. illus. Reviewed in *North Country Life,* Winter 1960, 14:no.1:64. 10640

Wilson, Charles Morrow. Crown Point, the destiny road... N.Y. McKay, ©1965. 191p. map. Fiction. 10641

APPENDIX I: UNLOCATED TITLES

Note: This list includes those titles listed on p.295 of the *Adirondack Bibliography* (1958) which have not been located.

Adirondack mountain reserve. President's report. Missing from the New York Public Library.

Adirondack stories. N.Y. William Wood. 6v. Listed under title in the *American Catalog*, 1876.

Adirondack traveler; a monthly magazine. Advertising brochure lists volume 1, number 1 to be published in Utica, N.Y.

The Adirondacker; a weekly. *The Resorter* for September 1907, v.7 no.3 announces publication.

Association for the protection of the Adirondacks. Report of the Committee to investigate truck trails. N.Y. 1936.

----. A sane forest policy for New York state.

The bucaneer of Lake Champlain...by Uncle Ben of Rouse's Point. Rouses Point, N.Y. D. Turner, 1854. In Imprint Catalogue, New York Public Library. The author has been identified as Rhoda Elizabeth (Waterman) White.

The Cardinal: yearbook of the Plattsburgh (N.Y.) Normal school, 1894? Issue containing: Baker, Bertha. Robert Louis Stevenson. Reference from Stevenson House, Saranac Lake.

Channing, William Ellery. Burial of John Brown. Boston, 1860. 8p. Cited in Donaldson, v.2,p.316, as title from Villard.

Colden, Cadwallader David. Memoir containing the history and description of the State of New-York. N.Y. Davis, 1825. 408p. Cited in Ludewig, Hermann Ernst. The literature of the local history of New York.

Cole, Hiram. Washington county business directory. Albany, J. Munsell, 1859. Listed in Munsell catalogue.

Goodenow, Sterling. A brief topographical and statistical manual of the State of New York; 3d ed. Cited in Ludewig.

Gordinier, Herman Camp, comp. List of plants collected on Mount Marcy, August 17 and 18, 1855. Troy, N.Y. 1885. 1p. Cited in House (N.Y.S. Museum. Bulletin 328-29). Copy missing from New York State Museum.

Holden, Austen Wells. Early voyages of discovery. First attempts to establish a colony in Canada. Albany, J. Munsell, 1851. Listed in Munsell catalogue.

New York (state). Laws, statutes, etc. Game laws of the State of New York. N.Y. Association for the protection of game, 1875. Listed in Phillips, John C. American game mammals and birds.

New York. Board of trade and transportation. A proposed bill to remodel the Forest, fish and game commission...Jan. 1901. Listed in Donaldson, v.2, p.313.

New York central and Hudson river railroad. America's winter resorts. (Four Track Series). Missing from the New York Public Library.

New York Saturday journal. Dec. 3, 1881, no. 612 containing: Whittaker, Frederick. Milo Romer, the animal king.

Paine, Silas H. and Watts, W.G. Points of interest for Silver Bay guests... n.d. 19p. Listed in Carr catalogue.

A summer in the forest; or, Slender hands in the stone quarries. American tract society, 1871. Title from Leslie Rist, Newcomb, N.Y.

Warren county teacher's association. Catalogue of officers and members...for 1861 /62... Albany, J. Munsell, 1862? Listed in Munsell catalogue.

Wild wood notes, by Scope. Cited in Grady, Joseph F. The Adirondacks: Fulton chain - Big Moose region.

APPENDIX II:
ADDITIONS AND CORRECTIONS
TO THE ADIRONDACK BIBLIOGRAPHY (1958)
ARRANGED BY NUMBER

Note: Reprinted as separates: 31, 156, 426, 427, 428, 438, 461, 462, 1722, 4984, 5113, 7459.

17 Advertising circular: Century company. A history of the Adirondacks, by Alfred L. Donaldson... N.Y. 1917? Broadside printed on both sides and folded into 6p. illus. port. The first edition appeared with the last page blank; in the second edition a review by Morris Longstreth appeared on the last page. Donaldson was reprinted by I.J. Friedman, Port Washington, N.Y. 1963. 2v. illus. (Empire State Historical Publications no. 12) Reviewed in *York State Tradition*, Spring 1963, 17:no.2:57.

18 Date of appearance in Glens Falls *Daily Times* is 1885, not 1855.

24 An earlier edition published in Cleveland, O. Burrowes Bros. Co. 1896.

37 Translations: *French* - Paris, 1874; translated by Countess Gédéon de Clarmont-Tonnère; *German* - Stuttgart, 1878; translated by Friedrich Kapp.

40 Reprinted in the *Tahawus Cloud Splitter*, Feb. 1964 - Summer 1964; 15:no.2:10-11; 15:no.5:15; 15:no.6:8,13.

53 Extracts in *North Country Life*, Winter 1959 and Spring 1960, 13:no.1:46-48; 14:no.2:4-9,17,22 illus. The Naming of the Chazy River; The Tragic Story of Father Jogues.

58 Reviewed by Paul F. Jamieson in *Adirondac*, July-Aug. 1954, 18:76.

89 Also published by Doubleday, Page, Garden City, N.Y. 1923.

101 Dates should be 1755 and entry should be classified under French and Indian Wars.

103 Reprinted in *Gentleman's Magazine*, Oct. 1755, 25:473-74.

121 Reprinted with title "A Rogers Ranger in the French and Indian War, 1756-59", 12p. illus. undated.

226 Should be classified under Archeology. P.S.M.

227 Paging should be 125-461. Reprinted by I.J. Friedman, Port Washington, N.Y. 1963. Reviewed in *York State Tradition*, Spring 1963, 17:no.2:58.

242 Omit, not in Adirondack area. P.S.M.

288 In title, add "s" to "valley".

304 Second edition, Burlington, Vt. 1894. 190p. plates, map.

387 Also in *Vermont Life*, Summer 1947, p.14-17, with additional plan.

426 Abridged in *North Country Life*, Summer 1957, 11:no.3:53-56, 65, illus.

432 Excerpts in *Quarterly*, April 1964, 9:no.2:23, illus.

452 Change name of the periodical to *Broadway*.

463 The author is Jervis McEntee. W.C.

526 Condensed in *York State Tradition*, Summer 1965, 19:no.3:2-5,10. illus.

541 Also issued in 1929 and 1959.

608 Mountain name is given as "Vanderwhacken". Author is Cecil Clay. L.R.

612 Month should be August.

628 Abridged in *North Country Life*, Summer 1961, 15:no.3:44-50.

673 Author's middle name is Joel.

677 Condensed under title "118th N.Y. Volunteers, and the Men of Essex County" in, *Reveille*, Dec. 1961, 6:no.23:1,3-4.

704 Add "unpaged". Another edition with title "Constitution, Officers, Committees, Members, etc." published in Hartford, Conn. Plimpton mfg. co. 1904. 19p. maps (one folded) Copy at the Adirondack Museum.

722 Variant edition published in New York by the Beacon press, undated, unpaged, illustrated.

755 Transfer to archaeology. P.S.M.

774 Similar title issued separately by the Fort Ticonderoga Association in 1955, unpaged, illus. maps.

796 Reprinted for the Fort Ticonderoga Museum, 1951, 112p. illus. ports. facsims. folded map.

802 Excerpt separately printed for the Fort Ticonderoga Museum Library, 1920, 98p. plates; 3d ed.

815 Also printed in 1933, 28p. Copy in the Rutland Free Library.

832 Asa Post letter reprinted in *Reveille,* Nov. 1958 and Mar. 1959, 2:no.14:3-4; 2:no.15: 3.

842 Inscription in the Loomis copy at the Keene Valley Public library reads: Lucy Fountain is pseudonym of Kate Hilliard, actress and summer resident of Keene Valley, with cottage near Putnam camp.

869 Extract with title "Ransom Noble & the 'Battle of the Boquet River' " in *Reveille,* June 1963, 30:no.8:4.

885 Also issued in 1851, 1862, 1865 and 1868.

931 Also issued for 1954 and 1958.

950 Variant edition issued by Houghton Mifflin, Boston, 1923. Volume I was also issued by Blackwell, Oxford under title: "With Burgoyne from Quebec", arranged for modern readers.

977 Omit chapters 4 and 5, not on Adirondacks.

1005 Undated, one-volume edition published in London by Bentley, 284p. Copy at the Adirondack Museum.

1034 In title, after "Adirondack" add "motor".

1043 Published in London by J.W. Parker & son, 1856, 2v. Copy in the Library of Congress.

1044 Copy in the Saranac Lake Free Library has "Effingham H. Nichols" written on the title page.

1084 Also published in Albany, 1870, by Weed, Parsons & co., 345p. illus. map (differs from that in the 1865 printing) Extract reprinted with title "Legend of the Water Lily" in the *Quarterly,* Jan. 1960, 5:no.1:12-14.

1087 Another edition issued by the New York Central & Hudson River R.R. Co., N.Y. 1892, 32p. illus. (Four Track Series)

1095 Undated edition published in Edinburgh by Gall and Inglis, 256p. col. front. with title "Sketches and Incidents; or, Summer Gleanings of a Pastor's Vacation". Another edition published in Northampton, Mass. by Bridgman and Childs, 1872.

1103 Extract abridged in *York State Tradition,* under title "Old Mountain Phelps", Summer 1964, 18:no.3:14-19, port.

1115 Change author's first name to Daniel.

1154 Report of George E. Hoffman, p.17-22.

1167-1168 Reports also issued as follows: 1956. Cover title: Trends and Developments in Resources Conservation. 1957. Cover title: Legislative Progress in the Development and Conservation of Natural Resources. Section II, Legislative Progress in Improving the State Forest Preserve; Section VII, Recommendations. Appendix B and C, Concurrent Resolutions Affecting the Forest Preserve. 1958. Cover title: New Challenges in Natural Resources Conservation and Development. Section III, The Changing Needs of the State Forest Preserve and State Reforestation. 1959. Cover title: Eight Years of Study and Action on the Development and Conservation of New York State's Natural Resources. 1960. Section II, Wilderness Areas. Reviewed by Henry Young in *Adirondac,* Mar.-April 1961, 25:39. 1961. Cover title: Long-Range Planning for the Forest Preserve and Other Studies in Conservation. 1962. p.16-19, The Forest Preserve, followed by statistical summary of 1961 studies on accessible Forest Preserve tracts. 1963. The Forest Preserve, p.14-24,28-35. 1964. The Forest Preserve, p.13-17; Socio-economic Characteristics of Adirondack Campers, by Elwood L. Shafer, jr. and Neil J. Stout, p.56-64 (abstract)

1178 Also published in 1843, 96p. map.

1179 1840 edition, 156p. listed in Morrill catalog, 1959.

1191 Another edition, 1895? 50p. illus.

1195 Reviewed in *Lake George Mirror,* July 23, 1943, 40:no.4:5,8.

1197 1897 edition, 118p. in Plattsburgh Public Library.

1204 1875 edition advertised by Pytell, Fall 1959.

1206 1909 edition located in the library of Ronald Allwork, Lake Placid.

1207 Also published in 1874, 210p.

1208 Copy of 1900 edition advertised by Samuel Weiser, Inc. in 1962.

1215 Variant edition, 1894?

1222 Another edition with title "In the Adirondacks", ©1901.

1223 1885 edition advertised by Cedric L. Robinson; 1895 edition in the Feinberg Library, State University College at Plattsburgh.

1225 1891 edition advertised by the Carnegie Book Shop.

1227 Add: Broadside printed on both sides and folded into 24p.

1231 Also an undated edition.

1232 1913 edition, 72p. illus. in the Adirondack Museum.

1240 Change copyright notice to E.A. Knight. Another edition ©1916, 151p. illus. map (front.)

1242 Earlier edition published by Santway at Star Lake, N.Y., 1917, 68p. illus. (part col.)

1244 Another undated edition, Fenton Press, Auburn, N.Y., 70p.

1250   Add: illus.

1274   Change publisher to McDonald & Foy.

1280   1960 edition advertised by Charles E. Tuttle.

1803-1804   Author's name is Hauptmann.

1884   Author's surname is Ketchledge.

1934   Also issued in 1956, 1958, 1959, 1960, 1963 and 1964.

2015   Add: Supplemental brief, signed by Marshall McLean, published by the Pandick Press, New York, 1945? 6p.

2055   Last report issued in 1965. Superseded by its "Conservation Highlights".

2056   Earlier edition: Conservation law...as amended to the close of the regular session of 1914. Albany, 1914. 239p.

2157   Add: Author's edition on heavy calendared paper, gilt edges, bound in brown leather with gold lettering, limited to ten copies. Autographed copy no.8 in the library of Maitland C. De Sormo.

2261   Reprinted in letter of Leslie Rist, *Tahawus Cloud Splitter*, June 1965, 17:no.4:5,10.

2271   Reprinted in *North Country Life*, Summer 1956, 10:no.3:64-68.

2276   6th edition published April 1950 by the Schenectady County Conservation Council.

2413   1942 edition at the Adirondack Museum.

2825   In title change "waterpower" to "water power".

2929   Author is Oliver St. Marie. L.R.

2973   Author is Betten

2981   Author's name is Jamnback.

2988   Omit

3037   Issued previously in the U.S. Geological survey, 16th annual report, 1894-1895, Part I, section e, p.543-70.

3134   Abstract in *Dissertation Abstracts*, 1955, 15:no.3:393.

3255   Bulletin number is 297.

3352   Date is 1822.

3638   Facsimile edition privately printed, New York 1925, limited to two hundred copies.

3677   Extracted in *Forest & Stream*, May 4, 1876, 6:200-201.

3708   Author's middle initial is S., not L.

3839   Also published for the northern area, 1955, 38p. and 1962, 20p.

4031   Reprinted in New York State Fisheries, Game and Forest Commission, 2d annual report, p.501-21.

4071   Author's full name is Nelson Titus Samson.

4149   Copy in the Adirondack Museum has two maps - Essex County, by E.N. Horsford and The Iron Deposits.

4384   In note change "Heritage" to "Hermitage".

4506   1847 edition, 32p., published by S.N. Dickinson & co., Boston, in the Adirondack Museum.

4529   Variant edition published in Boston by S.N. Dickinson, 1851, 13p.

4552   Add note: R., C.H. "Dear Stockholder..." *Railway Progress*, May 1952, 6:no.3:45. Comment on annual report.

4568   1883 edition, 100p. illus. folded map, advertised by John Skinner in 1957.

4639   Author's surname is Elli.

4714   Extract with title "The Lake of the Broken Heart" in *York State Tradition*, Summer 1963, 17:no.3:27-28.

4740   Printing date is 1898, not 1889.

4764   Ceased publication with no.33, 1964.

4771   Volumes one and two now in the Adirondack Museum.

4779   Add: illus. including p.145.

4809   Reviewed by William H. Burger in *North Country Life*, Winter 1956, 10:no.1:56-57; by Howard Zahniser in *Living Wilderness*, Spring 1956, no.56:12-13; by D.A. Plum in *Adirondac*, May-June 1956, 20:60.

4820   Reviewed by G. Glyndon Cole in *North Country Life*, Fall 1956, 10: no.4:53,55 and by D.A. Plum in *Adirondac*, May-June 1956, 20:60.

4843   Change Deavitt to De Witt.

5032   First word of title is "Do", not "So".

5057   Reprinted in New York (state) State library. *The Bookmark*, May 1963, 22:223-25.

5081   Extract with title "Mitchell Sabattis" reprinted in *York State Tradition*, Spring 1964, 18:no.2:24-29, port.

5162   Reprinted "slightly abridged and edited" by Dover Publications, N.Y. ©1963, 105p. illus. port.

5184   Author is Jeremy G. Case. L.R.

5230   Also issued in 1921, 14p.

5271   Month is May.

5273   Also issued in 1929, 1956, 1958-1961.

5295   Author's surname is Pritchard.

5320   Reprinted in 1964.

5321   Also issued in 1929, 1954, 1956, 1959-1961, 1964.

5324   Also issued in 1932 and 1939.

5366   Reprinted in *Appalachian Trailway News*, Sept. 1957, 18:39.

5381 Reprinted with title "Reading a Map" in *Appalachian Trailway News*, Sept. 1957, 18:37-39.

5536 Also issued in 1958-1961, 1963-1964. 1929 in Plattsburgh Public Library.

5539 Second edition, 1882 (School Bulletin Publications) Also an undated edition, published in New York by Orange Judd co.

5542 1928 edition in Keene Valley Public Library.

5616 Excerpt entitled "Keeseville in 1854" in *North Country Life*, Summer 1962, 16:no. 3:21-24, illus.

5617 Published in London by Beadle, 1862 under title "Hunting Adventures in the Northern Wilds, or, A Tramp in the Chateaugay Woods". (Beadle's Sixpenny Tales no.4) W.C.

5618 Another edition published in Philadelphia by John E. Potter & co., ©1863.

5629 Also in *Catholic World*, Oct. 1885, 42: 10-20.

5645 Locale is Cranberry Lake area, Cat Mountain, Town of Fine.

5689-5692 The following information is supplied by Warder H. Cadbury. Romance of natural history; or, Wild scenes and wild hunters, by W.C. (sic) Webber. London, T. Nelson & sons, 1852. 447p. Reprinted under title: Wild scenes in the forest and prairie, same publisher and pagination, in 1855 and 1858. An abridgment which excludes the Adirondack materials was also published in England: The romance of forest and prairie life... London, Vizetelly, 1853, 239p. published without author's name. Date supplied by the Library of Congress. There may be also a later printing, also anonymous and undated, published by Clarke, Beaton & co. German printings including the Adirondack chapters: Romatik der naturgeschichte; oder, Wildes land und wilde jaeger. Dresden, Kuntze, 1853, 1855, 2v. Jaeger und naturforscher. Leipzig, Kollmann, 1854. 3v. Also printed in 1855.

5914 Author is Batchelor.

5929 Author's name is Jeremy G. Case. L.R.

6040 Another edition published by the Ticonderoga Chamber of Commerce, undated. mimeographed, seven leaves.

6192 See letter by C.C. (Clay) and comment by E.K. Wilson in *Forest & Stream*, Mar. 23, 1876, 6:103 and April 13, 1876, 6:149.

6292 Also in: A book of sports, ed. by J.C. Dier, N.Y. Macmillan, 1912, p.15-17 entitled "Motor Sleds on Saranac Lake".

6489 Treasurer's Report for year ending Mar. 8th 1906 in Saranac Lake Free Library.

6509 Variant edition entitled "The Adirondack Mountain Club. Purposes and Scope", 1922.

6512 Also issued in 1956 and 1965.

6517 Also issued in 1957-1959.

6519 Also issued in 1929. The 1965 edition of "Constitution and By-Laws" was combined with the Roster of members.

6522 Issued in 1960 and 1964.

6594 In author entry change "educational" to "education". New edition issued in 1957, 31p. illus. port.

6605 Author is Jeremy G. Case. L.R.

6646 Author is probably Jeremy G. Case. L.R.

6655 Extract in *Living Wilderness*, Spring 1956, no.56:26.

6673 Also issued in 1931 and 1934.

6682 Author is Jeremy G. Case. L.R.

6718 "The Life of Ethan Allen", by Jared Sparks was reprinted in Burlington, Vt. 1858.

6759 Author's name is Featherstonhaugh.

6779 Insert "Capt." before "John Brown".

6789 Also issued by Doubleday, Doran & co. inc. Garden City, N.Y., 1929.

6837 In title insert "seer:" after "Melvil Dewey".

6872 Date is 1903.

6881 Reprinted in *Adirondac*, Mar.-April 1964, 28:26.

6892 Brief reference and quotation, accompanied by etching after a painting by Jesse Talbot, engraved by W.G. Jackman in *New York Illustrated Magazine*, Feb. 1847, 3:no.2:94, under title "Lake Scene Among the Adirondach (sic) Mountains". W.C.

7138 Supplement 3 (printed) is in the Saranac Lake Free Library.

7177 Change author's surname to Lusk.

7188 Another edition, illustrated, published in Garden City, N.Y. by Doubleday, 1916.

7244 "A-Hunting of the Deer" is in Roy Chapman Andrews's My favorite stories of the great out-doors... N.Y. Greystone press, 1950, p.171-78. "A Wilderness Romance" in *Good Company*, Sept. 1879, 4:1-6; "What Some People Call Pleasure" in *Good Company*, Sept. 1880, 6:1-7.

7246 Also published in London, by Victor Gollanz Ltd. 1952.

7263 Middle initial is G., not C.

7282 Reprinted in: American local-color stories, ed. by Henry A. Werfel and G. Harrison Orians. N.Y. American book co. 1941, p.179-87.

7313 Also published by Grosset and Dunlap.

7326 Another edition, published in London, by Richard. D. Dickinson, 1878. Text the same as the 1877 edition.

7327 Reprint "The phantom of Phantom falls," in *North Country Life,* Summer-Fall 1962. 16:no.3:46-50; 16:no.4:35-41.

7330 Also printed by Cupples & Hurd, Boston, 1888. Folio.

7331 In *Harper's Weekly,* Dec. 22, 1883, 27: supp.:825-32. illus. Also in *Plattsburgh Sentinel Annual,* 1894.

7336 Reprinted in *North Country Life,* Summer-Fall 1962, 16:no.3:46-50; 16:no.4:35-41.

7348 Also an undated edition, issued by the New Amsterdam Book Company, 104p. illus. Crepe paper wrappers. Illustrations differ from those in the original edition. W.C.

7353 Author's surname is Sherwen.

7361 Also issued with title: Scouting in the wilderness: the fort in the forest, N.Y. Appleton, 1924. (American Scouting Series)

7364 Date of publication is 1901.

7372 Juvenile.

7416 Add: Jamieson, Paul F. A note on Emerson's "Adirondacs". *NE Quar,* Mar. 1958. 31:88-90.

7423 Second, limited edition published in Schenectady by Riedinger & Riedinger, 1963. Reviewed in *York State Tradition,* Winter 1965, 19:no.1:55-56, port. Extract, "Sabael" reprinted in *York State Tradition,* Winter 1965, 19:no.1:46-49.

7496 Reprinted in *Adirondac,* July-Aug. 1958, 22:81-84.

7537 First published in 1911.

SERIALS AND SOURCES CITED

This list is arranged alphabetically by the citations used in the Bibliography. Periodicals included in the *Union List of Serials* or *New Serial Titles are listed by title only.*

Acadiensis. Acadiensis...a quarterly devoted to the interests of the maritime provinces of Canada.

Ad Life. Adirondack Life. Magazine supplement to the *Lake Placid News* and other north country newspapers.

Ad Phys. Advances in physics.

Adir Peeks. Adirondack peeks; published by the Adirondack Forty-Sixers.

Adirondac. Adirondac (Adirondack Mountain Club, inc.)

Advance Thought. Advance thought; a general news monthly published by Marcus M. Pomeroy. N.Y.

Alb Church. Albany churchman.

Aldine. Aldine.

Alpenstock. Alpenstock.

Am Agric. American agriculturist.

Am Ant Soc Proc. American antiquarian society. Proceedings.

Am Assn Pet Geol Bul. American association of petroleum geologists. Bulletin.

Am City. American city.

Am Field. American field. Changed to Field and stream (1874/75), Field (1875/76) and Chicago field (1878/81).

Am Fish Soc Tr. American fisheries society. Transactions.

Am For. American forests.

Am Geophys Union Tr. American geophysical union. Transactions.

Am Gun. American gun. N.Y. 1961-

Am Heritage. American heritage.

Am J. Sci. American journal of science.

Am Leg Mag. American legion magazine.

Am Min. American mineralogist.

Am Misc. American miscellany. A magazine of complete stories. Boston.

Am Mus Nov. American museum of natural history, New York. American museum novitates.

Am Nat. American naturalist.

Am Rev Tub. American review of tuberculosis.

Am Ski Ann. American ski annual.

Am Soc Hort Sci. American society of horticultural science. Proceedings.

Am Sportsman. American sportsman. Changed to Rod and gun and American sportsman.

Am Weekly. American weekly.

Am Wildlife. American wildlife.

Am Wood. American woodsman.

Amat Nat. Amateur naturalist; a monthly magazine for all nature students.

Anal Mag. Analytic magazine.

Anglers Club. Anglers club bulletin.

Appalachia. Appalachia.

Appalachian Trailway News. Appalachian Trailway news.

Appleton. Appleton's journal.

Aramco. Aramco world; published by the Arabian American Oil Company.

Archery. Archery.

Argosy. Argosy. N.Y.

Art Bul. Art bulletin.

Assn Boys. Association boys.

Atlan. Atlantic monthly.

Audubon Mag. Audubon magazine.

Backwoods J. Backwood's journal. Paradox, N.Y.

Ballou. Ballou's pictorial.

Beadles M. Beadle's monthly.

Berry thesis. See no.8633.

Bet Crops. Better crops with plant food.

Better Camping. Better camping. Milwaukee, Wis.

Bookmark. The bookmark; published by the New York State Library.

Box Mark. The box mark; published by the A. Sherman Lumber Company, New York City.

Bul Schools. New York (state) University. Bulletin to the schools.

Bus N Y. New York (state) Department of commerce. Business in New York state, 1960-

Camp. Camping; published by the Camp directors' association of America. Superseded by Camping magazine.

Camp Mag. Camping magazine.

Camp News. Camp news.

Can Mo. Rose-Belford's Canadian monthly.

Cath World. Catholic world.

Chr Advocate. Christian advocate. N.Y., Chicago. 1826-

Chr Sci Mon. Christian science monitor. Weekly magazine section.

Christ Union. Christian union.

Cloud Splitter. Cloud splitter: published by the Albany Chapter of the Adirondack Mountain Club.

Compact News. Northeastern fire protection commission. Compact news.

Con. Conservationist, formerly New York state conservationist.

Con Council Com. Conservation council comments; published by the New York State Conservation Council.

Copeia. Copeia.

Country. Country, 1879-

County Gov. County government.

Craftsman. Craftsman: an illustrated monthly magazine.

Crayon. The crayon. N.Y.

Curator. Curator; published by the American museum of natural history.

Dance Mag. Dance magazine.

Deke Q. Deke quarterly; published by the Council of Delta Kappa Epsilon, New York, N.Y.

Demorest. Demorest's Illustrated monthly magazine.

Diamond Dig. Diamond digest; published by Diamond Gardner Corporation, New York, N.Y.

Diss Abs. Dissertation abstracts.

Ecology. Ecology.

Econ Geol. Economic geology.

Ed & Pub. Editor and publisher.

Ellery Queen. Ellery Queen's Mystery magazine.

Emp State Geo. Empire state geolgram; published by the Geological survey, New York state museum and science service.

Empire. Empire: the magazine of central New York. Sunday supplement to the Syracuse Herald-American, Post-Standard.

Eng. & Min J. Engineering and mining journal.

Essex Co. Essex county farm & home bureau news.

Family Weekly. Family weekly.

Farm Res. Farm research, 1932- New York state agricultural experiment station, Geneva.

Fed Gard Clubs N.Y. Federated garden clubs of New York state, inc. News.

Field & S. Field and stream.

Fin World. Financial world.

For & Stream. Forest and stream.

For Hist. Forest history; published by the Forest history society.

For Leaves. Forest leaves. Sanatorium Gabriels, Gabriels, N.Y.

Ford Times. Ford times; published by the Ford motor co., Detroit, Mich.

Fortune. Fortune.

Four Tr News. Four track news. Changed to Travel.

Fr Leslies Pop Mo. Frank Leslie's popular monthly. Changed to American magazine.

Franklin Hist R. Franklin historical review.

Friends. Friends; published by Ceca publishing company, Detroit, Mich.

Friends In. Friends' intelligencer.

Ft Ti Mus Bul. Fort Ticonderoga museum. Bulletin.

Fur-Fish-Game. Fur-fish-game.

Gard Club. Garden club of America. Bulletin.

Gard J. Garden journal of the New York botanical garden.

Gent Mag. Gentleman's magazine, London.

Geol Soc Am Bul. Geological society of America. Bulletin.

Gold Hours. Golden hours: an illustrated monthly family magazine.

Good Comp. Good company.

Gr Mom. Great moments in sports.

Happy Days. Happy days: a paper for young and old. N.Y.

Harper. Harper's magazine.

Harper W. Harper's weekly.

Health News. Health news.

Herbertia. Herbertia. American amaryllis society.

Hist News. History news; published by the American association for state and local history.

Hist Today. History today.

Holiday. Holiday.

Home Office. Home office; published by the Metropolitan life insurance company, New York, N.Y.

Indian Forester. Indian forester.

J Econ Ent. Journal of economic entomology.

J For. Journal of forestry.

J Geophys Res. Journal of geophysical research.

J Hist Ideas. Journal of the history of ideas.

J Home Econ. Journal of home economics.

J Mam. Journal of mammalogy.

J Pet. Journal of petrology.

J Wildlife Man. Journal of wildlife management.

K N Akad Wet Proc. Akademie van wetenschappen, Amsterdam. (Koninklijke akademie Nederlandsche) Proceedings

Kingbird. The kingbird; published by the New York state federation bird clubs.

Knick Mag. Knickerbocker magazine. Changed to Foederal American monthly.

Ladies H J. Ladies Home journal.

Lake Pl Club Life. Lake Placid club life.

Lapidary J. Lapidary journal.

Leslies Illus. Leslie's illustrated weekly newspaper.

Life. Life.

Limn & Ocean. Limnology and oceanography.

Lines. The lines; published by the New York state electric & gas corporation, Binghamton, N.Y.

Liv Wild. Living wilderness.

Long Tr News. Long trail news; published by the Green mountain club, inc.

Lumber Camp News. Lumber camp news. Changed to Northeastern logger.

Maine Coast Fish. Maine coast fisherman. Combined with National Fisherman.

Mas Outlook. Masonic outlook.

Mast Detect Mag. Master detective magazine.

Min Eng. Mining engineering.

Min Mag. Mining magazine.

Moshers. Mosher's magazine.

Motordom. Motordom.

Mt Club Md. Mountain club of Maryland. Bulletin.

Munsey. Munsey's magazine.

Mus Am. Musical America.

Mus N. Museum news.

N Logger. Northern logger. Formerly Northeastern logger.

NE Home. New England homestead.

NE Quar. New England quarterly.

NJ Hist Soc Proc. New Jersey historical society. Proceedings.

NY Fish & Game J. New York fish and game journal.

NY Folk Q. New York folklore quarterly.

NY Gen & Biog Rec. New York genealogical and biographical record.

NY Hist. New York history.

NY Mirror. New York mirror: a weekly gazette of literature and the fine arts.

NYS Con. New York state conservationist. Changed to Conservationist.

NYS Con Council. New York state conservation council. Bulletin.

NYS Ed. New York state education.

NYS Ranger Sch. New York state ranger school. Alumni news.

NY State Hist Assn Proc. New York state historical association. Proceedings.

NY Times Mag. New York times Magazine. Sunday supplement of the New York Times.

Nat Fish. National fisherman.

Nat Geog M. National geographic magazine.

Nat Tub Assn Tr. National tuberculosis association. Transactions.

Nat Parks. National parks bulletin and National parks magazine.

Nat Skiing. National skiing.

Nature Con News. Nature conservancy news.

New Eng Hist & Gen Reg. New England historical and genealogical register.

New Yorker. New Yorker (1840)

Newsweek. Newsweek.

Niagara Frontier. Niagara frontier; published by the Buffalo historical society.

Niles. Niles national register.

No Country Life. North Country life. Changed to York State Tradition.

No Country Notes. North country notes; published by the Clinton County historical association.

Northeast Log. Northeastern logger. Changed to Northern logger.

Nutt Orn C Bul. Nuttall ornithological club. Bulletin. Changed to The Auk.

Old & New. Old and new.

Open Road. Open road for boys.

Our Town. Our town: the story of Diana, Lewis county, New York.

Outdoor Life. Outdoor life; outdoor recreation.

Outdoor Maine. Outdoor Maine.

Outdoors. Outdoors: the magazine of outdoor recreation. Columbia, Mo.

Outlook. Outlook. Changed to New outlook, N.Y.

Pa Mag. Pennsylvania magazine.

Perspect USA. Perspectives USA.

Pittman R Q. Pittman Robertson program. I-R. Quarterly report.

Pop Mech. Popular mechanics magazine.

Pop Sci. Popular science monthly.

Pot App Trail Club. Potomac Appalachian trail club. Bulletin.

Princeton Alum. Princeton alumni weekly.

Prog Fish Culturist. Progressive fish culturist. U.S. Fish and wildlife service.

Pulp & Pa. Pulp and paper magazine of Canada.

Pure & App Geophys. Pure and applied geophysics.

Quar. St. Lawrence county historical society. Quarterly.

Rail & Loc. Railway and locomotive historical society. Bulletin.

Railway Progress. Railway progress.

Recreation. Recreation.

Redbook. Redbook magazine.

Reveille. Reveille; published by the Essex county historical society.

Rocks & Min. Rocks and minerals.

Rod & Gun. Rod and gun and American sportsman.

Roy Soc Canada Proc. Royal society of Canada. Proceedings.

Saga. Saga: the magazine of true adventure.

Sat Eve Post. Saturday evening post.

Sch Co Hist Rev. Schoharie county historical review.

Sci Mo. Scientific monthly.

Scrib M. Scribner's magazine.

Shoot & Fish. Shooting and fishing.

Sierra Club Bul. Sierra club. Bulletin.

Ski Life. Ski Life.

Ski Mag. Ski magazine. Cover-title Ski.

Skiing. Skiing.

Soc Am For Proc. Society of American foresters. Proceedings.

Soil Sci Soc Proc. Soil science society of America. Proceedings.

Speleo Dig. Speleo digest; published by the National speological society.

Spirit Times. Spirit of the times and the New York sportsman.

Sport NY. Sporting New Yorker. Early issues have title: The new sensation.

Sports Illus. Sports illustrated. N.Y. 1954-

St Law Univ Bul. St. Lawrence university. Bulletin.

Staff. Staff; published by the Bank of Montreal, Montreal, Can.

State Gov. State government.

Summit. Summit magazine.

Sup News. Supervisors' News; issued by the Supervisors' association of the state of New York, inc.

Tahawus Cloudsplitter. Tahawus cloudsplitter; published by the National lead company, Tahawus, N.Y.

Tel Rev. Telephone review.

Tip Top. Tip Top weekly.

Todays Liv. Today's living. N.Y. 1956-

Top O' the World. Top o' the world news; published by Top o' the world mills, Lake George, N.Y. 1936-1939.

Tower. The tower; published by the International paper company, Ticonderoga, N.Y.

Trailmarker. Trailmarker; published by the Trailmarker corporation, Utica, N.Y. 1962-63.

Trains. Trains.

Travel. Travel. N.Y.

True. True.

U S N Inst Proc. United States naval institute, Annapolis. Proceedings.

Union Coll St. Union college studies in character research.

Union Worthies. Union college, Schenectady. Union worthies.

Univ Cynic. University cynic; published by the University of Vermont.

Vassar Misc. Vassar miscellany. Poughkeepsie N.Y. 1872-1915.

Ver Hist. Vermont history.

Ver Hist Soc News. Vermont historical society. News and notes.

Ver Hist Soc Proc. Vermont historical society. Proceedings.

Ver Life. Vermont life.

Vermonter. Vermonter.

Villager. The villager; published by the Bronxville (N.Y.) women's club.

Weekly Novelette. Weekly novelette.

West World. Western world.

Wilkes Spirit. Wilke's Spirit of the times. Changed to Spirit of the times and the New York sportsman.

Womans H C. Woman's home companion.

Woods & Wat. Woods and waters.

Wings of Love. Wings of love; published by St. John's church, Charlestown, Mass.

Yachting. Yachting.

Yester. Yesteryears; for the appreciation and study of New York regional history. Scipio Center, N.Y. 1957-

York State Trad. Before spring 1963, North country life.

Yorker. The Yorker; published by Junior historians of the New York state historical society.

INDEX

Numbers refer to entries, not pages.

Bold face numbers indicate main references. Numbers
before 7340 refer to the main volume of the Adirondack Bibliography. An asterisk following a number
indicates an addition or correction: See p. 124-128
of this volume.

A., J.D., 5695
A., P.H., 2879
ADK corner, 4772
A.N.C., *see* Cheney, Albert Nelson
Abbott, Robert W., 4606
Abbott, Henry, Birch bark books: *Anthony ponds;
Anxious seat; Camping at Cherry pond; Camps
and trails; The chief engineer; Cold river; Fish
stories; Fishing brook; Lost pond; Muskrat city;
North bay brook; Old bare-back and other stories;
On the bridge; Pine brook; Pioneering at Rowan-
wood; Psychology of the lost; Raquette river;
Tirrell pond; Wild cat mountain:* 7236
Abbott, Karl P., 10077
Abel, G.W., 3864
Abel, Hilde (Mrs. David Albert Davidson), 7246,
7246*
Aber, Frederick C. *see* Aber, Ted
Aber, Ted, 7839, 9256
Abercrombie, Major General Sir James, 85
Aborigines, **225-45,** 286, 6786, 7583-84, 7589, 7681-
83, **7684-98;** St. Regis, 10331
Academy of Political Science, 1648
Achilles, Laurence, 3560
Adam, Samuel F., 1584, 2786
Adams, Charles Christopher, 2064, 2880, 3561, 5335
Adams, Charles Francis, 6747
Adams, Frank Dawson, 3042, 6947
Adams, Howland K., 8282
Adams, Joseph, 7096
Adams, Joseph H., 10156
Adams, Samuel Hopkins, 6460, 10444
Adams, Spencer Lionel, 225
Adams, William R., 2020-21, 8391d. *See also* Black
River Regulating District: lawsuit
Adams, Zab Boylston, 5563
Adirondac (village), 848, 866, 899, 984, 5628; letters
relating to, 856; Masten's *Story of,* 397, 864; mining,
8954
Ad-i-ron-dac, 6507, 6558
Adirondac wilderness, The, 1105
Adirondack, pseud.: *An Adirondack table-land,* 932;
Assocation for the protection of the Adirondacks,
6565; *Death of Martin Moody,* 6984; *Destruction
of young spruce,* 3867; *Extending state owner-
ship,* 1523; *The Hermitage,* 4630; *Natural selec-
tion,* 8507; *New York's great forest and mountain
park,* 1538; *Protection of the Adirondacks,* 1541;
Reply, 8801; *State land purchases,* 1540
Adirondack, 4478
Adirondack, first use of name, 2985
Adirondack Al, pseud., *see* Young, Albert A.
Adirondack & St. Lawrence Railroad, 4540-41, 9187
Adirondack and state land surveys, **1117-52, 8120-21**
Adirondack Association, 2324
Adirondack bibliography, 4, 7540-43
Adirondack Bill, pseud., 7247
Adirondack Bureau, Plattsburgh, 708, 1243
Adirondack Camp and Trail Club, 6601
Adirondack Center Museum, 7897, 9238, 9514, 9517-
19, 9524-25, 10323
Adirondack Chamber of Commerce, 1244, 1244*,
9534

Adirondack Civic League, 8373
Adirondack Club, 5623, 6476, 10052
Adirondack Club, Lake Placid, 6603
Adirondack Communities Council, inc., 7902-903
Adirondack Company, 8991
Adirondack Company (railroad), **4478-97, 9165-70**
Adirondack Cottage Sanitarium, 4829, **4830-66,**
5054, 9352
Adirondack Development Corporation, 8957
Adirondack directory, 1274
Adirondack Enterprise, 4739-40, 4740*, 9286-88,
9535
Adirondack Farm and Forest Club, inc., 10022
Adirondack Forest Products Association, 3908
Adirondack Forestry Council, 3868
Adirondack forestry tour, 2234
Adirondack Forty-sixers, 5181, 5347, 6604, 6638,
6644, 6655, 6669, 6685-88, 9697, 9703, 10029, 10038,
10042-43, 10045-50, 10057, 10063; publications:
Adirondack forty, 10023; *Adirondack Peeks,* 9291;
Climbing, 10024
Adirondack French Lewie, *see* Seymour, Lewis
Adirondack Girl Scout Council, 9431
Adirondack Good Roads Association, 8135
Adirondack guide, ed. by Arthur S. Knight, 1241
Adirondack Guide Company, 1240, 1240*
Adirondack Guides Association, 2371, 5196-97, 5206,
5223, 5227; *Season of 1897,* 5198
Adirondack House, Keene Valley, 4371, 8993
Adirondack Inn, 9026
Adirondack Iron and Steel Company, 4149, 4154,
8938
Adirondack Iron Company, 4157
Adirondack Iron Ore Company, 4158
Adirondack Iron Works, 18, 398, 899, 6610, 8936
Adirondack Jim, pseud., 4669
Adirondack League Club, **6489-6506;** lawsuit (Black
River Regulating District), 2020-22, 2024-39
preserve, 281, 485, 5092, 5783; deer, 2704, 3776-
77, 5734; flora, 3494; history, 10025; lichens and
mosses, 3416, 3418-19, 3426; trees, 3507
publications: *Annual report,* 6489, 6489*; *Bul-
letin,* 6490; *Brandon,* 8499; *Club manual,* 6491;
Code, 6492; *Deer management,* 8522-23; *Fishery
management,* 2472, 8492; *Fishery survey,* 2471;
Handbook, 6493; *Prospectus,* 6494; *Seventy-fifth,*
10025; *To the members,* 6495; *Yearbook,* 6496
Adirondack Library, Saranac Lake, 5051
Adirondack Life, 9289, 9829
Adirondack Lodge, 252, 7193, 8994, 10012
Adirondack Lumber Manufacturers & Shippers As-
sociation, 3869
Adirondack Lumbermen's Club, 3870
Adirondack Moose River Committee, 1817-18, 1840,
1861, 1971; lawsuit, 2022, 2024, 2028, 2032, 2038
Adirondack Motor Club, 3821
Adirondack Motor Bus Company, 8145
Adirondack motor guide, 8134, 8138
Adirondack Mountain Authority, 9900, 10311
Adirondack Mountain Club, 5347, **6504-64, 9933-
10005;** annual meeting, 1348
chapters: Adirondak Loj chapter, 6526, 9947;
Bulletin, 6525; Albany chapter, 6532-35, 6537,

10486; *Domesticated*, 8531; *Forest preserve*, 8340; *Modern lumbering*, 10487; *Mountain names*, 8176; *Scenic wilderness*, 10488

Allen, J.C., 2600; *Adirondack deer*, 2596, 5699; *Adirondack game notes*, 5567; *Incidents of the woods*, 5568; *Romance of two ponds*, 417

Allen, Joseph Dana, 300

Allen, Merritt Parmelee, 7505

Allen, Paul W., 8944, 8946

Allen, Richard Sanders, 9182-83

Allen, Shirley Walters, 3872

Allen, Stanton P., 9363

Allen Mountain, 5496, 5527; winter ascent, 6394

Allen's bear fight up in Keene, 7378

Allerton, Reuben C., 6076

Alling, Harold Lattimore: *Adirondack anorthosite*, 3106; *Adirondack graphite deposits*, 3284; *Adirondack magnetite deposits*, 3118; *Ages of the Adirondack gabbros*, 3097; *Feldspars*, 3100; *Genesis of the Adirondack magnetites*, 3088; *Geology of the Lake Clear*, 3240; *Glacial geology*, 3246; *Glacial lakes*, 3064; *Metasomatic origin*, 3113; *Origin of the foliation*, 3085; *Pleistocene geology*, 3242; *Some problems*, 3075; *Stratigraphy of the Grenville*, 3091; joint author, *Geology of the Ausable*, 3249

Allis, J. Ashton, 6368

Alpina, 60, 72

Alpine Valley, 9057

Altamont Club, 10028

Altavista Lodge, 8998

Altitudes, 920, 923, 1142

Altmann, Heinz C., 8663

Altsheler, Joseph Alexander: *The hunters of the hills*, 7506; *Lords of the wilds*, 7506; *Masters of the peaks*, 7506; *Rulers of the lakes*, 7506; *Shadows of the north*, 7506; *A soldier of Manhattan*, 7507; *Sun of Quebec*, 7506

Amadon, Arthur F., 2267

Amateur, pseud.: *First visit to the Raquette*, 5060; *Long lake, Newcomb*, 5061; *North woods Walton club*, 6607; *On to "G" lake*, 5062; *Saranac route*, 418; *Sport near Lake Champlain*, 5569; *Swinging round the circle*, 5063

Amberg, C.R., 3285

Amendments (proposed), 1903, 1918, 1920, 1933, 1957

Amendments and constitutional conventions, **1935-74, 8380-91**. *See also* names of amendments, i.e. Burd amendment, etc.

American Association for the Advancement of Science, 1157, 2883

American Bison Society, 2391-92, 2395

American Canoe Association, 5255, 5281, 5311, 9604, 9617

American Forestry Association, 1462, 1608, 1651

American forests, 4741

American Geographical and Statistical Society, 4451

American Legion, New York: mountain camp, 4867, 6608, 8029; Plattsburgh chapter, 709; Saranac Lake chapter, *Jubilee book*, 729

American Legion Auxiliary, 4881

American Olympic Committee, 6341

American Management Association, 7963

American Planning and Civic Association, 2028, 2032, 2038

American Scenic and Historic Preservation Society, 1323

American Trudeau Society, 9337

Ames, C.H., 1298, 2736

Amherst, Jeffrey Amherst, 1st baron, 83, 108, 7565, 10065; *Journal*, 106; *Letter*, 7578

Amherst, William, 106

Amherst, Fort, *see* Fort Amherst

Among the Adirondacks, 937

Ampersand, pseud., 2536, 5700

Ampersand Hotel, 8999

Ampersand Mountain, 610, 620, 628, 1059, 5559; ascent, 5445, 5473, 9706

Ampersand Pond, 1551

Amphibians and reptiles, 3522, **3554-59**

Amrach, pseud., 2554

Amstuz, John O., 3822

Anburey, Thomas, 949-50, 950*

Anderson, C.O., 4230-32

Anderson, George Baker, 633

Anderson, George Pomeroy, 302

Anderson, John, 8439

Anderson, Richard, 8575

Anderson, Robert, 9000

Anderson, Robert V., 9810

Anderson, Sven A., 4201

Anderson, W.P., 5701

Anderson-Bartlett bill, 8391

Andia-ta-roc-te, 545

Andrews, Arthur L., 1985

Andrews, Buel C., 7704

Andrews, Mary Raymond (Shipman), 5508

Andrews, Roy Chapman, 5072, 7244*

Andrews, William A., 6506

Angell, George W., 9432

Angler, pseud., 1999, 6077

Animal Land, 8806

Anthony, Theodore Van Wyck, 9952

Anthony Ponds, 7236

Antlers, The, 9088

Apatite, 3292, 4237, 8692, 8695

Appalachian Mountain Club 3005, 5358

Apperson, John S., 1737, 1753, 1911, 1965, 8391c, 10083-91; *Adirondacks are*, 6255; *Better forestry*, 2297; *Comments*, 1747, 8204; *Confusion*, 8215; *Conservation*, 2084; *Forest preserve*, 1819; *Forests upstream*, 2251; *"Forever wild"*, 8335; *Given before*, 8208; *Land utilization*, 2070; letter, 8427, 8543-45; *Man-made*, 2071; *Minority report*, 1787; *Missing islands*, 2875; *New York state*, 8187; *New York's*, 8126; *Perpetual*, 2276, 2276*; *Preservation*, 8211; *Proposed*, 8380; *To the editor*, 8303; *Twenty-fifth*, 8212; *Withhold*, 1875

Applegate, Howard Lewis, 9460-62

Apples, 8966-71, 8977

Appleton, Thomas Gold, 419, 951, 10489

Appleton, William, 61

Appleton's Companion hand-book, 1187, 1209

Appleton's General guide to the United States, 1212

Appleton's Hand-book of American travel; northern and eastern tour, 1209

Appleton's Hand-book of American travel. The northern tour, 1194

Appleton's Illustrated hand-book, 1187

Appleton's Illustrated hand-book of American summer resorts, 1210

Appy, John, 7595

Arabella, pseud., 7379

Arbutus Lake, 6086

Archaeology, **211-24, 7676-83**

Archery, 9541, 9578

Architecture, 8838

Argument showing why the state, An, 4467

Arietta road, 8291

Aristocrats, The, 7248

Armchair mountaineer, 5131, 5404, 10436

Armstrong, Dick, 8843

Armstrong, George R., 3873, 8844, 9467

Armstrong, Louis Oliver, 303, 7691

Armstrong Mountain, 5495

Arnold, Allan, 10574

Arnold, Benedict, 6725, 7554, 10064, 10092-93; *Regimental memorandum book*, 7603

Arnold, Ed, 10094

Arnold, R.W., 8965

Arnold, Seward, 825

Arnow, Theodore, 2873

Art and literature, **7213-7502, 10405-10641**. *See also* Essays; Fiction; Poetry

Arthur, Helen, 9514

Arthur, L.W., 5910, 10423

Artists, 7214; Frederick Baylies Allen, 7994, 9589, 10407; Archibald Brown, 7230; Lewis Stacy Brown, 6793; Thomas Cole, 10413; Albert Tatum Davis, 10166-67; Arpad Geyza Charles Gerster, 5611, 6702, 10189; Winslow Homer, 7218, 7233, 10406,

Brown, William H., 7840
Brown-Serman, W., 423
Brown bill, 1515-16
Brown Swan Club, 10036
Browne, Marion Josephine, 5018
Browne, Stewart R., 6091, 6171
Brownell, Baker, 5345
Brownell, Catherine J., 8807, 9003
Brown's Tract, 289, 989, 1092, 5633, 9281; beaver liberated, 2493; camping 5550, 5560, 6235; canoeing, 5161; ferns, 3437; fishing, 5161, 5571, 5941, 5959, 5992, 6019-20; geology, 2984; history, 51; ponds, 7794; settlement, 297; trapping, 6235
Brown's Tract Association, *see* North Woods Walton Club
Brown's Tract Guides Association, 2376, 2741, 5236; reports of meetings, 5196, 5199, 5205
Bruce, Dwight Hall: *Adirondack deer hounding,* 5723; *Adirondack jottings,* 5075; *An Adirondack trail,* 5259; *The Adirondacks,* 966, 2338, 4352; *Cranberry lake country,* 424; *In the Adirondacks,* 5579; *In the wilderness,* 7756; *Letter* (on moose), 2401; *Syndicating the Adirondacks,* 4540
Bruce, Eugene Sewell, 2116, 2122, 2141, 2185
Bruce, Wallace, 400-1, 967, 7394, 7745, 8126
Bruen, Edward T., 4786
Brundage, Frances, 7504
Brunowe, M.J., pseud., *see* Browne, Marion Josephine
Bryan, Charles W. Jr., 425, 7757
Bryant, F. Hastings, 8082
Bryant, Fitch C., 518
Bryant, Ralph Clement, 2120, 3896
Bryant, William Cullen, 968-69
Bryce, A.W., 8183
Bryce, Viscount James Bryce, 308
Buchner, Marion Yates, 7758
Buck, pseud., 5510
Buck, C.J., 3897
Buck, David, 10131
Buck, Robert J., 3824
Buck Island (Cranberry Lake), 3519
Buck Mountain, 3458, 5319
Buckham, John Wright, 309
Buckheister, Carl W., 8326
Buckley, John Leo, 2891, 3753, 3898
Buddington, Arthur Francis, 8614; *Adirondack igneous rocks,* 3114; *Adirondack magmatic stem,* 3104; *Chemical petrology,* 3138, 3140; *Composition and genesis,* 3131; *Correlation of rigid,* 8636; *Foliation,* 3238; *Geology;* Santa Clara, 3257, Saranac, 3281; *Granite phacoliths,* 3098; *Gravity stratification,* 3107; *Interrelated precambrian,* 8640; *Origin of anorthosite,* 3111; *Origin of granitic rocks,* 3126; *Regional geology,* 8653; *Some problems,* 3112
joint author: *Degrees of oxidation,* 8655; *Geology;* Lake Bonaparte, 3252, Willsboro, 3266; *Iron and titanium oxide,* 3142; *Iron ores,* 8691; *Iron titanium,* 8665; *Lake Bonaparte,* 3239; *Micro intergrowths,* 8648; *Ore deposits,* 8662; *Remanent,* 8667; *Thermometric and petrogenic significance,* 3147; *Titaniferous hematite,* 8669
Budlong, Percy E., 533
Buffalo, 2391-93, 2395
Bug Lake, 2012
Bugbee, Willis N., 7395
Bulger, John D., 426-27, 426*, 1172, 5260
Bulkley, C.H.A., 4884
Bulkley, E.A., 9367
Bull, Henry J., 4885
Bullard, Herbert F., 3501, 5448
Bulletin (Saranac Lake, N.Y.), 9324
Bulletin: digest of business, 8809
Bullhead Mountain, 9674
Bump, Gardiner, 2505, 3577, 3795
Buntline, Ned, *see* Judson, Edward Zane Carroll
Burch, Barbara J., 9203
Burd amendment, 1638, 1641
Burden, William Douglas, 9754
Burger, William H., 240; *Adirondack Coney island,* 3826; *Coll Bay,* 7999; *Father Mac,* 6966; *The first*

Adirondackers, 230; *George Morgan,* 6992; *George Webster,* 7201; *The Hands of Elizabethtown,* 6697; *Melvil Dewey,* 6836; *Shambles at Shattucks,* 5346; *Sidewheelers on Lake Champlain,* 4612; *Some conservation men,* 6698; *Tom Peacock,* 7030 joint author: *Camp Dudley,* 4940; book reviews, 857, 4808, 4809*
Burgoyne, John, 145, 153, 171; fiction, 10478; *Letter,* 7610; *Orderly book,* 7611; *State of the expedition,* 7612
Burgoyne invasion, 10472
Burgoyne's campaign, 153, 171, 7602, 7606-607, 7613, 7618, 7627-29, 7632; poetry, 10550; surrender, centennial, 7638; poetry, 10552
Burham, J.T., 5924
Burke, Martin, 5580
Burke, Raymond, 10132
Burnand, Eugene, 62
Burnett, Charles Howard, 4541
Burnett, William H., 2348, 6795
Burnham, John, 2072
Burnham, John Bird, 1562, 2383, 6796-98, 10133; *Adirondack animals,* 2396; *Adirondack caribou,* 3783; *Adirondack deer hounding,* 2633; 2635; *Adirondack deer hunting conditions,* 5724; *Adirondack deer law,* 2583, 2624; *Adirondack notes,* 2892; *Ben Jourdon,* 6938; *Boquet river,* 5925; *Eastern Adirondack winter,* 2893; *Echoes of the New York show,* 4682; *Elijah Simonds,* 7103; *Errors in the official Adirondack map,* 1482; *Fishing in northern New York,* 5926; *Future of the Adirondack state park,* 1790; *Gens des bois,* under name of biographee; *George McBride,* 6964; *Guy Brittell,* 6746; *Guy Ferguson,* 6854; *History of the Adirondack deer,* 3784; *James M. Wardner,* 7199; *Joseph McGuire,* 6969; *Lake Champlain fishing,* 5927; *Lake Champlain pollution,* 2770; *Maple sugar,* 3827; *Martin Van Buren Moody,* 6985; *My mountain home,* 10491; *Outing in the snow,* 5449; *Panthers in the Adirondacks,* 3674; *Plimsoll line,* 3793; *Plumadore,* 7048; *Simeon J. Moody,* 6988; *Spring in the Adirondacks,* 2894, 5511; *Told at the sportsmen's show,* 4683; *Two days' hunt at North Hudson,* 5581; *Winter camp on Wadleigh brook,* 6260
Burnham, Koert D., 3285, 3899, 4266, 8958
Burnham, Stewart Henry: *Additional notes,* 3456; *Additions to the flora,* 3457; *Admirable Polyporus,* 3396; *Braun's holly fern,* 3434; *Charles Horton Peck,* 7033; *Ferns of the Lake George flora,* 3435; *Flora of Buck mountain,* 3458; *Hepaticae,* 3410; *Lake George flora stations,* 3436; *Lichens,* 3411; *Mosses,* 3412; *The Naiadales of the flora,* 3459; *Notes on the flora,* 3460; *Quadrilliums,* 3461; *Sedges,* 3462; *Supplementary list,* 3413
Burns, George P., 2880
Burns, James C., 184
Burr, C.G., 4684
Burr, David H., 1277
Burrell, A.B., 8977; *Effect of,* 8966; *Effectiveness,* 8967; *Further pollination,* 8968; *Immediate,* 8969; *Pollination,* 8970; *Response,* 8971
Burroughs, John, 5076, 5138, 6799, 6800; *A bed of boughs,* 5512; *Locusts and wild honey,* 5512; *A night-hunt,* 5725; *Wake-robin,* 3578
Burroughs, Julian, 5076
Burrows, George, 4606
Burt, C.H., 35
Burt, Olive (Woolley), 10115
Burton, Harold B.: *The commissioner,* 7027; *Forty acres,* 4634; *Holiday hand book,* 9542; *I'm glad,* 8467; *Inside Dannemora,* 8000; *Lake Placid,* 691; *More about,* 9956; *Mountaineering,* 6405; *Placid's,* 9875; *"Pro" Whiteface,* 1797; *Rock climbing,* 5500; *Ski touring,* 6404; *To the editor,* 8297; *What a way,* 5347; *Whiteface,* 9876; *Why do,* 9877
Busbey, Hamilton, camp, 4630
Bush, Robert, 310, 428
Bushnell, Frances Louisa, 7396
Bushnell, Horace, 907, 5080
Butcher, O.L., 8577